# PEREGRINA

BOOK SIXTEEN

Louann Atkins Temple Women & Culture Series
*Books about women and families, and their changing role in society*

Alma M. Reed

*Edited and with an introduction by* Michael K. Schuessler

*Foreword by* Elena Poniatowska

UNIVERSITY OF TEXAS PRESS AUSTIN

# *Peregrina*

## LOVE AND DEATH IN MEXICO

Printed in the United States of America
First edition, 2007

The Louann Atkins Temple Women & Culture Series
is supported by Allison, Doug, Taylor, and Andy Bacon;
Margaret, Lawrence, Will, John, and Annie Temple;
Larry Temple; the Temple-Inland Foundation; and the
National Endowment for the Humanities.



∞ The paper used in this book meets the minimum
requirements of ANSI/NISO Z39.48-1992 (R1997)
(Permanence of Paper).

*Library of Congress Cataloging-in-Publication Data*
Reed, Alma M.
Peregrina : love and death in Mexico / Alma M. Reed ;
edited and with an introduction by Michael K. Schuessler ;
foreword by Elena Poniatowska. — 1st ed.
p. cm.
Includes bibliographical references and index.
ISBN-13: 978-0-292-72615-4

1. Reed, Alma M. 2. Carrillo Puerto, Felipe, d. 1924.
3. Carrillo Puerto, Felipe, d. 1924—Relations with women.
4. Yucatán (Mexico : State)—History—20th century.
5. Journalists—Mexico. I. Schuessler, Michael Karl. II. Title.
F1376.R42 2007
972′.65082—dc22

2006023444

To Alma M. Reed, "La Peregrina," and to all the extraordinary women of the United States whose contribution to the life and culture of postrevolutionary Mexico has been overlooked and undervalued for more than seventy-five years.

—*Michael K. Schuessler*

# CONTENTS

# FOREWORD

I REMEMBER ALMA REED WELL: DURING THE 1950'S AND 1960'S WE WOULD often share the elevator going up to the editorial offices of *The News*, a U.S. daily associated with the Mexico City newspaper *Novedades*. She used to sing to herself during the ride up from the first to the third floor, keeping her eyes closed, and only opening them when it was time for both of us to get off the elevator. She wore old-fashioned dresses, always covered with lace and frills, and when she wore black, she looked quite lovely, because her face was quite pale and the dark apparel made her seem still more distinguished. Some mornings I would happen to ride up standing in between Alma and Yucatecan poet Rosario Sansores. They seemed to be engaged in a duel of hats, and theirs were always covered with veils, flowers of all sorts, and even stuffed birds. I regret that I never spoke to Alma, because there was always a smile fluttering on her lips, but as she was always singing quietly to herself, I didn't dare interrupt. Now that I know how important Alma Reed is, I am astonished that *Novedades* did not pay more attention to her. I never heard any comments regarding her articles, nor did anyone mention that she was a good journalist. Fernando Benítez, the director of the supplement *México en la Cultura*, never asked anyone to write an article about her. In a way, they treated her in the same disdainful way they did Rosario Sansores, who was considered gaudy and passé. Rosario had come from Cuba as the chronicler of Sociales[1] for Mexico. No one mentioned her poem "Sombras," which was made into an emblematic song for the Yucatecan *trova*. Rosario Castellanos once wrote that she felt very grateful to her son, Gabriel, because he was the only one who never confused her with Alma Reed. Like Sansores, Alma Reed did not belong to the Mexican intellectual establishment; the only women who had access to such elite groups were Frida Kahlo, Elena Garro, and, naturally, Sor Juana Inés de la Cruz.

If I ever knew that Alma Reed had written José Clemente Orozco's first biography and supported him during times of hardship in New York, I forgot. If someone ever mentioned to me that Alma had written such important books as *The*

*Ancient Past of Mexico* or *The Mexican Muralists,* I don't recall. Now, through the publication of her autobiography with a preliminary study written by Michael Schuessler, I learn that for several years I used to ride the elevator up and down with a fabulous personage.

At the Windsor School, we were always taught to sing two songs: "Caminante del Mayab," by Guty Cárdenas, and "La Peregrina," written by the Yucatecan poet Luis Rosado Vega and set to music by Ricardo Palmerín. Over the years, when I heard the line "Peregrina of clear and divine eyes," I never associated it with Alma Reed. Indeed Alma was a foreign woman, but I used to attribute the song to all the female tourists who came to Mexico. Now I see that the only person truly worthy of the ballad was Alma Reed, the great love of the Yucatán governor Felipe Carrillo Puerto, known as the "red dragon" of southeast Mexico.

As a columnist writing under the pseudonym "Mrs. Goodfellow," Alma Reed defended the outcasts of San Francisco in her weekly column that appeared in the *San Francisco Call,* a left-wing newspaper, during the first two decades of the twentieth century. She was the defender of migrant workers—Mexico's *braceros*—as well as the promoter of the art of Orozco, Edward Weston, and Ansel Adams. Alma Reed fully transcends the blond *gringuita* who falls in love with a revolutionary from the Mayab.

Hired in 1921 by the *New York Times,* Reed defended and uncovered Mexico's archaeological heritage through a series of articles in the newspaper's *Sunday Magazine.* She chronicled the excavations of Sylvanus G. Morley in Yucatán, and when Sir Edward Thompson confided to her that he had secretly sent the archaeological treasures retrieved from the sacred *cenote* of Chichén Itzá to the Peabody Museum via diplomatic pouch, Reed did not hesitate for an instant in making it known. Thanks to her and her journalistic and political campaigns, Mexico was able to recover at least half its treasures. Also thanks to her and to her contacts with Mexico's revolutionary government, Reed was able to obtain the necessary preliminary information so that Adolph S. Ochs, the owner of the powerful *Times,* could write an editorial in favor of President Álvaro Obregón, thus heralding official recognition by the United States government.

Orozco owes Alma Reed not only his first biography but also the sale of his *Mexico in Revolution* series in the United States and, later, commissions to paint murals in the New School for Social Research, Claremont College, and Dartmouth College. Through her friendship with Eva Palmer, wife of Greek poet Angelo Sikelianos, and the Delphic Society that they founded together in New York in 1928, Reed was able to give Orozco the exposure that he would have never obtained otherwise, as well as the opportunity to meet personalities such as Kahlil Gibran and Thomas Hart Benton. Later, Reed founded her Delphic Studios Gallery on East Fifty-seventh Street—then and now the most prominent address for art galleries—with the sole purpose of exhibiting Orozco's work and, later, that of other Mexican artists such as Emilio Amero, Miguel Covarrubias, Roberto Montenegro, and Adolfo Best-Maugard.

Reed was part of a group of bold North American women who arrived in Mexico seeking to learn about the revolution and there devoted themselves to the study and promotion of Mexican culture. Among them are Frances Toor; Alice-Leone Moats; Anita Brenner, who was born in Aguascalientes, lived in the United States, and exposed her splendid backside to Edward Weston; Emily Edwards, who commissioned Manuel Álvarez Bravo to take photographs of Mexican murals; Tina Modotti; Grace and Marion Greenwood, who painted murals in the Abelardo Rodríguez Market alongside Fermín Revueltas and Pablo O'Higgins. Later arrivals were Mariana Yampolsky; Margaret Shedd, who gave impetus to the Centro Mexicano de Escritores; Irene Nicholson, translator of Juan Rulfo's work; Ione Robinson, who substituted Modotti in Edward Weston's amorous relations; and Katherine Anne Porter, whom Reed never befriended, because Porter had spoken disparagingly of her and both had been girlfriends of Carrillo Puerto.

Michael Schuessler has already published *La undécima musa: Guadalupe Amor* (*The Eleventh Muse: Guadalupe Amor,* 1995) and *El universo de Sor Juana* (*Sor Juana's Universe,* 1995), as well as *Elenísima: Ingenio y figura de Elena Poniatowska* (*Elenísima: Facts and Fictions of Elena Poniatowska,* 2003). It was only to be expected that Michael would be interested in Alma Reed, especially after he discovered her autobiography along with Felipe's love letters in a semi-abandoned apartment in Mexico City. I recall that when Michael first told me he had found the autobiography of "La Peregrina," I thought that perhaps it might be apocryphal, as Reed had been dead for forty years and nobody seemed to remember her. Nevertheless, one day he stopped by my house on his way home from the gym with the first chapters in his backpack. These documents were a fascinating read because they portrayed the Mexican Revolution in Yucatán (which is very unusual) and described the impressions of a young U.S. journalist who would soon fall in love with a fascinating man who was already a part of the history of Mexico, Felipe Carrillo Puerto.

Since the era of the marquise Fanny Calderón de la Barca, travel writing has become enthroned in Mexico, but no work to date has been as instructive as Alma Reed's, which describes in detail her adventures in Yucatán as well as her fascination with Carrillo Puerto's socialist utopias; she considered him her true soul mate, referred to him as a "Greek god," and was given a Mayan equivalent of her name by him.

Reed's friend Ethel Turner—the widow of John Kenneth Turner, who wrote *Barbarous Mexico*—helped Reed revise her book and recommended that in the last two chapters she include details such as the reactions of the people of Yucatán to the assassination of Carrillo Puerto, as well as the honor guard ceremony held each year at the place of his death. Reed was unable to follow her friend's advice because she fell ill. Thinking it was just "Montezuma's revenge," she checked into the British hospital in Mexico City. There the doctors discovered she had intestinal cancer, something she would never learn but which caused her death only a few days later, on November 20, 1966, the anniversary of the Mexican Revolution. Therefore she was unable to write the last lines of her book, which, as Schuessler explains, was also to become the script for a movie made in the United States about the meaning of Yucatán in her amorous and ideological existence.

In his preliminary study, Schuessler, an extraordinary scholar, uncovered many intimate details about Alma Reed and tirelessly searched archives—often alongside his friend and mentor Miguel Capistrán—to document the life and work of this extraordinary woman. He also interviewed the recently deceased Swedish painter Rosa Lie Johansson and Joe Nash, the veteran U.S. journalist who arrived to Mexico on his bicycle over half a century ago and would become a close friend of Reed's. However, it was thanks to Richard Posner, perhaps Reed's best friend and confidant during the last ten years of her life, that Schuessler was able to rescue this valuable text, for after La Peregrina's death Posner hid her memoir in the back of a closet, behind stacks of musty sheets and pillows.

Michael Schuessler is a passionate scholar of Mexico, and in this sense he has followed in the footsteps of Egon Erwin Kisch, Carleton Beals, Malcolm Lowry, the brothers Gutierre and Carletto Tibón, and many others who came to Mexico for a short visit but stayed on for many more years than they had ever imagined. We of Mexico are indebted to people like them for their loving and critical vision of our country. They deserve high honors, for, in the words of José Martí, *honrar honra*—it is honorable to honor.

—*Elena Poniatowska*

# ACKNOWLEDGMENTS

A FULBRIGHT–GARCÍA ROBLES FELLOWSHIP AND A MINI-GRANT FROM Barnard College, Columbia University, allowed me to spend the 2003–2004 academic year in Mexico City, where I completed the research for my introductory study as well as the notes to Reed's text. The following individuals made important contributions to my research and to the preparation of the manuscript: Ramón Arzápalo, Patricia Sawtelle Berman, Donna Brodie, Jim Budd, Mrs. Elsy Bush Romero, Ligia y Virginia del Socorro Cámara, Miguel Capistrán, Elizabeth Castelli, Helen Delpar, Adelina Erosa, Tita Escudero, Norma Franchi, Elisabeth Garrett, Amparo Gómez, Kim Haney, Luis Irabién, Rosa Lie Johansson (†), John Maxim, Sandra E. Miller, Joe Nash, Juan Bruce Novoa, Steve and Mimí Novom, Lois Parkinson Zamora, Lisette Parodi, Elena Poniatowska, Ruperto Poot Cobá, Sara and Manuel Poot Herrera, Richard Posner, Tynisha Rue, Salvador Rueda Smithers, Gail Schuessler, Herbert Sloan, Rhona Statland de López, Philip Stein (Estaño), Luis Terán, Pat Vano, Alejandro Varderi, Ileana Villarreal, Elizabeth Wade, Christopher L. Winks, and Nancy Worman.

# PEREGRINA

# INTRODUCTION

*Life has so many chapters . . .*
ALMA MARIE SULLIVAN REED (1889–1966)

THE FIRST TIME I HEARD OF ALMA REED WAS IN 1992, IN THE LOBBY OF the Gran Hotel in Mérida, capital of the state of Yucatán. I had arrived after a twenty-six-hour bus ride from Mexico City, which included frequent stops in towns and villages along the way. Upon my arrival, I was immediately captivated by the once-imposing surroundings of the hotel, which, as I would soon discover, was a local landmark in the cultural and political history of the city. As the receptionist, Don Eusebio, handed me the key to my room, he mentioned that Fidel Castro had occupied my suite many years before, when he and his rebels were searching the Gulf Coast for a boat to take them back to overthrow Batista's Cuba. Encouraged by my interest, he rattled off the names of several other foreign celebrities who had once stayed there: Charles Lindbergh, Sergei Eisenstein, Douglas Fairbanks Sr., and so on until he happened upon a woman popularly known as La Peregrina. When I failed to show any enthusiasm, he quickly explained that La Peregrina was a *gringa* from San Francisco, California, whose name was Alma Reed. He was astonished that I had never heard of this locally revered figure, especially given that we were *paisanos*, or countrymen, and he proceeded to narrate the story of her tragic romance with the revolutionary hero and martyred governor of the Yucatán, Felipe Carrillo Puerto (1874–1924). Alma Reed met, fell in love with, and became engaged to marry the Yucatán's charismatic populist governor, known to his detractors as the "red dragon with eyes of jade," while on assignment for the *New York Times Sunday Magazine* in the early 1920's.

Immediately after their formal engagement, Reed returned to San Francisco to gather her trousseau and make plans for the wedding. Although she had been previously married to Samuel Payne Reed, Alma was again in love and willing to face the consequences of this union, as Felipe was a married man. In January 1924, a week before the marriage was to take place, Alma received a telegram with devastating news: her fiancé, three of his brothers, and nine of their followers had been executed by a firing squad.

*Portrait of Felipe Carrillo Puerto, wearing his "Governor's Stetson." The photo is inscribed in red ink with the following note in Spanish: "Alma, my most lovely little woman: I send you this, for they say that it looks like me, and if you agree, keep it as my portrait."*

Carrillo Puerto had fought alongside Emiliano Zapata for "Land and Liberty." In the spirit of the Mexican Revolution, the governor made great attempts during the early 1920's to modernize his distant state, whose land barons were members of *la casta divina*, the "divine caste." This landed aristocracy had steadfastly resisted agrarian reform and other social advances put into practice by the new constitutional government. In the Yucatán, these included the creation of feminist leagues, led by Felipe's sister Elvia, which instituted the first family planning programs with legalized birth control in the Western Hemisphere, as well promoting women's suffrage, which was obtained far earlier than in the rest of Mexico.[1]

The radical governor also founded more than four hundred local schools to educate Maya youth, until then virtual slaves held by debt peonage on the enormous henequen haciendas of the ruling class. Indeed the coat of arms of the all-powerful Montejo family, which adorns the facade of their sixteenth-century palace in Mérida, is composed of a Spanish foot planted squarely on the head of a Maya slave. In clear defiance of the status quo, the socialist governor revived the *ejidos,* or communal villages, characteristic of pre-Hispanic Mexico, arguing that the land of the Yucatán was the inhabitants' legal birthright. He also reformed

*Alma in Mérida with members of the Feminist League of the Southeast, including Felipe's sister Elvia Carrillo Puerto (standing on right).*

*Carrillo Puerto's funerary bust in Mérida's Panteón General. It bears the following phrase in Spanish: "Do not abandon my Indians." The memorial was constructed directly in front of the wall where Carrillo Puerto, three of his brothers, and nine of his supporters were executed by firing squad on January 3, 1924.*

the prison system and constructed roads into Mérida from numerous villages, so that farmers could transport their goods to the market more efficiently.

Despite his towering height and green eyes, Carrillo Puerto was said to be a descendant of Nachi Cocom, the last indigenous cacique of the Mayapán federation, who in the mid-sixteenth century had steadfastly resisted the invading Spanish.[2] Whatever the case may be, as a result of his childhood spent in the countryside and his regular contact with indigenous peasants, Carrillo Puerto was fluent in Yucatec Maya and in his youth even translated the Mexican Constitution so that the non-Spanish-speaking majority could know their rights.

As a direct result of the socialist-inspired reforms enacted during his governorship, which lasted only twenty months, the first democratically elected governor of the Yucatán was murdered on January 3, 1924, along with his brothers Edesio, Benjamín, and Wilfrido and nine political confidants, including Manuel Berzunza, Carrillo Puerto's closest adviser.

The assassins were agents of the Delahuertista rebellion, led by Adolfo de la Huerta and headed in the Yucatán by Colonel Juan Ricárdez Broca, from the northern state of Sonora. The Delahuertistas supported the efforts of the Yucatán's ruling class to regain the henequen haciendas and de facto slave labor they were forced to give up as a result of the Mexican Revolution. This once-privileged group, supported by the Catholic Church, openly challenged the presidency of Álvaro Obregón, Carrillo Puerto's staunch ally, and would later unsuccessfully attempt to overthrow him. Although de la Huerta condemned the executions the same day they occurred, shortly afterward Ricárdez Broca was promoted to general and named acting governor of the Yucatán. His provisional—and illegitimate—government was short-lived, due in part to the immediate response of the important Ward Line—its suspension of cargo service to and from the region paralyzed the henequen industry, whose revenues were the backbone of the local economy.

In a stirring attempt to emphasize the improbable couple's everlasting love, Don Eusebio intoned the first lines of the popular ballad through which Reed is still remembered in Mexico and abroad.[3] The ballad was composed upon Carrillo Puerto's request by Yucatecan poet Luis Rosado Vega and arranged by Ricardo Palmerín:

LA PEREGRINA

Peregrina de ojos claros y divinos,
y mejillas encendidas de arrebol,
peregrina de los labios purpurinos
y radiante cabellera como el sol.

Peregrina que dejaste tus lugares,
los abetos y la nieve virginal,
y viniste a refugiarte en mis palmares,
bajo el cielo de mi tierra, de mi tierra tropical.

Las canoras avecitas de mis prados
por cantarte dan sus trinos si te ven,
y las flores de nectarios perfumados
te acarician en los labios, en los labios y la sien.

Cuando dejes mis palmares y mi sierra,
peregrina del semblante encantador,
no te olvides, no te olvides de mi tierra,
no te olvides, no te olvides de mi amor.[4]

Don Eusebio didn't recall how the song was conceived, only that it was dedicated to Carrillo Puerto's American sweetheart, the reporter Alma Reed. Ten years later, in a letter dated May 1951 from the composer to *La Revista Ilustrada* director Ramón Ríos Franco, I discovered the "Only True Account Concerning 'La Peregrina.'" In it Rosado Vega recounts that Reed, Carrillo Puerto, and he were driving through Mérida on a warm summer evening en route to a dinner party. It had just rained, and the poet describes the origin of the song:

> Upon perceiving that fragrance which emanated directly from Nature and which has no equal, Alma, widening her brow, breathed in deeply and exclaimed:
>
> "What a lovely bouquet!"
>
> I immediately answered: "That perfume is because you are passing by and the earth, trees and flowers wish to caress you."
>
> Alma laughed in her distinctive crystalline way and Felipe immediately remarked, looking at me:
>
> "You shall tell that to Alma in verse."
>
> "I will tell it to her in a song," I answered.
>
> "I have your word," replied Felipe.

Throughout my first visit to Yucatán, Reed's ghost would appear on numerous occasions, most often in this famous song but also in the collective memory of the *emeritenses,* residents of Mérida. As I would later discover, the images conjured up by the ballad "La Peregrina" aren't always pleasant, and during a recent interview with a granddaughter of Carrillo Puerto, she was quick to point out that her grandmother always changed the channel whenever the song was played on the radio, as it inevitably reminded her of that "gringa oportunista" who stole her husband's love.

Ever since that first visit to the Yucatán in 1992, I have been captivated by this woman. Before becoming a living legend in Mexico, she had begun her journalistic career in San Francisco under the pseudonym "Mrs. Goodfellow," a columnist for the leftist *San Francisco Call.* Under this byline, she documented the tragedies and injustices suffered by the disenfranchised, earning her the dubious sobriquet of "sob sister."

Reed's reputation as a champion of human rights and as a journalist was established in 1921 by her celebrated defense of Simón Ruiz, a seventeen-year-old undocumented Mexican worker who was sentenced to death by hanging after being advised by his state-appointed lawyer—in incomprehensible English—to plead guilty to trumped-up charges. As a result of Reed's campaign, which lasted several months and produced many impassioned articles in the *Call,* the state laws of California were amended to prohibit the execution of minors. The law, passed in 1921, was popularly known as the Boy Hanging Bill.

The legal amendment attained as a direct result of Reed's efforts is a clear case of how journalism could lead to tangible advances in government and society, and Reed was a visionary in this sense. Indeed her absolute support of Álvaro Obregón's revolutionary government, as reflected in several articles written for

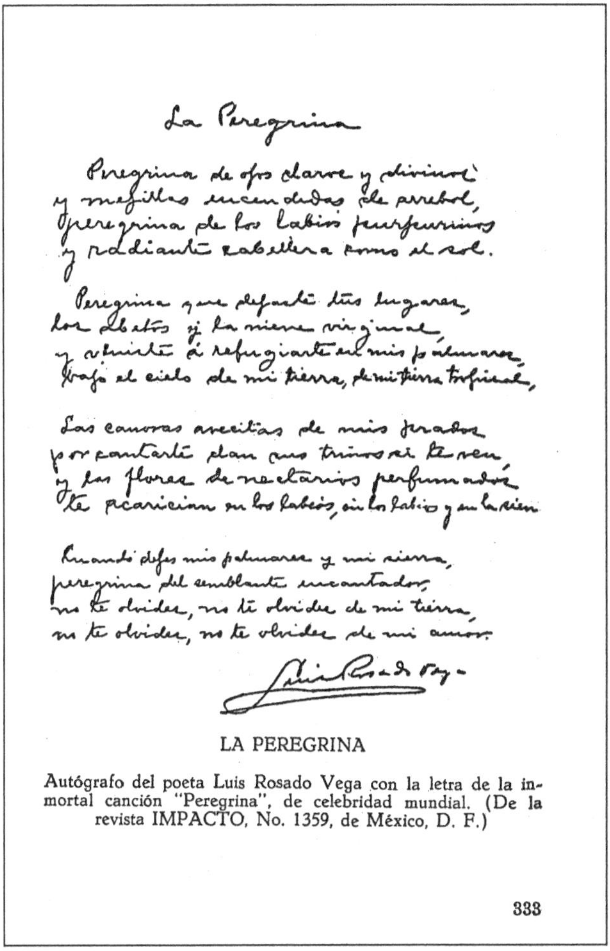

La Peregrina

Peregrina de ojos claros y divinos
y mejillas encendidas de arrebol,
peregrina de los labios purpurinos
y radiante cabellera como el sol.

Peregrina que dejaste tus lugares,
los abetos y la nieve virginal,
y viniste á refugiarte en mis palmares
bajo el cielo de mi tierra, de mi tierra tropical,

Las canoras avecitas de mis prados
por cantarte dan sus trinos si te ven,
y las flores de nectarios perfumados
te acarician en los labios, en los labios y en la sien.

Cuando dejes mis palmares y mi tierra,
peregrina del semblante encantador,
no te olvides, no te olvides de mi tierra,
no te olvides, no te olvides de mi amor.

Luis Rosado Vega

LA PEREGRINA

Autógrafo del poeta Luis Rosado Vega con la letra de la inmortal canción "Peregrina", de celebridad mundial. (De la revista IMPACTO, No. 1359, de México, D. F.)

333

*Original manuscript of the ballad "La Peregrina," by Luis Rosado Vega, reproduced in the Mexico City magazine* Impacto, *no. 1359.*

the *Times* as well as the Hearst papers (under a pseudonym), would soon result in the official recognition of Mexico's new government by the United States. Given her defense of the disenfranchised, which, in the case of Ruiz, resulted in a major change in the California legal system, it may be argued that Reed heralded a type of reporting that had nothing to do with the antics of "daredevil girls" such as Nellie Bly, popular at the time. This was in part thanks to Fremont Older, "who gave newspaper women extraordinary opportunities on the *San Francisco Call Bulletin* and backed them in many original exploits, and believed that editors did not employ enough women."[5]

Reed's crusade to save Simón Ruiz attracted the attention of Mexico's new

*The back of this curious photomontage reads as follows: "Alma as Mrs. Goodfellow distributing gifts to poor Mexicans in San Francisco before her first visit to Mexico." The other person has not been identified, but her image was cut out and pasted on top of the original photograph, which probably dates from 1919–1920.*

revolutionary government, and in September of 1922 Reed traveled to Mexico City for the first time as the semiofficial guest of President and Mrs. Álvaro Obregón. Upon her arrival, Reed was treated like royalty; her suite at the elegant Hotel Regis was festooned with flower bouquets and caged songbirds, while a chauffeur waited outside to take her to her various official engagements, which included a trip to the pyramids of Teotihuacán, tours of the schools constructed by the new government, and luncheon with the president and first lady at their residence in the former castle of Emperor Maximilian and Empress Carlota, perched atop Chapultepec Hill.

At the time, Mexico had just emerged from a revolution that had left thousands dead but that, upon its triumph, had distributed arable land to the peasant population, for this had been the greatest demand of the landless majority. The

*Alma as a young woman in her native California, wearing a pendant given to her by Felipe: a pre-Hispanic Mayan copper bell set within the red triangle of the Resistance League of the Southeast.*

new government was also attempting to overcome a long history of educational neglect and undergoing a cultural transformation spearheaded by Secretary of Education José Vasconcelos. It was said at the time that just as the revolution had handed over large tracts of land for cultivation, Vasconcelos had given to the artists enormous public walls to adorn with images of such changes. This official sponsorship gave rise to the Mexican mural movement, whose main exponents (Diego Rivera, José Clemente Orozco, and David Alfaro Siqueiros) would soon transcend Mexico's borders.

Upon Reed's triumphant return to San Francisco, Adolph S. Ochs, owner and editor of the *New York Times,* contacted her at the *Call,* where she had gone back to work. Like many journalists of the time, Ochs had followed Reed's successful campaign to change California's capital punishment law, and he now wanted her to write for his daily. The two met face-to-face, and the newspaper magnate offered her the position of California correspondent. Duly flattered but having been bitten by the bug, Reed explained that what she really wanted was an assignment that would take her back to Mexico. Ochs was surprised by such a request, especially as she was then enjoying a growing visibility in the United States. However, he had also come to California looking for someone to cover an important upcoming archaeological expedition to the Yucatán.

After a series of brief negotiations, Reed was hired to cover the Carnegie Expedition to the Yucatán Peninsula, where she would document the activities and discoveries of American archaeologists, including Harvard Mayanist Sylvanus G. Morley. His plan was to excavate the ruins of the classical Maya city of Chichén Itzá, located on the former henequen hacienda owned at that time by legendary American explorer and archaeologist Sir Edward Thompson, who had lived there with his family since 1885.

As Reed recalls in her autobiography, Thompson considered her to be "simpática," and he admired her professionalism and work ethic. Soon after, he would choose Alma as his confidant, revealing to her that over the years he had dredged up countless treasures from the sacred *cenote,* or sinkhole, of Chichén Itzá and had gradually sent them back to the Peabody Museum at Harvard University via diplomatic pouch. When Reed's exclusive story broke in the *New York Times* on April 8, 1923, under the title "The Well of the Maya's Human Sacrifice," the taking of the artifacts at once became an international event. Mexico demanded repatriation of the items or the payment of a large indemnity, and Reed actively championed this petition. Nearly ten years later, in 1930, the Peabody Museum reluctantly returned a portion of Mexico's national treasure, largely as a result of Reed's efforts in journalistic and legal circles.

It was also upon her first visit to Mérida, in February 1923, that Reed became enamored of the Yucatán's governor, Felipe Carrillo Puerto. Their passionate ro-

*Sir Edward Thompson, American archaeologist and owner of the Hacienda Chichén Itzá, in a photograph he probably gave Alma during their groundbreaking interview in 1923.*

mance would last for less than a year but would leave an indelible mark on the life and work of La Peregrina and also on the history of twentieth-century Mexico.

According to her own recollections, Reed first met Carrillo Puerto at an official reception attended by all the North American "Yucatologists," as they were soon christened by the local media. After being introduced to the governor—who worked out of the "Casa del Pueblo,"[6] having converted the Governor's Palace into a cultural center and archaeological museum for the residents of Mérida—

*The back of the photo reads: "Alma and Felipe—Alma departing from Yucatán, October, 1923." This is the last known picture of the engaged couple. Note that Felipe is carrying Alma's purse by its straps while the latter bears a large bouquet of roses, surely a parting gift to his beloved "Pixan Halal."*

Reed shared her impressions with Brigadier General William Barclay Parsons, an American railroad and subway engineer who accompanied the expedition. According to Reed's autobiography:

> A Carnegie Trustee and the senior member of the group, he voiced what was obviously the amazed reaction of his fellow expeditionaries when he whispered: "This is the most personable red dragon I've met with in any of my safaris . . . What do you think, young lady?"

> With total conviction, I unhesitatingly answered: "He's *my* idea of a Greek god!"

The intensity of their love and utopian dreams is fully documented in the letters and telegrams, composed mainly in Spanish, that Carrillo Puerto sent to Reed in New York and San Francisco between April and December 1923, which I will reproduce in a scholarly edition to be published in Mexico. As I explain in detail below, the henequen bag in which I found one version of Reed's memoir also contained three manila envelopes labeled "Felipe's Letters and Telegrams," "Letters of November, 1923," and "The Final Letters and Maya Poem." These original materials—a total of twenty-seven telegrams and thirteen letters, many written in red ink on the official stationery of the Liga de Resistencia del Sureste (Alliance of Resistance of the Southeast)—cast an entirely different light upon the governor of the Yucatán. As his correspondence reveals, Carrillo Puerto was utterly captivated by his "idolatrada Alma,"[7] although it was rumored that he had pursued affairs with other women, including an American he had met in Mexico City a few years prior and an alleged mistress in Mérida.[8] His love for the "niña periodista,"[9] whom he soon gave the Mayan name "Pixan Halal,"[10] was apparently so genuine that in his letters he regularly informs her about the status of the divorce he had requested from his first wife and the mother of his four children, María Isabel Palma de Carrillo, so he and Reed could marry in San Francisco on January 14, 1924. The wedding would never take place, for Carrillo Puerto was assassinated on January 3 of that year. His last missive, in Spanish and dated December 10, 1923, sets the ominous tone for his violent death, which occurred less than one month later. His last words to his "linda niña"[11] were these:

> With all tenderness I send you greetings and I hope that you realize how desperately unhappy I am that you are not at my side. I have no one to comfort me, nor the slightest caress. Receive all the kisses from my lips and all the love from this poor man who is thirsting for happiness. Yours until death.

Underlining his pressing situation, at the bottom of the typewritten letter, which had been interrupted by a bomb that exploded nearby, he scrawled: "Communicate our matters by aerogram until I can send you a code."

In the notes for Katherine Anne Porter's unpublished novel *Historical Present,* "a full history of a period as seen by certain people that moved through it," the author records Reed's "dramatic account of how she was standing by what chance she never explained in the hotel lobby, in full white satin with veil and orange blossoms rehearsing in her wedding dress, when the news came of Felipe's death."[12] The novelist "was both envious and contemptuous of Reed's notoriety," according to Thomas Walsh, Porter's biographer of her Mexican sojourn: "In fragments of *Historical Present,* a novel she was working on in 1930, she planned to begin with Reed's 'cashing in on Felipe's death' and go on to her gradual building up the legend to become 'patroness of all Mexico.' " This hurtful remark, as well as the women's shared romantic interest in Carrillo Puerto, explains why Reed never attended Porter's well-publicized lectures in Mexico City during the 1950's and 1960's.

After Carrillo Puerto's assassination in January 1924, Reed traveled to North Africa, again as a correspondent for the *New York Times,* and reported on the archaeological excavations in Carthage led by Polish count Byron Khun de Prorok. A series of five articles, bearing such intriguing titles as "Science Ferrets Out Carthage's Secrets," " 'Curse' Still Hovers over Carthage," "Science Hunts for the Lost Atlantis," "Under-Water Camera Films Ruins of Deep," and "Explorers Seek Traces of African 'Joan of Ark,' " appeared in the New York City daily from October to December 1924 and bear witness to Reed's renewed interest in classical studies, an area that had fascinated her since childhood. While studying archaeology for a year in Naples, Reed translated G. Consoli Fiego's archaeological treatise, *Cumae and the Phlegraean Fields,* which was published in Naples in 1927. She later traveled to Greece as a guest of her childhood friend Eva Palmer, wife of the Greek poet Angelo Sikelianos, and translated Sikelianos's works as *The Delphic Word . . . The Dedication,* published the following year. During this period, Reed continued to write for the *Times* and in 1926 published two articles dedicated to one of the greatest mysteries of the Greco-Latin world: "Virgil's Hades Gives Up Its Secrets" and "Sibyl Renews Her Challenge to Man." While in Athens, Reed participated in the first Delphic Festival, which was organized by Palmer and Sikelianos in May 1927 as a way to return Greek culture and traditions to their rightful heirs.

Inspired by this Hellenic spirit, Reed and Palmer traveled to New York later that year to found the Delphic Society's first colony in the United States. In early 1928 they moved into an apartment once occupied by celebrated Russian author Maxim Gorky, located at 12 Fifth Avenue. The flat, near Washington Square and its triumphal arch, was baptized "the Ashram" in homage to the "apostle of pacifism," Mahatma Gandhi, whom both Palmer and Reed greatly admired.[13] Like Gandhi's settlement, Reed's New York apartment was the center of communal activities while also serving as headquarters for a cultural movement born of ancient philosophy, both Eastern and Western. Eventually Reed's Delphic Studios Gallery would emerge as the most enduring product of their initial collaborative effort. Unfortunately, only a few photographs survive that evoke the cosmopolitan atmosphere of their innovative literary and political salon.

*(left) Reed dons Greek-inspired attire at the Delphic Society, ca. 1928. (Underwood and Underwood Studios, 417 Fifth Avenue, New York)*

*(below) "Artists in Alma Reed's Apartment, ca. 1932." (Courtesy of the Enrique Riverón Papers, 1918–1994, in the Archives of American Art, Smithsonian Institution)*

One day in 1928, Reed received a telephone call from Anita Brenner, a young woman from Aguascalientes who shared her fascination with Mexico and whose parents had immigrated to San Antonio, Texas, at the beginning of the Mexican Revolution. Later, Brenner would return to Mexico on numerous occasions, first to complete research for her well-known books, which included her study of religious syncretism and Mexican art, *Idols behind Altars,* published in 1929. During their conversation, Brenner informed Reed that the artist José Clemente

Orozco had been living in Manhattan since December 1927 and was a bit down on his luck.

During Reed's second visit to the Mexican capital, in 1923, when she and Carrillo Puerto were the toast of the town, Secretary of Education José Vasconcelos showed Reed the murals then being painted by Diego Rivera in the Public Education Secretariat, as well as those recently begun by Orozco in the National Preparatory School. In her 1956 biography of Orozco, Reed remembers that as she and Vasconcelos "approached the main patio of the *preparatoria,* where Orozco was engrossed in the decoration of a high vault, Vasconcelos called up to him: 'Orozco, this is the North American *periodista* (journalist), Alma Reed. She likes your painting. I don't! It's the worst yet. But it's your wall, *hombre,* not mine, so go ahead.' "[14] Surely Orozco's powerful images of peasant struggles, warring revolutionary factions, the dissolute upper classes, and ruthless critiques of the Catholic Church made a great impression on the young journalist, and statements made during her first visit reveal a budding fascination with Mexico. In an interview with one of the capital's most important dailies, *Excélsior,* Reed announced: "Mexico should be the Mecca of all the world's artists: here every object and every scene is an occasion for art and beauty."[15] This developing interest would soon lead her to join the ranks of other North American women who arrived on the heels of the revolution, including Katherine Anne Porter, Ione Robinson, and Frances Toor, founder and editor of the magazine *Mexican Folkways.* Although their activities have yet to be fully documented, these women were all actively engaged in important cultural endeavors during a period referred to as the Mexican Cultural Renaissance, when the artistic and educational ideals born of the revolution were being put into practice.

Reed immediately volunteered to assist Orozco and planned to visit him at his "parlour-floor studio on a shabby Chelsea block somewhere in Manhattan's West-Twenties" (Reed, *Orozco,* 3).[16] In a letter written to his wife, Margarita Orozco de Valladares, in June 1928, he mentions Reed for the first time:

> The other day Anita [Brenner] told me that there are possibilities that I might sell a drawing and a small picture of those I have made here. Apparently, a Miss Alma Reed, who was the fiancée of Carrillo Puerto, the governor of the Yucatán who was killed, likes my works a lot, but naturally I was not introduced to her. Ms. Reed is a close friend of [José Juan] Tablada, but that cad hasn't introduced me to her or to anyone else.[17]

Two months later, according to a note dated August 2, 1928, Orozco had apparently still not met Reed, but in a second letter written later that same day, he informs his wife that she is interested in visiting him at his studio:

> I have just received a letter from Alma Reed, whom I haven't met, but who is a friend of Tablada and the person Anita [Brenner] showed my drawings to a few days ago. She tells me that she has been a profound admirer of mine for a long time, and that "The entire series on the Mexican revolution holds a very intimate appeal to me, but one of them, 'Cemetery Scene,' is irresistible,"[18] and she includes 20 dollars towards the $100, which is the price of the drawing. She wants to come to my studio with a friend to talk about the publication of who knows what. My luck is changing a little bit, Miti. From your mouth to God's ear![19]

After visiting Orozco at his improvised studio for the first time, Reed recalls: "The next morning I resolved to help the Mexican painter pursue his career in the U.S. I did not try to rationalize the inner compulsion that had shaped my decision." She also confesses: "I had no precise idea as to what I might do—if anything at all—to further his career in New York. But I could at least buy a picture, perhaps induce my friends to do likewise."[20]

In a letter to his wife dated August 15, 1928, Orozco's reaction to their meeting is equally enthusiastic:

> On Sunday night, Anita introduced me to Alma Reed, who is a lovely woman and seems quite cultivated. She says that she is a great admirer of my work. She told me that she wants to illustrate a book she is writing with some of my Revolutionary drawings, and that tomorrow (Thursday) she will come to my studio with a woman she says is involved in some 40 magazines, in order to see my works, and that perhaps there will be business, that she wants a poster to announce some festivals in Delphos, Greece, patronized by a woman millionaire, that is celebrated every two years and is attended by people from all over the world. She says that there is some kind of group of literati and philosophers I will be presented to next winter, with a conference and projections of my paintings, and that they have spoken about me to all of their friends.[21]

Soon afterwards, Reed convinced her friend Eva to commission a portrait of herself from the painter, who set up his easel in a small room of the Ashram that he dubbed "the Pulquería," in honor of the notorious Mexican watering holes.

As Reed recalls in her biography of Orozco, first published in Spanish in 1955 by the Fondo de Cultura Económica, the artist later painted odd pieces of homemade furniture and completed two canvases for the decoration of what he called the Ashram's "Mexican Sector." He also painted Reed's portrait but soon destroyed it in a paroxysm, provoked by what he considered to be a far superior

*"Photograph of a party at Alma Reed's Delphic Studios, ca. 1936." Alma Reed is squarely in the center, and muralist José Clemente Orozco is standing on the right of the picture. David Alfaro Siqueiros, another Mexican muralist, is standing at the extreme left, while Kahlil Gibran stands in front of him. Although the other guests are unidentified, they are most likely members of the Delphic Society. (Courtesy of the Enrique Riverón Papers, 1918–1994, in the Archives of American Art, Smithsonian Institution)*

rendering by Lebanese poet and engraver Kahlil Gibran, another famous habitué of her salon. The latter's admirable likeness includes the following dedication: "For Alma Reed: My dear and gracious friend, whose heart dwells in the world of truth and beauty. K. G. 1928."

In his autobiography, Orozco recalls frequenting the Ashram and the great impact its cosmopolitanism had upon him:

> When I met [Alma Reed] and Mrs. Sikelianos, they were living in a spacious place on lower Fifth Avenue. They had come to New York to secure financial aid for the cause of Greece's resurgence and to organize an excursion to the festivals that were celebrated every two years in Delphi. . . . The literary-revolutionary salon of Mrs. Sikelianos was extremely well attended. Some days the Greeks came, among them Doctor Kalimacos, patriarch of the

*Alma Reed as envisioned by the artist and philosopher Kahlil Gibran, a frequent guest at the Delphic Society. This image was reproduced from an in-depth article dedicated to La Peregrina that was published in the* Mexico City News *immediately after her death in 1966. The drawing has apparently been lost (or sold); the frame, donated to the Museo Nacional de Historia by the nieces of Rosa Lie Johansson, now contains only the artist's dedication to Alma.*

> Greek Church in New York. There one heard Modern Greek spoken to perfection by the owners of the house. On other days bronze-colored Hindus with turbans arrived, champions of the cause of Mahatma Gandhi. . . . Alma Reed recited her translations of Sikelianos's epic poems, some of which had already been collected in a volume entitled *The Dedication.*[22]

Orozco held his first solo U.S. exhibition in that fabled Greenwich Village apartment in September 1928, and some sixty guests attended the opening. A testimony of Reed's keen desire to promote the Mexican artist is to be found in a letter she sent to Orozco, dated September 26 of that year, which he transcribed in a letter to his wife, Margarita. In it Reed informs him of several developments and potential opportunities that had come about as a result of this first solo exhibition:

> The interest in your exhibit grows. Yesterday we had several very important people here, some of whom are returning today with the owners of galleries and with wealthy prospective purchasers. We feel that in view of this continued interest that it would be wiser to keep the exhibition here until Friday night. There is likelihood too of some portrait orders, so we think that it would be well to have your marvelous portrait of yourself here. Several very distinguished critics who viewed your work yesterday made the same comment independently and quite spontaneously: "Orozco's grouping and anatomy would pass for that of Michel Angelo."
>
> I have never seen such enthusiasm aroused by the work of any artist as was shown here yesterday. Many of our guests on Monday telephoned us yesterday to express their profound admiration again. . . .
>
> There will be interesting developments, I am sure, in regard to your work very soon, for so many influential friends are deeply interested now. We are working towards obtaining a "pretty wall" for you at the "Architectural Exhibit" in January. There will be some heads of galleries here today, including Marie Sterner. I think that I shall have some news for you tomorrow evening.[23]

The success of his first show led to a two-week exhibition of his *Mexico in Revolution* series, curated by the upscale Marie Sterner Gallery. The show opened on October 10, 1928, and, according to Orozco, Reed herself paid for the framing of his canvases as well as the printing and mailing of exhibition catalogs. Unfortunately, most of the guests had attended the opening in deference to the gallery owner, and they appeared more interested in Sterner's Biederman furniture than Orozco's revolutionary canvases.[24] According to Alejandro Anreus, author of *Orozco in Gringoland*,[25] "much to the disappointment of Reed and Orozco, the exhibition received no critical notice, and not a single work was sold."[26] However, as Orozco himself points out in another letter to his wife dated October 11, 1928, Mrs. Sterner asked that his drawings not be sold, as they would "cause a sensation" in Paris, and asked Mrs. Sikelianos to take the "entire collection of drawings" with her to Europe on her upcoming trip.[27]

Nevertheless, Reed didn't give up her hope for the artist's commercial possibilities, as she considered herself Orozco's self-appointed "mother, sister, agent, and 'bootlegger.' "[28] Shortly after this first exhibition, she gathered enough funds to rent a space on the top floor of the same East Fifty-seventh Street building and there established Delphic Studios, her own formal gallery dedicated to the promotion of various artists, but principally Orozco.[29] The Mexican painter designed the furniture and chose the colors to complement his work, which would be there on permanent display. In a letter to Mexican artist Manuel Rodríguez Lozano dated October 11, 1929, Antonieta Rivas Mercado, patroness of the arts, intellectual, and a tragic figure,[30] describes Reed's new gallery while indirectly criticizing its founder:

> Clemente [Orozco] met Alma Reed on November 10, 1928, quite by coincidence. Alma Reed is an Antonieta who never met a Rodríguez Lozano: all goodwill and disorientation.[31] Until then, Cleme[nte] had done nothing. Alma, who is well connected, embroiders her tragedy with Carrillo Puerto with red thread and thus holds great interest in Mexico. Clemente, a Mexican, unprotected and brilliant, allowed her to avenge herself over Mexico, which killed her Carrillo eight days before the wedding. She adopted him, and the last three or five days has done nothing but create a reputation for Orozco in the United States: articles, exhibitions, lectures, etc. She has now rented a flat on Fifty-seventh Street, where all the best art galleries are, half a block from Fifth Avenue, where she will open a gallery (Clemente mentions it sotto voce) that will be dedicated to Orozco. He is going to paint a fresco on the façade that will be visible from Fifth Avenue and in February will hold an exhibition (it's the best month).[32]

In *An American in Art: A Professional and Technical Autobiography*, U.S. muralist Thomas Hart Benton also recalls the Delphic Studios, an organization to which he felt obliged to belong and whose originator he describes:

> The Delphic Gallery was founded by Alma Reed, who, as a buxom and attractive blonde reporter for some press organization,[33] had found herself in Mexico at the time of the first successes of the Mexican School of painters.

*"Alma Reed being serenaded by Los Hermanos Hernández in New York, ca. 1936." (Courtesy of the Enrique Riverón Papers, 1918–1994, in the Archives of American Art, Smithsonian Institution)*

> Alma envisaged a resuscitation of the Greek mysteries of Delphi in a new and modern form. This was considerably too esoteric for me, but because Alma had the Mexican painter Clemente Orozco in tow and because I had great admiration for his work, I joined her organization.[34]

In a letter dated November 15, 1930, and included in her autobiography, *A Wall to Paint On,* North American artist and Diego Rivera's assistant Ione Robinson also comments on the Delphic Society and its eccentric cofounder:

> There is an extraordinary woman by the name of Alma Reed, who has a gallery called the "Delphic Studios"! She is going to sponsor Orozco. Mrs. Reed originally came from California, and I'm afraid that she carried with her some of the mystic ailments that sometime befall the people out there. Mrs. Reed is a very fat woman and wears long black dresses, but she has the face and hands of a Madonna! She belongs to a secret Greek order called the Delphic Society. (I only hope that she concentrates on selling Orozco's work!) The other night she invited me to one of the meet-

> ings of the Delphic Society. A Mrs. Hambridge, the wife of the man who is supposed to have discovered Dynamic Symmetry (a system of drawing mathematical forms), was there, dressed in white veils, and she wore Greek sandals. The rest of the people (all women) wore long chains with Greek crosses. The lights were dimmed—and the discussion of "Art on a Higher Plane" commenced. I was really frightened.
>
> When Mrs. Reed is talking, she waves her hands in the air and the words go up and down, all according to the dramatic incident she is recalling. The most dramatic part of her life was her engagement to Felipe Carrillo Puerto, the martyred governor of the state of Yucatan, Mexico. But in spite of her foolishness, Mrs. Reed has a rare quality. No matter what cause she is devoted to, she makes the most of every moment in order to arrive at some climax. She is determined that Orozco will paint a fresco in New York, that his genius will be recognized, and that with his recognition, Diego Rivera will fall into oblivion.[35]

The stock market crash of 1929 caused an abrupt decline in the art market, of course, but it did not mean the end of Reed's first venture into the gallery business. Indeed, on October 15, 1930, Reed's Delphic Studios presented Edward Weston's first solo exhibition in New York City. The idea had been born during a trip to Carmel, California, where Reed and Orozco met the photographer—recently back from his Mexican sojourn—and where Orozco posed for Weston's now-famous portrait of the artist. According to Orozco, Weston was "the first surrealist photographer," and there he proposed the idea of an exhibition in New York. Later that year Orozco himself hung the fifty photos making up the show. Reed would exhibit the work of other up-and-coming American photographers at her Fifty-seventh Street gallery, including that of Ansel Adams, who later complained that he never was paid for the eight prints Reed sold for him.

The California visit had been a professional venture, for earlier that year Reed had negotiated a commission for a mural by Orozco from Professor José Pijoan, head of art history at Pomona College in Claremont, California.[36] The work, titled *Prometheus Bound* and informed by the ideas and individuals Orozco had encountered during many hours spent in conversation and debate at the Delphic Society, was completed in 1930. Soon after, Reed secured another commission for Orozco from the New School for Social Research in Manhattan. Thomas Hart Benton, in his autobiography, recalls Reed's role in what would be Orozco's second U.S. mural:

> At this time, Alvin Johnson, founder of the New School for Social Research, had raised enough money for the erection of a building for the school on

*Detail of Orozco's mural at the New School for Social Research in Manhattan's Greenwich Village, showing the artist's rendition of Carrillo Puerto and Lenin.*

> West Twelfth Street near Fifth Avenue. Hearing of this, Alma visited Johnson and offered Orozco's services as a muralist. They were accepted. Orozco would paint a mural for the New School's dining room for the expenses of execution.[37]

The work was inaugurated on January 19, 1931, and its principal mural was entitled *Table of Brotherhood.*

Among the images included in the fresco cycle is a portrait of Felipe Carrillo Puerto, depicting him in the same pose as that of a photograph that the martyred governor of Yucatán had inscribed and sent to Alma after their first encounter in the Yucatán. In the background, Orozco painted the main pyramid of Chichén Itzá, which Alma and Felipe had climbed together almost ten years earlier. Below, the artist painted groups of women, recalling the progressive Feminist Leagues headed by Felipe's sister Elvia in Mérida. Other world leaders depicted by Orozco at this universal supper were Gandhi and Lenin, but in 1952, censorship brought about by McCarthyism forced school authorities to cover up not only Lenin's portrait but Carrillo Puerto's as well. In 1932, a year after the New School commission, Orozco was invited by Dartmouth College to paint what was to be his last U.S. mural, *Indian Prometheus.* Its title was a clear allusion to his growing fascination with the concept of the "cosmic race," an idea first proposed by José Vasconcelos in the early 1920's and certainly shaped by the numerous Delphic Society events Orozco had attended.

That same year Reed published the first book dedicated to the art of Orozco. The large volume contains a five-page introduction to the artist and his work, in which Reed describes Orozco's art as "an integral part of the drama evoked by the crash of age-old systems and the reversal of once immutable scientific laws."[38] The book also includes "Biographical Notes of the Artist," as well as more than one hundred black-and-white reproductions, many of them photographs of the artist's frescoes taken by such essential photographers of Mexico as Tina Modotti, Edward Weston, and José María Lupercio, all acquaintances of Reed. It should be pointed out that Reed herself published this landmark book in her Delphic Studios press, which would later publish such works as *Photographs of Mexico,* by Anton Bruehl (1933), a book chosen by jury for an exhibit of American book illustrators held by the American Institute of Graphic Arts; *Art Young's Inferno: A Journey through Hell Six Hundred Years after Dante,* by Art Young (1934);

*On the back of this photograph Reed has inscribed the following heading: "Felipe Carrillo Puerto, martyred governor of the Yucatán, known as the 'Abraham Lincoln of the Mayab.'"*

*Three Dollars a Year,* by G. Russell Steininger and Paul Van de Velde (1935), the account of daily life of a Oaxacan Indian; *Bowery Parade and Other Poems of Protest,* by Stella Wynne Herron, with illustrations by Orozco (1936); *System and Dialectics of Art,* by John D. Graham (1937); *Book of Job Interpreted,* by Emily S. Hamblen, with illustrations by William Blake (1939); and *I, Mary Magdalene,* by Juliet Thompson (1940).

In 1997 I returned to Mérida, this time with a group of professors and students from the United States International University in Mexico City. Among the people I met during the trip was Lindajoy Fenley, a specialist in traditional Mexican music who was traveling with her mother. She too was fascinated by the legend of Alma Reed and, given her interest in Mexican popular ballads, had already begun to investigate Reed's life, motivated by the ballad that bears her name. During the course of our excursion, which took us to major Maya archaeological sites, as well as to the ruins of various henequen haciendas, we discussed this unique figure in Mexican history: Reed's life and fate had been caught up in the political designs of a country that, having overthrown the dictatorship of Porfirio Diaz, was in the middle of an ideological and artistic renaissance, with a special emphasis placed on Mexico's cultural heritage. During our stay in Mérida, Ms. Fenley visited Reed's grave, which had been strategically placed near that of her beloved Carrillo Puerto, himself interred next to his parents, siblings, and estranged wife, from whom he had filed for divorce at the time of his execution, to the shock and disdain of the traditional Catholic majority of Yucatán.

As previously mentioned, Alma herself had been briefly married to the businessman Samuel Payne Reed in 1915, but the marriage was annulled when he became hopelessly ill soon after their wedding.[39] Nevertheless, she liked the name "Reed" and kept it all of her life. Over the years, this decision has caused some confusion, leading at least one researcher to assert that Alma was the sister of John Reed, author of *Insurgent Mexico.*[40] Obviously, this is not the case, as her last name is Sullivan, one that she is said to have traced back to England's Mary Tudor.[41] Although she was brought up in an Irish Catholic household, Alma had distanced herself from Catholicism from an early age, according to her close friend Richard Posner, when her mother told her that her pet dog would not go to heaven. More tellingly, while kneeling in prayer at the Vatican, Alma was once accosted by a priest. This was, as Posner recalls, the final "nail in the coffin," as she would later adopt a keen interest in Unitarianism.[42]

Recently I had the honor of accompanying Sr. Ruperto Poot Cobá, former director of Mérida's Panteón General and the person responsible for placing Reed's funerary monument, on an excursion to visit her grave. There I was able to photograph it and appreciate its discreet proximity to Carrillo Puerto's monument.

Upon reviewing Alma's correspondence shortly after her death, Reed's friend

*Funerary monument in honor of Governor Felipe Carrillo Puerto, located in Mérida's Panteón General. His brothers and the other members of his political party who were murdered as a result of the Delahuertista revolt also repose here.*

and flatmate Rosa Lie Johansson discovered a letter dated a year before, in which Reed requests that "if anything happens to me, Rosa Lie, I want to be buried as close to Felipe Carrillo Puerto as possible."[43] Upon learning that Alma's ashes had been kept for a year by the Gayosso funeral home in Mexico City because of lack of payment, Johansson contacted Reed's friend and patron Pablo Bush Romero, founder of the *Club de Exploraciones y Deportes Acuáticos de México* (CEDAM),[44] which employed Alma as official historian.

In his unpublished memoirs, Joe Nash, senior *Mexico City News* reporter and a resident of Mexico City for more than fifty years, divulges the mystery of Alma's ashes as well as that of her lost autobiography, an enigma that was partially revealed upon his first encounter with Mr. Bush Romero in 1967:

> I had never met Bush but enjoyed a warm welcome, being advised that CEDAM's Chairman of the Board was a constant reader of the decades-old Sunday travel section of *Vistas,* "perhaps mainly because that's where Alma regularly appeared."
>
> "Don Pablo, do you have any idea where in the world Alma's ashes might be?"
>
> "Right over there on the mantle."
>
> One mystery had been solved. For the second question there was no answer. He too was puzzled as to the disappearance of the text of her autobiography.
>
> Bush said he was glad I had dropped in, for the following week there

*Sr. Ruperto Poot Cobá (left), former director of the Panteón General in Mérida, with the editor at Alma Reed's tombstone.*

would be a brief ceremony at the Mérida Cemetery, where Alma's ashes would be placed in a small pink concrete shaft he had provided. He invited me to attend at the lot the governor had given across the pathway from the center of the mammoth hemicycle erected to the memory of and marking the grave of her intimate friend, Felipe Carrillo Puerto.

I asked how Bush happened to acquire the urn of ashes. The courtly gentleman of the "old school," friend to the end, said: "It was simple. They had been at Gayosso's for more than a year with the family having no interest at all in acquiring them, so with their permission, I paid the bill and there they are."

Being advised that I had reservations for a travel trade exposition in London but was sure my editor would make it a point to cover the Mérida event, Don Pablo had one more thing to say: "By the way, tell him not to mention the governor's gift of the lot. There are still Carrillo Puerto descendants, as there are Orozcos in Guadalajara, and they're mossbacks about Alma."

The editor was so advised but spiced up his report with mention of the governor's kindness to the memory of a patrician lady. The newsmen still reside in Mexico City. Don Pablo chose to retire in El Paso, where he died at the turn of this century.[45]

The director of the cemetery was able to comply with the governor's wishes, and he carved out a space for Reed's cenotaph directly in front of Carrillo Puerto's tomb, under the canopy of a large tree and separated from her true love only by a narrow road that passes between them. One side of the rose-colored shaft bears the following epitaph: "Alma Reed: prolific writer and engaging lecturer. She deeply loved Mexico, and Mexico honored her with the Aztec Eagle in recognition of her merits as promoter of the arts, critic, historian, and humanist. Greece and Lebanon also distinguished her with their highest decorations."

From this discreet angle, Alma and Felipe are, albeit obliquely, united in death.

For my part, I didn't forget the legend of Alma and Felipe's tragic romance, although five years would pass before they would again appear, this time in the pages of her lost autobiography, which I found in an abandoned apartment in Mexico City in August 2001. Several colleagues accompanied me, including Lois Parkinson Zamora of the University of Houston, whom I had managed to get involved in this "search and rescue mission" during our frequent "sit-downs" at Mexico City's time-honored restaurants, where I would describe the life of this exceptional woman whose fascination with Mexico was mirrored by our own. The succession of events that culminated in the recovery of Reed's autobiography is a complex one, as it involves more than a few people and places. However, the key figure who eventually led to the discovery of the 110,000-word typescript was Mrs. Lisette Parodi, whom I met in 1994 through her daughter Claudia, professor of Spanish linguistics at the University of California, Los Angeles. Mrs. Parodi was born in Poland but came to Mexico in the aftermath of World War II and there married an Italian businessman. From the very start, she was active in the cultural and social life of Mexico City. In that context in 1958, she met Richard

*Close-up of Reed's funerary monument, showing one of the inscriptions provided by Pablo Bush Romero, director of CEDAM. It reads: "Alma Reed: prolific writer, emotional speaker; she loved Mexico dearly and Mexico honored her with the Aztec Eagle in recognition of her merits as a promoter of art criticism. Greece and Lebanon also distinguished her, bestowing upon her their highest honors."*

Posner, an aspiring playwright from New York who had recently arrived to teach drama at Mexico City College—now the Universidad de las Américas, located in Cholula, near the city of Puebla. Mrs. Parodi and Mr. Posner lived in the same apartment building where I eventually recovered the typescript, located on Melchor Ocampo Boulevard, in the Cuauhtémoc neighborhood. Mrs. Parodi recalls that she first perceived Mr. Posner melodically, as he had the habit of playing classical music at a high volume, something that she quite enjoyed. One evening they met at a cultural event, realized they were neighbors, and soon became fast friends.

Several years prior to their encounter, around 1956, Posner had met and befriended Alma Reed at a reception held by a woman who had shown interest in producing one of his plays. As he recalls, there were few people at the gathering, but among them was a woman who stood out because of her striking figure and rather unusual attire. As Posner would later learn, Reed never wore anything but the most extravagant satin ensembles, many of which she had designed for her by a local tailor, who created her trademark ample, flowing gowns, capes, and other garments. Such outfits, often combined with wide-brimmed hats trimmed with

*Close-up of the monument's Maya-inspired design. Note the incorrect date of birth.*

*Reed in a satin gown and laurel-crown hat, later years.*

a feather, netting, or a silk rose, never failed to call attention to this older woman, who still conserved the radiant blue eyes and milky complexion so celebrated in her ballad.[46]

Later on, when the two had become better acquainted and Posner worked up the nerve to ask Reed about her eccentric apparel, she demurely admitted that she suffered from "arrested development" when it came to contemporary fashions, preferring the styles in vogue around 1912. However, as may be noted in several of the reproductions included in this book, Reed also regularly donned indigenous Mexican dress and jewelry, the first of which was the legendary *traje de mestiza,* the traditional Yucatecan costume that Carrillo Puerto had had made for her upon her first visit to Yucatán in 1923 and which is now conserved in Mexico's National History Museum. In two of her surviving portraits, the first painted by Philip Stein—also known as Estaño, a name given to him by Mexican muralist David Alfaro Siqueiros—and the second by Roberto Cueva del Río, Alma dons native gear, including what appear to be pre-Hispanic earrings.

Her wardrobe later included embroidered *huipiles,* silk *rebozos,* and other out-

*Reed wearing one of her signature hats. (Photo by Alice Reiner)*

*Portrait of Alma Reed by Philip Stein, oil on canvas, 1957. (Courtesy of Elsy Bush Romero)*

fits still worn today by many Mexican women. Sometimes she would top off such attire with an enormous rosary made of gold filigree, a gift from her beloved Felipe. Immediately before his abduction by de la Huerta sympathizers, Felipe sent to Alma, through a trusted courier, an engagement ring set with a large garnet. The ring is now apparently lost, although it might turn up among the items recently donated by the nieces of Rosa Lie Johansson to the National History Museum in Mexico City.

Before arriving in New York City in the late 1920's, Reed had spent four years studying classical archaeology in Greece and Italy. In 1933 she traveled to Chicago with Orozco, who had been invited to show his work at the Arts Club, one of the conservative bastions of the midwestern art world.[47] Up to this point, Reed's activities are well documented, but little is known of her life between 1933 and 1941 when, at the age of fifty-two, she accepted a five-year stint as cultural editor of the *Press Register* in Mobile, Alabama. During this period, she also hosted a weekly radio program, dedicated to various cultural themes, and founded the Society for the Friends of Mexico.[48]

Details of Reed's activities during this period have recently surfaced in the file that the Federal Bureau of Investigations (FBI) maintained on her activities

*Portrait of Alma Reed by Roberto Cueva del Río, oil on canvas, 1966. Note the Maya-inspired jade necklace, ear spools, and traditional headdress. (Courtesy of Museo Nacional de Historia, Mexico City)*

*Reed dressed as a "flapper," wearing the gold filigree crucifix given to her in 1923 by Felipe Carrillo Puerto.*

in the United States and Mexico through the 1940's and 1950's, an expurgated version of which I obtained through the Freedom of Information Act. According to an office memorandum sent to the director of the organization and dated December 16, 1948, one of its informants

> advised that she suspected Mrs. Reed might be connected with Communistic activity and suspected her of Communistic tendencies because of

> her treatment of colored people and also because she had been connected with the [George] Wallace campaign, having been away from Mobile about two months last fall working for the Progressive Party. When asked about Mrs. Reed's treatment of colored people and in just what way it would indicate that she is a Communist, [blank] explained that Mrs. Reed is a Northerner and that the "Northern people like to stir up the colored people."

Six years later, on September 21, 1954, another anonymous informant mentioned that "Mrs. Reed had attempted to have [blank] attend a meeting of an interracial organization whose members included [blank]" and stated that "this, in addition to several other things she observed in Mrs. Reed indicating a 'strange' attitude of friendship between Mrs. Reed and the colored people of Mobile, had raised a question in her mind as to Mrs. Reed's sincerity and reliability."

Reed's alleged involvement with Communist activities in the United States and Mexico is detailed in a later memorandum, dated August 18, 1954, in which another unidentified FBI informant

> reported that Miss Reed is reportedly a former member of the Communist Party and was an active promoter of anti-Catholicism in Mexico in the early twenties. During a trip from New York to El Paso, a period of nine days due to engine trouble, Miss Reed, according to [blank], consistently defended Russia and the Communist Party. He stated that she attempted to persuade [blank] to join the "Movement for World Peace," and made the statement to the effect that [John Foster] Dulles and the United States wish to destroy what is basic Christianity, the faith which has been given to us by Lenin, Stalin, and all such great men.

As illustrated by several notations in Reed's FBI file, many of these informants were less than reliable, and some of them even had criminal records or were described as compulsive liars. The lack of integrity on the part of the FBI's local informants—combined with the fervent anti-Communist atmosphere that in many ways defined the mid-twentieth century and was fueled by now-discredited politicians like Senator Joseph McCarthy—must be taken into consideration when determining Reed's supposed affiliation with such potentially incriminating political organizations. At the same time it will be recalled that, beginning with her "soul mate," Felipe Carrillo Puerto, Reed consistently supported socialist governments but, at least on the surface, would always identify herself as a Democrat, having been—according to the organization's cofounder, newspaper reporter Joe Nash—a charter member of Democrats Abroad, established in Mexico City in 1942.

*Personalized Christmas card with a portrait of Reed at an unidentified pre-Hispanic archaeological site, addressed to Richard Posner. It reads: "For Dick with all my best wishes and affection from Alma. Xmas '63."*

In 1952 Reed finally returned to her beloved Mexico for good, where she was still a living legend and where her eponymous ballad was customarily performed by local musicians upon her arrival at a restaurant or cultural event.

There Reed was soon hired by the owner of the Mexican daily *Novedades,* Rómulo O'Farrill Sr., as a columnist for his recently founded English-language daily, *The News,* which, after almost fifty years, only recently ceased publication. She wrote a weekly column entitled "Alma M. Reed Reports" for its Sunday edition as she had for the *New York Times* in the 1930's, when she published many articles in its *Sunday Magazine,* often dedicated to pre-Hispanic and classical archaeology.

It was at this time that Richard Posner and Reed, who lived around the corner from one another, became friends, and he would often accompany her to various social and professional engagements in the capital. Dick, as she called him, would become one of her closest confidants: "everything but lovers," as he would later recall. He would remain so until Reed's unexpected death on November 20, 1966, the anniversary of the Mexican Revolution: a fitting coincidence, given Reed's extraordinary passion for freedom and democracy. As her friend Joe Nash recalls in his unpublished memoirs: "Had she been able to designate a date to terminate her militant career, that would have been it."

Several weeks before her death, Reed began to experience severe stomach pains, and when they became unbearable, her friend and flatmate Rosa Lie Johansson referred her to a Swiss doctor who shared Alma's political views and sense of humor. Evidently, he misdiagnosed her condition, believing it to be a severe case of "turista," a common bacterial infection that often assails foreigners in Mexico. When the pains worsened, Reed checked herself into the American British Cowdray (ABC) Hospital, where a few days after exploratory surgery revealed widespread intestinal cancer, she died.[49] In a conversation in 2002, Richard

*Reed with Richard Posner (standing on the right) and Rosa Lie Johansson (sitting next to Posner) and other colleagues from the* Mexico City News.

Posner recalled Alma's last words: "Dick, I never regretted writing anything, even things that I never published." For his part, Joe Nash remembers:

> Few of her friends knew Alma was in the ABC Hospital. One of her reporter friends visited her on November 19, and when questioning her about the manuscript, she said she was being released the following day, a Friday, that it was in her apartment and she would be sending it to her publisher on Monday. She died early in the morning on the 20, a national holiday commemorating the Revolution. A long-standing law in Mexico decrees that burials will be within twenty-four hours, so it was early in the afternoon on the day after that friends gathered, notably on Sullivan Street, at Mexico's most famed funeral home. Her brother, Stanley, on being escorted from the airport to the Continental Hilton, a block from the Sullivan Street wake and meeting a welcoming committee in the lobby, said he was particularly ingratiated that he had come, not realizing the popularity of his sister. She was cremated beside the double circle of Mexico's illustrious personalities in the Dolores cemetery.[50]

The day Reed passed away, Posner entered her duplex apartment on Río Elba #53, where he recovered many of the author's papers and other documents, including one version of her life story, which provides part of the contents of this book. As mentioned earlier, he apparently stuffed all of her assorted papers and folders—which neatly contained the first twenty-one chapters of "Peregrina," along with Felipe's love letters and numerous telegrams—into one of her many henequen bags, or *sabucanes,* as they are called in Mayan. It was there that I found them in the back of a bedroom closet, hidden behind several mildewed pillows and blankets. On two previous occasions, accompanied only by Mrs. Parodi, I had unearthed a copy of Alma's last will and testament, as well as several Christmas cards with her photo and salutations, but the fabled typescript was nowhere to be found in the grimy flat.

But the third time was a charm: this valuable material had remained hidden in Posner's closet for almost forty years, and I was fortunate to have found it when I did. As it turned out, the apartment had a leaky roof, and all of the contents in the bedroom were ruined during a strong rainstorm only two weeks after I retrieved them. A few days later they were carted off to a local garbage dump.

After living in Mexico City for almost seven years, in the summer of 2000 I moved to New York City, where I had been offered a professorship in the Department of Spanish and Latin American Cultures at Barnard College, Columbia University. Upon my departure, Mrs. Parodi recommended that I contact Richard Posner,

*One of Reed's signature Christmas cards found in Richard Posner's Mexico City apartment. It message reads: "Merry Christmas and a prosperous New Year."*

who had returned to Brooklyn from Mexico City in the early 1980's because of his mother's illness. She passed away soon after his return to the United States, and because of his own developing heart condition, Posner was unable to return to the high elevation of Mexico City. After settling into my flat on the Upper West Side, I called Posner and explained that I was a friend of Mrs. Parodi and that, given my interest in Mexican culture, she had recommended I contact him. We set up a meeting for the following week at a Chinese restaurant near his apartment on Ocean Parkway, in Brooklyn. In the meantime I prepared my interview;

I wanted to learn more about the personal and professional life of the Mexican writer Salvador Novo, his close friend who had died in 1974. Posner was notably enthused upon meeting someone with a common acquaintance who was also very interested in Mexico's cultural milieu during the mid-twentieth century. We immediately became friends and began to meet—always near his apartment in Brooklyn—on a regular basis.

Reed's name never came up during our first conversations, as I was interested in Novo and his relationship with other key writers, including Federico García Lorca, with whom Novo was rumored to have been romantically involved. After we had met on several occasions, Posner briefly mentioned Reed, assuring me, however vaguely, that "there was a story there." Still focused on my interest in Novo, I failed to react, and my new friend apparently decided to wait for a better moment to reveal his long-kept secret. This happened late one December evening in 2000, when, as he was reminiscing about his friendships with various Mexican artistic and cultural figures, including actress Dolores del Río and writer Celestino Gorostiza, he again mentioned Alma Reed. After coolly reminding me that he had already hinted at a special story regarding his dear friend "La Peregrina," Posner began to discuss their unique friendship in detail, recounting how he was one of only two people that Reed trusted to read her proofs at *The News* and how, on many occasions, they traveled together to different parts of Mexico, often in the company of her favorite niece and literary heiress, Patsy Berman, or such noted figures as the archaeologist Eulalia Guzmán, who had allegedly discovered the remains of Cuauhtémoc, the last Aztec emperor. Posner also recalled their long conversations about Reed's past and described the way Reed would close her eyes and throw back her head when speaking, especially when remembering her days with Carrillo Puerto, a topic that would invariably put her into a trancelike state. I assume this must have been a special attribute, because Elena Poniatowska also confessed to me one day that she was always afraid to approach Reed when they coincided along with Yucatecan poet Rosario Sansores in the elevator at the *Novedades* offices, because the former had the strange habit of closing her eyes and humming to herself during the lift upstairs, perhaps intoning the lines of "La Peregrina" and evoking her cherished moments with Felipe.

During our conversations, Posner recalled the names of other people—many now deceased—who had also enjoyed a friendship with Reed during the last years of her life. First and foremost, he mentioned Reed's flatmate, the Swedish painter Rosa Lie Johansson. After the two met during a trip to New York City, Reed later invited Johansson to reside in her Mexico City apartment when she was away on numerous lecture tours in the United States, often speaking about Mexico for such organizations as the Columbia Lecture Bureau. Ms. Johansson, who had been a student at New York's Art Students League and in the 1950's was a regular at the celebrated Cedar Bar, where she often accompanied Willem

*Reed standing guard at Carrillo Puerto's monument on the anniversary of his assassination, January 3, 1963.*

De Kooning and Jackson Pollock, was eager to explore new horizons. She gladly accepted Reed's invitation to come to Mexico, arriving in 1960 and living there until her death in August 2004.

Following Posner's clues, I called the Swedish Embassy in Mexico City to request information about Johansson. Unfortunately, the personnel at the embassy had no knowledge of her, and it wasn't until Mrs. Parodi happened to read an article about one of her exhibitions in the Mexican daily *Excélsior* that I was able to track Johansson down. I headed to the Salón de la Plástica Mexicana in the Roma neighborhood, where I inquired about the artist. Indeed she had held several exhibitions at the gallery, and upon my request the receptionist agreed to phone Maestra Johansson and tell her that I would like to speak with her about her good friend Alma Reed. After a brief conversation, the young woman wrote down her telephone number on a scrap of paper. Later that afternoon I called Ms. Johansson, and she agreed to meet me the following Wednesday at her apartment, also located in the Colonia Cuauhtémoc, Reed's old neighborhood. At one time or another, Juan Rulfo, B. Traven, Juan José Arreola, Juan Soriano, Octavio Paz, Pita Amor, and Gabriel García Márquez all resided on the jacaranda-lined streets bearing the names of the rivers of the world: Nilo, Ganges, Hudson, Elba, Ebro.

That Wednesday afternoon an elderly woman with watery blue eyes, wearing traditional Swedish clogs and a tiny black ribbon pinned to her silver hair, received me with an inquisitive smile. Upon entering her apartment, I was immediately met by Reed's gaze, for there on the mantelpiece sat the bronze bust cast in 1924 by Vincenzo Miserendino, a photogram of which I had recently uncovered in an issue of the *Brooklyn Standard Union* published that same year. There were also portraits of Reed hanging on the walls of the sunny flat, in particular a canvas painted by Johansson of Reed standing in profile, with the pages of various newspapers incorporated as a reference to her journalistic activities in Mexico and abroad.

In the living room, the *maestra* had laid out a smorgasbord of various sweets, cakes, and other treats on the coffee table, along with the ever-present coffeepot—covered with what appeared to be the lid of a tin can. After we sat down, Ms. Johansson inquired as to my interest in Alma Reed.

At first the *maestra* was reserved about discussing the life of her dearly departed friend, because, according to Johansson, she had told the author of *Passionate Pilgrim,* Reed's biography, many things that later weren't recorded correctly, and she was particularly incensed about the suggestion that Alma Reed and artist José Clemente Orozco might have been romantically involved during the time they worked together in New York. Ms. Johansson couldn't bear the fact May had suggested they were "two lonely people" who came together during a time of emotional necessity. Indeed Orozco himself was obliged to clarify his relationship with Reed, and in a letter to his wife, Margarita, dated November 16, 1928, he cautiously describes their unique friendship:

> Your last two letters make me sad for various reasons. I see that you have formed a very wrong idea regarding my relationship with Mrs. Sikelianos and Alma Reed. It is true that they greatly esteem and care for me, but it does not go beyond the purely intellectual plane, professional, that is, and has nothing to do with the family. There is no reason that we might have a personal relationship, and less with the dry and grim character of these

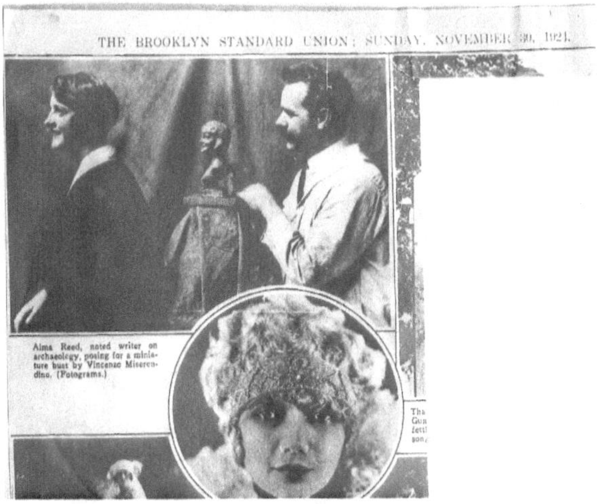

*(above left) Bronze bust of Alma Reed by Vincenzo Miserendino, 1924. This is a reproduction of a "Fotogram" that appeared in the* Brooklyn Standard Union *on November 30, 1924.*

*(left) Portrait of Alma Reed as a journalist by Rosa Lie Johansson, oil on canvas. This was Johansson's favorite portrait of the three or four she made of her admired friend and flatmate Alma Reed. (Courtesy of Museo Nacional de Historia, Mexico City)*

> people whom you already know something about. And you know very well that they don't understand favors or anything like that.[51]

Joe Nash would later inform me that Reed had confessed to him on several occasions that she and Orozco were indeed in love, but that he was a married man and Alma, who had lost Felipe—also married—several years prior, was unwilling or unable to pursue this impossible romance.

Ms. Johansson's initial reservations about my project were assuaged when I

*From left to right: Senator Bohorques, Alma Reed, Ethel Turner (widow of John Kenneth Turner), and Mr. and Mrs. Harold Coy in Cuernavaca. Mrs. Turner was involved in the final correction of Reed's memoir, and her commentary has been annotated in the last two chapters.*

happened to mention that I too was of Swedish ancestry and proceeded to tell her how my great-aunt Esther, who lived to be 103, used to make coffee with egg whites, often accompanying it with such delicacies as *kroppkakor,* diminutive meatballs, and other Nordic specialties. Johansson paused for several minutes in midsentence, apparently surveying my alleged Swedishness, and suddenly exclaimed; "Yes, now I remember. That's how the farm people used to make their coffee!" From that point on, she was more comfortable and insisted that because I was a "good Swede," I could be trusted with the information and materials she was about to provide me. When she inquired as to my interest and knowledge about Reed, I explained how I had come upon part of her autobiography. She expressed astonishment that Posner also possessed a copy of the typescript, because the *maestra* thought that she was the only one with a copy. As it turns out, more than one version of the document exists, but thanks to Johansson's copy, I was able to piece together what I believe to be the final edition, which is the contents of this book. I soon discovered that Posner's copy was missing the last three chapters, which deal with the death of Felipe Carrillo Puerto, and that the only reason Johansson had them in her possession was because they were given to her shortly after Reed's death by Ethel Turner. The widow of John Kenneth Turner, who wrote *Barbarous Mexico* to document the extreme abuse endured by Maya peasants during the height of the henequen industry in the Yucatán, Mrs. Turner had volunteered to edit Reed's autobiography and apparently had just finished correcting the last chapters when she received word of her friend's death.

After several initial meetings, Johansson agreed to lend me her copy of the typescript in order to compare it with the one I had already found in Posner's apartment. She also mentioned that there was more material to be had, but that in order for me to gain access to it, I would have to secure a written contract from a U.S. publishing house, thus guaranteeing that the book would finally be published. Ms. Johansson handed me a rejection letter that she had received in the late 1960's from Crown Publishers of New York, which was preceded by others sent to Reed herself, claiming that although Reed's was undoubtedly a fascinating story, it really held little appeal for wide audiences, as it covered a very particular time and place mainly unknown to U.S. readers. This was a severe blow for Reed, who had spent many months writing her life story, a saga that was supposed to be adapted for the big screen by producer and writer Budd Schulberg, author of the award-winning novel *What Makes Sammy Run?* and screenwriter of the critically acclaimed film *On the Waterfront,* starring Marlon Brando and Eva Marie Saint. Apparently, Reed had even proposed that Elizabeth Taylor play the role of La Peregrina.

Posner, a longtime friend of Schulberg's, had always believed that Reed's life would make a wonderful film, and he knew very well that she didn't want a Mexican production of her memoirs, because she feared it would water down the political aspects of her relationship with Carrillo Puerto and highlight only their tragic romance. Posner contacted Schulberg and told him about Reed, who had already begun her autobiography, which was also a biography of Carrillo Puerto and a political history of the Yucatán. They soon met at one of Reed's fabled "crèche parties," held at her apartment on Río Elba street during the Christmas season and attended by such local celebrities as painters Raúl Anguiano, José Segura, and Fito Best-Maugard; Howard Phillips, editor of the magazine *Mexican Life,* where Reed sometimes published her articles; and José Luis Ramírez, owner and founder of Editorial Diana, which would later publish a posthumous translation of Reed's last volume on Mexican archaeology, entitled *El remoto pasado de México.* Once assembled, Reed would introduce everyone at her party, while presiding on the staircase above the crowd. According to Posner, Reed and Schulberg

*Reed with writer and producer Budd Schulberg at the entrance to Chapultepec Park, Mexico City, in a photo taken by her friend and confidant Richard Posner.*

got along from the very start and would often meet at a Polynesian restaurant in the Zona Rosa for dinner and to discuss plans for the future film.

According to the producer, his interest in this project was sparked because of the way the story was at once individual and collective. In an interview published in *The News* on September 15, 1962, Schulberg explains:

> Alma Reed's personal story is tellingly intertwined with the struggle of the Mexican people to achieve mature and liberal statehood in the face of countless tragedies. As a longtime admirer of Mexican life and culture, I have long been attracted to the relationship of two people from opposite sides of the border who meet and work with common purpose to fight against man's inhumanity to man.

As I later discovered, Mr. Schulberg had been providing Reed with a stipend in order that she complete her life story, an income that greatly aided her financial situation, which was always precarious. Indeed, Posner himself was worried that the project would never come to fruition because Reed kept postponing the completion of her autobiography in order to finish what would be her last work, *The Ancient Past of Mexico*, a survey of the archaeology of Mesoamerica, published in 1966 by Crown Publishers and, as mentioned above, by Mexico's Editorial Diana in 1972.

Upon Reed's death, the manuscript of her autobiography disappeared, and the portion that Schulberg had already received is said to have been lost in 1985 when a deadly earthquake struck Mexico City, leaving his Colonia Juárez studio condemned. According to Posner, the producer was never able to recover his belongings; he was prohibited from entering the structure, which was eventually demolished. Although his movie was never made, Reed's adventures in the Yucatán had already inspired the 1938 film *La Golondrina (The Swallow)*, directed by Miguel Contreras Torres. More than twenty years after her death, Reed's adventures in the Yucatán provided the subject of the movie *Peregrina* (1987), starring the Argentine actress and vedette Sasha Montenegro. The movie centered upon Reed's romance with Carrillo Puerto—just what she had most feared. Reed was also featured in Julio Bracho's 1973 film, *En busca de un muro (In Search of a Wall)*, the story of muralist José Clemente Orozco's life and struggles in New York.

Another essential link in the series of events that led to the discovery of this remarkable document, as well as its historical contextualization, was the information provided by aforementioned journalist and longtime Mexico City resident Joe Nash. After traveling to Mexico on bicycle in the early 1930's with Frances Toor's groundbreaking guidebook under his arm, he had returned to live in Mexico City soon after. He met Reed at *The News* during the early 1950's, where at the time he was a cub reporter specializing in cultural and historical topics. Mr. Nash, now in his early nineties, has recently begun to record some of his most vivid recollections of time spent working with Alma at *The News*, and these chronicles help illuminate certain aspects of Reed's character that would be otherwise forgotten. One of his most revealing vignettes documents Alma's forays into the heart of macho Mexico: the cantina, where, until recently, "decent" women were not allowed. As Nash recalls in his memoirs:

> No one knows who introduced her to the comeliness of the Negresco cantina. At first sight of the first woman to patronize them, no one dared evict such a patrician person. So without any formal introduction, her acquaintance took root and grew as a meeting place far less stuffy than the newspaper office, whose owners had no contract with the employees to pro-

vide a den of inspiration. Following Alma's passing, one of her confrères asked for permission and provided a small envelope-size bronze plaque, which read, "In this booth sat Alma Reed, 'La Peregrina,' who leveled yet another barrier." The sign prohibiting women is long gone. No one knows what happened to the plaque in a city known for the wanton theft of bronze ID's large and small.

In another passage describing the inauguration of Acapulco's International Film Festival, Nash documents Alma's keen interest in cinema, while divulging a little-known incident that illustrates how La Peregrina could be roused to action:

> *Anatomy of a Murder* was one of the films shown in the several nights of the festival and [Otto] Preminger, as the director of that film, participated. Some cub reporters for Mexico City papers were so awed by the Preminger presence, they asked no questions. A dishwater blonde whose father was posted at the Uruguayan Embassy and who did an occasional column for *El Universal,* the oldest Spanish-language daily in the capital, was widely unknown but there. A well-seasoned reporter, Alma started the jolly afternoon with: "Mr. Preminger, do you suppose you will ever do anything for cinematic art's sake? I was so tired of having dirty panties rubbed in my face through *Anatomy.*"
>
> "I might. I accept assignments to make money, and this film is certainly doing that."
>
> Strangely, there was no newspaper photographer there. The cub reporters were so overwhelmed, they asked no questions. Alma sat to Preminger's right, and Miss Uruguay stood to his left until she directed a suggestion to the dowager lady of legend: "Why don't you shut up, you old bag, and give someone else a chance?"
>
> All hell broke loose. Alma, half-rising from her deep-seated deck chair clambered over Preminger to get at Miss Uruguay; the Mexico City editor grabbed Alma's skirt and tugged mightily to keep her seated; and Preminger doubled over with his hands protecting his head. That well ended an otherwise drab session of inconsequential questions.

Fortunately, Reed's sustained dedication to Mexico and its culture didn't go unnoticed by Mexican authorities, and in 1961 she became the third woman inducted into the Orden del Águila Azteca in recognition of her outstanding contribution to Mexican culture over a period of almost fifty years. Other women to have received the honor were aviator Amelia Earhart and opera diva Grace Moore. That year was pivotal for Reed because she was also inducted into the

*Reed bearing her Águila Azteca medal.*

Order of Welfare by the Republic of Greece in acknowledgement of her contribution to the recovery of classical Greek culture through the foundation of the Delphic Society in New York, as well as her translations of the poetry of Angelo Sikelianos.

She was later awarded the Cross of the Holy Sepulcher by Patriarch Damianos as well as the Order of Merit from the Republic of Lebanon. It is my hope that through the recovery and publication of this most extraordinary autobiography Reed's place in the cultural histories of Mexico and the United States will

*Reed receives the Order of Welfare decoration from the ambassador of Greece to Mexico, her close friend Leander P. Vourvoulias.*

be duly recognized and that the still unexplored contributions of other outstanding US women—such as Frances Toor, Margaret Shedd, and Ione Robinson—to post-revolutionary Mexican culture will be object of future documentation and study.

*About This Edition*

Throughout the preparation of Reed's autobiography, a complex process that began with the transcription of the twenty-three typewritten chapters that make up *Peregrina,* my principal goal has been to respect the author's perceived intent, knowing that she had planned to send the manuscript to her publisher at Crown the day after she was released from the hospital, thus confirming that, in Reed's opinion, her autobiography was practically complete. The changes I made to her text were to correct typographical errors and the misspelling of several Spanish words, as well as several inconsistencies in dates, names, and titles. Some additional minor copyediting changes were also made.

As Mr. Posner's copy of "Peregrina" was missing the last three chapters and Ms. Johansson's was complete, I relied heavily upon the material contained in the latter, as I believe that it was Reed's final edition. After comparing both versions, often side by side, I detected corrections made in Alma's hand to Johansson's copy of what, in the first twenty chapters, was essentially a facsimile of Posner's document. However, I spliced two versions of chapter 21 because they were both fragmentary but, when combined, created a coherent unit. As the last three chapters bore no title, I inserted my own, while attempting to replicate the kinds of titles Reed had employed in her preceding chapters, often borrowing a phrase that the author had used in the body of the chapter. As mentioned previously, I have included endnotes throughout the text designed to assist readers unfamiliar with Mexican Spanish or Mexico's pre-Hispanic, colonial, and modern history, particularly that of the Yucatán. I have also provided bibliographical information where necessary, as Reed often refers to other historical and political works, especially in her re-creation of the events leading up to the death of Carrillo Puerto, the only event described in her autobiography that she did not witness herself.

The photographs included in my edition are principally those given to me by the late Rosa Lie Johansson, which I selected from more than five hundred images that she had inherited from Reed and stored in a cardboard box in her living room. They include an early photomontage depicting Reed as Mrs. Goodfellow, pictures taken by official photographers during her first trip to the Yucatán with the Carnegie Expedition, often accompanied by Carrillo Puerto, as well as studio portraits taken of her to accompany her books or publicize lecture tours in the United States. Several of the photographs I took myself during my research in Mérida, Yucatán, and at the National History Museum in Mexico City, while some I located in other archives, particularly that of the Smithsonian Institution. Where possible, the provenance and appropriate acknowledgment of all photographs is noted in each accompanying caption.

—*Michael K. Schuessler*

MEXICO CITY AND MANHATTAN, 2003–2005

# SELECTED BIBLIOGRAPHY

WORKS BY ALMA M. REED

*José Clemente Orozco.* New York: Delphic Studios, 1932.

*Orozco.* Translated by Jesús Amaya Topete (Spanish translation). Mexico City: Fondo de Cultura Económica, 1955.

*Orozco.* New York: Oxford University Press, 1956.

*Los cronistas de México.* Translated by Jesús Amaya Topete. Puebla: Grupo Literario Bohemia Poblana, 1957.

*The National University of Mexico: The Story of University City.* Mexico City: Editores Asociados, 1957.

*A Man and His Liberal Heritage.* Mexico City: M. Casas, 1958.

*The Mexican Muralists.* New York: Crown Publishers, 1960.

*Uxmal and the Cities of the Yucatán's Low Hills Region.* Mexico City: self-published, 1960.

*El cenote sagrado de Chichén Itzá cede de nuevo antiguo tesoro* [The Sacred Well of Chichén Itzá Gives Up Ancient Treasure Once More]. Publicación Club de Exploraciones y Deportes Acuáticos de México, no. 8. Mexico City: P. Bush, 1961.

*The Ancient Past of Mexico.* New York: Crown Publishers, 1966.

*El remoto pasado de México.* Mexico City: Editorial Diana, 1972.

*Works Translated by Alma Reed*

Fiego, G. Consoli. *Cumae and the Phlegraean Fields.* Naples: Mary E. Raiola, 1927.

Sikelianos, Angelo. *The Delphic Word . . . The Dedication.* New York: H. Vinal, 1928.

MONOGRAPH ABOUT ALMA REED

Finer, Neal. *Alma Reed: A Unique Bicultural Bridge between North American and Mexican Cultures in the Twentieth Century.* Tempe: Arizona State University Press, 1979.

WORKS CITED IN THE INTRODUCTION

Anreus, Alejandro. *Orozco in Gringoland: The Years in New York.* Albuquerque: University of New Mexico Press, 2001.

Benton, Thomas Hart. *An American in Art: A Professional and Technical Autobiography.* Lawrence: University Press of Kansas, 1969.

Delpar, Helen. *The Enormous Vogue of Things Mexican: Cultural Relations between the United States and Mexico, 1920–1935.* Tuscaloosa and London: University of Alabama Press, 1992.

Givner, Joan. *Katherine Anne Porter: A Life.* New York: Simon and Schuster, 1982.

Glusker, Susannah J. *Anita Brenner: A Mind of Her Own.* Austin: University of Texas Press, 1998.

May, Antoinette. *Passionate Pilgrim: The Extraordinary Life of Alma Reed.* New York: Paragon House, 1993.

Orozco, José Clemente. *Autobiografía.* Mexico City: Ediciones Era, 1970.

———. *Cartas a Margarita,* 1921–1949. With introduction and notes by Tatiana Herrero Orozco. Mexico City: Ediciones Era, 1987.

Rivas Mercado, Antonieta. *Obras completas de Antonieta Rivas Mercado.* Ed. Luis Mario Schneider. Lecturas Mexicanas, no. 93. Mexico City: Secretaría de Educación Pública, 1987.

Robinson, Ione. *A Wall to Paint On.* New York: A. P. Dutton and Co., 1946.

Ross, Ishbel. *Ladies of the Press: The Story of Women in Journalism by an Insider.* New York: Harper and Brothers, 1936.

Smith, H. Allen. *The Pig in the Barber Shop.* Boston: Little, Brown, 1958.

Walsh, Thomas F. *Katherine Anne Porter and Mexico: The Illusion of Eden.* Austin: University of Texas Press, 1992.

# PEREGRINA

*by Alma M. Reed*

# AUTHOR'S FOREWORD

A MORAL OBLIGATION TO HISTORY IS INCURRED BY ANYONE WHO HAS shared the hopes and aims of a great public leader sacrificed to the causes he courageously served. In writing *Peregrina* I have attempted to discharge a sacred responsibility of this character. The idealist who entered my own life to embody for me the archetypal reality of the Good, the True, and the Beautiful was Felipe Carrillo Puerto, martyred Governor of Yucatán, often referred to as the "Abraham Lincoln of Mexico."

My commitment was assumed with his full knowledge during the autumn of 1923, when we decided to unite our destinies. In that ecstatic hour of faith in our common future, we planned to collaborate on a book for which Felipe Carrillo had provided the title. The proposed autobiography, "Details from the Life of a Socialist Leader," was designed to project the fruits of his years of intensive labor and study, of incessant struggle and constant peril. The work was to have contained his educational, social, and economic program for lifting within a generation hapless millions of the five continents out of their age-old Karma of ignorance and fear, superstition and desperate poverty.

The world is gradually catching up with Felipe Carrillo's vision and initiative. Many of the ideas and movements he pioneered in Yucatán are taking root in contemporary thinking and action as well as in the policies of government and the declarations of the United Nations. Simple justice demands that the creator be identified clearly with his significant creation.

Still another consideration impels me to "give testimony" now. A lie in history has been likened to a fly embalmed in amber. There comes a day when the organism is so firmly imbedded in the solidified mineral and the falsehood in the hardened human consciousness that to dislodge either one becomes a virtually impossible task.

Despite the homage that Felipe Carrillo's name evokes in every part of the Mexican Republic and indeed, far beyond Mexico's national boundaries, sinister reactionary forces persistently strive to tarnish his memory. They are the same forces that conspired to end, through a hideous crime, his invaluable public service. They are, too, the same forces that destroyed Hidalgo, Morelos, Melchor Ocampo, that defamed and continue to defame Benito Juárez, and for identical reasons! Like Felipe Carrillo, these Mexican patriots were champions of the lowly and the dispossessed, the "inarticulate ones" as Felipe used to refer to them. An analogous situation exists today in certain sections of the United States with respect to Abraham Lincoln. How often one hears the Great Liberator designated by epithets that do not bear repetition in print. In each country the venom of the slave owner suddenly deprived of his slaves has been voiced in similar fashion. Through the slave owners' egocentric frame of reference, Abraham Lincoln in freeing the Negro slaves on the cotton plantations of the Deep South and Felipe Carrillo in initiating the emancipation of the Maya and other slaves on the vast henequen empires of Yucatán are guilty of an unpardonable offense. Both dared to challenge the sanctity of "private property," however illegitimately acquired. Both refused to accept the slave owner's contention that human beings are to be regarded as negotiable chattels.

Obviously, "Details from the Life of a Socialist Leader," as Felipe Carrillo and I had planned it, will never be written. But the final chapters of his heroic epic embrace certain chapters of my own personal story. In consequence, *Peregrina* is both biographical and a partial autobiography. But I have always thought of the happenings the book records as part of a larger story of our world in transition—a phase in humanity's revolutionary ascent from the predatory violence of the jungle to the practice of the Golden Rule. More specifically, I feel that the biographical aspects outline the story of a major American continental effort in the never-ending endeavor to rescue man from the inhumanity of his fellow man.

There has been no attempt to separate or divert the various currents that flow in the mainstream of the narrative. I have merely set down events as I encountered them and have evaluated situations as they impressed me against the background of my youthful emotional and rational awareness and inevitable prejudices.

I venture to hope that both the documentary and the subjective elements of *Peregrina* will provide or at least indicate the existence of new sources of information and illumine already known facts in the life of Yucatán's humanist apostle. In any case, I am confident that future historians will be occupied increasingly with research on his radiant personality, his bold vision of a happier scheme of things and his enduring contributions to a worthy concept of true civilization. One distinguished historian-economist, Dr. Ernest Gruening, long in the high echelons of the United States government and who knew Felipe well, has already written of him: "Like a great comet he came out of age-long darkness, lifting men's eyes and hearts, a fiery token of cycles reaching out into the vast unknown, a vision unforgettable. He was a cosmic figure. He linked in his single person the far-flung epic of the great American race and the undying epic of man's quest for freedom."

Throughout all the years that have passed since that fateful dawn of January 3, 1924, Felipe Carrillo has retained, for me and for all who truly knew him, his creative force in the living present. I find no yesterdays at journey's end. For the images that have vanished from physical sight still dominate the inner prospect and are more intelligible for heart and mind than the concrete realities of the passing hour. "That which was can never cease *having been.*" These words of the sixteenth-century Spanish philosopher Saavedra de Fajardo are now recalled with fresh poignancy, in the "ceaseless" quality of everything that relates to Felipe Carrillo. But while his spiritual presence and influence function in continuum for the Maya race, the Mexican people, and for tomorrow's world, the date at which "it all began" for me is clearly noted between the purple leather covers of my 1923 diary. As I read its pages, memory reconstructs this "beginning" and all the unutterable magic and pain that followed, as distinctly as though I were viewing the sequence on a TV screen.

*And so,*

# OUTLINE OF BOOK, BY ALMA M. REED

*Peregrina*

THIS BOOK OF APPROXIMATELY 110,000 WORDS, WHICH I HAVE TENTATIVELY called *Peregrina,* concerns my first visits as a young journalist to Mexico, my significant experiences there during the so-called Renaissance following a decade of Revolutionary chaos, and mainly the tragic involvement of my own life with that of the historic personage Governor Felipe Carrillo Puerto of Yucatán, known as the Abraham Lincoln of Mexico.

The opening chapters deal with my own youthful newspaper crusading on behalf of the unjustly treated Mexican nationals in my native California and my meeting with Governor Carrillo in February 1923, when I visited Yucatán as a member of the Carnegie Expedition to survey the Maya ruins, as a feature writer for the *New York Times Sunday Magazine.*

Felipe (as I shall henceforth refer to him) had invited the Carnegie archaeologists to explore the ruins of the ancient capital of Chichén Itzá, which he had made accessible by fine highways. As a direct descendant of Nachi Cocom, the last Maya king to make a stand against the invader and to resist the Spanish Conquest, Felipe was regarded as the natural leader of his people, as a race, enslaved on the great henequen plantations, or *haciendas,* of Yucatán, under a perpetual debt of *enganchado* systems.[1] He had lived a life of sacrifice for them—statements by his heroic mother to me reveal that the work of redeeming his people began in his childhood—and had served various terms in the Penitentiary for defiance of the Díaz Dictatorship. Once, he served several years for translating the Mexican Constitution into the Mayan language, the only one that the enslaved Indians could understand.

After Felipe had obtained their freedom, the Maya Indians and the Mestizo[2] Yucatecans, representing 95 percent of Yucatán's population, elected him Governor by an overwhelming vote. As Governor he was able to put into practice his dreams and longings for the advancement and resuscitation of the Mother Race of the American Continent. He encouraged the revival of ancient arts and crafts, the colorful ritual dances, and now was determined upon a long-range program for restoring the great palaces and temples, which according to the eminent American archaeologist Dr. Herbert J. Spinden of the Peabody Museum represent "one of the four really great and coherent expressions of beauty that humanity has produced since the dawn of history."

But Felipe's concern with antiquity was rooted in his hope of reviving the crushed spirit of his people and equipping them for a more dynamic role in contemporary life. He instituted not only the most modern type of government but the most advanced economic system and educational methods known in Mexico. He organized and maintained the first Birth Control Clinic in the entire New World (under state auspices); he established a university where humanist philosophy dominated. He built model villages with roads for the small farmers to carry more conveniently their produce to market. Of major importance was the fact that his program was universal in scope. He aimed to lift by an educational "shortcut" the millions of the earth to a point where they could compete with a complex civilization. Discarding, for the time being, "the mid-Victorian learning," he planned to teach these millions whom he called the *inarticulados*[3]—people without newspapers or radios—the essentials of modern living (hygiene, basic science, etc.), to enable them to live a full and productive life. Thirty years after Felipe's time, this very thing is happening to the great masses of the world's population. Even the Vatican has come out for most of his reforms.

Our mutual attraction was instant and potent at our very first meeting. I saw him for the first time when I went with the distinguished North American archaeologists—Dr. John C. Merriam, President of the Carnegie Institution; General William Barclay Parsons; Dr. Herbert J. Spinden; Dr. Marshall H. Saville; Dr. Sylvanus Morley; and others—to make our official call immediately after our arrival in Mérida. He received us at the headquarters of his Liga de Resistencia,[4] the humble office he preferred to the pompous Governor's Palace, where so many of Yucatán's exploiting chief executives, under the pay of the multimillionaire *hacendados*, land barons who controlled the enormous henequen industry, had ruled.

We saw Felipe dispensing "compassionate justice," suggesting a kindly father among his own children. His radiant personality, his physical beauty, poise, his quiet authority, above all, his naturalness and his evident sense of mission, made a profound impression on the entire group, especially since he had been described to us aboard the Ward Line steamer *Mexico*, by the Yucatecan "aristocrats" who were returning home for the Carnival celebration, as a "red dragon with eyes of jade," a "monster" guilty of unidentified crimes.

I had no sooner returned to the elegant home of my host, Felipe G. Cantón, relaxing in a hammock prior to dressing for the brilliant festivities of the evening—the banquet, official reception, and departure by train at daybreak for the ruins of Uxmal—than the servant rushed excitedly up the great marble staircase to announce, "The Governor of the State is here!" Felipe had come to ask me to accompany him to his model Socialist village at the far end of the new highway, which he had just completed to replace a stony trail, and "to enjoy the unusually beautiful sunset." Two chapters are devoted to the "Road to Kanasín," to the three unforgettable hours in which I learn of his achievements, his aims, his sincerity, and become unalterably convinced of his true greatness and his congenital right to leadership. Before the end of the trip, I realize how outrageously he has been maligned by his political enemies and the forces of the reaction. I am completely on *his* side and know that I shall always remain there. He leaves me at the gate of the Cantón mansion. I want to remain there, to relive each ecstatic moment, to pin down the thoughts and the emotions that possessed me, in *poems,* rather than in journalistic reports. But there was time for only one brief entry in my diary that evening. It read: "He is a miracle of Goodness and of Beauty!" I used the Spanish word *milagro*—"miracle" seemed weak and inadequate. I describe the ball, my lovely opalescent sequined and emerald chiffon gown, and the Yucatecan aristocracy. Felipe "breaks his rule" to dance with me. My swift realization that I am hopelessly in love.

A magical two weeks follow. Dances, native festivals staged in honor of the visitors, trips by train, automobile and horse-drawn coach to the majestic Maya ruins, Chichén Itzá, Uxmal, Kabah, Labná, etc., to the pueblos where the *ejidos,* or communal lands, were given back to the villagers in colorful ceremonies, lands of which their ancestors had been robbed. A visit to the great caves of Loltún, where the lights fail and our party is believed "lost," until Felipe with words of command in his native Maya quells the panic and orders the guides to find a way out, to the admiration of the frightened scientists. Part of a chapter is devoted to a review of the various theories on the origin of the Maya, the opinions of the visiting archaeologists, their feuds and rivalries. A review of the period—the heyday of archaeology, the popular interest in Tut-Ankh-Amen and the golden treasure flowing from his tomb, accompanied by far-reaching curses on the despoilers. Felipe's new roads and invitation to United States science to explore the Maya ruins send a thrill through the travel bureaus as well as the halls of science. The "confession" made to me by Edward J. Thompson of his recovery of a half a ton of ancient treasure from the Cenote Sagrado, or Sacred Well, on his *hacienda* at Chichén Itzá. He confesses to me because "the story must be told sometime," and because I am "the most *simpática* American journalist" he has ever met. He tells me how he learned the diver's art, when he realized that his Cenote was the well of sacrifice of maidens of flawless beauty, educated with an ideal of sacrifice for their people, drowned in a mystical wedding ceremony that united them to the deity they wished to appease, while the nobles rimmed the great circular well and threw in their most precious jewels, at the moment the priests flung the maiden into the Cenote's depths. Thompson told how, as American Consul, under an appointment secured by the American Antiquarian Society, he sent back the treasure he had retrieved, in the Consular mail pouches each month, to the Peabody Museum, over a period of years. My story claimed eight-column headlines in the national and metropolitan papers and was hailed as the "greatest archaeological adventure of the New World."

My return to New York with the Carnegie party—my articles in the *Times,* the first to describe the long-neglected Maya ruins and sympathetically the Socialist "experiment" of Governor Carrillo in a New York newspaper series, both angles arousing tourist interest in the Yucatán.

Felipe's daily letters and telegrams were filled with his dreams and plans for a "new order," the resuscitation of his people—and his love. I quote several of his extraordinary letters, my own fears and strange premonitions of doom. The natural conflict born of conservative traditions and convent education, a passionately patriotic home where all national holidays were observed with American flags decorating the dinner table. Despite my own liberal convictions and personal emancipation from church dogma, I could not really shake off the rather sinister connotations that the very word "Socialist" held for me. But I realized that Felipe dominated my heart, that he claimed my total admiration as a man, a leader, an authentic voice for humanity. Yet what seemed to me at the moment a break with the past loomed as too great a step. I tried to evade destiny. I asked Mr. Ochs, the *New York Times* publisher, to send me to Turkey to interview Kemal Pascha, but he insisted that I return to Mexico to interview President Obregón, Calles, and others, for, as he explained, the cultural articles I had written for him during my first Mexican visit and the Yucatán series, had convinced him that the new Obregón administration was "serious and permanent" and that he was considering announcing his support and recognition of the Mexican Revolutionary Government by the United States.

At the time, Felipe was staging the greatest reunion of the Maya race since the Conquest, at a ten-day Festival in the one-thousand-foot-long Ball Court at Chichén Itzá. He had invited the entire Indian population of Yucatán, arranging for their transportation to Mérida from distant places, and providing for them during the Festival. The event was the first and only authentic revival of ancient dances, music, ritual dramas, and costumes of the Maya in modern times. He was most eager to have me present at the historic occasion. I sailed again for Mexico and did not disembark at Progreso, but Felipe had anticipated my decision and sent out a little launch decked with floral arches and carrying an orchestra, to greet me. His English-speaking secretary, Manuel Cirerol, who is one of the personages of the story, handed me a letter urging me to leave the ship and come to Mérida. I explained that I was not free to do so, and then a second letter was handed to me, which announced that if I could not accept his invitation, Felipe himself would come to the Mexican capital at the conclusion of the Festival. He *did* come on the next boat, and we became formally engaged on the day after his arrival. A marvelous month followed—idyllic visits to Xochimilco, the pyramids of San Juan Teotihuacán, the elaborate dinner parties arranged in his honor by his great admirers, President and Sra. Obregón and the cabinet ministers, including the man later responsible for his assassination, Adolfo de la Huerta. Everywhere Felipe was acclaimed as a devoted public servant, a friend of the Indians, a truly worshipped public figure. The warning of the remarkable seeress Doña Juana, who had foretold the deaths of Madero, Pino Suárez, Carranza, and other officials, and before whose house on Donato Guerra Street there was always a long line of carriages, had told me of past and current events in my own life, and I insisted that Felipe visit her. Despite his rationalistic viewpoint he saw her to please me. He emerged pale. She had told him of situations of which he alone was aware, of present dangers, machinations of political enemies, in great detail, and warned him that his life was in grave peril. She did not know Felipe's identity, for he had not been in Mexico City for three years.

At the end of his month's annual leave, Felipe returned to Mérida to prepare to receive hundreds of delegates to the first American Continental Press Conference, which he arranged for mid-September. I returned to Yucatán as a delegate, representing the *New York Times Magazine* and the United Press. At Veracruz, our little party of North American press representatives from Mexico City was met by the South and Central American delegations, and we all boarded the Mexican battleship *Jalisco,* bound for Progreso. The North American party included two journalists in the pay of Adolfo de la Huerta, who were attending the congress for the specific purpose of influencing delegations against Felipe and to initiate propaganda for de la Huerta as Obregón's successor to the presidency. Felipe favored General Calles. The trip from Veracruz to Progreso in a terrible "norther." All are reported "lost" in the press of the capital, but the *Jalisco* rode the storm that night, and in the raging hurricane, I was to hear for the first time the lovely strains of my song, "Peregrina," played and sung outside my cabin by a quartette, which Felipe had sent to Veracruz to give me a surprise serenade. I already knew the words of this song, which had been written during my first visit to Yucatán by the eminent Yucatecan poet Luis Rosado Vega, on Felipe's suggestion and inspiration. The musical accompaniment had been completed after my departure by the beloved Ricardo Palmerín. Today, "Peregrina" is one of Mexico's most cherished songs and is known, in fact, all over the Spanish-speaking world. While full of tenderness, its underlying nuances suggest infinite sadness, and the antiquity and mystery of the land of the Maya. Our arrival in Yucatán, Felipe's welcome, elaborate entertainment, his eloquent appeals for continental solidarity, visits to the pueblos, ruins, etc. At an official banquet given in our honor by the city of Progreso, Felipe dramatically reads a telegram, announcing the recognition of Mexico by the government of the United States. My own desire to kneel in thanksgiving, aware of my own share in the historic event. Earlier I had written the editorials, for which I managed to obtain the necessary advance information on the Obregón 1924 budget, for the *New York Times* and a series of articles for the Hearst papers when, in view of the position of the *Times,* they decided to switch from "intervention" to "recognition." I remain in Mérida for a month after the departure of the journalists and during this period arrange with Felipe for our future home, the Villa Aurora. Felipe secures a divorce from the wife he had not seen for three years and who was living in Cuba, while his mother acted as his official hostess. Conflict between *man* and *leader,* his sense of pain that his own "easy divorce" laws might be interpreted by political enemies as a move to obtain his own marital freedom, despite the fact that they were framed more than a year before he met me . . . My return to New York and then to San Francisco to prepare for our wedding there, for which invitations were engraved and arrangements completed, with the Consul General Alejandro Lubbert serving as "best man." The strange premonitions of catastrophe communicated in Felipe's wires and letters a whole month before the so-called de la Huerta revolt paid for by the rich *hacendados,* whose vast holdings — the smallest, four square miles — Felipe had reduced, in conformity with the Mexican Constitution, giving the uncultivated lands to communities of small farmers for the production of other crops beside henequen, to enable them to meet the needs of their daily existence. A small garrison, made up of troops from the North, specifically planted by de la Huerta, and armed with machine guns, suddenly turns upon an unarmed population, since Felipe was a pacifist and was so certain of the devotion and loyalty of his people that arming them seemed unnecessary. He had been warned repeatedly, however, by such hardheaded realists as Crossette, Herbert Hoover's representative in Yucatán, with whom Felipe was then negotiating for direct exchange between the farmers of the United States and of Yucatán for the "green gold," or sisal hemp, upon which the binding of our own grain crop depended. On the outbreak of the military revolt for which the commander of the garrison received $250,000[5] from the *hacendados,* Felipe, his three brothers and a small group of followers left Mérida en route to Cuba, where they planned to await the arrival of Manuel Cirerol, who had been sent to New Orleans a few days earlier to purchase arms for the defense of the unarmed populace. This was a difficult decision for the pacifist Felipe to make, but he faced the situation realistically when warned of the conspiracy and its threat to throw back into slavery the people to whom he had dedicated a life of struggle and sacrifice. I document every incident from the time Felipe left Mérida, the brief stops at stations along the route when the Maya came out by the thousands with their machetes, offering their aid. But he told them that their machetes were powerless against machine guns and begged them to remain calm until he returned with adequate defense weapons. I give eyewitness accounts of the treason of the owner of the launch, who disconnected the engine so that Felipe and his followers were prevented from reaching the ship that was to take them to Cuba, how Felipe was urged by his brother to shoot the small detachment of soldiers who advanced to capture them and how he refused to give permission for "violence," merely saying, "let us be taken." I give descriptions of Felipe wading through the water, carrying high his sombrero in which was sewn my photograph—the one he called the *periodista*—the journalist—his favorite photograph. I give eyewitness accounts of his ten-day imprisonment at the Juárez Penitentiary, which he had converted into a model prison that had aroused the admiration of prison officials everywhere, even in New York. I include summaries of the mock trial, record of his eloquent pleas for the lives of his three younger brothers, his efforts to send letters to me, the singing of "Peregrina" outside his cell as an added torture, the night before his assassination. I include descriptions of his last moments, his final words and his last recorded act—his stepping forward to ask a soldier of the firing squad to deliver to me my "Maya" wedding ring, a triangular-shaped garnet. I record the heroism of his remarkable mother, who said to the messenger of Ricardo Broca, who ordered the execution of Felipe, his three brothers, and his six assistants against a wall in the Mérida Cemetery at dawn on January 3, 1924: "Go tell your master that, in the last hours of my sons, he would not permit me to console them even for a moment and that I am *strong enough not* to look at their mangled bodies *now.*" Doña Adela, who was then 70 years of age, designed Felipe's tombstone—a white marble slab, bearing his name, date of birth and death, and the simple red marble triangular emblem of his Socialist Party and its slogan "Tierra y Libertad"—"Land and Liberty." Under the rigid restrictions of her son's murderers, she had fully condemned them and told the story of his heroic martyrdom in three words.

In a "throwback" chapter, the material of which is drawn from his own words, the accounts of his mother, brothers, and sister Elvia, much of it in their own handwriting, I tell the story of his extraordinary childhood and young manhood, the renunciation by his father of the high and lucrative post of *jefe político*[6] under Díaz, because he found that his "chief duty was to return escaped Maya slaves to their owners." There is an account of Doña Adela's heroism, when she used to keep vigil at night in the days when Felipe and his brothers were organizing the Ligas . . .[7] When bombs were left in front of the family home in Motul, she would go out and with her bare hands, pick them up, and deposit them in the plaza.

The text also relates the aftermath of the tragedy. My own visits to Washington to interview Samuel Gompers, who was instrumental in causing the United States to place an arms embargo on Mexico following the assassination of Felipe, to foil the de la Huerta rebels, who were crushed in order, since the movement represented no just revolutionary or popular cause, but merely personal ambition. Accounts of how Franklin D. Roosevelt, then Secretary of the Navy, one of Felipe's admirers, "swept the seas" in the hope that Felipe had escaped, as the thoroughly frightened "rebels" announced to avoid vengeance . . . My own return to Yucatán on the first boat, sailing on the *Rajah* with the Carnegie scientists to resume work as a newspaperwoman and to face all the terrible facts of the tragedy "for history." Only on the very last day of my three-months' stay in Mérida was I capable of looking at the Villa Aurora, the home he had so beautifully adorned in "puro Maya" style with such love and hope.

In addition to the documented story of Felipe's life, excerpts from his letters, his public addresses, and recorded conversations, the book gives a picture of post-Revolutionary Mexico, of the men whose vision and initiative were responsible for the so-called Renaissance, most of them alive and still serving Mexico—Dr. Manuel Gamio, Jorge Enciso, Rivera, Orozco, Siqueiros, Francisco Valladares, Luis Montes de Oca, Roberto Casas Alatriste, Aarón Sáenz, Juan de Dios Bojórquez, Vasconcelos, Dr. Atl, and many others.

Despite the severance of all means of communication with the outside world, Felipe's faithful Maya Indians nevertheless tried to advise me of the tragedy. Braving the shark-infested waters off Progreso, a group of them swam out to a British ship anchored some distance from the docks, to send me a radio cable. Their message never reached me, for they had sent it addressed to "Pixan Halal," my name in Mayan, the only one they knew . . . Months later, the cable was recovered in the Mackay radio offices of the Fairmont Hotel, where I resided.

Alma M. Reed

# 1. Yucatán Assignment

The friendly assistant editor wished me luck as he handed me last-minute cable instructions. But in his Tennessee drawl there was unmistakable disapproval of the project that claimed his publisher's keen personal interest.

"For a quiet girl out of the Far and Golden West," he said, "you've certainly picked yourself the most incongruous pair of assignments around this man's office since 'Rum and Romanism.' "

When I asked him why, he answered: "That one is not hard to figure out. Have you ever heard of a more absurdly mismatched copy team than archaeology and free love? If you can name one, I'll buy you a nice luncheon at Delmonico's the day you land back in town."

I reminded him of the well-known attraction of opposites, but I admitted frankly that on the spur of the moment I couldn't think of a more flagrant case of incompatibility myself. Obviously, he would be spared the frightful expense of the Delmonico affair.

I seriously doubted that the "free love" angle, a favorite theme of current yellow journalism when dealing with Yucatán, would meet the authenticity requirements of the respectable *New York Times.*

It struck me as just another one of those distorted slants so easy to get on our nearest Southern neighbor. During my three months' stay in Mexico the previous autumn I'd seen clever, even brilliant newspapermen become perfect dupes of the oil interests. Unconsciously or otherwise, they were serving the highly financed effort to overthrow the new Obregón Government. Their reports, for the most part, were confused, inaccurate or thoroughly prejudiced, containing little or no information on the immediate progress or constructive achievements of the Social Revolution following the restoration of order after eight years of bitter, bloody conflict. But I didn't stop to argue the point. It was nearly eleven o'clock. A registering taxicab was waiting downstairs, and I was scheduled to sail at noon.

Yet the assistant editor's rather flippant references to the venture that marked the most important step to date in my young professional life bothered me considerably. I kept mildly brooding over it all the way to the Ward Line pier where the steamship *Mexico* was already taking passengers bound for Gulf and Caribbean ports. It annoyed me most that not even a flash of Thackerayan "cab wit" had appeared to taunt me with a scintillating reply I might have made to him. Still worse was the sneaking thought that he might be *right.*

It was a clear, vivid morning—a Thursday—and the date was February 8, 1923. A southwest wind was gently stirring the winter numbness into a premature *joie de vivre* of spring. Before going aboard, I stood in a brief, sentimental leave-taking of Manhattan at the foot of Wall Street, my glance following its deep, narrow canyon to where the dwarfed and unrelated steeple of Old Trinity closed it on Broadway. I had been in New York for less than two weeks, barely long enough to skim more than the dazzling surface enchantment. But the great city on such short acquaintance had been cordial and exciting. I arrived from my native San Francisco with a few established friendships among stage folk and in the literary world. At the home of George Creel and his wife, Blanche Bates, I met the Barrymores, Henry Miller, Ruth Chatterton, and other celebrities. Several of my former colleagues, transplanted to the metropolitan newspaper row, were flourishing in top editorial posts. Life soon became a festive sequence of formal dinners, theater parties, intimate luncheons, and *thés dansants.* I loved every instant of it and was looking forward to my return and to closer acquaintance with the town's myriad wonders almost as eagerly as I anticipated the high adventure of the Yucatecan jungles.

Romantic lingering in farewell of Wall Street was prompted by nostalgic thoughts of my father. In all the hectic rounds of daily sightseeing, nothing had evoked a deeper emotional impact than this same downtown district, which he had so often feelingly described to me and his seven other children as a sacred national shrine. The whole area was intimately associated in my mind with his intense patriotism. It recalled the little American flags that always decorated our family dinner table on national holidays, even for the observance of the less heralded anniversaries such as the Battle of Bunker Hill on June 17. It brought into new and more appreciative focus the big steel engravings that adorned the walls of our old-fashioned dining room—*Franklin Before the House of Lords* and the *Delaware Crossing,* balanced by full-length portraits of Henry Clay and Patrick Henry in heroic attitudes, while, on either side of the tall mirror above the white marble fireplace, George and Martha Washington looked benignly down upon our evening meals from their oval-shaped walnut frames. The real memory link between my distant home and Wall Street's mighty canyon was Fraunces Tavern. For, tucked in among the skyscrapers at Pearl and Broad, stood the small, white-porticoed square brick building in which General Washington bade farewell to his officers in 1783. I can still hear my father relating the historic episode with colorful detail, his voice vibrant with feeling that brought us all to the verge of tears, especially the moving line that invariably closed the narrative—"and then, with thoughtful mien and slow step, he walked silently down to Whitehall."

But the appeal of the glamorous present and of the unknown, vaguely perilous future soon broke in upon my reveries of cherished past things. With my favorite traveler, George William Curtis, the poetic Howadji of the *Nile Notes,* I could jubilantly announce that "to our young eyes, everything was picture." Through my charmed perspective even the huge mechanical forms assumed outlines of beauty against the clouds. Diffused in white sunlight, they became challenging symbols. I likened their great towers to silver spears piercing heights of the uttermost quest, demanding fulfillment of youthful dreams and ambitions. And I knew that they would gracefully rise in my memory forever.

The sailing of the *Mexico* was a quiet, rather casual affair. There was none of that flower-laden gaiety of sailing days I had known since childhood, when I would accompany my parents to the San Francisco wharves to watch our friends and relatives depart on the queenly Pacific liners for Hawaii, Australia, and the far Orient. On deck, I noted but one familiar trace of bon voyage atmosphere. It was provided by the reporters and their attendant cameramen, who, on the trail of "close-ups" and interviews, had cornered several distinguished scientists representing American museums, universities, and learned societies. The scientists, like myself, were journeying to the ruined cities of the Maya in Yucatán. They had been invited to assist in a preliminary survey for the large-scale explorations to be launched the following year by the Carnegie Institution of Washington, D.C., at Chichén Itzá, most renowned of the ruined Maya cities.

I accompanied the party as *New York Times* correspondent. Mr. Adolph Ochs, the publisher, had engaged me to write a series of special feature articles for the *Sunday Magazine,* and the managing editor, Mr. Carl Van Anda, wanted cabled news coverage for the regular daily editions of the paper. I held, besides, an order from *Collier's Magazine* for a personality story on Yucatán's Socialist Governor, Felipe Carrillo Puerto, whose radical labor and divorce legislation ("free love" program to the assistant editor) was then causing widespread and heated controversy.

The early twenties represented the archaeologists' heyday in practically every corner of the globe. From Sweden to Mesopotamia, discoveries of ancient civilizations were numerous and startling. The archaeological theme all but monopolized the daily press. Front-page headlines announced that the silence of centuries had been broken at Carthage, Nineveh, Baalbek—that Ethiopia's desolate wastes had been invaded by the armies of science. Special editions in rotogravure and in color were required to handle, adequately, accounts of the spectacular "finds." Whole pages were devoted to descriptions of the dazzling avalanche of treasure pouring from newly opened Egyptian tombs. Columns under famous bylines were given over to the vanished splendor of Tut-Ankh-Amen and the attempts to trace to their fated denouements his far-reaching curses on the desecrators of his golden sarcophagus. Even *New York Times* editor Van Anda turned Egyptologist to write a book on the exploits of Lord Carnarvon and Howard Carter near ancient Thebes.

To all this massive publicizing a captivated popular imagination responded with postwar gusto. Isis-inspired headgear and scarab jewelry became the vogue. The ultra-fashionable managed to conform to mummy-case silhouettes. But throughout this unprecedented archaeological activity—much of it financed and engineered by United States expeditions—little or nothing was known by the average American of the magnificent Maya temples and palaces within comparatively easy reach of New York and our southern ports. The apathy of the general public in regard to these ancient monuments had long been, in fact, something of an international scandal. As far back as 1831, a leading London gazette had superciliously commented that if the Maya ruins were located in a country accessible to *British* travelers, they would have created a sensation unrivalled by Pompeii or Herculaneum.

There was no lack of literature on the subject. Commentaries on the Spanish Colonial chronicles of priests and navigators were plentiful. Outstanding was the research of the French abbot Brasseur de Bourbourg, who in 1863 found in the archives of the Academia Real de la Historia in Madrid, the manuscript to which we owe our knowledge of the Mayan alphabet. The manuscript, *An Account of the Things of Yucatán* was by Fray Diego de Landa, a Franciscan who served in Yucatán between 1549 and 1562 and, during the later years, Bishop of the Province. Moreover, there existed numerous works in many languages on the history of the Maya and their pre-Columbian way of life. There were fascinating accounts by such scholarly travelers as A. P. Maudslay, Désiré Charnay, the Baron Alexander von Humboldt, to mention only a few. Paradoxically, North American scholars were the major recent contributors to our knowledge of the Maya culture. One of the most vital discoveries in the field of Middle American research had been made by the California journalist and publisher J. T. Goodman, who, after years of painstaking study, first deciphered, in 1890, the so-called Initial Series method of dating, from hieroglyphic inscriptions on the monuments, basing his findings on Maudslay's detailed reproductions of the Maya sculpture. Incidentally, Goodman, as editor of the *Virginia City, Nevada, Enterprise,* also enriched English Literature, when, with encouragement and guidance, he helped the young Samuel Clemens to develop into the brilliant humorist known and loved as Mark Twain. Even the standard book on the Maya ruins, *Incidents of Travel in Central*

*America, Chiapas, and Yucatán* was written by an American explorer, John L. Stephens. The notable work, published in 1841, was profusely illustrated by the British artist Frederick Catherwood.

With the Carnegie-sponsored Maya survey, made possible through the initiative of Governor Carrillo, our national interest in the age-old architecture and sculpture suddenly awakened. Public curiosity, finally shaken from its unconcern, now focused the spotlight of information full glare upon the buried treasure of the New World. We were no longer indifferent to our own archaeological heritage. At last, it became a widely publicized theme. Press releases received by the *Times* told of months of preparation for the survey in Yucatán. A year before the event, the local archaeological society, headed by Governor Carrillo and composed of prominent Yucatecans and one American woman—Mrs. W. James—met in Mérida, the Yucatecan capital, to draft plans for the visit of the archaeologists and to initiate organized tourism. At a meeting held at the home of Sr. Felipe G. Cantón, Governor Carrillo announced his intention to construct immediately a twenty-five-mile highway between the railroad terminal at Dzitas and the ruined city of Chichén Itzá, where only a stony trail led through the jungles. As a repercussion of the announcement in the United States, a thrill of hope ran through the halls of science as well as through the travel bureaus. And both hailed the survey as the prelude to the greatest archaeological adventure of western hemispheric research.

Keenly alive to the momentous possibilities involved, I looked forward to the outcome with the greatest eagerness. Naively, I anticipated results, confident that the excavator's spade would in no time lay bare the secrets of the American mother culture—secrets more baffling than those of forgotten Nile dynasties. If the origin of the Maya race were definitely known, whole pages of recorded history would be subject to revision, countless pages of prehistory would no longer remain blank. The enigma of our own continental beginnings had completely captured my imagination and directed much of my reading. I could hardly wait for the time-defying riddles to be solved and the wordy battles of the archaeologists settled without further discussion.

A few years earlier, two members of the survey party, Dr. Sylvanus G. Morley of the Carnegie Middle American Research Program and Dr. Herbert J. Spinden of the Peabody Museum, independently established the earliest date on a Maya monument that could be regarded as historical. The time glyph engraved on the nephrite carving known as the Tuxtla Statuette and found in the state of Veracruz, coincided, according to Dr. Morley, with our year 96 B.C., while Dr. Spinden's correlation fixed the date as 100 B.C. To the more academic gropers in the Maya darkness, this decade—a century before the Christian era—loomed as a solitary guidepost, and against it they leaned heavily. Meanwhile, however, they conceded that an equation derived from three identical ancient calendars—the Aztec of the Valley of Mexico, the Cakchiquel and Quiché of Guatemala—gave November 10, 3,485 B.C., as the first day of the Maya era. Between these widely separated time markers and far beyond them and coherent history, speculation was free to wander uninhibited along a choice of alluring paths. For, on all the major problems of the Maya genesis, one man's guess was still as good as another's. No one could make any unchallenged statements as to the *whence, when,* and *how* of the Maya's advent into Central America. The cradle of this mysterious people had been variously placed in Asia, Africa, Polynesia, and North America. Dr. Ales Hrdlicka of the Smithsonian Institution, whom I had interviewed, believed the Maya had crossed over from Asia either by way of an existing land bridge north of the Bering Strait or by way of Kamchatka, using the Aleutian Islands as their "stepping-stones." This theory received the widest scientific acceptance. But other anthropologists insisted that the Maya was a true autochthon of America, that he had evolved from lower forms on the continent and had carried his culture to Egypt and other Mediterranean lands. There were, too, many adherents of the "realist" school. A prominent one, D. G. Brinton, held the Maya to be of remote Appalachian stock, a blood brother to our Seminole and Creek and hailing from no more distant a provenance than Florida or the Mississippi Valley. In another camp, under heretical ban, outside the wall of the scientific dogma, was the large following of a "mystical" cult, influenced more or less by Rosicrucian teachings. The mystics penetrated into shadowy realms where fact and fable merge, clutching fervently at tenuous legends that linked the Maya to a Lost Atlantis or to the allegedly sunken continent of Mu.

The sources advanced for the unique architecture were equally divergent. It was generally classed as an "exotic"—transplanted to Yucatán late in the Maya's development. But Mesopotamia, Egypt and China, Japan and Buddhist India, Ceylon, Cambodia, and the Malay Peninsula could all put forth plausible claims to the honor of nurturing an art regarded by Dr. Spinden and other eminent authorities as "one of the few really great and coherent expressions of beauty so far given to the world."

The *Mexico* was late starting on her ten-day cruise. But now, it was time to sail. Amid the laughter and tears of last-minute "good-byes," the "all-ashore" gong sounded. But before the visitors hurried off toward the gangplank, a stronger hand impulsively tightened its grip over my own on the deck rail. Into my private ear a man's husky voice whispered: "Dearest in all the world, go for a little while that will seem eternity, and keep me in your heart." Then the anchors were lifted. We moved out into the open waters. From the receding dock, the charming romanticist who met me at the boat and who had been an admirable friend and guide—if unreliable philosopher—since my arrival in New York, was waving a final "bon voyage."

This was my first Atlantic voyage. The occasion seemed to merit postal cards to my family in San Francisco, all bearing the single news item that I was about to pass the Statue of Liberty. The event, I knew, would give them as great a thrill as it would give me. Far Western Americanism of the day paid ardent if distant devotion to the goddess whose arms extended generous and perpetual welcome to the oppressed of the earth from the Eastern edge of the continent. California's patriotic orisons may, it is true, have included the postscript: "Let the oppressed of the earth stay right there on the Atlantic seaboard, dear Lord! We already have far too many foreigners on the *Pacific* Coast." But as we sailed down the bay and approached ever closer to the torch that lights the world, my own homage to the gracious symbol of our national meaning was uncomplicated by doubts or question.

A distinguished-looking young Mexican cut short my reflection with deck pleasantries. He introduced himself as Roberto Casas Alatriste, member of the Chamber of Deputies and chairman of the Committee for the Settlement of Mexico's National Debt, then meeting with the International Bankers in New York. We talked about his country, which I had left only six weeks before. I learned that Liberty's light-shedding torch was a symbol tragically entwined with his own story and his present unexpected trip. He had just been advised of the death of his mother, who was a member of the family of Aquiles Serdán, the Revolutionary leader and martyr. He related how she had escaped almost miraculously, when, on November 18, 1910, nineteen of her relatives and dearest friends were massacred in the Serdán home in Puebla, with the discovery of the impending Madero revolt. Plotted outbreaks scheduled to occur simultaneously over the Republic on November 20 had been revealed when Madero's correspondence was seized. Sr. Casas Alatriste, a youth of eighteen at the time, went to the railroad station in Mexico City to board the train, intending to join the Puebla Revolutionists according to plan. Boys at the station were selling the evening newspaper, headlines announcing the shooting of his cousins Aquiles and Máximo, with seventeen other "Anti-Reelectionists"; when outnumbered and surrounded by the Díaz police, Aquiles had stood to the very last, shouting defiance of the despot. Roberto did not go to Puebla that day. On his father's side, Sr. Casas Alatriste was descended from the brother of Bartolomé de las Casas, the revered humanitarian Bishop of Chiapas who devoted his life to the cause of the exploited Indians after the Conquest. Tall and of robust build, the young official had the regular features, brown hair, and clear, fair complexion of pure European ancestry. But the intense pride that flashed in his dark eyes, whenever, during the voyage, we discussed "Revolución Social," left no doubt as to his faith in a Mestizo Mexico. His plans were shaped and his hopes were colored by the conviction that the merging of two venerable cultures in the "Third Race" and the achievement of a stable *patria*[1] represented his country's highest destiny.

Another Mexican, Sr. Luis G. Molina, was seated at my table in the dining salon. In appearance, temperament, and viewpoint, he was the direct opposite of Sr. Casas Alatriste. A Yucatecan, Sr. Molina had long been a resident of New York. He was returning to his native Mérida for a brief holiday during the Carnival season. Apparently in his mid-forties, he was short and muscular, with sandy hair and light hazel eyes. Glistening thick-lensed glasses heightened the contrast of a tropical pallor and emphasized a general misanthropic aura. He was the grandson of Olegario Molina, Yucatán's multimillionaire governor in the Díaz regime. I was already aware that the name "Molina" was synonymous in Mexico with the iron rule of the *hacendado,* or landed proprietor. I had heard and read of the able executive and his unbridled pre-Revolutionary power. He had organized an oligarchy of fifty land barons and had solidified the peonage labor system, under which the *hacienda,* or estate, yielded its vast revenues in sisal hemp known as the "green gold" of Yucatán. His condemnation of Indian communal lands in his capacity of Governor, for personal aggrandizement in the capacity of *hacendado* owning fifteen million acres of land in Yucatán, was a notorious and often cited case in the struggle for agrarian reform. In my long talks with Sr. Molina he would invariably extol the greatness of his state in ancient, colonial, and *científico*[2] times and dismiss the present as a "hopeless muddle." His disapproval of all governments since the fall of the dictatorship and particularly that of the Partido Socialista, was sweeping and complete. To Governor Carrillo, the head of the party, he attributed serious faults and shortcomings as well as destructive social and economic policies. It was from him I first learned that the Governor was known to the *hacendados* as the "red dragon with eyes of jade." He felt, he said, that it was his duty to warn me against the "dragon's" wiles. I did not doubt Molina's sincerity, but he did not deceive me. His evaluation of any Socialist, or, as he called it, "Bolshevist," government, was of little worth; his reasoning seldom strayed beyond class interest. Nevertheless, I welcomed his opinions and wrote them down for future reference. It indeed seemed a streak of luck to learn in advance from so authoritative a spokesman the arguments and political views of the *hacendados.* We discussed the henequen market and philosophies of government.[3] Impersonal issues—but before Carnival season came again, they would enmesh our personal destinies. In all the years ahead, this quiet, uninspiring fellow voyageur would call up tragic memories for me. Yet no premonition of a star-crossed future disturbed our deck conversations. Cultists of the dead past who, with a blind faith, worshipped the name of Molina had already marked its victim. But through those pleasant Caribbean hours, no warning was flashed of an onrushing doom, impelled by *lex talionis,* the law of revenge.

# 2. Southward

On board the *Mexico* were several other Yucatecans, all of them members of the landed aristocracy and shareholders in the one-hundred-million-dollar sisal industry. It seemed logical that they wished to be known as Yucatecos, as their feeling for Mexican nationality was, at best, lukewarm. They showed, at least, no enthusiasm for the progressive currents then quickening the Republic into vigorous life. The boundaries of their "patria chica,"[1] or little country, defined their patriotic horizons. One might easily suppose them to be citizens of a foreign land or of some isolated racial group about as remote from happenings in the Mexican capital as our own Aleuts from the affairs in Washington, D.C. All appeared to share Sr. Molina's prejudice against the Socialist regime. Some were openly bitter. But no one of the group was willing to be pinned down to specific charges or to be quoted on the new government's alleged "flagrant injustice" and unidentified "crimes." Their mystifying innuendos aroused my curiosity but failed to stir indignation.

I was not unprepared for the existing hatred of the old reactionary against the new Revolutionary order. Fortunately, I had read a remarkable book, *Barbarous Mexico,* by John Kenneth Turner, which exposed the shocking conditions during the Díaz dictatorship with particular emphasis and documentation on the virtual enslavement of the Maya and Yaqui Indians to the lords of the henequen empire of Yucatán.[2] And while in Mexico a few months earlier, I chanced upon a detailed study of the current Yucatán situation in *The Pulse of Mexico,* a small English-language review published monthly in the capital.

The author, Mr. A. G. B. Hart, analyzed the program of Yucatán's Socialist administration, of which Felipe Carrillo Puerto had assumed control as Governor on February 5, 1922, having been elected to office by an overwhelming popular vote. The article gave a brief historical background of henequen development and distribution and an account of the fluctuating fortunes of the *hacendados* since the First World War. His article, Mr. Hart modestly claimed, "made up in truth what it lacked in craftsmanship," and unlike much American reporting on

Mexico, often from an easy chair in some comfortable office many miles north of the Rio Grande, it had been written in an atmosphere of personal experience and had come "hot forged from the anvil of immediate contact." For me the article was a determinative event. I thought it tremendously exciting and profoundly significant that such a forward-looking, courageous system as the author indicated was being given a trial anywhere on the American continent, although Mr. Hart was careful to point out, everything was either quite tentative or in an incipient stage. Maurice Becker's caricature sketches, which illustrated the article, contained no element of propaganda. They were decidedly unflattering to Governor Carrillo, the Socialists, Feministas, Maya Indians, and all concerned. Yet my imagination was intrigued by this New World Ultima Thule.[3] I wanted to know more about it, to investigate it for myself.

During my first Mexican visit I had written weekly articles for the *New York Times Magazine.* Before my departure from San Francisco on that trip in late August 1922, Mr. Ochs had requested a series on the nation's new cultural, social, and economic trends. While in Mexico City, I learned of the proposed Carnegie Survey to be launched the following spring. The prospect of accompanying the expedition as a journalist was a glamorous temptation. But while I informed Mr. Ochs of the project, I did not seek the assignment. Nothing could have appealed to me more at the time than a visit to Yucatán's ruined cities, even though the trip would upset an established order. None too willingly, I had been granted by my editors a three-month leave of absence from my San Francisco newspaper commitment and in addition there were public activities, university study courses, and even an incipient political career to be considered. Common sense and conscience dictated my return to the daily routine at the conclusion of my brilliant Mexican holiday. I doubtless would have obeyed these "practical urges," if the Hart article had not reached me at a psychological moment, even though a letter from Mr. Ochs suggested that I come to New York immediately after Christmas to make the necessary arrangements to accompany the Carnegie scientists to Yucatán. It was the Hart article that had definitely sounded an inner summons, determining all my "important" actions. I wired acceptance of the plan and returned to San Francisco on Christmas Day to announce my temporary withdrawal from journalistic and social activities there.

The sudden decision to break with the pleasant rhythm of work and study, and the promising future career I had so painstakingly fostered, was partly due perhaps to a growing awareness that my life pattern was to be involved with Mexico. Promptings far more cogent than expediency or acquired habit interpreted as duty had been steadily if unconsciously drawing me southward since young girlhood, when I first became an earnest student of Mexico's past and present.

As we sailed through tranquil Antillean seas—in those days, Havana was a five-day journey from New York—I indulged in mental and emotional stocktaking when not conversing with the scientists or my new Mexican friends. One by one I reviewed the links in the chain of events that finally attracted me to the land constantly dominating my imagination and to which I was now returning. I knew that the first steps in Mexico's direction, like most of my deeper urges, could be traced to the influence of my father. As a young mining engineer, he had spent some months in various parts of the Mexican Republic. He had learned to speak a passable Spanish and had carried away with him happy memories of the country and a warm regard for its people. His fascinating accounts of village *fiestas* and of the quaint charm of old colonial cities captivated my childish fancy. Later, my intensive reading of travel books and cursory archaeological studies fanned my interest into an absorbing hobby.

But the predestined road to Mexico began to assume concrete shape when I started a daily feature column in the *San Francisco Call*, with the aim of various forms of social service. Significantly, the general period of my newspaper activities was marked by rampant scheming of the interventionists. The Mexican in the United States and particularly in California received no coddling and scant sympathy. In most quarters he was regarded as an inferior being and, in the common usage of the day, was referred to as a "greaser." When he was unfortunate enough to clash with the law, he was often the victim of questionable justice. Usually, he found himself at the mercy of intolerant jurors, the logical spokesmen of a biased public opinion. Popular prejudice was heightened by the keen competition that followed the influx of cheap Mexican labor across the international boundaries during and after the long period of Revolutionary chaos.

Many refugees from Mexico's violence and insecurity were stranded in different parts of the Pacific Coast and were financially unable, after peace had been restored, to return to their homeland. Wherever labor competition was especially intense, these uprooted Mexicans formed deeply resented minority groups. Jobs were particularly scarce in the Bay region, where discharged veterans of the First World War swelled the ranks of the unemployed. Hundreds of ex-servicemen in Oakland and in San Francisco were still living on the free meals doled out by civic relief agencies. Aggravating the tense situation were the recurrent echoes of the familiar threat: "Let's send the military into Mexico and protect American investors." The chauvinistic slogan was frankly voiced in the statewide California press and in the street meetings of the rabble-rousing "one hundred percenters." Wealthy Mexican exiles—die-hard reactionaries of the ousted Díaz regime—ever hopeful of staging a comeback, subsidized the more belligerent journalism and the curbstone Ciceros. Often their efforts at stirring up hatred met with success, since border raids on neighboring states were still fresh in public memory. The new Obregón Government had not yet had sufficient time to demonstrate its stability and constructive policies.

Under these conditions, needy Mexican families were daily being brought to my notice, and I always welcomed a chance to help them. I was not only interested in Mexico but also admittedly prejudiced in its favor, sympathetic with the struggle of its people for release from exploitation and enormously intrigued by their mysterious past. Moreover, among our family friends were Mexicans of rare culture. I had come to know our Southern neighbors well—to appreciate and respect them. The injustices and discourtesies these "strangers in a strange land" were forced to endure and the growing threat to their national sovereignty ignited my congenital crusading spirit. I had inherited from the Irish poets of my father's ancestry a tendency to champion unpopular causes; from my mother's long line of Virginia Revolutionary patriots—framers of the Mecklenburg Declaration of Independence in 1775 and later Kentucky Abolitionists—the urge to remedy abuses. In cooperation with local and national labor organizations, I engaged, as a writer, in campaigns to benefit Mexican workers. One such movement attempted to improve the disgraceful living conditions of seasonal laborers in the Alaskan fisheries.

In my daily column, I described, under the pen name of "Mrs. Goodfellow," cases of want and suffering among San Francisco's impoverished families, a large percentage of whom were Mexican nationals. In several instances, the generous response to my appeals had resulted in the relief of immediate distress and had opened up for these helpless Mexicans opportunities for normal living.

The incident, however, that dramatically brought me in close touch with the Mexican government, and with the Mexican people, grew out of my interest in prison reform. It had been my practice for some months to visit San Quentin Penitentiary on Wednesdays, often with an older woman, who was a well-known social worker. When occasion arose we would make "last mercy" calls on men who were sentenced to die the following Friday morning. I learned from the celebrated Tom Mooney, during one of his frequent court appearances in San Francisco, that I was known to the inmates of San Quentin as "the Rose of Murderer's Row."

On my weekly visit of January 19, 1921, I saw quite by accident on the warden's desk an undelivered engraved invitation to the scheduled hanging of the sixteen-year-old Mexican boy Simón Ruiz. When I inquired, the warden, with a trace of compassion in his voice, informed me that the condemned youth spoke no English and that not a single person had called on him during his two months' imprisonment at San Quentin. Moved and shocked, I asked permission to see him, offering to forgo the privilege of my next week's prison visit. "Why not?" replied the warden as he signed my pass for my return to the prison yard. I questioned the guards, including the one chosen by lot for Friday morning's grim job. Some of them expressed sympathy as they commented on the incredible facts of the Mexican boy's trial, later confirmed by Simón himself when—never more thankful for my "workable" if un-academic Spanish—I interviewed him in the death house.

Simón's story disclosed that a year before he had come to Bakersfield from his home in Sonora to work as a carpenter's helper and that since his arrival his record had been flawless. His father had been killed in the Revolution and from his twelfth year he was the chief support of his widowed mother and several younger sisters and brothers. In a fit of anger provoked by an insult on his race—he had been called a "greaser"—and spurred on in his resentment by an older Mexican, Miranda, known as a "bad *hombre,*" Simón waylaid the foreman and assaulted him. The two fought for some fifteen minutes, and three weeks later, the foreman died of the effects of the blows. Miranda fled across the Mexican border. After two trials—the first ending in jury disagreement—the boy was sentenced to hang. But he entered San Quentin unaware that he had been condemned to death. He did not understand the verdict, and the court-appointed lawyer did not take the trouble to have the sentence translated for him. He learned his fate only a few days before the scheduled execution from a Spanish-speaking prisoner who sat with him in the condemned men's box at San Quentin's Christmas vaudeville show. Upon hearing the truth, Simón shrieked and fainted and had to be carried back to his cell. Believing that the boy, who looked even younger than his years, was doomed to die a horrible death within a few hours, I left him emotionally shaken and in tears. But I lost no time in telephoning my editor, Emil Gough, the kindly "boss" and the father of two young sons. As an enterprising newspaperman, he instantly saw the possibility of arousing strong public feeling over the imminent hanging. He gave me carte blanche to use all the "white paper" necessary for the telling of the whole story. Although "precious little time remained," he observed, "there was a chance in a million" for us to obtain a stay of execution.

My lengthy exposition of the case with its flagrant miscarriage of justice—which construed provoked manslaughter, carrying a ten-year sentence—together with the boy's story, an analysis of the state's outmoded penal code and my interview with the hangman, appeared on the front page of all six editions of the *San Francisco Call* the next day. The article opened with the line: "Invitations are in the mail today to the hanging of sixteen-year-old Simón Ruíz," and was followed by a stark, realistic description, as told to me by the hangman, of precisely what the state's guests would see at the ghastly function to which they had been formally invited. I had asked the hangman not to spare my feelings, and in my account I did not spare my readers. The newspaper was hardly out on the street when telegrams, letters, and telephone calls began to pour into the *Call* editorial rooms and to the Governor's office in Sacramento.

Before midnight, editor Gough phoned me to announce the good news carried in an Associated Press dispatch. At the last hour, Governor Stephens had granted a thirty-day stay of execution. I immediately decided to give up all other activities and devote myself exclusively to an intensive effort to save the young Mexican's life. I wrote daily articles, organized "mercy" crusades, and addressed scores of groups and organizations on the injustices involved in the Ruíz murder conviction. By the time the reprieve expired, so many protesting delegations of clubwomen, educators, humane societies, and religious bodies—several of which I personally led—had descended upon Sacramento that it was not too difficult to obtain three later reprieves.

But another youth—a few months older—committed murder before the expiration of Simón's final commutation of sentence, and in the emergency, I conceived the idea of changing California's law in regard to capital punishment for minors. Under the existing statute, the death penalty could be exacted at fourteen years of age. Accordingly, I framed the so-called Saylor Bill, the state's only woman legislator, Mrs. Florence Saylor, permitting me to use her name. A lobby, which I headed, was organized by the bill's supporters, and I went to Sacramento to direct the work of the committees and to write the arguments—based on statistics showing the inadequacy of capital punishment as a deterrent to crime—for the speakers. The moving eloquence of a family friend, Representative Roy Fellom, father of the state's Public Defender Act and other progressive legislation, secured passage through the Lower House. But in the Senate the measure was tied. The deciding vote belonged to the President, who was on record as strongly opposing the bill. He had once assured me that it was "just as final to be clonked on the head by a youth of sixteen as by one of eighteen."

Believing all hope was lost, I sat on the Capitol's steps and wept profusely. Fortunately, I had selected a spot near the gentlemen's cloakroom for giving emotional vent to my disappointment and profound sorrow. While I was weeping, a kindly senator, John N. Inman, stopped as he passed by to inquire the cause of my distress. Without even looking up, I answered through my sobs, "I've lost the Boy Hanging Bill!"

"And by how many votes, may I ask?"

His question brought on a fresh flood of tears. My head still buried in my hands, I managed to tell him—none too coherently—that the score was tied and I knew the president would cast a decisive negative vote.

"Well, young woman, since you are taking this matter so much to heart, I'll go back and change my vote, that I will."

Thus, by Senator Inman's ballot, Lieutenant Governor Young was prevented from voting and the way was opened for reconsideration. As a result, California's antiquated Penal Code—a survival of lawless "sheep stealing" days of the early 1850's—was altered by the slender margin of a single vote, and the minimum age for capital punishment was fixed at eighteen years. Before the drafting of the act, I had tried to extend it, to have it coincide with the age at which a citizen is qualified to exercise the right of suffrage. But in order to win any concession beyond the statutory fourteen-year minimum, I was forced to accept the compromise.

I was given public credit for the adoption of the humane act both from groups who approved and from groups who disapproved. Entirely unknown to me at the time, the Mexican press, which had closely followed developments, applauded my successful campaign. Shortly after the Simón Ruiz case and the passage of the "Boy Hanging Bill," as it became popularly known, I received a platinum vanity case that bore the inscription: "Respectfully presented by the Mexican Government to Alma M. Sullivan Reed, in high appreciation of her altruistic efforts." A few days later, the Consul General, Sr. Alejandro Lubbert, delivered to me an invitation from President and Señora Obregón to visit Mexico as a semi-official guest.

Friends and relatives strongly opposed acceptance of the invitation, predicting that I would be "murdered in my bed" or, at least, kidnapped as a result of such a foolhardy adventure. Even my father gently cautioned me, as he saw me board the train at the Oakland pier, against the "often fatal attraction of the exotic."

All the fears and doubts, however, proved to be groundless, even though I myself faced sad disillusion at the international border. I had eagerly been waiting to shout, "Beautiful Mexico," as I crossed over the Rio Grande from El Paso to Ciudad Juárez. Instead, I smothered the exclamation, "Poor Mexico!" At that period, the entire Juárez business section looked to be nothing more than a series of swinging *cantina* doors opening upon unpaved streets. The offensive odor of stale beer and the equally offensive jazz from wheezy phonographs further polluted the atmosphere. The few dwellings along the dusty road that led to the railroad station were ugly hovels. It did not occur to me then that American enterprise was largely responsible for the crude, unwholesome aspect of Juárez and that, far from being a typical Mexican town, it was merely the messy backyard of Texas. I learned later that the section I saw that day was maintained almost exclusively for "los gringos" and that "los gringos" owned most of the swinging-door establishments.

On the Pullman, the passengers—all Mexican men—had a very disconcerting, casual sort of way of throwing their pistols about as they arranged their luggage or overcoats for the journey. The dismal prophecies of friends and relatives, which I had so lightly laughed off, now started to ring in my ears with nerve-wracking insistence.

It was through blurred eyes that I took a parting glance at Old Glory waving from the top of the Hotel Paso del Norte on *our* side of the frontier bridge.

An executive of the National Railways who occupied the seat opposite, trying to cheer me, said: "Don't look so downhearted, young lady, just because you are going into a country where no man's afraid of a traffic cop and where each man believes he's an emperor!" His well-intentioned analysis of Mexican psychology was hardly reassuring. Yet it carried more comfort than my father's haunting words of farewell: "Mexico is enchanting, but it is also a land of illusion!"

But once past the dreary "coyote lands," the enchantment became a reality. Gradually, the unique Mexican pageant unfolded in fleeting, ever ascending glimpses of distinguished old cities and of humble pueblos—warm with color and vibrant with the music of guitars that drifted after the moving train. One little group of *mariachi* singers, at the Aguascalientes station, I think it was, sang "Alma de mi Alma" with such an appealing note of personal welcome in their voices that I decided to do my gift shopping on the spot and, from the car window, I stocked up with enough opals to bring years of disaster upon any normally superstitious household. By the time I reached the luxurious altitudes of "la capital," I felt thoroughly at home—never more conscious of being in an *American* country or of my New Worldishness. I was met by a small caravan of automobiles and carriages, and when, at the head of a triumphal procession, I arrived at the Hotel Regis, I found my apartment and bathroom bulging with huge bouquets of gorgeous flowers, with a birdcage or two added for good measure. Almost accusingly, I asked myself: "Where have you been all your life?"

# 3. Antillean Interlude

The five and a half sailing days separating Manhattan's Broadway and Havana's *malecón*[1] were passed in avid pursuit of "background" material. During the early sun-drenched hours, I read absorbing books on Mexico's ancient and modern history. I would interview, in the long afternoons, archaeologists on their previous findings in the Middle American field or question them about their theories of Maya origin. In frequent conversations, I gathered from totally different viewpoints—represented by the Yucatán reactionary Don Luis Molina and the progressive young economist Sr. Casas Alatriste—opinions on the Reform, the Revolution, the Constitution, and on all the tragic events and the top-level treachery that had stained the pages of the Mexican story between Madero and Obregón. A note in my diary, dated February 11, indicates the seriousness with which I regarded the *Times* assignment. "I have determined to work today as never before," I wrote. "My one desire now is to prove myself worthy of the confidence that Mr. Ochs placed in me. I *will* not, *must* not, let him down."

But at night in my cabin all the energetic efficiency of youthful ambition dissolved into waking dreams. Romantically, I lingered over flattering memories of the recent past—hearing again the endearing words of the husky-voiced charmer who had accompanied me to the dock and who eagerly awaited my return. Or, picturing myself at the side of the great Unknown Beloved, I fashioned an ideal future scheme of things.

At moments, I felt I was drifting—helplessly yet willingly—towards some immense reality that would suddenly divert the currents of my thought and action to broader, deeper channels. Then, with an ever-present spirit of self-criticism, I would reprove my imagination for its reckless Icarian soaring towards the regions of the wing-singeing sun. Hope and desire, however, continued to color uninhibited speculation. I kept wondering what new knowledge, what life-shaping events and personalities, I would encounter on this second visit to the country that had already so mysteriously yet so definitely seemed related to my individual destiny.

And, half in promise, half in warning, a new awareness spoke in my heart: "You are sailing to Ultima Thule to keep your most decisive rendezvous with fate." Yet even in the land of the enigmatic Maya, it would be difficult, I realized, to recapture the magic of that first Mexican visit, which I could now appreciate in clear perspective. I began to see, too, that Mexico's tremendous emotional impact had been due not merely to my own temperamental responsiveness, but to historic reasons that were constantly being clarified for me by my new shipboard acquaintances.

My arrival six months earlier in the Mexican capital—it gradually dawned upon my Antillean reflections—had coincided with a golden moment in the national existence, a moment without precedent or possibility of duplication. Now, as I looked back, it all seemed as though I had been watching a great century plant, that aggressive, symbolic *agave,* so indispensably a part of the Mexican pattern, burst suddenly into magnificent flowering to fill the scene with joyous repercussions of its release to the light after a long darkness. And this, I now understood, was its appointed hour of florescence, Mexico's true Centennial!

Exactly a hundred years had passed since the birth of national freedom. Independence dated from September 16, 1810, but the violent conflict of separation from Spain lasted for another twelve years, and it was not until 1822 that the first Mexican Congress met to draw up a Constitution and lay the cornerstone of the future Republic.

The deck conversations with Sr. Casas Alatriste, whose own background was dramatically entwined with every period of post-Conquest Mexican history, clarified social, political, and economic situations that had previously seemed vague or obscure. His illuminating facts also served to highlight new aspects of Mexican character and heroism. Now more than ever Mexico became for me not only the scene of an eager professional interest but the object of my sincere admiration and affection. With poignant awareness, I could now fully appreciate the generous hospitality that had been showered upon me from the moment of my arrival in the Mexican Republic. For knowing at first hand the people and their emphasis on human values, on the things of the heart and the spirit, I could more readily understand the gracious invitation of President Obregón to visit his country. It no longer seemed extraordinary but merely a Mexican gesture that, burdened as he was with heavy responsibilities and grave perils, he should have reached out from his war-torn land across a continent, to a nation that still withheld recognition from his government, to acknowledge gratefully the sympathetic understanding and the acts of friendship of a young and relatively unknown newspaper writer.

With fresh emotion, I recalled, as we sailed, all the enchantment I had absorbed during those three eventful months. I responded anew to the high adventure of nation building in which I had been a privileged spectator and, on occasion, even a participant. I relived the vivid experiences of the officially arranged tours under ideal and, for the period, unique conditions. At that time, Mexico could count on very few friends anywhere. I was spontaneously received as one of the small company and, wherever I went, was received as a "goodwill ambassadress." But I carried no portfolio other than my little inscribed platinum vanity case. I did not have the slightest need of any formal title or sponsorship. For, on all my travels, poetic accounts of the Simón Ruíz incident, which had been featured in the press of the capital and of the larger cities, preceded me. Even in the isolated villages of Jalisco, Oaxaca, Guerrero, and Puebla, where newspapers were scarce, some primitive yet remarkably functional "grapevine" must have been responsible for the *fiestas* and the *banquetes* given in honor of "la niña periodista," as they called me.[2]

At the time, I was a tall, slender young woman with an oval face, chestnut brown hair, classic features, fair skin, and very large dark blue eyes. Despite an early idealistic marriage that had soon ended in divorce and despite my almost daily contact with life's misery and tragedy as a journalist and as an apprentice social and prison worker, I was continuously being assured: "You have such a happy, angelical, 'little girl' look, as though you have never known sorrow or had ever been in love!"

But the most important consideration, perhaps, in establishing my popularity was the elusive, inexplicable fact that Mexico had found me personally *simpática*. In official circles, the federal departments arranged *conferencias* and invited me on expeditions to distant places, so that I might have "eyewitness" information on the nation's problems. On several occasions, I was received at Chapultepec by Sra. Obregón and at the National Palace by the President, with whom I led the grand march at an Armistice Day Ball on November 11, 1922. I was frequently entertained at the homes of cabinet ministers and members of Congress. Under the potent spell of Mexico's Renaissance, I had discovered among the Mexicans unimagined levels of individual and collective inspiration. An irresistible surge of creative effort in all fields of constructive activity accompanied public elation over the end of bloodshed and the restoration of order. It was the moment at which the Mexican people first realized that they could counterbalance their terrific losses with material and spiritual gains. Victory had cost nearly a decade of destruction, misery, and sorrow and the toll of approximately two million lives. The prevailing courage to reshape an unsatisfactory scheme of things could hardly have been more in evidence at any time, anywhere.

An atmosphere of political calm apparently provided a smooth course for the return of normalcy. President Álvaro Obregón had assumed office in December 1920, and during the year and a half that followed, there had been a steady swing to public order. Fortunate internal and external events combined to hasten stabilization. Restored railroad service and property protection were among the more encouraging first results of the process. Business flourished—the oil output of the year just ended breaking all records, due to Supreme Court decisions in favor of the petroleum companies, without loss of Revolutionary "face." In June, Mexico had assumed full obligation for the principal of her foreign debt and for the defaulted interest; technical details of the agreement were later worked out in New York by the committee of which Sr. Casas Alatriste was chairman. Treaties had just been concluded with France and England, and friendly relations with the United States had not yet been strained by the implementation of the administration's oil and agrarian policies. Newspapers of the capital were carrying statements from the Mexican Embassy expressing hearty approval of Washington's moves on behalf of persecuted Mexican laborers in the Texas oil fields. The important Mexico City daily, *El Mundo,* ventured the first prediction of early recognition. Secretary of War Serrano reported a definite trend towards peace, the only statement of its kind to come from his office in many years. Interrupted momentarily by a flurry of charges and denials that Catholic priests were supporting Fascism with the aim to control the government, there was, in effect, a truce with the church, while enforcement of the anti-clerical provisions of the Constitution still remained in abeyance.

Labor organizations again came out into the open with increased memberships and added influence, after their drastic suppression under Carranza.[3] Rival unions freely aired their quarrels in spirited demonstrations. From my window in the Hotel Regis, I watched daily parades along Avenida Juárez. The objective of the workers, carrying red-and-black CROM[4] banners, was the plant of *El Universal,* where the entire staff of 250 members had just formed a new union of newspaper writers and pressmen. The owner, Sr. Félix F. Palavicini, intellectual leader of the Renovators[5] during the Constitutional debates of 1917, closed down his paper for a week in protest against an attempt by Luis G. Morones to force his staff to join the politically powerful CROM. When I visited *El Universal* in late September with Sr. Elías G. de Lima, the building was still barricaded against further assaults and we had to take a roundabout way to Sr. Palavicini's editorial sanctum. But publication had been resumed and, for the time being at least, "freedom of the press" was triumphant.

Outside of a few permanently irreconcilable elements, whose spokesmen I occasionally met at social functions in the Casino Español or in the home of Díaz regime families, President Obregón appeared to be the idol of a united people. His ruddy "Irish" face, genial smile, and thoroughly human personality, and his one arm marking him as a hero and identifying him with sacrifice for his country, became a rallying point for popular enthusiasm whenever he appeared in public. Everywhere, there was faith in his promise to educate Mexico in the practice of democracy. This faith grew stronger as it became daily more apparent that he shunned military dictatorship and hastened political rehabilitation. It was capped in December 1922 by the passage of a bill granting amnesty to all political prisoners. The fervor of Indian orators at pueblo celebrations, particularly at *fiestas* connected with the *ejidos*[6] programs, their prolonged and vigorous *¡vivas!* for government officials, individually and collectively, indicated a new spirit of confidence. It was evident that the masses, encouraged by the fulfillment of old promises to distribute lands, emerged hopefully from the cataclysmic wreckage of the peonage system to duly exercise their guaranteed rights and liberties.

During the first months of his administration, General Obregón established some twelve thousand elementary schools, most of them developed from the "Missionary" units.[7] Practical rural education was under the direction of Ramón P. de Negri, Minister of Fomento y Agricultura,[8] whom I had known in San Francisco when he was Mexican Consul General there. The forceful official, with the swarthy complexion, broad shoulders, and compact build that distinguished many of the Mexican Revolutionary leaders, was almost as prominently in the limelight as the administration's "strong man," General Plutarco Elías Calles himself. With pronounced and radical convictions, de Negri dealt boldly with the agrarian question, upon which the current peace and hopefulness rested. In several interviews he had outlined for me his proposed development of land grants, cooperative organizations, speedy return of *ejidos* to Indian communities, and his daring plan of complete nationalization of the land.

With the engineers of the Department of Forestry and Fisheries, I journeyed into mountain regions of the state of Hidalgo to see how the government worked, through the reforestation and preservation of timberlands, to prevent "dust bowls" for future agriculturists.

Unforgettable mornings were spent in the recesses of the National Archives, examining Mexico's documentary treasures. The director, Don Rafael López, the Jaliscience poet-author of that thunderous invective against "the Monster of the North"—"La Bestia de Oro"[9]—would take from their intricate wrappings age-yellowed parchments containing Papal Bulls, Royal Edicts, and Vice-Regal Decrees and the faded manuscripts and letters of *cronistas*[10] and *Conquistadores* for my study. We were often joined in these sessions by the frail co-director, Don Luis González Obregón, whose volume of tales, *Las Calles de México,* tracing the legends and dramatic events behind the names of the capital's streets, was the inevitable companion of my frequent tours of the city's old colonial sections.

I went with Dr. Manuel F. Gamio and his group of experts—ethnologists, sociologists, linguists, economists, and archaeologists—on their first field survey of Oaxaca. We climbed to the heights of Monte Albán that overlooked the city. On the terraced "White Mountain," where excavations were in progress among the mounds and vaulted chambers, the youthful and scholarly head of the Department of Anthropology formally launched his study of the region. Marking the occasion with a brief address to the members of the little group, he said: "Any turn of the spade now may reveal the tombs of Zapotecan kings. But, *compañeros,*[11] what is more important for us and for Mexico is the light that these excavations will throw upon the humble lives being lived in the valley below."

The great purpose that lay beyond their immediate effort was to form a coherent and definite nationality out of Mexico's many racial units, differing widely in characteristics and in historic antecedents. The task that Dr. Gamio began that day in Oaxaca with the triple vision of the scientist, humanitarian, and patriot, he had already accomplished in the Valley of Teotihuacán. His monumental work, *La Población del Valle de Teotihuacán,*[12] representing ten years of unremitting research throughout changes in government and the chaos of revolution, had been published earlier that summer and had served as my chief source of information on many aspects of both the ancient and contemporary Mexican scene.

In the field of esthetics, from the start, Dr. Atl[13] was recognized as the true pioneer of the mural movement, organizing before 1910 the *Centro Artístico,* the nucleus for the Syndicate of Painters, Mechanical Workers, Engravers, and Sculptors, whose members had been given public walls in 1922 shortly before my arrival.

His studio was in the old *ex-convento de la Merced,*[14] in the ancient quarter back of the Cathedral. To attend night parties there, I would have to pass through interminable corridors and grope my way through dark, deserted patios, while my art-conscious escort would light matches to show me the beautiful carved columns. Then we would ascend great stairways and pass along other corridors before reaching the far end of the enormous edifice where our host held court.

Rumor associated Dr. Atl with fantastic adventures and escapades and curious personal habits. It was said that he slept nightly in a coffin in order to accustom himself to the "feel of death," and that he had resented the rumor as "half truth." He explained that he slept in a coffin merely because he "rested *better* that way." I used to look with suspicion upon every covered object in the huge candlelit room, cautiously lifting the edges of tapestries thrown over the furniture, to make sure I was not sitting on any long, narrow, black box that might serve the versatile scholar as a bed. Topics of studio conversation ranged from early Chinese landscape and the influence of St. Francis of Assisi on the painters of his day, to the Freudian whimsies of ecclesiastical architecture. There were spirited discussions over technical problems, which usually culminated and ended in arguments over efforts of the leading muralists—José Clemente Orozco, David Alfaro Siqueiros, Diego Rivera, Francisco Leal, Jean Charlot, Carlos Mérida, Fermín Revueltas, Xavier Guerrero, Ramón Alva Guadarrama, Roberto Montenegro, Adolfo Best-Maugard, Ramón Alva de la Canal, and of course, Dr. Atl—to rediscover the *buon fresco* of Giotto, or at least to find in the Mexican shops ingredients equivalent to those mentioned by the Italian master's son-in-law, Cennino Cennini, in his treatise on fresco technique.

Sometimes, the young Nahui Olin (Aztec for the "four winds"), daughter of the well-known Díaz *militar* General Mondragón, would recite her *Poemas Dinámicos.* The artists and the literati, who were seated on the floor against the walls, already knew what she explained for my benefit, that "the words made no pretension to sense, but were rich in plastic values," a virtue I was not in a position to appreciate until some years later through my reading of Gertrude Stein and James Joyce. Her thick blonde hair, worn in a long Egyptian bob, was severely banged across her wide forehead, and her large round eyes, with iris rims as black as India ink, were fathomless, suggesting the eyes of one of Foujita's introspective cats. In the mellow, flickering candlelight, there was both a striking and a gossamer quality to her strange beauty. Somehow she impressed me as a graceful symbol of at least one aspect, and a fascinating one, of the Mexican mood, of an elusive glamour that was as poignant as a moonflower at midnight, radiant with a white intensity that was uncertain of its tomorrow. Her personality seemed a composite of all the lively mental curiosity, the dazzling unfinished projects, the feverish haste, and the impetuous plunging into the untried that characterized much of the impassioned, often quixotic, "direct action" of the post-Revolutionary era and which no one more vividly than Dr. Atl himself summarized when he explained: "Our object is to purify knowledge already acquired and to fling a new missile through a new space."

In any other country, the "Bohemia" of the Mexican capital might have bankrupted fantasy. But in its own setting it was all a very natural expansion of the popular psychology and the general spirit of rapture, in which the "carryings-on" of the oversouls were not etched in any bold or bizarre relief. A surrealist mood permeated the social gatherings of the *intelligenzia,* but it was the same mood that had produced Mexico's very original popular arts. If, according to New England standards, the Normal at times in this circle suffered severe dislocations from historic backgrounds or violent wrenchings from their accustomed settings, so did many phases of the ordinary daily life that one encountered in the streets. On my way, for instance, to luncheon at Sanborn's, the famous House of Tiles, I would pass three stages of human evolution telescoped into a sun-drenched moment, and a foot or two of stone pavement on Avenida Francisco Madero. For there, as travel writers were to record years later, an Indian *peladito* wrapped in a red *serape,* his head and shoulders all but hidden in the protecting depths of a big straw sombrero, ground his midday meal on a *tezontle metate* of the Neolithic period.[15] He leaned against the wall of a resplendent blue-and-gold tile built under the feudal system of Colonial times for feudal purposes. Part of the façade had been transformed into a store and behind its plate-glass show windows were displayed electric irons, refrigerators, automatic heaters, and other gadgets of the Machine Age.

The surrealist attitude asserted itself most vigorously perhaps in the amazing decorations of the butcher shops and the *pulquerías*.[16] Above the doors of the latter appeared such typical firm names as "Wise Men Who Never Study," "The Magnificent Jewess," "The Errors of Cupid," "No One Will Ever Know," and "Who Cares, Anyway?" But the uniquely Mexican brand of fantasy found its most typical and uninhibited expression in the toys and candies sold at the *puestos,* or stands, of the Alameda Central and elsewhere for the approaching feast of "Los Muertos" (All Souls' Day) on November 2. These decidedly different candies were little sugar skulls and cadavers, brightened with bits of gold and silver paper. The toys were gaily adorned hearses and other miniature trappings of the grave and the funeral parlor. And dramatizing the acceptance of death as a fact of life, and the general casual approach to it, were the tiny white coffins—*real ones*—for which people shopped, as they did for other household commodities, from the stacks that were piled high on the sidewalks around the Zócalo, the great central Plaza of the Constitution. When President Obregón assumed office, the infant mortality rate in the Republic, I was informed by Health Minister Alberto J. Pani, was 85 percent. Only fifteen out of every one hundred babies born survived their first year.

Within the short period of two years, the mural movement, initiated by the progressive Minister of Public Education, Licenciado José Vasconcelos, had developed the greatest figures of contemporary art.[17] Summoning the nation's outstanding painters from different parts of the country and from their studies abroad, he turned over to them the walls of new public buildings and those of certain colonial churches, which had been converted into workers' libraries and classrooms. There was no attempt to dictate propaganda or to impose technical specifications. The artists organized into a *sindicato,* or union, and, working as day laborers at a modest wage, were regarded as responsible creators over whose output no committee, politician or contractor had the slightest control. On one occasion, when, with Vasconcelos, I visited the patio of the National Preparatory School where José Clemente Orozco was then painting his powerful frescoes, the official called up to the muralist on the scaffold: "I heartily dislike what you are doing. It is terrible! But the wall is yours—Go ahead!"

In 1922, Orozco was still experimenting with the fresco medium, which the Mexicans had revived for monumental muralism for the first time since the great Italians. His theme was the laborer, or *obrero,* a carpenter of Galilee or Cuautla, about to swing an axe into a heavy wooden cross that he had already partially destroyed. A work of serenity, of ample volumes, characteristic economy of line and controlled dynamism of inner action, it represented a supreme plastic interpretation of the *renovación* theme. Uncompromisingly, Orozco had projected the idea of the necessary abandonment of whatever in the tradition had lost its integrity, or had been perverted to ignoble uses, becoming like so much dead wood in relation to its original meanings.

The *obrero* must reject the symbol that inspired his mission of brotherly love, because now it is borne by priests advancing amid the bayonets of battle to urge men to slaughter their fellow men in causes just and unjust. The *obrero* will find a new symbol through his contemplation of nature's miracles—the stars, the sun, the planets—one of which now serves as a halo. Or, he will take from the ether some immutable sign of order, beauty, and ultimate justice in the universe—the geometric form of pyramid, cone, sphere, or cube. Orozco's significant *obrero* was partially destroyed, but the idea survived intact and assumed even greater dimensions ten years later at Dartmouth College. On the walls of Baker Library he painted a flayed Christ whose cross has already been chopped down and thrown upon the Calvario of discarded, junked emblems of humanity's physical and moral bondage.

On a vaulted surface of the National Preparatory School patio Orozco interpreted the eternal evolutionary process. I watched him as he painted "Man" leaping over an abyss, hurled forward by an inner force that forever drives him onward, the means and end of his own striving. There is no knowledge that Man may not wrest from the remote eons, even that well-guarded secret of his very existence, by an Olympian plunge into the cosmos of his own consciousness. This essential idea that underlies many of Orozco's universal concepts is a plastic synthesis of the exalted thought and bold action of that little band of Mexican idealists who, motivated by Mexican grievances, ceaselessly hacked away at the bases of Mexican despotism between 1900 and 1910, until the formidable structure toppled and opened up the road for Madero[18] and liberation.

For hours at a stretch, the muralist in complete oblivion to all about him, and enwrapped in creative silence, labored at covering the venerable ecclesiastical walls of San Ildefonso with the revitalizing symbols of a humanistic faith. It was the faith of the precursors of Revolución Social, and, with equal dedication and purity of purpose, he was registering the precise nuances of their honest words and courageous deeds, his genius enriching the synthesis until it glowed with the splendor of a fixed star for the guidance of history in the making. Like most Mexico-conscious California journalists, I knew that the trailblazers of the New Order had looked to Ricardo Flores Magón, intellectual anarchist, for spiritual leadership. Magón had been an exile in Southern California and between 1906 and 1910 published his celebrated *Regeneración* there. But I was still uninformed as to the significant role played by Felipe Carrillo Puerto, Socialist, in the national emancipation. At the time I was not even aware of his association with the brothers Flores Magón and other organizers of the Partido Liberal,[19] whose ideology was first articulated by the young poet Praxedis G. Guerrero of León, Guanajuato, when he wrote: "I am action. Progress and Liberty cannot exist without me!" Later, this same Humanistic Faith, the real foundation stone on which the structure of a modern Mexico was laid at the turn of the century, was defined by Ricardo Flores Magón himself, then a hunted and often hungry man in the United States with a price on his head. Through *Regeneración*, the Liberal Party organ, he flung out this challenge: "We are moving from illusions towards life. Yesterday Heaven was the People's objective. Today, it is the Earth!"

Ricardo Flores Magón's public funeral in Mexico City marked the emotional climax of a year tempered to the highest pitch of national consciousness. His death on November 21, 1922, in Leavenworth Penitentiary, Kansas, tugged at Mexico's heartstrings, releasing long pent-up tears of private and general grief. The event revived memories of unwept *noches tristes*[20] and dramatized the tragic power of the indomitable spirit that has sustained a people through their prolonged agonies. During the five years of his imprisonment for violation of the wartime espionage act—he had consistently preached Peace—Flores Magón had been failing in health and was gradually going blind. Millions of his admirers in the United States and in Mexico fought for his freedom. Many urged him to apply for a pardon, which was his for the asking. But he steadfastly refused liberty that required an admission of guilt. In the demonstration with which Mexico paid him posthumous honor, his austere black coffin was borne through the streets, followed by a throng carrying "Land of Liberty" banners and singing his moving *Songs of Deliverance.* I saw Mexicans to whom the word "Anarchist" or even "Socialist" was anathema, reverently standing with bared heads as the simple cortege passed, in tribute to the nobility of Flores Magón's life and death. Old Revolutionaries forgot his fiery, whole-souled denunciations of "compromise" or "sell-out" on the various proposals that had been submitted to the people as solutions, including the "Plan of San Luis Potosí."[21] They remembered only his innately Mexican yet timeless and universal dream, which, like a dirge and a paean, echoed in their hearts: "Life should be full of poetry; full of passion that runs through the veins. Life was never meant to be put in the straightjacket with which monopoly has bound it. Consent no longer by your submissiveness that idle hands become masters of what belongs to you, of what belongs to all humanity. Take possession of this earth to which you have given your toil and of its fruits, which have been denied you, with humanity's supreme cry, 'Land and Liberty!' "

I, too, recalled Flores Magón's stirring message, but in my nationalistic outlook it was translated for me into the words of another American—our immortal Thomas Jefferson, who declared: "The earth belongs to him who tills it!"[22]

# 4. Caribbean Reflections

At Nassau, some nine hundred miles from Manhattan, the *Mexico* made its first stop, anchoring close enough to the big coral island of New Providence to permit one to verify the claim of the Ward Line folder that the capital of the Bahamas "faces the ocean smilingly." In the pale light of the early morning, the town was as vivid and as economical of detail as a Raoul Dufy gouache. In a few deft strokes the sensitive artist might have caught all the elements of its insouciant charm—an emerald hill in the background crowned by the gray walls of the old Fincastle fortress; a fringe of coconut palms in the foreground, bordering the prim lawns around a wooden Georgian structure, the new Colonial Hotel; here and there, the white dot of a low building; and, with just a tilt of cocksure bravado in their gay sails, nestled the tiny craft of the "mosquito" rum fleet in the turquoise harbor.

During the waiting interlude, when several passengers disembarked, the history-minded archaeologists exchanged tales of the turbulent past of the Bahamas—legends of early buccaneers who seized passing Spanish galleons, of the hidden loot of later pirates, among them the notorious Blackbeard, terror of the British merchantment. There were stories, too, of the blockade runners who landed arms and military supplies for the Confederate States, receiving for England cargoes of cotton and other products of the South.

Again, we headed southward, and for the rest of the day the *Mexico*'s course lay over the "tongue of the ocean," a deep chasm west of Andros, largest island of the group. Occasionally I would run up to the skipper's bridge, where Captain Peterson, poring over his navigation charts, would take time out to trace our route through the intricate channels and around the shoals and coral reefs of the West Indies, sometimes dramatically describing the more sensational features of the pelagic landscape below us. We were skirting the Great Bahama's banks, the vast submarine plateau that forms the base of the islands and their innumerable cays and reefs, where islets and atolls by the hundred have been known to emerge and vanish overnight. Soon we would leave the shallow waters and veer due west into depths of a thousand fathoms, to sail along the northern coast of Cuba.

The West Indian archipelago had always attracted me, but chiefly, up until that time, because of its historic background and external beauty. When I thought about that far-flung island group at all, it was mainly in terms of the lugubrious chronicles of two or three humane friars and their shocking account of the cruelty of Spanish colonists against the defenseless natives, or the glowing descriptions of modern travel writers, most of whom pictured a fanciful paradise of palm-lined avenues, glistening strands of sheltered coves by moonlight. In general, the Bahamas and the Greater and Lesser Antilles existed for me as points on a map, representing a vast domain that begins fifty miles off the Florida coast and stretches southeastward from the Mexican Gulf for fifteen hundred miles, according to certain flamboyant Latin American poets, like a crescent of diamonds in a sapphire sea. Except for several outstanding personalities—literary figures or heroes of independence movements—I was only vaguely aware of the contemporary spiritual stature of the Antilles, of the many vital contributions stemming from the rich and varied currents of tradition and art that have met and mingled and flowered into significant new patterns of life on the windswept ocean, shored by the oldest and the youngest of the continents.

Yet I did recall *one* Antillean dream with reverence for the dreamer. At the close of the nineteenth century, the Cuban Apostle, José Martí, in his exalted vision of continental solidarity, conceived and labored for the plan of an Antillean Confederation as part of his larger aim to "unite with inviolable bonds the Latin American Republics of the New World." Martí was the moving spirit in a group of West Indian patriots and intellectuals who attempted to merge the political and economic fortunes of the Greater Antilles—his beloved Cuba, Santo Domingo, Puerto Rico, Haiti, Jamaica—islands which, he insisted, "must stand together or disappear from the roster of free peoples." America he saluted as "the continent of human hope." Fixed in his constructive ideas, unswerving in his pure purpose, the poet-statesman struggled throughout his entire life span of forty-two years for human rights and the dignity of man. He failed to unite the Greater Antilles, and as a result of the epochal lost opportunity, age-old social problems that might then have been solved have since weighed down upon the West Indian peoples as their dark heritage.

The leisurely seafaring days, however, were destined not only to broaden the dimensions of my individual work outlook but also to give stimulating direction to my personal and professional activities. It was there, for instance, on the vessel's forecastle deck, studying maps of the underwater topography or gazing down on the dolphins as they cavorted in the swirling foam that trailed the starboard prow, that I experienced intense desires which later found realization in absorbing pursuits. I longed to know firsthand the "feel" of that motionless, silent world beneath the sunlit surface, the mysterious realm that occupies that major portion of the global area. I can trace my enthusiastic involvement with submarine archaeology, as well as persistent research into the extraordinary career of the gentleman-privateer Jean Laffite, to those hours of tranquil detachment aboard the *Mexico.* Viewed through a magic sextant in which yesterday and tomorrow loomed on an equally remote horizon, these immediate new interests captured my imagination and left their deep and lasting impressions.

Suddenly, on the fifth day of the voyage, like a mirage in alabaster, appeared Havana's mingled mass of cupolas, spires, and battlemented walls. Suspended in diaphanous light between the dark blue of the water and the unflecked azure of the sky, the city's arresting contours glowed with an ethereal splendor. In my initiation to "tourist culture," however, the Pearl of the Antilles proved to be realistic enough when, docking shortly after dawn, the *Mexico* allowed its passengers a whole day to explore Havana's widely heralded attractions. I was invited to join a party consisting of an Austrian woman psychiatrist, two Yucatecan *hacendados,* Sr. Casas Alatriste, and Mr. and Mrs. John F. Barry of New York. As the editor of *Commercial Mexico,* a national business journal, Mr. Barry was keenly alive to the expansion in tourism and henequen trade that would likely result from the Carnegie Expedition publicity and was, in fact, making the Yucatán trip in order to submit an advertising program to Governor Carrillo.

Even at that period, two years before the Machado dictatorship, sightseeing in Havana was rigged to conform to what some wishful-thinking guide assumed was American taste in entertainment.[1] After a visit to "Sloppy Joe's" for spurious if delectable "native" beverages, our own guide, Pedro, rushed us through the main thoroughfares and along the elegant Prado and Malecón Boulevards as though bent on saving time for his idea of worthier objectives. These turned out to be Havana's breweries and cigar factories, and apparently his aim was to impress us with their number and size.

In any event, our first stop was an American-owned beer garden in a tropical setting; the second, a rambling establishment where an army of skilled and unskilled workers were engaged in sorting and rolling brown tobacco leaves into choice *puros* or mass-producing machine-made *cigarrillos*—an industry that next to the island's sugar refineries was the chief source of its flourishing economy. En route to these and similar places of his personal and doubtless pecuniary interest, Pedro would grudgingly pause to point out some celebrated Cuban landmark.

Fortunately his sketchy itinerary included Havana's immense Hispano-American-style Cathedral with its uninspiring Tuscany façade and dismal interior. With the enchantingly decorated and architecturally superior Mexican churches still fresh in my memory, the pompous structure suffered by comparison. Begun in 1704, the ecclesiastical edifice was nearing completion in 1796, when the supposed coffin of Columbus arrived from Santo Domingo and was encrypted in its walls. Prolonged and solemn ceremonies attended the event. The sepulcher of the Great Navigator, so inextricably a part of the opening chapter of the Cuban story, became a revered national shrine. The remains were continuously honored until Spain claimed them a century later. Only after Cuba had surrendered the venerated bones was the deception of "error" admitted; they were not those of Christopher but probably of his son, Diego Columbus.

Havana was at its gayest, lustily enjoying the season of the February *fiestas* then in full swing. The pageantry of extravagant masquerades and colorful processions—the traditional *comparsas*—was staged only at Carnival time, and the pleasure-loving populace was making the best of its eagerly anticipated annual event. In the evening, we joined in the street revelry, visited the elegant National Casino and, after dinner, danced until midnight on the roof terrace of the Plaza Hotel, thus completing, according to program, the "perfect day" of the travel agency. In compliment to the American guests, the Plaza orchestra played the tuneful and rollicking "Mr. Gallagher and Mr. Sheen," the current song sensation of New York's Ziegfeld Follies. The musicians—moon-faced young men flashing rows of white and gold dentistry in perpetual smiles—wore beige satin toreador jackets with wide yellow or scarlet cummerbunds. Their jet black hair shellacked to a scintillating brilliancy, the gleaming chrome of the ornate bandstand on which they rhythmically gyrated and performed clownish antics, added up to an apt symbol of the prevailing mood—one that reflected the smugness of the night spot's chief patrons, the affluent subsidized sugar planters and the North American owners of the fabulously lucrative gambling establishments. In the effusive deference to the tourists from the United States, there was everywhere an obvious recognition of Uncle Sam's generous benefactions and a bid for their continuance. Between rumbas and daiquiris, table conversation turned hilariously upon our "personally conducted" adventures of the afternoon. The topic suggested other tales about professional guides who totally misrepresented their countries.

Among the more amusing stories in this vein was Sr. Casas Alatriste's account of his first visit to the United States. In his school days, he dreamed of traveling through the rich, powerful land across the Rio Bravo that loomed so formidably in the imagination of Mexican youth. In preparation for the momentous event, he diligently applied himself to the study of English, even reading our poets and economists. The long-anticipated day for his crossing over the international boundary line finally arrived, and one morning at the beginning of the First World War he found himself in San Antonio. But a weird sight greeted his unbelieving eyes. He felt there surely must have been some terrible mistake and that he had landed in Darkest Africa instead of the neighboring Lone Star State. For, under a torrid noon sun, lined up in front of a gaudily ornate tattoo parlor, stood a double queue of soldiers and civilians patiently waiting their turn at having their bodies decorated like so many Ubangi savages. Happily, as the courteous Sr. Casas Alatriste explained, he remained long enough in Texas to correct his first startling picture of "typical" American customs.

In sharp contrast to the Plaza's dazzling gilt and glitter was the small candlelit hideout at Guanabacoa Beach, several miles beyond the city, where, at the invitation of a Cuban painter friend of one of the Yucatecan *hacendados*, we dramatically ended the evening's revels. Here, in a thatch-roof hut, in the cavernous region that local superstition associated with the nocturnal prowling of *zombies*, or newly disinterred dead, the gaunt, Negroid devotees of Ñáñigo, outlawed cult of Santa Bárbara, performed exotic ritualistic pantomime.[2] Bare-legged, but trailing bizarre, multicolored draperies from their loins or shoulders, they swayed to the scarcely audible rattle of the maracas and the muted thumping of the bongo. At intervals, they intoned the hypnotic sounds and meters of the Antillean *tun tun de pasa y grifería*, the "Danza negra," and the "Lamento," or improvised plaintive incantations.[3] That night, the voice of the Caribbean masses reached me as profoundly human rather than as purely literary expression. I had but lately become aware of Afro-Cuban poetry through the occasional *sones* published in the "Little Reviews" for the consumption of the intelligentsia of the Parisian Left Bank or Manhattan's Greenwich Village.[4] But in the black, shifting shadows of the secret Guanabacoa rendezvous, the poetry of Negrismo made articulate for me the primitive emotions of inarticulate peoples everywhere. Through a universally understandable idiom triple-rooted in the continents of Africa, Europe, and America, it spoke for the exploited and helpless millions of the earth.

Evidently our Cuban artist escort enjoyed the full confidence of our exotic hosts, for they appeared to be oblivious to any intrusion upon their private voodoo rites. Quite casually, they even asked us to join the "sacred circle" for the baptism ceremony and then, in the most matter-of-fact way, proceeded to tie the left leg of each female spectator seated in the magic ring to the right leg of the male beside her. Meanwhile, the ebony-hued neophyte chosen for the sacramental waters lay stretched out in the center space, writhing as one possessed of a demon. During the drama-packed two hours that followed, the Ñáñigo cultists were intent only on expressing an enormous racial capacity for joy and anguish through uninhibited dance movements or, in conveying in bold onomatopoeic verses, awe and reverence before the mysteries of love and birth and death. Often, leaping sharply above the low, steady rhythm of dry seeds rang a cry of fear at the menacing elements or the perils of jungle and swamp. Again, a wail of physical pain at the brutality of "civilized" overlords through the centuries. When not smothered in sigh of despair, the cry became a shrill call to revolt. But there were moments when, as if in complete release from hurt and humiliation and forgetfulness of ancient wrongs, the pulsating rhythms swung in wild abandon to the orgiastic, combining in Ñáñigo's ecstatic sensuality the rumba's sultry passion and the volcanic intensity of the conga—those whom the god of the heights had forsaken, seeking god in the depths.

Delayed loading and unloading of cargo won for the *Mexico*'s passengers another half-day stopover. Despite the strenuous festivities of the previous night and lack of sleep, a few of the same intrepid members of the "sightseeing" party decided to take advantage of the early morning hours to "get acquainted with the *real* Havana." This time, Sr. Molina offered his services as guide, and we started out in an open carriage, amid the furious cacophony of multi-toned bells, clanging simultaneously all over the city. We drove slowly through narrow, winding streets, pausing wherever and as often as we wished to admire some colonial *balcón,* an interesting wrought-iron grille or an impressive old gate still bearing its half-erased armorial escutcheon. We were free to look and listen at leisure, and there was plenty to see and hear during the colorful procession of food vendors who usher in Havana's ten o'clock *café con leche.*

For miles, our road followed white beaches and then turned to the open country through rows of royal palm and gorgeous flowering trees. On either side stretched vast sugar and tobacco plantations varied with well-kept *fincas,*[5] each with its broad terraced villa, or virgin hectares of lush, tropical forests. Over all this luxuriance that flourished under the Cuban sun, and that in its decay returned to enrich the Cuban earth, seemed to hover the spirit of the Discoverer, whose eloquent letters were imperatives of my preparatory reading. For notwithstanding his sense of inadequacy, Columbus will always remain for the perceptive traveler the most vivid interpreter of that "loveliness his tongue could not express nor his pen describe."

The report made to their Spanish majesties after his landing near the Bay of Nuevitas in late October 1492 is unrivaled both for accuracy of detail and feeling for the soil. "The clearness of the water," he wrote, "through which the sand at the bottom may be seen; the multitude of palm trees of various forms, the highest and most beautiful I have met with, and an infinity of other great and green trees; the birds in rich plumage and the verdure of the fields, render this country of such marvelous beauty that it surpasses all other in charm and graces, as the day doth the night in lustre."

Nothing had changed, it occurred to me, and I almost expected the original inhabitants of this Elysium to emerge shyly from the groves of "lofty palms and flowering trees." Columbus had described the natives—the *Cubeños*[6]—in a letter to his friend, Sant Ángel, Treasurer of Aragon, observing: "If anything they have and it be asked for, they never say 'no,' but do rather invite the person to accept it, and show as much loving kindness as though they would give their hearts." And once the Discoverer was quoted as saying: "These people are very gentle, knowing not what is evil nor the sins of murder and theft . . ." Peter Martyr, the Italian scholar at the Court of Isabella and later member of the Council of the Indies, had also described the Cubeños and their Utopian confraternity that might have been planned by St. Francis of Assisi himself. "It is certain," wrote the erudite churchman, "that the land among these people is as common as the sun and the water; and that 'mine' and 'thine,' the seeds of all mischief, have no place among them. They are content with so little that in so large a country they have rather superfluity than scarceness, so that they seem to live in a golden world, without toil, living in open gardens, not entrenched with dykes, divided with hedges or defended with walls. They deal truly one with another, without laws, without books, and without judges. They take him for an evil man who taketh pleasure in doing hurt to another; and albeit they delight not in superfluities, yet they make provision for the increase of such roots whereof they make bread, contented with such simple diet, whereby health is preserved and disease avoided."

Where were these gentle *Cubeños?* In that spot, marveling at such beauty in Nature and in the human soul, I might have absentmindedly inquired of the huge Negro—jet black son of African slaves—who shuffled along the dusty road. But I remembered Fray Bartolomé de las Casas and his *Brief History of the Destruction of the Indies,* that humane priest whose life was spent in a fruitless effort to alleviate the sufferings of the Cubeños and to prevent their final, total extermination.[7] For, in the thirteen years after the Conquest of Cuba by the Adelantado Diego de Velázquez in 1511, Fray de las Casas and other eyewitness chroniclers relate that between 300,000 and one million *Cubeños* disappeared in a mass murder, which for hideous cruelty had no parallel, until the Hitlerian genocide, in history. Enslaved—*encomendado* is the official word—and put to work at labor beyond their physical endurance in the rivers and among the rocks where the Spaniards believed there was gold, starved, tormented, they died or committed suicide, unable to bear the agony of life. Other thousands were killed outright or through slow torture. Fray Bartolomé de las Casas records that it was not an uncommon sight to see "processions of slaves chained together like droves of pigs to furnish food for the dogs. The more humane of the captains killed them first, but others turned the hungry dogs loose upon the terrified living victims." He describes the hanging of thirteen Indians in a row, strung up at a height where their toes barely touched the ground, "prodded with sword points, care being taken to prolong their agony." This episode, he adds, "was in honor of Christ and the twelve apostles, for it was a feast day."

Another *encomienda*[8] sport, which he describes, was the "roasting of Indian captives wrapped in straw at a slow fire." "Have I really seen these things or were they horrible dreams?" asked the bewildered priest as he penned his account of the atrocities, which he did not permit to be published until forty years after his death. "No, they were not dreams," he assures his future readers. "All these things, alas, my own mortal eyes have beheld . . ."

I recalled another priest, Luis Bertram, and his moving chronicles of the Cuban Conquest. Like Fray de las Casas, he tried, but in vain, to protect the *Cubeños* from the savagery of the *encomenderos,* or holders of allotments of lands and of Indians, in keeping with the colonization system of Hispaniola. Through those evil years there must have been many others, I thought, whose names one would never know, *inedited* names, but breathed in gratitude for some act of kindness by a dying *Cubeño,* as he crumpled under the lash or perished at the stake.

Yet in comparison with the long-continued, enormous grievances, I could count in the historic record very *few* protectors, not only in the Caribbean lands but also in the whole problem of Indian peoples in my own country. Compassionate thinkers of courageous action, true friends of the friendless, defenders of the disinherited heirs of the American continent, these formed a pathetically small group. Was the man I would see tomorrow—Socialist Governor of Yucatán—numbered among them? A passage in the Hart article, which I had just reread in order to phrase a question for my first interview, led me to believe that he might belong to that heroic company. "The Mayas," Mr. Hart had written, "have deified Felipe Carrillo, the man they have elected to govern them in Yucatán. Is he the very savior of the Indian in his state, a man whose feet are set firmly upon a rock and whose ideals will surely materialize in glowing deeds?" Mr. Hart stated that on the night he wrote that particular passage, he fell asleep wondering also "about their god, Felipe Carrillo, and the pedestal on which he stands."

I wondered about him, too, that afternoon, as once again we sailed westward while Havana receded into the flood of white sunlight from which on the day before it had so dramatically emerged . . . And far into the night, Maya idols dominated the pensive hours, as, through the luminous darkness and the vibrant silence, we followed the route of the earliest Conquistadores—Hernández de Córdoba, Juan de Grijalva, the Montejos, Hernán Cortés—over those storied sixty leagues that forever separate—forever *link*—the Isle of the Cubeños and the Maya peninsula of Yucatán.

The playful dolphins of the open sea were replaced by menacing sharks at the *Mexico*'s waterline when anchors were dropped in the roadstead off Progreso, Yucatán's port of entry, about three miles from shore. Waiting on deck for the ship's tender, some of the Mérida-bound passengers amused themselves by watching the wide-jawed man-eaters. I was not amused. I even shuddered with a strange superstitious revulsion at the sight of what Mr. Barry called our "official welcoming committee." Later, in my diary, I noted this sensation of dread, interpreting the presence of the ugly creatures as an evil omen. But the unpleasant feeling dissolved in happy excitement when, borrowing Dr. Merriam's binoculars, I studied the coastal bank fringed by trees and scattered buildings on the faintly discerned "low, level plains" mentioned by the Spanish navigators.

Courteously rushed through the customs and medical inspections, we boarded the electric trolley car and sped for an hour past great *haciendas,* planted row on row to the limit of vision with Yucatán's "green gold." Piled high alongside bulging warehouses, bales of henequen, all ready for export, indicated the prosperity of the state's basic industry.

Our arrival in Mérida was ceremoniously greeted by native bands and local archaeological groups and children bearing flower-entwined *bienvenida*[9] banners. In a fleet of automobiles, Governor Carrillo's English-speaking personal representative, Manuel Cirerol, had us whisked off to the headquarters of the Liga Central, where, as he explained to us en route, the Governor carried on both the affairs of the state of Yucatán and the business of the Partido Socialista del Sureste,[10] of which he was founder and president. Sr. Cirerol also informed us as we passed the impressive stone structure of the Palacio de Gobierno[11] that his chief had turned over his sumptuous official chambers there to the people as a public library and archaeological information center.

At the modest wooden two-storied Liga Building, we climbed up a narrow stairway and entered a long, sparsely furnished assembly room. We were welcomed with warm but simple phrases by a man of exceptional magnetism and rare physical beauty. He was attired in a crisp white linen suit and, in his over six-foot height, towered head and shoulders above the assistants and petitioners who crowded around him. To each of the fourteen members of our party he heartily extended his hand with a cordial expression that embraced some personally directed word or two and the hope that our stay in the "Land of the Maya" would be both joyous and rewarding.

He asked our permission to return momentarily to his desk while we "made ourselves at home," explaining that he wished briefly to dispose of a couple of matters that were under consideration when we arrived at the *Liga.* One was a Maya mother's appeal for a scholarship for her son in the newly opened Mérida technical school. After reading the reports and recommendations from the boy's teachers, he assured the gratefully smiling woman that the desired scholarship would at once be arranged. Next was the petition of a delegation of five Inditos[12] from a distant pueblo. They wished to form a local orchestra and asked for musical instruments. This request, too, was swiftly granted but not without a paternal caution, which Cirerol translated for us. The petitioners would receive their trombones and their drums, but only on the condition that they solemnly promised to make *sweet* music, not ear-splitting noise that disturbed the sleep of their hardworking neighbors.

Standing beside me was Brigadier General William Barclay Parsons, the eminent construction and railroad engineer. A Carnegie Trustee and the senior member of our group, he voiced what was obviously the amazed reaction of his fellow expeditionaries when he whispered: "This is the most personable red dragon I've met with in any of my safaris . . . What do you think, young lady?"

With total conviction, I unhesitatingly answered: "He's *my* idea of a Greek god!"

As guests of the state, the Carnegie party members were housed in leading hotels or in luxurious private homes. I was escorted by Sr. Cirerol to the mansion of Felipe G. Cantón, a rich scholarly *hacendado* who was president of the Yucatán Archaeological Society. Within a half hour after my arrival there, I was relaxing from the tensions of the eventful day in a hammock on the terrace outside my elegant quarters. Suddenly, I heard an uproar in the patio below. Three Maya servant maids rushed upstairs in clamorous excitement to announce: "Señorita, Señorita, el Gobernador del Estado . . . The Governor of the State is here to see you!" With equal if less articulate excitement I rushed into my room to change my lounging robe for a more appropriate costume in which to receive my official caller.

# 5. The Road to Kanasín

Antonio, *ayudante particular,*[1] was at the wheel. I sat beside the Governor of Yucatán in the big red official car. In animated mood we freely admitted finding each other more congenial than we had reason to expect from the "advance publicity." I assured the handsome, dynamic Don Felipe—in Spanish bristling with adjectives but deficient in verbs—that the project of interviewing "a crimson dragon with green eyes" had caused me anxious moments. It was a relief to see that I would be spared this perilous ordeal. For his part, he was enchanted to discover that the *periodista* Alma Reed was no female version of those formidable American journalists one encountered during the Revolution. A number, he confided, turned out to be genuine—*verdaderos*—monsters of the North.

He beamed at my rambling praise of Mérida's Old World charm, at my comment that quite justly the beautiful capital of his sovereign state was known as La Ciudad Blanca.[2] His startling eyes—in some lights gray, in others a clear jade—flashed instant response to my effervescent delight in the sunset pageantry, flooding to the distant horizon vast expanses of sisal with rose-tinged gold. And in the play of luminous shadow over his broad forehead, vigorous chin, and firm, generously modeled mouth, the mellowing splendor highlighted the kindliest expression I had ever seen on a human face.

Clusters of stunted palm and lofty *ceiba* trees . . . the thatched roofs of pink and blue adobe *naas,*[3] half hidden beneath vermilion showers from the flamboyant tree . . . low stone fences splashed with the royal purple of bougainvillea . . . forever they border the white road to Kanasín, then as now, my personal symbol of the questing spirit that moves towards its dimly descried joyous fulfillment.

I kept trying to remember what passing moment in my life had been dramatized by an equally immediate recognition of spiritual worth in any individual. I could think of none, nor of a single occasion when mere proximity had left me with a deeper sense of related destinies.

Quite abruptly the man beside me said: "From the moment you entered the *Liga,* I was desperate to talk with you . . . I am lonely . . . *solo . . . solo!*"

His candid words cut sharply through the laughter and our defensive clichés, those self-conscious pleasantries that at a first intuitively significant meeting screen emotion with the chatter of conventional "normalcy." The earnest intensity of his voice made me long to give some sincere, sympathetic reply. Instead, I discreetly pursued our mildly bantering mood to observe that lonely men in my country seemed less cheerful than those in the land of the enigmatic Maya.

"I am too busy, it is true," he said, "to write *versos melancólicos*[4] . . . I am lonely nevertheless . . . and *alone!* Even my brothers to whom I am devoted and who are devoted to me are only soldiers in my cause."

He had seemed surprisingly youthful when we first met earlier in the afternoon. The natural elation in his open countenance, his spontaneity and frank directness, heightened the illusion that he was years younger than his age, which—I learned from the Hart article—was forty-six. But during our unhurried visit with him at the *Liga* when with unstudied formalities he welcomed us, his guests, I had been observing him closely as he moved among his Indians and the heads of renowned American institutions. Before we left the *Liga,* I had another impression of him.

Within a few moments I became aware that a gentle paternalism was his dominant psychic quality and the motivating urge of his action. I felt his power to shape the environment—quietly and without effort, to fill the atmosphere with a calm yet incisive personal force. I studied him in moments of thoughtfulness, as he gravely put on his glasses to read some communication, his face assuming a judicial expression as he read. I observed his poised bearing and cordial dignity when speaking with the scientists, his patience and kindness when dealing with the humble folk who sought favors. Above all, I was conscious of his own sense of mission, the acceptance of his inherent right to leadership. There were moments when he looked the patriarch and my imagination endowed him tentatively with a flowing beard and clothed his commanding over six-foot stature in classical robes.

And now . . . as we drove along his new highway, I was trying to reconcile the various aspects of him. It dawned upon me that they were not in conflict. Like diverse themes of a symphonic orchestration resolving into ultimate harmony in a stirring coda, his qualities merged and integrated in a unique personality. The discovery held for me the dramatic implications of some phenomenal happening. A suggestion of unreality flared in the very notion that here in this far-off corner of the world on the margin of Caribbean jungles, I was chatting with a charming man in tailored business attire, a veritable synthesis of twentieth-century culture and a highly evolved modern attitude, yet who personified the immemorial Orphic concept of unity that made athlete, priest, and prophet One.

But, through all the tingling excitement occasioned by his unexpected visit to the Cantón residence, newspaper instinct had not failed me. I had, in fact, delayed my impetuous caller long enough in the patio to locate a list of questions that I had prepared aboard ship. I brought it along in the hope that there would be an opportunity to interview him during the ride. The pointed queries were based on the Hart interview and other published articles, some of them quite unfavorable. Showing him the list, I assured him that it was an invaluable paper. "It will enable me to check up," I explained, "on how well you have kept the promises made a year ago!"

Keenly amused, he assured me that however seriously tempted, he would not rob me of such a treasure. But he urged me to take the precaution of hiding it from him until Friday. On that day . . . at the hour arranged for the formal interview, he would, with the greatest pleasure, place himself entirely at my disposition to answer all the "embarrassing interrogations." He would, moreover, provide me with volumes of facts and figures . . . so many . . . that I would finally "plead for mercy . . ." but *today* it would make him so happy if "without a single preoccupation" we would visit the model Socialist village at the far end of the new road. It was no *ordinary* sunset . . . the trip would take only an hour or two . . . and if I wished, while we were driving, he would tell me something of his aims and give me an idea of what had already been accomplished but, with my permission, in his "own way."

His voice was rich in poignant resonances and in tender, lingering inflections. Long after the sound of it had faded, the overtones remained with me like the rhythmic measures of a poem, helping me to remember his words.

"You may, and I hope you will," he began, "find the *living* Maya and their progress as deserving of your study as their ancient monuments. Unfortunately, we cannot carry out all our plans at once. We must work hard and unceasingly for another generation. But we move steadily forward. We have made much progress in a year. You learned at the Liga that our slogan is 'Land and Liberty.' These words are not only emblazoned on our banners. We have carried them in our hearts for many years, through bitter struggle and countless sacrifices. They have guided the very purposes of our lives. They are stern objectives that will give us no rest—no *peace*—until they are won!"

Ordinarily, the warnings of Sr. Molina and his *hacendado* friends concerning the Governor's "wiles," together with my own distrust of panaceas acquired through newspaper training, would have influenced me to withhold judgment on the Socialist program until after personal investigation. But I had already grasped the quality of the man who had conceived and executed it. Intuitively, I knew that he was utterly sincere. This certainty and his absolute humaneness bridged our brief acquaintance, and without doubt or hesitation my allegiance made the crossing to *his* side. In a flash of perception, I knew, too, that it would remain there.

Any possible doubt of his integrity implanted by the innuendos of the reactionaries or his political opponents had, at our very first meeting, been uprooted from my mind. I was now fully conscious of the presence of a great man—one who had been *born* great. And in some inexplicable yet decisive way, I felt a deep personal kinship with him. Even his face looked familiar—a vague, bewildering composite of dearest facial expressions at home.

He did not remotely suggest the "foreigner" in our provincial use of the term, and I found him closer to my native California than to his own Yucatán in that real or fancied relation that people bear to locale. I could not easily identify him with these austere, calcareous plains sweltering beneath a relentless sun. I pictured him in our high Sierras hiking over mountain trails, or camping in cool groves of sequoia. I placed him—and it seemed poetically flawless—against the mighty profile of El Capitán, that Yosemite rock with enough granite in its towering mass to rebuild New York and which, after summers spent in its shadows, had become my favorite symbol for all that was dependable and sure of itself.

I told him that if I were to guess his nationality by looking at him, I would say that he was an American from the West or Southwest and that his ancestry, like my own, was Scotch-Irish. My hypothetical guess intrigued him. "That is most curious," he exclaimed. "Mother Jones—perhaps you know the marvelous *viejecita*[5]—told me the same thing when I talked to her miners once, in Colorado."

I scarcely realized that he was not speaking English. His language had the lucidity one might hope to find in some universal tongue. It occurred to me that anyone, anywhere, would be able to understand him. He addressed me as "Almita," often adding *niña* (child), and asked, *por favor,* to call him "Felipe."

"It is the custom among our Socialist *compañeros* to use the first name," he said. I conceded that it was a nice, *human* custom. I could think of no one, except my father, who had given me so profound a sense of spiritual security. As we talked, it seemed we were merely resuming a fated conversation interrupted, I forgot just *where,* or *how long* ago!

One of Felipe's more kindly critics aboard the *Mexico* had described him to me as "idealistic and visionary" by way of censure. I was willing now to admit that he was *both.*

His words, evidently impelled by an inner necessity, were clothed at times with the fervor of the zealot. His extraordinary eyes, so large and luminous that they almost created the effect of a halo, reflected nevertheless precise nuances of thought and emotion. They were compassionate when he described the bondage of his people, flashing with decision when he pledged their redemption. Yet whatever his passing mood, one could readily tell that he was no ineffectual *soñador,*[6] no wishful thinker "after the dawn." His enthusiasm served to clarify rather than to obscure the sharp outlines of his thought, to throw into bolder relief the solid structure of realism beneath his eloquent arguments.

Through journalism, social service, and activity in public movements, I had been brought into almost daily contact in San Francisco and in the Mexican capital with orators of various types. My ears were quick to detect the dogmatic harangue that throws an audience into nervous tension but fails to persuade the heart. In Felipe's attitude, I found no trace of that hard, dry fanaticism or the hollow note of the builder of purely theoretical castles. His "ideals and visions," I realized, were workable and of the kind that would demand concrete action and material form. They would never be content to languish indefinitely in the astral sphere of the unborn. Thought and action seemed balanced in his intention and performance like the equal wings of the great bird that soars serenely through contemporary Greek poetry.

Felipe sketched the background of his problem — the exploitation of the Maya in Yucatán. I recognized the old familiar pattern of moral and physical enslavement, common scourge of the Antilles and of all the lands washed by the Caribbean. The purple splendor of the tropical sunset had mellowed now into golden gloom. Something in the sad monotony, in the nostalgic spell of mists that gathered and encroached upon the low-growing shrub, made me suddenly "map conscious." I looked out over the vast, level spaces, and the San Francisco hills seemed very far away. As one might remark at a play when the scene has shifted for the next act: "Well, here we are now, in the latitudes of *slavery.*" All my feverish reading in preparation for this and my first Mexican trip suddenly coalesced into a twilight mirage of the tragic past of these lands. From the letters of the explorers, the chronicles of friars and conquerors, from commentaries and statistical reports, emerged and passed before me, on the stage of New World history, debased men and women — helpless beings herded into cattle-holds of ships, delivered into strange, distant environments at so much per head to brutal overlords, into lives of toil and suffering without hope of relief.

As though the Great Disc that records all sound in its endless repercussion through the Cosmos were broadcasting for my special benefit, the wail of Caribbean peoples over the centuries echoed and re-echoed across the peninsula. Out of the Gulf, up from the coastal jungles, it rose in an anguished cry or in passages that registered wild, flaring shrieks of revolt. It died amid the hissing of bullets, the heavy thud of blows, with a sob of despair that filled the vault of All Hearing. Slavery no longer seemed a settled issue of historical geography. Bodies and dreams broken through the greed of "civilized" races became the living *dramatis personae* in the still unfinished tragedy of the Caribbean — a tragedy in which the unassuming authoritative man beside me was playing a hero's role.

"Our Indians" — Felipe always referred to them as Inditos or *pobrecitos*[7] — "though nominally free, were owned body and soul by the *hacendado* heirs of their Spanish conquerors. They lived on these vast henequen plantations under the watchful eye of the *mayordomo*.[8] They labored inhumanely for long hours in our burning sun. Their reward was humiliation, misery, cruelty. They had no possessions. Food and clothing were doled out to them as to incompetents. Even in the most sacred relations of life the Indian was left no power of decision. Speaking only Mayan, he knew nothing of his rights under the law. Like a tree, he was rooted to the land he tilled. Like a tree, he went with the land when it was sold."

I mentioned that some Yucatecans of the *clase aristocrática,* who had sailed with our party from New York, had spoken of schools for the Indians, in a more favorable portrayal of *hacienda* life.

"Yes, there were schools," Felipe replied, "but for the Indian none worthy of the name. In fact, every effort was made to prevent him from gaining knowledge that would further his mental development. The church fostered his ignorance. The priests attached to the *haciendas* filled his mind with superstitious fear. Many of them were propagandists for the capitalist tyranny that kept the Indian enslaved. They taught him that obedience was the chief virtue, that the *mayordomo,* as Christ's representative on the *hacienda,* must be implicitly obeyed. The Indian was caught in an iron trap of skillfully organized labor control. He was helpless and defenseless."

Felipe's words brought forcibly to mind one of the statements he had made in the Hart interview, which, almost intact, had persisted in my memory. "I shall not rest content," he had said, "until I have eradicated ignorance, superstition, and priestcraft and have driven them disgraced from my country. While there is one child in this state who cannot read or write, I shall strive untiringly until he can. I intend to take the school to the child and *not* drag the child to the school."

Months before, when I first read this statement in the Mexican capital, I welcomed it as a fearless reaffirmation of the principles of Benito Juárez and Melchor Ocampo.[9] It had a positive, serious ring to it and provided no loophole for *vaciladas,* freely translated as "monkey business." I took it as an indication that in one Mexican state, at least, the local government proposed to "follow through" with the great Benemérito's[10] essential objectives.

Every American journalist in Mexico at the time knew only too well what powerful and subtle pressures were being exerted on both sides of the border to pull teeth from the Leyes de la Reforma. Felipe's picture of pre-Revolutionary collaboration of priest and *hacendado*—their mutually helpful offices in cementing common bonds of interest—not only illumined his own clear-cut position, as quoted by Mr. Hart, but also served to define boldly and frankly for me, for the first time, an analogous situation in my own country.

In some parts of the Mexican Republic, one could still see at pitiless close range the "iron trap" of skillfully organized "labor control" in clumsy, noisy operation. Or one could witness, as I was now doing, naive and primitive mechanisms being smashed to bits and exposed in public warning. But in New York or Chicago, Detroit or San Francisco, and in other cities of the United States, the mechanism was a far more intricate and complex device, which ran smoothly and with a disarming precision. The names of respectable people, great corporations, and celebrated institutions lent it a false glamour. Yet here, in the perspective of distance, one recognized it as the same ruthless trap—under a gold veneer—describing the same circle of operations with the identical objective of "labor control." Colossal wealth building, equipping, maintaining churches and colleges. Churches and colleges condoning, ignoring the essential injustice of colossal wealth. Both conniving to mold the embryonic shape of collective thinking and feeling to "acceptable" patterns, plotting cold-bloodedly to kill off at birth all "different," construed as "dangerous," tendencies.

I did not share these thoughts and impressions with Felipe then. He had finished with the negative side of the Yucatecan picture, and his mood swung to hope and optimism. There was hearty emphasis in his voice as he said: "You shall see, Almita, that inhumanity to man is doomed here. The Maya has awakened. His old civilization is proof that he can build things of beauty and of permanence. It is our guarantee of his future. It is the promise of his fulfillment, of his ability to make Yucatán an example not only to Mexico but to all the world." He leaned forward and gripped Antonio's shoulder with the easy gesture of old comradeship . . . "What do *you* say, Antonio? . . . Speak up . . . *hombre!*"

Antonio murmured ecstatic affirmatives. With joy unutterable, his typically broad Maya face seemed to expand to greater width. His massive features and the array of golden dentistry between his full lips suggested an ancient sculptured mask smiling in bliss perpetual from a temple façade. Yet his fine, dark eyes were ever watchful, roving as he spoke, from side to side, on the lookout, one suspected, for the *enemigos.*[11] And fires kindled—one knew instantly—by unbounded faith in Felipe, and undying loyalty smoldered in their depths. He had been listening as he drove us at leisurely speed, straining to catch every word. He must have heard the Socialist program expounded many times before, yet it still held novelty and fascination for him. Occasionally, in his own excitement or out of sensitive consideration for my note taking—carried on unsteadily and at times even surreptitiously—he had brought the car to a full stop.

A *camión* passed us on its way to Mérida. As it rattled by, I saw that it was an old Ford converted into a bus, its seats running lengthwise on either side. The passengers—ten or more—were all Indians in spotless white *camisas* and wearing sombreros of *paja.*[12] Felipe and Antonio called out to them in Mayan. In mild voices, the Inditos returned Maya greetings and smiled and waved at us, gently. Baskets filled with fruit and vegetables were bulging from the vehicle at all angles, attached between fender and radiator and tied to the top. "You will see others,"

Felipe said. "They take their products into market at this hour. Before the road was finished last September, these *pobrecitos* used to walk the long distance, in all the heat, carrying their heavy baskets over the rough, stony trails. It used to take them an entire day, and after the toil and the fatigue they received only a few centavos or a peso at most. Now they even enjoy themselves, while carrying heavier loads. They are earning more and the housewives of Mérida buy their vegetables at lower prices. We are building several roads that will connect Mérida with still more distant pueblos and bring similar benefit to other Indians."

Felipe related how the ten-kilometer road happened to have been so quickly completed. He said that when the people of Kanasín learned that the Socialist Government intended to construct highways for the betterment of the state, they organized through their Liga a committee to determine the most effective way that the community as a whole could contribute. After various meetings, the outstanding Liga members presented their resolutions, which Felipe described as "very simple, very practical, and probably unique." He explained that each day squads of fifty men, selected by vote, were required to labor in the project and without compensation. In case any one of those selected did not wish personally to give his services, he could name a substitute, paying him a wage not less than $2.50 pesos a day. After the motion had been unanimously approved, Felipe directed Ingeniero Rafael Gasque to take the first steps for the building of the road. In appreciation of the town's attitude, he ordered a squad of one hundred men to begin work from the Mérida city limits so that the two groups would unite at the middle of the road. This plan made it possible for the first stretches to be in use the previous June.

There were slight changes in the landscape as we neared Kanasín, although its low, even sweep continued, unbroken, to the azure rim of the horizon. Small *milpas*,[13] with their fertile vegetable patches and gay, flowering gardens, varied now the dull stretches of sisal. Broad, cultivated fields appeared. Their abundant crops were tubers and maize and squash of strange varieties—"grown only in Yucatán," Felipe announced with visible local pride. Windmills silhouetted against the sky revealed the presence of underground streams and the secrets of hidden *cenotes*,[14] with deep caverns through which the rivers flow on their way to the sea. Felipe promised that I would be shown "some wonderful *cenotes* . . . the great Sagrado at Chichén Itzá, of course, and another one, not large, but very lovely . . . a perfect jewel of a *cenote*." It had been converted into a swimming pool, with electric lights and stairs leading down. The little *cenote* had been the favorite swimming hole of his boyhood. It was in Motul, where he was born and where his mother lived. He would take me there to meet her . . . not because she was his mother, but because she was "a truly remarkable woman."

Imperceptibly, the dazzling white of adobe walls softened to palest gray. But highlights still straying in the distance were caught by the slow-wheeling arms of the windmills and waved aloft like flamboyants.[15] The scroll of that "larger Maya destiny" unfolded; Antonio and I followed as Felipe traced for us the steps by which a race after centuries of neglect—even deterioration—may again ascend the heights. The spiritual authority for his task, he pointed out, was the life-giving earth. Endlessly renewed and renewing, it had inspired his dream of *renovación:* "A just redistribution of the land is basic to any attempt to build solidly for the future. It is the very foundation of our Socialist program." He explained how the Ligas were returning to the villages, the *ejidos* or group holdings, from which they had been driven in the course of the centuries—"For this our Revolution was fought." He described the process of restoring the *ejidos,* stating that "within a year the Maya Indians, ninety-five percent of Yucatán's population," would, according to his schedule, "repossess the land of which their fathers, one by one, and their ancestors, as a people, have been despoiled."

But the land—Felipe was careful to make the distinction clear—was given to *groups,* not to individuals. It could neither be bought nor sold. "It is held in common by little communities," he emphasized, "for our Maya have always been a communal people." He said that already about half of the villages of the state, some eighty or more, had received their lands, the allotment having been made on the basis of fifty acres for the head of each family. On Thursday, he would invite the members of our party to accompany him to the pueblo of Suma for the distribution of *ejidos.* There, I would see for myself "the happiness of the Indians as they realized they were free men—free at last to build their own homes in their own village, free to reap harvest of their planting."

I inquired about the condition of the *hacendados* after the appropriation of their lands. He answered: "Please do not believe they are plunged into swift and abject poverty. The *hacendado* is left a very large estate—some fifteen hundred acres at least. Naturally, this looks small to him compared to the little empire over which he once ruled. All of the Yucatán was formerly owned by a few multimillionaires. But time moves and evolution is at work. We no longer live in the feudal age. It is as necessary for the *hacendado* as for the Indian to face squarely the changed conditions of our epoch."

The *hacendado,* however, as Felipe informed me and as I already knew from the Hart article and official sources in Mexico, was reimbursed for the lands taken from him, in compliance with the federal agrarian laws. The value of the land was fixed by his own declared tax valuation, to which the state added another 10 percent. Payment was made in land bonds for the amount involved, and the *hacendado* could redeem them at the end of twenty years. This system, Felipe observed, should give him a personal stake in the stability of the government, and he expressed the wish, in fact, that the *hacendado* might eventually see the advantages of closer cooperation with the Socialist order. A certain cooperation already existed, he said. It had saved the sisal industry from the financial disaster that had overwhelmed the Cuban sugar planters when the inflated and artificial prices obtained during the war dropped back to normal. He outlined briefly the functions of the state-controlled Comisión Exportadora,[16] through which sisal became a public utility. The highest prices were thus obtained, and prosperity, he said, was returning to Yucatán despite the generally unfavorable market conditions throughout the world, which "could hardly be held against the Partido Socialista of the Southeast." For the present, he would continue to encourage, in every way, the development of henequen "since it was the state's most important financial resource."

"But I do not wish to create a false impression," Felipe added with an amused smile, "not even if I were to receive full absolution and special benediction from Wall Street and many columns of eulogy in your capitalist newspapers. We are looking forward to the day when henequen will be of *less* importance. Our aim is a *new* agriculture, with a diversity of crops. We already raise, as you can see, our own corn, our own fruits and vegetables. We are experimenting with other export products such as tobacco and cotton, with good results. Eventually, each pueblo must be dependent upon its own food supply grown on its own lands."

I was now in a mood to compliment myself, satisfied that my intuition in supporting Mr. Hart's judgment had been sound from the beginning. I recalled the postscript written to his article as he sailed away from Yucatán—after weeks of careful investigation of general conditions there. When I realized that he had been in close daily association not only with Felipe and the Socialists but with Mérida's "aristocracy" as well, the words of his "afterthought" reached my mind and heart with new impact. "Felipe Carrillo," he wrote, "—and I care nothing for the opinion of his avowed enemies when I say this—is, I believe, animated by sincere and honest ideals: he can look one in the eye fearless and unashamed and true; and a *big* thing, he can be relied upon to keep his word and to extend, if he has promised them, guarantees to any and all." I had not met Mr. Hart during my stay in Mexico City, but I decided then and there to write him a *fan* letter, telling him that already the predictions he had made less than a year ago were well on their way to fulfillment. I felt, too, that I must congratulate him on his astute and courageous journalism—a commodity that was at the time in extremely scarce supply in every part of the Americas.

Mr. Hart's appraisal of the Socialist educational program indicated that Felipe had faithfully kept his promises about bringing the school to the child in Yucatán. The writer had stated that the scope and quality of the Partido's work in this field was an incredible achievement in so short a time. When I cautiously inquired about developments since Mr. Hart's visit, Felipe unhesitatingly outlined the past performance and the immediate plans of his administration.

There were, he explained, the usual schools for children from seven to fifteen years, which were now available to every child in the remotest pueblo and *hacienda.* Night schools for adults had been organized all over the state by the Liga Central and the village Ligas—each a combination of labor union, educational center, and a farmers' cooperative. Monday evening sessions—called *Lunes culturales,* or cultural Mondays—were held in the main and local Ligas. The weekly programs were devoted to lectures on current and historic topics—art, scientific discoveries, and hygiene, illustrated with motion pictures. Music, poetry, dramatic sketches. and dancing were, of course, included. At the conclusion of each session, there was a brief talk on the evils of intemperance because, as Felipe assured me, "alcohol has been harmful to the Maya; encouraged under the *hacienda* system, it has been one of the factors in his racial retrogression." The temperance campaign, he said, was under a sincere and able director, Maestro[17] Eligio Erosa—whom he would have me meet. In Mérida, there had recently been established a modern agricultural college, a new industrial school and one for specializing in the mechanical arts. He spoke proudly of the University of the Southeast, founded within the year by arrangement with the national government. Its curriculum adopted a rationalistic viewpoint and, in addition to the usual professional departments, had made available courses in evolution, astronomy, the modern sciences and Socialist Economy. He hoped its students would go forth as leaders in the work of *defanatización,*[18] for only with the "elimination of the fear complexes of the Maya can we build a happy and clear-minded citizenry in Yucatán."

Encouraged by his willingness to discuss his program, at least in outline, even before our formal interview, I told Felipe that prison welfare was one of my particular interests and that I had been working both personally and with organizations on this question for the past two years. I was anxious, I said, to go very thoroughly into his reforms, which, he should know, if not already advised on the matter, were attracting considerable attention in the United States, especially, as I had learned just before my departure, with important prison workers in New York.

"*That,* Alma, you will have to *see,* not *hear,*" he insisted. "It is difficult to convey atmosphere with words. One must *feel* the atmosphere of the Juárez Penitentiary to understand the innovations there."

But some things he would tell me *now.* He had done away with locked cells; the prisoners had been given access to the yards and open gardens at all times. Stripes and mail censorship had been abolished. Prisoners were permitted daily visitors and, once a week, allowed to receive wife or sweetheart in complete privacy. Primary school education was compulsory; a model trade school had been established in the prison, and the inmates were being taught lucrative trades. They sold the articles they made, keeping the larger share of the proceeds for themselves. The balance was turned over to the prison welfare fund partly administered by the prisoners themselves. "The penitentiary as an institution will entirely disappear," he declared, "when we uproot the social evils that create lawbreaking, crime. Meanwhile, we do our best to help the prisoners face responsibility and become better citizens instead of making more hardened criminals to send back to the world."

It all seemed so civilized . . . so *moral!* I kept naively wondering why his courageous effort to right ancient wrongs had caused such national and international consternation. The entire program obviously adhered to the sound democratic principles of the Mexican Constitution. Much of the so-called radical legislation was already operating in enlightened Scandinavian countries and in Holland. His own original humanitarian contributions would soon be copied in *other* places. After all the newspaper scandal about the "Maya Bolshevists" and the "Mexican Russia," I had frankly expected to find some rather bizarre—however idealistic—approach to political, economic, and social organization, instead of this straight, clean cleavage between conditions no longer tolerable and those which must inevitably supplant them, not only in his own state but everywhere else in the world. I had no knowledge of Karl Marx other than the current journalistic perversions of his philosophy and naturally did not think well of him. The word "Communist" held for me vaguely sinister implications, and I rejected its emphasis on the mechanistic and regimentation of life. But, like many other young university women of the postwar period, I read with stirring acceptance Bernard Shaw, Tolstoy, Ibsen, Carlyle, John Stuart Mill, Havelock Ellis, Olive Schreiner, our own Emerson, Jefferson, and Thomas Paine. Influenced by my father, I was an ardent "Single Taxer," and Henry George's *Progress and Poverty* was regarded as a family bible in our home. One could hardly be a devotee of such teachers without admiring the structure and objectives of Felipe's program and arriving at similar conclusions.

I had been waiting for Felipe to explain the social program by which he was being mainly judged *outside Yucatán.* My desire for firsthand information was impelled less by the *Collier's* commission to gather feature story material than by my own earnest search for new psychological directions. For a long time, I had been preoccupied with conflicts resulting from changed beliefs and the gradual awakening to an "emancipated" outlook. Yet despite growing mental convictions, I was still what might be called "biologically Catholic." Nor had I yet freed myself from certain subconscious vestiges of an early convent training. I wanted to rid myself of them but not at the sacrifice of my emotional and spiritual fiber. For this attitude I had found comforting support in my initial classical studies. Ever since second-year high school, the Greeks and their language had claimed my ardent admiration, due largely to the stimulating instruction of

Dr. John Nourse. Through the myths and tragedies, I also learned to appreciate that the Greek thinkers attributed greater validity to the "divine" imagination than did the Pragmatists of my current reading. After weeks of wrestling with Spencer and Darwin, I accepted Evolution. I continued to believe, however, that there must be an archetypal pattern towards which evolution moves.

Vaguely, too, I clung to the idea that survival, as demonstrated in the indestructibility of the cell, might apply in some form beyond our brief earthly experience. I hesitated to part with my essentially religious if wholly unorthodox views. I was hoping rather to identify them with some humanistic philosophy endorsed by reason and the highest concept of universal ethics. Like thoughtful young people everywhere in all epochs, I was inwardly groping for reconciliation between the ever-present physical facts of decay and death with that mysterious world of feeling and intuition, of longing for immorality and even premonition of development in an unborn future.

Following the example of Omar Kayyam's seeker after Wisdom, I had optimistically frequented the sanctums of local seers and sages—the Omnipotent Ooms of the Mazdaznan Society, the Hindu Swamis, the Rosicrucian Mystics and the Sunday Night Fellowship Centers. But while each group contributed something to my sense of the oneness of the human family—generously holding out hope of eternal peace even to the unbaptized—not one of them supplied the initiating spark or defined the course of effective "direct action" that would right the world's ancient wrongs.

But now, in Felipe's company, all the promptings that had incited and sustained my honest if "roundabout" search for reality, suddenly fused into exhilarating certainty. He was so sure of himself, of his values, of the importance and dignity and the lasting significance of his work and methods. His superb confidence had the effect of a magnetic force that picked up the stray fillings of my doubt and timidity to fashion the fragments into positive organic cohesiveness. Almost instantly, I saw in him my own completed spiritual "self-portrait"—an image of the soul I ultimately hoped to resemble when, as "the end and aim of life," I had achieved, in the words of the sensitive American novelist Caroline Munger, "improvement of the silent character." In any event, that day Felipe represented for me, on the secure plane of attainment, a synthesis of all the noble causes that had enlisted my own adherence and feeble personal efforts—prison reform, sane marriage and divorce laws, suffrage, economic justice, art encouragement, birth control, rationalistic education.

As I suspected, the daring sociological program, especially the aspects that had to do with the stimulation of new collective patterns and responses, demanded, as he confided, "his most serious thought." He gave, he said, these questions intense and constant study and was rewarded "with tremendous satisfaction." The program had been conceived not only with the aim of creating a changed viewpoint and a different mood, but to implant entirely new concepts of virtuous behavior among his people. Its success, he said, would depend largely upon the collaboration of the Yucatecan woman: "It is very necessary that women no longer be regarded, nor regard themselves, as slaves *(esclavas).* They are now *compañeras,* with all the rights and all the obligations of citizenship. With our coeducational system they may now enter the various professional fields, and here in Mérida, women are holding public office." In discussing the Ligas Feministas, in which his sister Elvia was very active, he said that such organizations would train women of special aptitude to fill elective posts in city and state government. With the cooperation of the Feminist Ligas, clinics for both prenatal and postnatal care had already been established.

His first interest in this line of work, he revealed, stemmed from his admiration for what was then being done in Sweden. He was in close touch with the Swedish scientists, and the program in Yucatán was under their direction. Recently, two birth control clinics had been organized in the state—"the first in the Americas conducted with government sponsorship." His clinics had been approved, he said, by the American Birth Control League, two of whose members, Mrs. Anne Kennedy and Mrs. George H. Rublee, had been invited to Yucatán and had been asked to make final suggestions. He expressed regret that they "sailed back to New York only yesterday." It was a pity that I had not met them, for both were "magnificent women and very *simpáticas.*" Felipe disclosed that already Margaret Sanger's *Family Limitation* had been translated and was being distributed to married couples. "A child is too precious a thing," he observed, "to trust its coming into the world to blind and ignorant chance. Parents are the ones who must decide when they should have children and how many they should have."

As gently as I could, I reminded him that his divorce law was a target for denunciation in the North American press and pulpit. Felipe answered that he thought the commotion was wholly unjustified. "If the principle of divorce is accepted—and it seems to be accepted throughout most of the world today—what valid objection can there be to keeping divorce simple and inexpensive?" he asked. I replied that personally, I saw no objection, once the problem of children was dealt with in a *human* way. I assured him, too, that while a strong opposition to easy divorce existed in the United States, there was, at the same time, a growing acceptance of it. Some of our foremost thinkers were going even further than his official attitude and were concurring with Bernard Shaw, who had said: "We shall have civilization *only* when divorce is as easy and as cheap as marriage!" The news pleased him and he remarked: "Ah, Shaw is a great Englishman!" And when I corrected him, saying, "Shaw is a great *Irishman,*" he exclaimed enthusiastically, "Better still! The Irishmen I met in your country—in New Orleans—were my favorite Americans!"

Felipe spoke feelingly and at length on marriage and divorce: "It is indeed hard to understand how anyone of even average intelligence and ordinary self-respect can continue to live with another who does not wish it. Such an arrangement is contrary to both common sense and common decency. But when two people have mutually decided that they no longer wish to remain married, that state's interference in their efforts to lead separate lives is both cruel and insolent. Mistakes are recognized and remedied in every human relation. Why exempt marriage? To fail to recognize the error of mismating is as heartless as and surely more devastating in its effect upon society than ignoring the physical agony of a person who has been injured in some automobile accident on the grounds that he had been struck through his own carelessness." He explained that the new Yucatán marriage law "emphasized *love* in the union of two people" and discounted the idea of possession with which marriage "most unfortunately" had become involved. "Certainly, children have rights," he said, "and their *first* right is to a home with an atmosphere of affection and love. If a child for any reason finds no pattern of love in its own home but only cold indifference or hatred, and the parents are unable to provide a substitute home, then it is the duty of the state to surround that child with the nearest equivalent to the tender care furnished by a happy and well-regulated family life."

Felipe confessed that at the moment this problem, the children of estranged parents, was his "gravest concern." He revealed that he was in the process of establishing a haven for orphans and the children of disrupted marriages—one entirely free of regimentation and the usual institutional errors. He was working on the details with experienced modern educators, but he would appreciate having *my* ideas on the subject . . . Would I talk with him soon about the Casa del Niño—the House of Childhood? I assured him that I would give most serious thought to his appealing plan and discuss it with him whenever he desired.

Felipe's project was close to my sympathies, for time and time again, in the course of my social service journalism I had encountered the pathetic figure of the child victim of the broken home. My native city of San Francisco held at that period a United States record for its proportionately high divorce rate. Not long before, my own brief marriage to a kindly inventive genius, more than twice my age, had been dissolved in an unpublicized divorce and by mutual consent. The experience left me saddened but not disillusioned nor embittered. I had suffered no psychic trauma nor severe emotional wrench, and there were no children involved. Believing that the perfect union of man and woman represented life's greatest success, I welcomed freedom, confident that love such as I had known only vicariously, through the example of lifelong, unswerving devotion set by my own parents and through the great loves of romantic literature, would one day come to me. I had perfect faith that I was yet destined to know the normal happiness that my youthful, idealistic experience of marriage had missed.

# 6. Ultima Thule

"Kanasín!" The ever-exuberant Antonio announced our arrival as the white road ended and we swung into the peaceful little plaza of the model Socialist village. It was arranged like a modern park and planted with orange and lemon and *tamarindo* trees. At the center, from a double concrete platform, arose to the height of twenty feet or more a glistening white monument to the Maya race. Enclosing the plaza were low stuccoed buildings and a modest church with a rounded façade and open bell niches. The buildings were painted a vivid shade of coral red, and in sharp contrast, pale ivory outlined the outer edge of the doors and windows. Masses of verdant foliage, waxen-leafed magnolia and luxuriant *guanábana* formed the background. The combined effect of coral, ivory and bright green was very gay and striking.

We left the car and briskly encircled the plaza, "for exercise," while the loud honking of Antonio's Claxton brought villagers from every direction. Felipe greeted them and inquired about their affairs. They trailed behind us in little groups, while we examined the monument from different angles. All had the same worshipful look I had seen in the eyes of Indians at the Liga Central. Apparently, they regarded him as some kind of Maya deity. The monument, Felipe said, was the work of two young Yucatecan sculptors, Leopoldo and Alfonso Tomassi. I found it convincing in design and symbolism, but regardless of its intrinsic merit as an art creation, I could see that it was ideologically functional. For I watched the people of Kanasín—Indian and Mestizo alike—as they gazed proudly and reverently upon their most cherished public possession. The square central shaft—a series of horizontal planes, suggesting the levels of a pyramid—was capped by a decorative frieze adapted from Maya motifs. The shaft was surmounted by the figure of an enslaved Maya Indian in the attitude of one about to rise. His facial expression was sad, but not without a faint gleam of hope. With rare sensitivity, the young sculptors had conveyed the mood of the "Sad Race," the "Raza Triste," awakening from the sleep of centuries and going forth fearlessly toward the dawn to claim its long-denied heritage of liberty and human rights.

The four sides of the monument were adorned at the base with the design of a triangular shield, set in red marble to represent the Socialist emblem. Each shield bore the name of a Maya leader who, at some epoch, heroically, but in vain, had striven for the liberation of his people. One of the shields carried the name of Cecilio Chi of Tepich, who fell in the Maya uprising against the whites in 1847; another, that of Jacinto Pat, who was sacrificed in the same hopeless struggle.

"The stones come from the quarries of Sotuta," Felipe said, as we examined details of the work. "My father was born in Sotuta. He was a man of strong and unusual character. His family had lived there for many generations. Sotuta is the city of Nachi Cocom, the last Maya king to stand against Spanish invaders." One of the archaeologists had told me that Felipe claimed direct lineal descent from Nachi Cocom, but neither one of us mentioned that fact then. I would ask him about it some other time.

Antonio had gone off in quest of *limonada.* Felipe warned me that this was a "temperance" village and that no other cold drinks were to be had, not even by "representatives of the press." The workers of Kanasín, he explained, had decided that there "shall be no *cantinas* and no churches in their pueblo. The church you see across the plaza has been converted into a public library and cultural center."

We sat on a tamarind-shaded bench, awaiting the *limonada* and admiring the stone symbol of the "Raza Triste."

"They call the Maya the 'sad race,' but do you think our Indians look any more depressed than Indians in other places?" Felipe asked. I answered that all Indians look a bit sad to me, but from what I had already observed of the Maya, he seemed healthier and certainly *cleaner* than Indians in other parts of Mexico or in my native California. "Yes," he agreed, "the Maya have kept many of their beautiful habits and customs through all their sufferings. Personal cleanliness is almost a religious obsession with every Maya."

I begged him now to tell me something of the initial stages of his program of racial resuscitation, how he had organized the movement and set it into motion, if he were not too tired and if there were still *time.*

Opalescent streaks against a gray-blue sky were the sole remnants of the glory of the sunset. I knew that we should now be on our way back to Mérida for the crowded and important evening with its official *banquete,* the reception for the archaeologists and last-minute preparations for the departure by midnight train for Uxmal. Even Antonio was beginning to worry and had already reminded us, "Ya es tarde,"[1] when he returned in triumph with a whole half gallon of *limonada.* But suddenly the word *time* took on a detached, almost irrelevant meaning in this place and at this hour. My reflections had veered away from the *clockwise* conventional demands and were heading direct and unhampered to the *timeless* metaphysical. I was thinking, for no accountable reason, of the old Theosophist at home and his lesson on the cosmo-conception of eternal recurrence, the theory that all lines, not merely in space but in time, finally close their circles. He had suggested that we try to visualize history *not* as a succession of events following a path of straight linear projection but rather as the course of a spiral, which in its descending return brings that far-off tomorrow of man closer to his remote antiquity than to the pulsating moment. Now, if ever, it seemed to me, the idea invited application . . . I *tried* it . . . Questions shot up around me like the sharp, spaded leaves of the sisal, bearing thorns! What Karmic law was Felipe obeying in his mighty effort to revive a dead civilization? From what obscure cycles had the impulse reached him to infuse the still-beautiful body with new life — a life of unimagined perfection? By what forces was he impelled in his consuming desire to restore "an organic power to become" to a culture which Spengler declared had not died "naturally" in some process of inevitable Western decline, but had met a "violent death . . . murdered in the full glory of its unfolding, destroyed like a sunflower, whose head is struck off by some ruthless hand in passing?"[2] My speculative musings dissolved of their own futility. But the hypothetical questions had evoked a strangely disturbing spell that then, or even later, I was unable to shake off. For always, Felipe seemed to be fatefully involved with their *unanswerable* answers!

So, in the orange-perfumed twilight, I listened to his epic dream. Remembrance and hope, ancient roots and new florescence, mingled their potent magic in the warm tranquil air. All the petty concerns that lay beneath the myopic frame of the self-seeking present — the vulgar clamor for profit and privilege — were swallowed in the immense silence. Out of the stillness came the Great Past and the Great Future like honored guests, to sit with us for a little while in the Plaza of Kanasín and to give solemn ear or, at times, lend their mute eloquence to the discussion . . . Felipe believed that if the Maya were ever to regain their vital functioning, it would be necessary first to erase "the many writings" four centuries had imposed upon the faded document of their racial heritage. He must work, he said, as on a palimpsest, lifting layer upon layer of unrelated impressions from the age-worn parchment until at last he reached the still-legible traces of the original hieroglyphs. . . . As with a palimpsest, he must search for the initial layer, the innermost core of *essential* Maya character, to which alone the creative impulse of the race would again respond. To the basic task of finding it, he disclosed, he was bringing scientific aid. He named archeological research and excavation of the ancient cities; the study of the Mayan language and the ancient inscriptions; development of surviving arts and crafts; revival of folk music and the dance, of the traditional festivals and other cultural expressions that had lived on, despite every effort to obliterate them.

It was primarily to give the Maya access to his ancestral cities, he admitted, that he was building roads to Chichén Itzá and Uxmal. Eventually, he would connect all the principal archaeological zones by a system of highways. "You may be sure," he added, "that we want the tourist in Yucatán. We are only too eager to have the world know about the splendid past of the Maya. But what is more important for us is that the Maya himself become aware of that splendid past—that he become *proudly* aware of it. His pride in race, his pride in its achievements, must be turned to account . . . With that, we shall light the spark of a new volition, create a desire to live, a passion to possess as a spiritual treasure all that was his in the past and that can be his in the future." He told me about the new archaeological museum under the direction of his good friend, the poet Luis Rosado Vega, where the most important discoveries of sculpture and other antiquities would be kept in Yucatán "so that the Maya would always have these unrivalled works of his ancestors where he might see them."

"It is necessary also," he went on, "that the Maya become a happy being and regain the capacity to feel both pride and joy after so long a period of humiliation and sorrow." He mentioned some methods being used to teach the Maya how to enjoy life. Sports and games of all kinds were encouraged. Every little Liga in the state had its own orchestra and its own baseball team. Baseball and boxing had been made a part of school training. Frequent contests were held in tennis and swimming and wrestling. There were colorful *fiestas* with prizes for dancing and singing—"not only their own sad songs but with lively, modern music." The Maya must learn to play; he has all but forgotten how . . . The expiring flame must be fanned into fresh vigor, "before it is too late."

Felipe revealed, unconsciously, that once he had tried to find the clue he was seeking by another, more personal method. In speaking of his travels "over the length and breadth of the Mayab[3] on foot and on horseback, through the Yucatán, into the wilds of Campeche, Tabasco, Quintana Roo, and the forest jungles of Chiapas, "hasta Guatemala," he casually mentioned that he had often stood before the majestic monuments in the silent and deserted cities, "wondering and wondering" how he might penetrate the age-old mystery and draw closer to the "soul of his blood brother, the Maya."

Through gleaming clouds of brilliant *luciérnagas*—my heart has no other word for fireflies, unless it be the Mayan name *cocay*—we virtually flew in the deepening dusk over the road to Mérida. My "invaluable" paper, that painfully worked-out list of questions, now seemed as foolish as it was useless. I would have quietly dropped it out of the speeding car to let it drift far out over the sisal, if I were sure that it would not first be blown back into my face like a boomerang, or pinned by the evening breeze to the windshield to cause me further embarrassment. In his "own way," Felipe had told me all that I needed to know about himself and his Socialist program. And in the deepest recesses of my consciousness, his total meaning as a man and as a symbol, and as an authoritative voice for humanity, had, in that brief space of time, been fully comprehended.

We would have that *formal* interview as arranged. But certainly I had no intention now of squandering any part of its priceless hour or two on *henequén.* I would not fail the financial editor who had asked me as a favor to gather information for him. I would inquire conscientiously about the latest "lowdown" on recent sisal developments, official statements on the intricacies of Reguladora[4] moratoriums, local and federal tax deductions, collateral guarantees, and the like. But for this and similar data, I would go to the English-speaking experts. There were several of them in Mérida . . .

My now eagerly anticipated Friday morning interview would be devoted, I promised myself, to conversation of a very different content. I must know more about Motul, about his boyhood and young manhood there, his "truly remarkable mother" and the father with the "strong and unusual character." I would ask him about his devoted brothers who were "soldiers in his cause" and his sister Elvia, the feminist leader . . . I would question him about those years of "bitter struggle and countless sacrifices," when he carried in his heart the words "Land and Liberty"—words that had guided his purpose and "gave him no peace until they became realities." I would entreat him to reveal what song the ancient temples sang to him—as once the statue of Memnon might have sung to the wayfarer in the Theban dawn—when, at early morning or at sunset, he had stood before them "wondering" in the silent and deserted cities of the Mayab . . . Was it a mystic chant . . . the severed head of the Great Lord Itzamná—father of the Holy Itzáes—singing of a day of Maya legend and of living Maya faith when "in a *single* day, if that day should come, will be shattered the silence of seven hundred years?"

"You are married, Almita?" he asked simply.

"No," I answered. "No longer . . . A few months ago I divorced my husband."

"That is too bad! . . . Is there a child?"

"No."

"What a great pity! . . . But you are young. You will marry again!"

"Someday . . . perhaps!"

I felt that his own status might be delicate ground. I did not expect him to refer to it. At least a dozen gossips aboard the *Mexico* and since my arrival had volunteered the news that he was living apart from his wife. It was obviously a very popular topic of conversation in Mérida. But he gave me the information himself. Without comment, he told me that he was married but had been separated for three years from Señora Carrillo, who was living in Cuba. There were four children. His eldest daughter, Dora, was married and living in Mérida. He had a "fine young son," who had a Mayan name, Zichilich . . . and a daughter who was just seventeen, "tall and lovely, a blonde, with eyes like my own, of jade" . . . She, too, had a Mayan name . . . It was Gelitzli . . . They were both away at school, in *my* country . . . He missed them . . . There was another little girl . . . the youngest child . . . She was with her mother . . .

Abruptly, with the exultant tone of one who has made a happy discovery, he said: "*Your* Mayan name is very beautiful! It is Pixan, for 'Alma' in Mayan means 'soul' . . . 'life.' I shall call you Pixan, sometimes. But I like the name 'Alma,' just as it is. It suits you!" He told me his own Mayan name . . . H'pil. He used it a great deal, he said, for it was what the Inditos in the distant villages always called him. He wrote it out for me with his fountain pen on a page of my notebook, in red ink. With a wistful smile he explained why he had written it: "When you are back in your huge New York and I, unhappy Maya, write to you in my infinite aloneness, you will know that the letter is from me, Felipe, even though I should happen to sign it this way."

I would recognize his letters, I replied, even though they were to reach me unsigned. I had an infallible way of telling that they were *his.*

"How could you tell?"

"Simple! By no remote chance would any of my other men friends even *think* of using red ink when they wrote to me . . . green or violet, brown, blue and even yellow, perhaps, but *never* red!"

"I shall not be able to deceive you then. I see it is useless to try!" He was laughing gaily. "Our Socialist *tinterías*[5] in Yucatán sell ink of only *one* color . . . a *very* bright red!"

The *luciérnagas* fell around us — enveloping the car, whirling in showers of infinitesimal stars. I had never before seen anything like it, and in my rapture I kept exclaiming, "¡Maravilloso!"

"Yes," he agreed. "*Luciérnagas* are always beautiful, and extraordinary *animalitos,* too. They are not phosphorescent, you know. That glow emanates from their own luminous cells. Their light comes from their *own* heat, their *own* intensity. They are a lesson to our puppet *políticos* . . . I know a Maya legend about them. It was told to me by Rosado Vega, the same dear friend who is director of our museum. For years, he has been collecting legends among the Indians in the pueblos. Would you like to hear the story of *cocay,* for this is the name of the *luciérnaga* in Mayan?"

When I assured him that I would love to hear it, he began the story in a droll tempo and with a trace of whimsical humor in his voice as though he were imitating someone telling a fairy tale to a young child: "Well then, here is the legend of the *cocay* . . . Once there was a very humane god who used to cure all the *pobres* — the sick, blind, and lame — who came from far and near. He made his remarkable cures with a little amulet of green stone. I am sure, *niña,* it was like *this* one." He showed me a tiny ancient Maya idol of nephrite attached to his watch chain. He prized it, he said, above all his earthly possessions, since it had been with him through all the *luchas*[6] of the Revolution and had become his lucky piece. He continued:

> Well, one day the god lost his miraculous green stone and he was desperate. He looked high and low, but it was nowhere to be found. Then he called on the animals to help him find it. The jaguar, the hare, the black *zopilote,*[7] and the deer, all answered his call. The deer found the amulet, but being a crafty animal—although he is such a prominent native of the Yucatán, I hate to tell you this—swallowed it, thinking it would give him the god's power of healing. But a hunter killed the deer and found the stone when he opened its entrails. The other animals kept searching in the woods, the marshes, and among the rocky places. At last, the *cocay,* then a very insignificant-looking insect, decided to join in the search. But *how?* He thought and thought, and so much thinking sharpened his wits. But he continued to concentrate until his mind finally became so clear that he felt a spark coming from his own being . . .
>
> "Now," said the *cocay,* "I shall find the amulet . . . for there is no darkness that I, myself, shall not be able to illumine."
>
> And he *did* find the amulet and brought it back to the god, who was very happy indeed and offered to reward the tiny creature. But the *cocay* did not wish any reward. It was enough for him to know that the god continued to cure the *pobres.* Besides, he was too humble an insect, he thought, for so great an honor from a god.
>
> "You are a very small animal, it is true," the god answered, "and the light that you shed is but a faint one by reason of your size. But *size* does not matter. The important thing is that beings produce of themselves the light that guides them through life."
>
> But the god rewarded the *cocay* by decreeing that the *animalito* should forever after emanate the glow that was born of himself, and the light that had served others so well would now serve his own needs. And as the grateful and happy *cocay* flew away in the dusk, throwing his light wherever he passed, the voice of the god followed him, saying: "It is better to be small and shine with your *own* light!"

When I told him that I loved every word of his story, he said he was deeply pleased, for it happened to be one of his favorites. I would hear many other Maya legends. We would meet Don Luis tonight at the reception and would arrange with him for an entire evening devoted to "puras leyendas y poesías mayas."[8] The legends, he explained, taught him much about the Maya, because they indicated a deep philosophy of life, a rare purity of soul united with a subtle and profound intelligence. They all betrayed, too, high moral and ethical concepts and were based on a true sense of justice . . . I noticed that an unruly forelock of his thick brown hair fell in a rebellious curl over his broad forehead. It was this, I suddenly realized, that had given him that cheerful look even when he had been relating very sad truths . . . I noticed, too, that his hands were strong and executive—though not large—and that there was a sensitive tension in his fingers, slightly squared at the tips. His two hands were clasped firmly over one of mine while he bid me "hasta pronto" inside the stately gate of the Cantón mansion . . . telling me that he would send Antonio and an escort—Manuel, perhaps—to accompany me to the Opera House, where he would join me in the foyer, at nine.

I hurried through the patio and up to my room. I wanted to remain there, undisturbed, to dream waking dreams. I longed to live over in visual memory each moment of those three amazing hours . . . to retrace every foot of the white road to Kanasín that led through the realm of the wondrous to the morning of the world! But I must run! It was after eight o'clock. Only half an hour remained in which to dress for the evening. There was no time now for transcribing my notes, no time to amplify them with impressions that were crowding upon me, rushing down the newly opened vistas of thought and emotion. I felt that I must preserve his every word—not only *what* he said but *how* he had said it! I had grave misgivings now about the story for *Collier's*. I was no longer an impartial judge of Felipe or his program, and I knew it. I wanted only to dash off pages on the Corona—but *poems*, not appraisals. I resented that everything must wait until tonight, on the train, or tomorrow, at Uxmal. Yet I *did* write nine words in my private diary. To the entry made that morning at sea, off Progreso, under the date of February 14, 1923—St. Valentine's Day—I added the line: "He is a miracle of Goodness and of Beauty!"

I used the Spanish word *milagro*. "Miracle" seemed too weak a word.

# 7. Uxmal: "The Thrice Rebuilt"

At the stroke of nine, the porter of the Felipe G. Cantón residence ceremoniously announced that Don Manuel Cirerol Sansores was waiting below at my disposition on the order of the Señor Gobernador. Still tingling under the blissfully disturbing impact of the twilight ride to Kanasín, I hurried down to the patio to meet the English-speaking secretary who had been assigned to escort me to the Mérida Opera House.

Felipe, in a crisp white *guayabera* dinner jacket and even more impressively handsome beneath the brilliant chandeliers than he had seemed in the earlier fading sunset, met us in the foyer. He greeted me with a single word, "Almita!" I instantly sensed, as he took my hand, an agitation that broke through his disciplined poise. His eyes conveyed his own awareness of an elemental bond already existing between us, though welded in the silence, as he led me to the table reserved for the honored guests—Carnegie members, state officials, and heads of the local archaeological society—and seated me at his right. On his left was Miss Frances Morley, the attractive blonde sister and able assistant of Dr. Sylvanus G. Morley, expedition director.

My reactions to that emotion-charged Yucatecan evening or, at least, the impersonal observations I could, as a journalist, share with my readers, were reported in the *New York Times Sunday Magazine* of March 18, 1923. The longer than full-page feature story was illustrated with a three-column photograph in which I appeared standing against a darkened entrance of the ruined "Nunnery" in the ancient Maya city of Uxmal. Under my byline I not only recorded immediate impressions of the international meeting—one of the most far-reaching in its effects throughout the annals of American archaeology—but analyzed background considerations that had induced the United States scientists to visit Yucatán. As a synthesis of our knowledge of the Maya civilization and the different theories concerning its origin and development advanced by the leading contemporary authorities in their own words, the article held, at the period, a certain historic as well as a timely news interest.

It read as follows:

*Reed at Uxmal, in a photograph originally published by the* New York Times, *March 18, 1923. On the back, she has written the following note: "Detail of the 'Temple of the Nuns,' Uxmal—showing artistic use of serpent motif, the basis of the Mayan decorative scheme."*

Less than a month ago a group of eminent American archaeologists sat at a banquet table in the foyer of the Opera House at Mérida—the colorful and altogether charming capital of the Mexican State of Yucatán.

With the last course of the sumptuous tropical feast—a veritable deluge of sweet-flavored oranges, pineapples, bananas, and luscious *zapote*—the host arose to greet formally his distinguished guests and to offer his good wishes toward the object of their long journey. He was Felipe Carrillo Puerto, Yucatán's Socialist Governor, who claimed direct descent from

Nachi Cocom, the last of the Maya kings and the valorous defender of his fatherland against the *conquistador* Montejo.

As poetically fitted the occasion—a "finale," it seemed, to the plaintive yet stirring strains of the "Jarana" played by the native orchestra—the Governor spoke in the language of his ancient race. It was the Mayan tongue, used today by more than one-half a million people, and, with the exception of the Guaraní in Paraguay, the only Indian language in the New World to dominate that of the conqueror. Most of the local guests understood it perfectly, and a few of the archaeologists.

With simple sincerity the Governor hailed this first expedition of American scientists and tourists as an epoch-making event in the history of his state. He expressed high appreciation of those great organizations represented at the official function—the Carnegie Institution, the Museum of the American Indian (Heye Foundation) and the Peabody Museum of Harvard University.

Then with a feeling that pierced the barrier of a strange idiom, he described a ruined Maya temple such as crowns the majestic pyramids of Uxmal and Chichén Itzá. "High up there in their sculptured halls," he said, "they are waiting—the ghosts of the Maya are waiting for you. They have been silent through the centuries. You will be the first to hear their story. Hear it and tell it to the world."

The descendant of Nachi Cocom, the big, handsome Mestizo whom the reactionary planters of sisal hemp execrate as "the red dragon with the jade eyes," and whom 300,000 workers of Southeastern Mexico have deified as their deliverer, protector, and infallible guide—touched with precision the hope of the scientific men from the United States. The Maya story is the end and aim of their endeavor. It is the ultimate goal of their present survey of those marvelous monuments that mark a wide, unbroken path from Mayapán, near the northernmost cusp of the Yucatán Peninsula, into the adjoining state of Campeche, some 100 miles southwest.

American archaeology in Yucatán insists that science alone will be able to communicate with the Maya ghosts. Its voice will be the sole medium for bearing across the chasm of the ages those significant questions of "How?" and "When?" and "Why?" and for carrying back to the world an answer that will illumine, perhaps, those shadowy beginnings of the human family.

But if science would learn the story of the Maya, warns Dr. John C. Merriam, President of the Carnegie Institution and a leader of the expedition, it must approach the sculptured halls with a wand instead of a pickaxe.

"The Maya will remain inarticulate forever," he explains, "unless the utmost care be exercised. Ignorant excavations and neglect to properly classify the excavated materials will only destroy the record for all time. Better by far to leave the cities beneath the soil for another hundred years and to sow maize over them than to expose them to the vandalism of careless handling. If the Maya is to tell his own story through his wonderful structures, his massive mounds, and his countless thousands of carved stones, it is imperative that the archaeologist know exactly where he is at each stage, and that he identify and classify the object wherever found. The story is there—the engineering, the philosophy, the literature of the Maya. But to use the pick and shovel without intelligence will shatter it beyond reconstruction. The Carnegie Institution realizes the full responsibility of giving the world the Maya story and of giving immortality to the Maya. Individuals die, but the work they accomplish is the most important fact of their lives. If what they have left behind them is destroyed, the loss is greater than the mere wiping out of a race."

This reverential attitude, with its slow, painstaking methods, will guide the American scientific bodies now surveying Yucatán's vast archaeological territory should they decide to undertake excavations.

The Carnegie Institution has a very definite plan. For nine years Carnegie experts, led by Dr. Sylvanus Griswold Morley, have been delving into the Maya field. They have gone through Guatemala, British Honduras, and the Yucatán Peninsula, studying the architecture, the sculpture, and the hieroglyphs, and in many instances dating monuments and the migrations of peoples. Their explorations have revealed a sequence of cultures, which coincide more or less accurately with these dates. In some sections they have found a single stage of culture. In others, two. In still others, several, in which one or more of the stages was missing.

Their next logical move is to ascertain where all of these stages appear in their sequence, and to work intensively here over a long period of years. So the Carnegie men, after looking about, are now focusing on Yucatán, to determine exactly where this course may be carried out most satisfactorily. They will be influenced, naturally, in their selection by the character of the place and by the working conditions there.

"Obviously," observes Dr. Merriam, "it will be necessary to have the fullest cooperation of the federal and state governments after we have presented to them the plan of the work we wish to do."

But although this plan involves the relation of the people of the United States to the people of Mexico, Dr. Merriam and General William Barclay Parsons, Carnegie Trustee, who is also a member of the party, fear no difficulties. Both express their confidence in the active support of Governor Carrillo and Dr. Manuel F. Gamio, Director of Anthropology for the

Mexican Government. And both agree that the ruined cities of Uxmal and Chichén Itzá should offer unrivalled opportunity for tracing back, step by step, or rather stone by stone, to the dawn of Maya civilization.

Science concedes that, judged as a whole, this civilization was the most remarkable expression of the Native American mind. Herbert J. Spinden, noted archaeologist, representing Harvard University on the Yucatán survey, asserts that the Maya "produced one of the four really great and coherent expressions of beauty so far given to the world, and that their influence in America was historically as important as was that of the Greeks in Europe." He maintains, further, that in perspective applied to the human figure the Maya excelled the Egyptians and the Assyrians.

Yet today absolutely nothing is known of the origin of the Maya people. Their record is lost in remotest antiquity. Even the lamp of tradition has withheld its vague, fitful glare from their beginnings. After centuries of study and exploration, conjecture and theorizing, not an authentic word has been written into the first chapter of Maya history. The earliest established date in the Maya hieroglyphic writing is 100 B.C., but even at this period, points out its discoverer, Dr. Morley, "the inscriptions literally burst fully formed, the flower of long-continued astronomical observations in a graphic system of exceeding intricacy."

It is true that the Maya date for the creation of the world is now accepted by the archaeologists as 3300 B.C. The discovery was made about thirty years ago by G. T. Goodman, a Pacific Coast editor, who also enjoys the distinction of having "discovered" Mark Twain. Goodman had never seen a Maya ruin, but correctly based his calculations upon the drawings of glyphs and inscriptions appearing in A. P. Maudslay's *Biologia Centrali-Americana.*[1] This date, however, in no way indicates the antiquity of the Maya race. It was arbitrarily fixed by the priests when they decided to adopt a starting point and to put a definite limit upon time. Consequently, Maya history was molded to fit within that limit, although the only happenings that can be deciphered with certainty are the conjunctions of the planets and other astronomical phenomena.

A fortunate inconsistency in an *auto da fé* is responsible for even this meager information of the ancient Maya times and for the chronology of the principal events from the colonization of the Yucatán Peninsula to the days of the Spanish Conquest. Bishop de Landa, one of the friars who accompanied Montejo, confesses in his *Relación de las cosas de Yucatán (Account of the Things of Yucatán)* to finding a great number of books written by the Maya priests on paper made from the roots and bark of certain trees and rendered indestructible by a lustrous white varnish. "I burned them all," he boasted, "because there was nothing in them that had not some superstition and falsehood of the devil."

But before destroying them, he gained a certain knowledge of the Maya writing, and although he left no translation, he made a copy of the alphabetical signs and of the hieroglyphs symbolizing the days and the months. The zealous monk also proudly boasted that he had burned all the books, "at which the natives were marvelously sorry and distressed," yet four managed to escape the flames, to be preserved to this day in European libraries, and his alphabet now serves as a key to their translation.

Through these native chronicles, known as the "books of *Chilam Balam*," and through the inscriptions on the monuments, archaeology has been able to follow the building and description of some of the Maya cities during the first fifteen centuries of the Christian era. It has been ascertained that Maya history may be divided into two general epochs, the Old and New Empire, each containing several distinct periods. The Old Empire, beginning only the Maya ghosts know when, lasted until A.D. 600. It embraced what are now the Mexican states of Chiapas and Tabasco, Petén and Izábal in Guatemala, and the adjoining western part of Honduras. The New Empire grew out of the Old in the fifth century, and flourished on the Yucatán Peninsula—although gradually declining—until the dominion of Spain in 1541. But while we know that the Maya migrated to Yucatán between the fifth and seventh centuries, it is likely that the sequence of cultures at Uxmal and Chichén Itzá—responding to the wand of science—will reveal the migration only as a return to sites abandoned generations before.

For many of the noble structures of these two cities and of others scattered throughout the peninsula defy the dating process. Speculation on their antiquity has completely disregarded the biblical guide as to the age of man. The scientists of the present expedition incline toward the most generally accepted theory that the Maya, coming originally from Northeastern Asia, settled in Yucatán during the Neolithic period. In discussing the source of this baffling fragment of the human race, Prof. Marshall H. Saville, internationally recognized Maya authority, who accompanied the expedition for the Museum of the American Indian, Heye Foundation, claims that his recent investigations only confirm his belief that the Maya civilization was not inherited, but that it independently developed the features of North African and Asiatic civilizations from a state of Neolithic culture. His verification some weeks ago of phallic worship among the Maya from temples explored at Uxmal and at Chichén Itzá is, according to Professor Saville, a significant point in establishing the theory that the same ideas will take root and grow in the same soil of the human mind without outside influence.

Dr. Augustus Le Plongeon, the eccentric French savant, who devoted thirty years of his life to the study of the Maya ruins, advanced the theory back in the 1870's that the Yucatán Peninsula is itself the cradle of human civilization.[2] He asserted that his knowledge of hieroglyphs (a knowledge that is doubted by some authorities) convinced him that the white-robed priests of Uxmal had carried their religion into Egypt, and that the Yucatán coast was merely the edge of that vast lost continent now submerged thousands of feet below the stormy Atlantic. Le Plongeon was of the opinion that the Egyptians received the rudiments of their culture from the Maya about one hundred and fifty centuries ago.

Many representations of human hands, actually found by him on temple walls, spelt to Le Plongeon the origin of Freemasonry in Yucatán thousands of years before King Solomon. He was also the discoverer of the famous statue of Chac-Mool,[3] the masterpiece of Mayan art. Chac-Mool, he asserted, was the Mayan for Abel, and it was the Uxmal priests who taught the people of Chemi about the creation of the world, the story of Adam and Eve, and of Cain and Abel.

Strange and fantastic seem these theories, but since no man speaks with authority on the origin of the Maya, who can positively refute them? Modern archaeology stands as helpless before the riddle as did Hernández de Córdoba in 1517, when he discovered the Yucatán Peninsula and wondered at the magnificent edifices outlining its coast. And until the wand of science breaks the long silence of the Maya ghosts, one guess, perhaps, is as good as another.

In the well-appointed dining car of the official train, the expeditionaries enjoyed their first "typical" Yucatecan breakfast when, shortly after dawn, we arrived at the Pisté railroad station. Avocado, or alligator pear, served in the regional style known as *guacamole,* was the feature of the feast. But as at the *banquete* of the previous night, a profusion of other tropical fruits—*mamey, mango, piña*—reminded the visitors of their debt to the ancient Maya agriculturists. At Pisté, a flock of little Fordingas—Mexican for "Fords"—were waiting to convey us to the nearby archaeological zone. The party comprised about fifty persons, including some ten members of the pioneer group of organized tourists—calling themselves Yucatalogists—to visit what was already being claimed by the travel agencies as "the Egypt of America."

Our arrival at the ancient city was greeted by substantially the same prospect that John Lloyd Stephens, exploring Uxmal in 1841, describes as his "first impressions" in his book *Incidents of Travel in Central America, Chiapas, and the Yucatán.*

"Emerging suddenly from the woods, to my astonishment," wrote the explorer, "we came at once upon a large open field strewed with mounds of ruins and vast buildings on terraces, and pyramidal structures grand and in good preservation, richly ornamented, without a bush to obstruct the view, and in picturesque effect almost equal to the ruins of Thebes."

Felipe, ever the courteous yet undemonstrative host, explained as he escorted us to the Fordingas, that our immediate objective was the great Castillo del Adivino, the Pyramid of the Magician, also known as the House of the Dwarf—he would tell us *why* later—which now loomed imposingly in sight. He was pleased, he observed, with a provocative grin, to see that we were all sturdy specimens, since we would have to climb 118 steps at a 65-degree angle, to reach the sanctuary that crowned the towering pyramid. But, reassuringly, he quickly added that it was not quite as bad as it sounded, since there were five different ledges where we could rest and catch our breath. Better still, there was a strong iron chain to cling to all the way up to the top. The levels, he said, were of different styles and belonged to distinct periods of construction.

In one of the earliest outside reactions to El Castillo del Adivino, Stephens wrote that he stood in its main entrance as the sun went down, "throwing from the buildings a prodigious breadth of shadow, darkening the terraces on which they stood, and presenting a scene strange enough for a work of enchantment." I was seeing the gigantic monument for the first time at sunrise, but my own vivid and enduring impressions check with his conclusion: "The whole forms an extraordinary mass of richness and complexity, both grand and curious."

Some of the scholars who had visited Uxmal on former occasions contributed facts or theories that helped us visualize the vast ceremonial center, as it must have looked in ancient times. Dr. Spinden told us that during its peak, the city probably had more than a million inhabitants. The buildings, too, he said, were originally painted—red, blue, green, yellow, white, and black—in striking color combinations. Dr. Saville noted that the Rain God, Yum Chac, whose mask appeared in an elaborately carved frieze above the five separate entrances of the lower west temple of the House of the Dwarf, was very similar to the Mexican Tlaloc.[4] According to Maya belief, all of Yucatán, he pointed out, was wholly dependent upon the bounty of this deity because in the entire peninsula there were no visible streams. The great subterranean rivers ran to the sea ninety feet below the ground level and in certain localities broke through to the surface, creating deep wells, or *cenotes*.

Whenever aspects of the old civilization were discussed, Felipe was a most attentive listener. But whether silent or expressively articulate, his commanding athletic figure, heightened by his distinctive wide-brimmed black felt "Governor's Stetson," was always the central presence. The humblest Indian and the most eminent savant seemed to be equally cognizant of his compelling personal magnetism. For me, at least, the mere fact of his nearness filled every void with ecstasy. I responded to hitherto undreamed-of sensate awareness at the touch of his hand as he helped me up pyramid steps or gently guided my way through the narrow passages of mystery-enshrouded masonry. But emanating far out beyond the area of mutual human recognition, his influence dominated my entire consciousness. It seemed to me that even those far-flung, impalpable fragments of archetypal self—dimly discerned hopes and aims for ultimate realization of truth and perfection—must somewhere be sharing my mortal happiness. I kept marveling that so many clear windows could have been opened to his character and temperament on such brief acquaintance. Suddenly, I understood the reason. For aside from the inexplicable laws of spiritual chemistry and their mysterious powers of attraction, Felipe, I believed, represented in his single person a grand-scale synthesis of my own youthful aspirations towards a better world, even the very movements that had claimed my devoted if feeble crusading efforts. In his solid accomplishment and well-defined goals, I perceived the finished design of what I hoped was my own potential, the kind of individual contribution I dreamed of eventually making to life's collection plate. Constantly evident, in his spontaneous words and in his kindly, paternal gestures, was a complete dedication to his Inditos, a sincere preoccupation with the lowly, "inarticulate ones," everywhere. This universal outlook ran parallel to, not in conflict with, his profound and proven love of country. It was his intense pride in the splendid monuments bequeathed by his gifted ancestors to our sense of beauty that sustained his faith in the great future role of Mexico's autochthonous peoples. His pride and his faith were reflected in his confident smile whenever the scientists or the tourists expressed their admiration of Uxmal's grandeur. His eagerness to have the visitors fully appreciate some architectural effect or sculptural detail he had discovered during years of familiarity with the site, frequently suggested the attitude of an adoring parent displaying the charms of a first offspring. He might even have been mistaken for an artist expounding the intricacies of his craft or the subtleties of conception that could otherwise pass unnoticed by the average spectator.

As we rested at the principal levels in our strenuous ascent of the huge "House of the Dwarf," the archaeologists obligingly outlined some of the events in Uxmal's history. At least, they pieced together for us as much of the dramatic story as the record had preserved. While only a few scattered legends, they admitted, shed light on the city's beginnings and remote past, the chronicles of the *Chilam Balam de Chumayel*—those four Maya books that escaped the flames of Bishop de Landa's *auto da fé*—did give a few meager details concerning later happenings. As to the founding of Uxmal, de Landa states in his *Relación de las cosas de*

*Yucatán* that, according to the tradition, "these people wandered for forty years through the wilderness of Yucatán without finding any water except what came from the rains, and at the end of that time they arrived at the edge of the mountains that descend in front of the city of Mayapán, ten leagues away from it, and they lingered there to till the earth like natives."

One of the chronicles of the *Chilam Balam* states that the year A.D. 1544 was "870 years after the destruction of Uxmal and the abandonment of the land." From this same source it is learned that the city was occupied twice, once toward the end of the seventh century and again three hundred years later. With Chichén Itzá and Mayapán, Uxmal was one of the three constituent cities of the Mayapán League, which flourished between A.D. 1007 and 1194.

Dr. Morley said that it seemed safe to conclude that during the last half of the tenth century, several groups of closely related peoples, probably of Mexican origin, though all spoke Mayan, entered the peninsula from the southwest and proceeded to assume the political direction of northern Yucatán, establishing Maya-Mexican dynasties at the capitals of the three city-states—the followers of Kukulcán[5] at Chichén Itzá, the Cocom at Mayapán, and the Tutul Xiu at Uxmal. He added that the Xius arriving in Uxmal—apparently from the Mexican plateau—had brought with them distinctive cultural traits and religious concepts, notably that of the cult of the Plumed Serpent.

It was Dr. Spinden who described the general prosperity that reigned during the period when the League operated as a peaceful confederation. Both at Uxmal and at Chichén Itzá, he said, the arts attained new importance. Uxmal became the model city of the Maya Renaissance and the architecture of the period, produced by what is known as the Puuc, or Low Hills Region, culture, achieved brilliant expression in the Palace of the Governor, which we were scheduled to visit later in the day.

Despite the semitropical heat and the unaccustomed effort in scaling rugged mounds and steep pyramids, the morning hours followed one another like the notes of some rapturous melody. But at noon I welcomed the chance to relax in the shade of the corbel arch of La Casa de las Monjas, the "Nunnery," where all the members of the party assembled for a picnic lunch. Because of the profuse latticework, the Spaniards, Felipe said, evidently believed the group of multiroomed structures surrounding a quadrangle, measuring over 259 × 250 feet, to be a convent. He observed laughingly that such an institution would doubtless be outlawed by Yucatán's present Socialist Government on the grounds that the Creator had made the female face to be seen and admired and not to be hidden behind concealing devices. However, he quite approved of the interpretation given the Nunnery by the chronicler Cogolludo, who referred to it as the dwelling of the Maya Vestal Virgins who kept the Sacred Fire, because keeping a fire anywhere, he felt, was usually a worthy form of sacrifice.

*The Nunnery of Uxmal, in a photo recovered from Reed's possessions inherited by Rosa Lie Johansson in Mexico City.*

On the inner walls of the arched corridor that functioned as our *al fresco* dining hall, red hands had been painted. Different versions of their significance were given by the archaeologists, but all admitted that the true meaning of the symbol was unknown. Dr. Alfred Tozzer quoted the French abbot Brasseur de Bourbourg, who maintained that by impressing the red hand upon the walls of their temples, the Maya believed they were invoking the spirit of Itsamatul, also known as Kabul, signifying the "Celestial or Creative Hand."[6] He said that other scholars regarded it as the mystical sign of some ancient political society, as evidence of murder in high places, or, as the mark of Kukulcán himself. "Murder!" . . . The word caused me to shudder with the same strange revulsion I had experienced the previous day when I looked down at the open-jawed sharks leaping around the prow of the *Mexico* while we were anchored off the Progreso roadstead. Whatever its meaning, the red hand struck as an ominous symbol—the only sinister note I had encountered in the Uxmal ruins.

But the fleeting intrusion of the red hand failed to mar the festive mood of our picnic luncheon, and no cocktails were needed to keep the spirits of the "Yucatalogists" and the scientists in a highly animated state. Delectable fruit cups—all nonalcoholic in conformity with Felipe's temperance campaign—accompanied the typical *platillos*, or dishes: *pollo pibil, enchiladas motul,* and others that make up the rich and varied Yucatecan cuisine. In their spotless white aprons, patterned someone mentioned on archaeological lines, the cheerful, broad-faced, bare-legged boys who served us, might have stepped down from a temple façade, so closely did their profiles resemble those on the sculptured walls.

The widely traveled, bilingual John and Vera Barry, who had been such interesting deck companions aboard the *Mexico,* again delighted everyone with their witty accounts of adventures on other continents. Felipe liked their happy camaraderie and their obvious pleasure in one another's company. From that day, he always spoke of them as "los simpáticos esposos Barry."[7] It was Mrs. Barry—the vivacious, blue-eyed, auburn-haired daughter of a Scottish baron—who reminded Felipe that he had promised to tell us why the Castillo del Adivino was known as the House of the Dwarf.

He replied that he would gladly keep his promise but, with her permission, some other day. He preferred not to dampen with a grim tale of black magic one of the most joyous occasions he had known in a long, long time. "Besides," he explained, to the amusement of the archaeologists who knew the popular legend, "it is rather hard on a Maya Governor, one of my predecessors, who ignominiously emerged with a badly cudgeled head and, worst of all, at the hands of a dwarf. Let us end our picnic on a more pleasant note—with music." He had come prepared, he announced, and his favorite troubadours, Alfonso and his *muchachos,* were ready with their guitars, to play and sing for us a few of the songs that Yucatán cherished most.

In cadences that throbbed with passionate longing, their plaintive voices, blending in flawless harmony, drifted out over the vast stretch of ruin. Felipe had suggested that we end our picnic with gaiety, but sadness was the undercurrent of most of the songs—"El rosal enfermo," "Flores de Mayo," "Un rayito del sol," "Las golondrinas," and others. Yet so completely did both words and music satisfy the heart, one could have gone on listening to them endlessly with undiminished enchantment. Curiously, these guitar-strummed melodies transcended the nostalgia of their personal themes to embrace the mystery of an ancient race, a vanished civilization. And despite their sensuous lyricism, they seemed poignantly attuned to the tragic mood of the dead city, abandoned in its full flowering. I could not help but relate their minor-keyed strains to Uxmal's desecrated altars, its dishonored deities, toppled in the dust. Nor to the unutterable sorrow of a richly endowed people, forced to endure centuries of oppression and humiliation.

On leaving the arched corridor of the Nunnery—in reality, the main entrance to the great central court—we followed a road that led past a unit of four buildings surrounding the Quadrangle of the Doves. Stephens believed that the title was derived from the high ornamented wall that ran along the top in such a shape that from a distance it looked more like a row of dovecots than anything else.

Nearby was the House of the Turtles, where we stopped for a few moments on our way to the Governor's Palace. This name the archaeologists attributed to the carved turtles on the lintel of the cornice. They classified the façade of one of the compartments as Chenes in style, representing an earlier period than the other buildings of the site, which belonged to the Puuc culture.[8] In balanced proportion and austere elegance, the structure recalled the classic Greeks.

Standing before the Palace of the Governor, we were now all quite willing to concede that its fame as ancient America's noblest building had been justly bestowed. But while the simple yet impressive architecture—crowning a triple terrace a little short of 600 × 500 feet at the base—was of striking esthetic appeal, the effect of timeless universality produced on the spectator was even more challenging. One could readily accept the tradition that this and other principal structures of Uxmal's ceremonial center had been "cosmically" planned—their foundations laid with the relative positions of the known planets in mind. Viewed from a distance, silhouetted against the southern sky, the monument defied dating. Ignorant of its geographical locale or historic background, no one except the experts, perhaps, could have guessed its American autochthonous origin. John Barry was of the opinion that, for a few thousand dollars, the entire building might again be made ready for occupancy and pass for modern streamlined construction. The imaginative Vera Barry expanded her husband's idea by suggesting that Felipe establish the Governor's Palace as a summer state capitol, especially since Uxmal between April and September was much cooler than Mérida.

"I'm afraid this is not a project for immediate realization," Felipe replied, "but it may well fit in with our general long-range program of Maya rehabilitation. Meanwhile, even in Mérida, we are always spiritually close to the builders of Uxmal in our effort and aims for the welfare of their descendants."

Ascending the broad stairway on the west and then a smaller one, we reached the level of the platform on which the enormous structure, occupying 320,000 cubic feet of space, rested atop a natural elevation. Felipe, who must have visited the Palace on innumerable occasions, and apparently knew every fact and fable concerning it that research, up to the time, had disclosed, led us through the double corridor with its two central halls and four lateral chambers, composing the large central unit. With picturesque analogies based on the deification of natural forces, he explained the significance of the motifs adorning the long, broad, well-preserved frieze of the east façade, stone carvings of the Rain God, repeated and combined in original and harmonious forms. Some twenty thousand mosaic elements, he said, had been used in the design—alternating Greek frets and latticework panels—while 200,000 cubic feet of solid masonry had gone into the structure itself.

With eager enthusiasm he developed the Maya theme so intimately involved with his life's pattern—his most compassionate impulses and most decisive remedial action. And as he spoke, Vera Barry's proposal to convert the Palace of the Governor into Yucatán's summertime state capitol seemed less fantastic and not altogether illogical. For by every inherent right, it occurred to me, this was *his* building. With lines of unpretentious dignity like those of his own confident, clean-cut personality, above all, through connotations of belonging to the ages and to all mankind, the architectonic values of Uxmal's ancient Palace of the Governor tellingly interpreted the twentieth-century Socialist leader Felipe Carrillo Puerto.

Dr. Morley noted that Stephens had found all the wood lintels at the Palace in place over the entrances.[9] The wood, which was very hard and rang under the blow of a machete, had come, he said, from distant forests, possibly three hundred miles away. He related that the pioneer American explorer found one wooded beam of *chicozapote*[10] in the southernmost outside room of the building. When he left Yucatán, he took it with him to the United States and shortly afterwards it was destroyed by a fire in New York City. The Carnegie director held this to be an irreparable loss, since Stephens believed that this wooden beam was the only carved one in the entire city of Uxmal and the "inscription could very well have been the date of this edifice, the most beautiful in ancient America."

Intriguing moments in our examination of the Governor's Palace were occupied in searching for clues to the whereabouts of the "Lost Maya Library." Felipe related that according to Le Plongeon—for whom he held deep respect—the Maya during the period of Bishop de Landa's vandalism had hidden the bulk of their sacred writings and that the great collection was still concealed in the temples of Uxmal and Chichén Itzá. As a result of this claim, supported by years of rumor and legend, three archaeological penetrations at different levels and at various periods had been made in the terraces but without result. Another penetration with improved scientific methods of detection was contemplated in the near future under state auspices, he disclosed. There was a chance that even though the Maya library failed to appear, other valuable information would doubtless reward the effort.

Dr. Saville said that he had known Le Plongeon's widow and had read several of the French savant's unpublished manuscripts, which she unfortunately had burned in despair at the contemptuous rejection of her husband's theories and discoveries. Dr. Saville expressed little faith in Le Plongeon's claim but explained that if the Maya books still existed in Uxmal, they should be found in good condition. Chroniclers of the period, he pointed out, recorded that the paper made from the bark and roots of native trees was rendered practically indestructible by a lustrous white varnish. The books were folded fanwise, and many of them measured a yard in length. The subject matter included treatises on history, religion, medicine, archaeology, astronomy, and the occult sciences, in the practices of which Uxmal was a recognized center.

Various causes for Uxmal's downfall and desertion were suggested by the archaeologists as we returned to the waiting Fordingas and headed for the Pisté railroad station. But there was general agreement that the disintegration of the tripartite League and the destruction of Mayapán in 1461 marked the beginning of Uxmal's end. As Dr. Merriam pointed out, it was the Uxmal chieftain Xipau Xiu, who, with the aid of other Maya leaders, had brought about the League's rupture. In its wake, internal disorders had so weakened the political and social structure that only a few final blows were needed to envelop the land in a long night of decadence and desolation. Pestilence, hurricanes, the frightful toll of war with the arrival of the Spanish conquerors, combined to decimate the large population.

"Would Uxmal, Phoenix-like, ever rise again from its ashes?" Vera Barry inquired of Felipe. "That's quite possible," he answered, "although, of course, any revival of the old creative spirit would seek and find different manifestations. Our present-day Maya, for instance, would not build pyramids for their ordinary daily functioning any more than would the modern Egyptians. But we are hopefully preparing for the new order, when Uxmal, 'The Thrice Rebuilt,' will again rebuild and once again be the scene of a vigorous, dynamic life. It's almost time, you know, for the reawakening and the fulfillment of the Maya prophecy, which says: "A day will dawn when in *a single day* will be broken the silence of seven hundred years!"

# 8. Land and Liberty

Preceded by a lively native orchestra and escorted from the railroad depot by a reception committee of some fifty leading citizens, we walked four or five abreast for a kilometer along an unpaved road to the village plaza of Suma, five kilometers from Mérida. Passing under an improvised cardboard arch adorned with painted Maya symbols and topped at the center with a big red triangle that bore greetings to Governor Carrillo and the members of the Partido Socialista, our little procession broke rank in front of the low wooden municipal building. In tropical cotton *camisa* and *calzones* and respectfully holding his coarse straw sombrero over his heart, the *presidente municipal* came forward to meet Felipe and his guests.[1]

It was clear to all of us that we were attending an event of the greatest importance, the most momentous, perhaps, as one of the Carnegie expeditionaries observed, since 1847, when at this same spot the grandparents of Suma's townsfolk gathered to play their part in the "War of the Castes," the bloody uprising of the Maya Indians against their Creole and Spanish masters.[2] This was the Thursday of which Felipe had spoken to me with such enthusiasm on our twilight ride to Kanasín, a memorable day in the modern history of every Yucatecan pueblo, the day of the *ejidos.*

Two hundred *campesinos*—Suma's entire adult male population—most of them attired like their Señor Presidente—massed around the table in the Plaza where Felipe, between local and federal Agrarian Commission representatives, was seated while he signed the document that restored to them communal possession of the public lands taken from their ancestors before and during the Díaz dictatorship.

On the sidelines stood an equal number of Maya women in the typical Mestiza dress of the Yucatán—a white cotton *huipil*[3] gaily embroidered with floral motifs at the neck and around the hem of the one-piece garment. Many held infants wrapped or swung in dark *rebozos* of fringed blue or brown jersey cloth while older children stood beside them or squatted at their feet.

Still another phalanx of women carrying *bienvenido* banners arranged themselves in semi-military formation facing the official group. These newly enfranchised members of the Feminist League watched the proceedings with a certain proud, proprietary air. As articulate and persistent agitators, they could claim active participation in bringing about the necessary measures that hastened federal action.

A delegation of Feministas headed by Felipe's vivacious younger sister, the brown-eyed auburn-haired Elvia, had accompanied us from Mérida. Distinctly Spanish in type, Elvia, I learned, was a most effective leader, who devoted full time to touring southeastern Mexico, organizing Maya women into Ligas and preparing them for civic responsibilities. Also in the Mérida Feminista group was *profesora* Rosa Torre G., a schoolteacher who had recently been made a member of the Ayuntamiento Council, the governing body of the Yucatán capital, the first woman in the Mexican Republic to be elevated to such an office. In appearance, Rosa presented a striking contrast to the tall, handsome Elvia Carrillo. The little bronze-skinned *regidora*[4] was evidently the well beloved of Antonio, Felipe's amiable, broad-shouldered personal assistant and chauffeur. In any event, his adoring glances seldom strayed from her classic Maya features. The union of two such perfect Maya types could have gloriously perpetuated the antique race, as Vera Barry remarked, the antique race whose silhouettes adorned the Yucatán's sculptured columns and temple walls.

The solemn *ejidos* act took place beneath a flat-topped wide-spreading flamboyant tree that afforded a natural canopy in the heat of the midday sun. And symbolically, as well as functionally, its huge, scarlet blossoms enacted a role in the ceremonies, flaunting the vivid Revolutionary color of the state's Socialist regime, sponsors of the reclamation of purloined civic rights.

On either side of the official table, chairs had been placed for the visitors, among them directors and principal stockholders in enormous U.S. corporations, large-scale employers of Latin-American labor. All were occupants of reserved seats at a significant performance—a preview of the drama of a changing world. For here, in this ancient, isolated land we were witnessing the sudden emergence into a new human and economic status of a people that for generations had existed—as millions on all of Earth's continents were still existing—for the exclusive benefit and profit of "big business." Here we were, all "close-up" spectators at the denouement of a torturous and drawn-out play of unequal forces in which humble, dispossessed men and women are finally seen in the act of acquiring a voice in the conduct of their affairs, coming again into the ownership of lands that their ancestors had tilled in remote millennia.

After the signing of the *ejidos* documents, the verification of the transfer deeds by the Agrarian Commission member, and the acceptance of the grant on behalf of the community by the local authorities, Felipe addressed the gathering in the Mayan tongue. And now, as at the reception to the Carnegie expeditionaries on the night of our arrival, he spoke with a depth of feeling that transcended language barriers. Again he succeeded in communicating with the intuitions, at least, of his foreign listeners. The Mayan-Spanish-English-speaking Manuel Cirerol made a running translation for me of Felipe's words, and as I had guessed from their mild yet decisive tone and their rhythmic quality of "joyous song," they carried encouragement and hope, with no trace of rancor. One of the archaeologists seated near me likened the talk to a rationalist-inspired Sermon on the Mount. He was deeply impressed, he said, by Felipe's wise counsel and the tolerant attitude conveyed in simple, clear, universal imagery as well as with the intimate "big brother" appeal that colored his voice and manner.

In essence Felipe lauded the great Social Revolution that had shaped new destinies for millions of Mexicans and for other millions still unborn. He explained that liberation had come about only through the love of a few men for man in the mass, through the sacrifice of their own lives that their fellow men might be freed from enslavement by despots. "We cannot all be equally heroic," he said, "but each can contribute something towards the transformation into a better, happier place, his pueblo, his *patria,* and consequently, the world of today and tomorrow." "Each one of us," he said, "can and should show gratitude for the gift of consciousness—that most precious of Nature's endowments, one that enables us to plan and fashion our environment along the pattern of our most beautiful dreams and highest ideals, if not for ourselves, then as a heritage for those who will follow us on the good Earth." He begged his Inditos to use their hard-won rights and new political power in a "generous" spirit without dwelling on past sufferings and injustices, but thinking only of their goal—an era of glorious opportunity. There is a fine example, he pointed out, to be seen in Nature itself as it revives with each morning's sunrise, forgetting the nocturnal darkness or yesterday's storms.

In a brief discussion of some of the immediate practical angles of the land distribution program, Felipe reminded the *campesinos* that two of their young men were already receiving instruction in modern farm methods at the recently organized Agricultural School in Mérida and would return to Suma as experts and teachers. In a short time, he said, tractors and other machinery essential for increased production would be made available to them through funds supplied by *ejidal* financing agencies.

But it was on the inevitable note of compassion that he concluded the informal talk to his Inditos. His thoughts were incorporated in his address to the workers of Mérida a few weeks later at the 1923 May Day observance, a newspaper account of which I received in New York.

"Use your freedom," he urged on both occasions his audience of former *hacienda* slaves, "to become better and freer citizens, never basely to revenge yourselves on some individual who is himself a victim of a wretched old order that is gone forever. Forget the past, except as a lesson for your future guidance. Hate corruption, hate vice, hate cruelty, hate the institutions that breed them, but not the individuals caught up in their meshes. Destroy the worn-out forms, expose the fallacy of ancient doctrines which have been used to enslave men, and a better day will dawn for all."

As I listened with rapt attention to his every syllable, and even more intently regarded his every move with the eyes of my heart, I could have found no words to interpret my own thoughts or express my emotional reactions in terms more accurate than those penned at the same period by Dr. Ernest Gruening, who knew Felipe well:

> Felipe Carrillo would have dominated his surroundings anywhere. His was a leadership almost unknown in this day and belonging rather to a legendary age. Straight, handsome, with keen yet kindly gray eyes; clean-cut features, and sparkling smile that could capture a child's faith or rivet the hearts of a vast multitude, taller by a head than most of his countrymen, he was truly a god among them. In any civilized society, a high-spirited, brave, and gallant gentleman. Never was the heritage of nobility that he believed to be his more fervently held as a high obligation, more worthily executed as a sacred trust. Yet he was a democrat to the core, a leader, a teacher, a big brother rather than a ruler. He lived simply and gave no thought to pomp, to personal power or its requisites. A great vision, a shrewd realism, intuitive sympathy, a loving sentimentality, militant ideals, and extraordinary physical energy combined with a rarely winning personality—these were the qualities which enabled him, virtually single-handed, to achieve a revolution.

The propitious moment with its captive audience was not lost for the cause of temperance, then a subject of a vigorous statewide campaign inaugurated by Felipe immediately after his election as Governor. The ardent and able crusader Professor Eligio Erosa, a fluent Maya orator and former schoolmaster, deftly connected sobriety with the "new deal" that the *ejidos* program would launch in Suma.

His interpretive gestures left no doubt that he was describing the helpless condition to which drunkenness reduced its victims, citing facts and figures that convincingly demonstrated the baneful effects of excessive drinking. Professor Erosa suggested that those who found it difficult to give up their harmful habits would find strength in unity, and he urged that they hold regular weekly meetings at their *Liga* to exchange effective methods of combating the vice, thus anticipating the system of Alcoholics Anonymous.

As I looked out over the bronzed faces turned toward their benefactor with expressions in which gratitude and a certain religious veneration were mingled, I remembered how enthusiastically on the road to Kanasín Felipe had described to me the joyous reaction in every Maya pueblo to the *ejido* programs. He had assured me that, at Suma on Thursday, I would see for myself the intense happiness of the Inditos when they realized they were in possession of the lands of which their fathers had been robbed. Certainly he had not overstated their elated awareness of a changed status, revealed in their broad smiles, in the light that gleamed in their tranquil, patient eyes.

But the very patience of these humble Maya folk, their evident childlike faith that the road of sorrow was about to make a fortunate turning, only stirred me to greater indignation when I recalled their tragic past. Suddenly, all that I had read in John Kenneth Turner's *Barbarous Mexico* came back to me in a flood of new resentment. Through his documented "eyewitness" account of the incredible misery that enveloped the daily lives of these same *campesinos* and generations of their forebears, the humiliation, suffering, and cruel exploitation to which they had been subjected, over a long and only recently terminated period, assumed for me on the scene of the brutalities an even more outrageous aspect.

My indignation would have been even greater had I realized that some of the *hacendados* who were among the worst offenders in their slaveholding days, but now members in good standing of the Cámara Agrícola de Yucatán,[5] attended the receptions and accompanied the archaeological tours arranged for the Carnegie expeditionaries. Since reading *Barbarous Mexico* several months earlier, I had forgotten the names of the plantation owners interviewed by the astute journalist on his visit to Yucatán in 1908, posing as a millionaire American interested in purchasing a large *henequén hacienda.* It was difficult for me to believe, for instance, when later I became aware of the fact, that the soft-spoken, cultivated don Felipe G. Cantón, president of the Yucatán Archaeological Society, in whose marble mansion in Mérida I was housed, was the same *hacendado* who had innocently made clear his philosophy of slave beating when queried by Mr. Turner on the subject: "Oh yes, it is necessary to whip them, yes, very necessary," Sr. Cantón had answered, with the same beguiling and perpetual smile I had observed in my own brief acquaintance with him. "There is no other way to make them do what you wish. What other means is there of enforcing the discipline of the farm? If we did not whip them, they would do nothing."

Names may have escaped me, but I would never forget Mr. Turner's pen picture of the first beating of a slave he witnessed on a *henequén* plantation—a formal beating before the assembled ranch toilers early in the morning just after the daily roll call. Here is his description:

> The slave was taken on the back of a huge Chinaman and given fifteen lashes across the bare back with a heavy, wet rope, lashes so lustily delivered that the blood ran down the victim's body. This method of beating is an ancient one in the Yucatán and is the customary one on all plantations for boys and all except the heaviest men. Women are required to kneel to be beaten, as are sometimes men of great weight. Men and women are beaten in the fields as well as at the morning roll call. Each foreman, or *capataz,* carries a heavy cane with which he punches and prods and whacks the slaves at will. I do not remember visiting a single field in which I did not see some of this punching and prodding and whacking going on.

Mr. Turner states that while he saw no punishments worse than beating in Yucatán, he had heard of them. He was told of men being strung up by their fingers or toes to be beaten, of their being thrust into black dungeon-like holes, of water being dropped on the head until the victim collapsed, of the extremity of female punishment being found in some outrage to the sense of modesty in the woman. He had heard also of planters who "took special delight in personally superintending the beating of their chattels." The journalist learned from a leading professional man of Mérida that the favorite pastime of one of the richest planters in the Yucatán was to sit on his horse and watch the "cleaning up," as they called it, of his slaves. He would strike a match to light his cigar. At the first puff of smoke, the first stroke of the wet rope would fall on the bare back of the victim. He would smoke on leisurely, contentedly, as the blows fell, one after another. When the entertainment finally palled on him, he would throw away his cigar and the man with the rope would stop, for the end of the cigar was the end of the beating.

Mr. Turner explained that he did not receive the word "slavery" from the people of Yucatán, though they were themselves the holders of the slaves. "The proof of a fact," he pointed out, "is to be found not in the name, but in the conditions thereof." He defined slavery as "the ownership of the body of a man, an ownership so absolute that the body can be transferred to another, an ownership that gives to the owner a right to take the product of that body, to starve it, to chastise it at will, to kill it with impunity. Such is slavery in the extreme sense. Such is slavery as I found it in Yucatán."

Mr. Turner asked, as did many others following his exposé: How was slavery possible in Yucatán when Article 1, Section 1, of the 1857 Mexican Constitution specifically states that in the Republic "all are born free" and that "slaves who set foot upon the national territory recover by that act alone their liberty and receive the right to the protection of Mexican law"?[6] This guaranteed freedom was reinforced by a later Constitutional Amendment, which provided that the state "shall not permit any contract, covenant or agreement to be carried out having for its object the abridgement, loss or irrevocable sacrifice of the liberty of a man, whether by reason of labor, education or religious vows. Nor shall any contract be tolerated in which a man agrees to his proscription or exile."

The answer, as Mr. Turner indicated, is to be found in the fact that the *hacendados* managed to circumvent the law of the nation by calling their slave system "service for debt." But the contrary was proven, he shows, by the habit of transferring slaves from one master to another, not on any basis of debt but on the basis of the market price of a man. Whenever, in his guise of prospective investor, he discussed the purchase of a *hacienda,* cash payment for the slaves was demanded exactly the same as for the land, the machinery and the cattle. The prevailing price fixed by the planters was 400 Mexican dollars apiece. Mr. Turner was told that before the panic of 1907, the price "had been much higher, at least 1,000 dollars."

The enslavement of the Maya described by Mr. Turner extended as well to some five thousand Yaquis who had ruthlessly been torn from their tribal lands and fertile *milpas* in distant Sonora and transported to the torrid *henequén* plantations of Yucatán, condemned to misery for the rest of their days. In most cases, however, the forced labor and its attendant horrors were of short duration, since two-thirds of the unfortunate victims of the Díaz "prosperity" system died of starvation, abuse, and sheer terror in the first year of their "relocation."

The Yaqui deportations were carried out under three Sonora Governors—Ramón Corral, who also served as Díaz's Vice President, Rafael Izábal, and Luis Torres—who rotated in office for more than a generation. Exercising absolute power, they were answerable only to the dictator himself. The Yaquis—believed to be an offshoot of the Aztecs—were goaded into war by the foulest means. The men at the head of the government wanted the lands, which the Yaquis had held under a patent signed by the King of Spain 150 years prior to their deportations. Up until the Díaz regime, the Yaqui claim to tribal lands was recognized by every ruler and chief executive of Mexico. The sequence of sanguinary events as reported by Mr. Turner begins with the harassment of the peaceful agriculturists by the Governors who sent bogus surveyors through the Yaqui Valley to stake off the land and inform the people that the government had decided to give it to foreigners. The officials confiscated $80,000[7] in a bank account belonging to Chief Cajeme. In their chagrin at not finding him when they came to arrest him, they set fire to his house and those of his neighbors and assaulted the women of the village, including Cajeme's wife. During the quarter of a century that followed, an army numbering from two thousand to six thousand men remained in Yaqui territory. Thousands of soldiers and tens of thousands of Yaquis were killed in battle, and many hundreds were executed after having been imprisoned. A few years later Cajeme was captured and publicly executed in the presence of a large body of his people who had been taken prisoner with him.

Among the worst atrocities was the mass hanging of men, women, and children on May 17, 1892, by General Otero in the town of Navojoa. With so many hangings, it is reliably claimed, the town's supply of rope became exhausted, requiring that each rope be used several times.

Many of the Yaquis had taken refuge on Tiburón Island. In reprisal Governor Izábal had ordered the Seri Indians to bring him the right hand of every Yaqui, with the alternative of the extermination of the Seris themselves. A Kodak photograph showing the Governor laughing at the bunch of hands dangling on a cane, which had been brought to him, was published by the Mexico City newspaper *El Imparcial* in proof of the official's brutality.

The four or five thousand Yaquis who refused to surrender their lands fled to the isolated strongholds of the Bacatete Mountains but were still hunted by an army of several thousand soldiers. They were classed as "renegades" because they refused to surrender without guarantees that they would be neither executed nor deported.

In an interview obtained by Mr. Turner from Colonel Francisco B. Cruz of the Mexican Army when they occupied the same stateroom on a trip between Progreso and Veracruz, the financial details of the flourishing business in human merchandise were clearly stated. The Colonel, who was in charge of the deportations to Yucatán, confessed to Turner that he had delivered 15,700 Yaquis during the previous three and one half years and would have delivered many more, except that the government never allowed him enough expense money to feed them properly and that 10 to 20 percent died on the journey.

For his services he received $10.00 for each Yaqui delivered, the remainder of the $65.00 going to the Secretary of War,[8] while "the land, the buildings, the cattle, everything left behind when the Yaquis were carried away by the soldiers, went to the Governor of Sonora."

Colonel Cruz complained bitterly about the high suicide rate among the Yaquis, stating that they "wanted to cheat him out of his commission money." He related that in February 1908, between the mouth of the Yaqui River and the port of Guaymas, scores threw their children into the sea and jumped in after them, first from the starboard and then from the port side of the gunboat *El Demócrata*. He said boats were lowered, but it was of no use because "they all went down before we could get to them."

During my first visit to Mexico I had gathered other details concerning the Yaqui deportations from my friend Ingeniero Juan de Dios Bojórquez, a member of the Mexican Senate well known as a writer under the pen name of Djed Bórquez, and who had been Carranza's Minister of Gobernación.[9] As a young engineering student from Sonora at the National University of Mexico, he used to visit the exiled Yaqui gangs as they arrived in the capital for an overnight stay at the army barracks before shipment by cattle car to Veracruz, where they were herded into the holds of boats bound for Progreso, Yucatán. He had known the Yaquis from childhood, spoke their language, and greatly admired their strong characters. In the concentration camps known as bull pens, they would confide in him, telling him of their misery and their anguish at being separated en route from their families. Ingeniero Bojórquez had visited, he said, about five thousand Yaquis, who had poured into Mexico City during this period at the rate of five hundred a month.

Supplementing Mr. Turner's on-the-spot reports and the personal reminiscences of Senator Bojórquez regarding the Yaqui deportations are those of Captain Blackadder of the Ward Line. I interviewed the doughty old red-haired Scotch mariner aboard his vessel, "The Yucatán," on July 6, 1923, on my second voyage from New York to Mexico. Among his impressions of the barbaric traffic in which he unwillingly became involved, he related the following:

> Just after the Spanish War seventeen years ago, I carried some five thousand Yaquis—men, women, and children—from Veracruz to Progreso, under guard of five hundred Díaz soldiers. Between Veracruz and Havana we carried cattle on the same deck, but the human cattle—for there seemed to be little difference in the way they were treated and herded together—were dropped off at Progreso. They put these poor creatures onboard at Veracruz just as they caught them, separating families—mothers from children and husbands from wives. Upper 'tween decks was roped off, and three times a day the stewards went below with buckets of food, which the Yaquis ate from their tin cups and plates. They all seemed very passive—never a word of complaint out of one of them, and they seemed mildly grateful whenever they were fed . . . I was impressed especially by the sad, brooding look of one couple. The man was a handsome fellow. He must have been nearly seven feet tall, and the woman was splendid. She looked like a Syrian, dark and straight-featured and almost as tall as the man, with great gold rings in her ears. They had a little child of seven, and the three were always together and apart from the rest. The transportation of the Yaquis took over a year, the largest shipment numbering thirteen hundred.

The cruel deportations were terminated with Carranza's decree abolishing peonage in December 1914. Later, when the First Constitutional Chief appointed Ingeniero Bojórquez to his cabinet, he ordered him to accompany the 20th Sonora Division to Yucatán to rescue from the *haciendas* two thousand enslaved

Yaquis and bring them back to Sonora, a task that was accomplished. Ingeniero Bojórquez found, however, that many of the exiles had escaped from their bondage. They had won their freedom by desperately plunging through tropical jungles and scaling mountain ranges and by actually walking around the entire southern and western coasts of Mexico—a distance of four thousand kilometers—before reaching Sonora and their native pueblos in the Yaqui Valley.

The rousing trumpet notes of "Diana," the military salute with which Mexico musically applauds the arrival and acknowledges the departure of a distinguished personage or announces some important event, cut short my melancholy reflections on slavery and marked the end of *negocios*[10] and the beginning of *fiesta* time.

On the broad verandah of the municipal building long tables had been set for a *banquete* that included the choicest dishes of Yucatecan fare—much of it brought from Mérida. In addition to the many delectable tropical fruits already sampled, we were now introduced to the *guanábana,* resembling in shape and color a huge, ungainly potato, but of the most delicious taste, and used as a flavor for the *sorbete,* or sherbet. Mr. Barry, ever on the alert for ways and means of exploiting Yucatecan products on the American market, suggested in his enthusiasm that the syrup of this delicious fruit should be bottled and distributed in the United States, where it would most certainly create a sensation with the vast ice cream-consuming public. Felipe beamed his agreement and added that the luscious *guanábana* was only one of the numerous contributions of use and beauty that the Maya had made and could still make to our modern way of life.

"We must not forget," he said, addressing the visitors, "that a large part of the colossal agricultural wealth of the United States—the greatest in human history—is rooted in discoveries made and processes invented by the Maya race. Our good friend here, Dr. Spinden, who has known us for a long while, will bear me out with his formidable list of fruits, vegetables, and other commodities that we now regard as prime necessities—many of them today forming the major crops of your own rich country. These are all the result of patient experimentation and devoted labor over unknown centuries by the ancestors of our Inditos." Dr. Spinden corroborated Felipe's figures and stated in a brief talk that the food products provided by Maya ingenuity and industry were, in fact, so numerous and so essential to contemporary diet that one wonders what Europe ate before the Conquest. He said that more than seven thousand species of the flora of Yucatán are listed in the Field Museum of Chicago.

Twenty young women in gaily embroidered *trajes de Mestiza* and wearing bright colored hair ribbons, pendant earrings, long gold chains with large filigree crucifixes attached—the typical *fiesta* costume—now formed in line opposite an equal number of young men attired in native garb, *camisas* and *calzones* of white cotton and *sombreros de paja.* With the first strains of the lively music played on ukulele-like instruments, brass horns, drums, and gourds of Cuban origin, the men claimed their partners. Facing one another, the couples zestfully plunged into Yucatán's most popular folk dance, known as the *jarana.*

With unsmiling faces, their bodies straight and hands behind their backs, the men dug the heels of their *huaraches* into the wooden floor, with special gusto in the *zapateado,* it seemed, in honor of the happy occasion. The girls, lifting their heavy lace-edged skirts a discreet few inches, kept up a steady, rapid shuffling. At intervals, they passed their partners with arms gracefully curving upward and snapping their fingers in the manner of Spain. An accelerated tempo in the music announced the "Torito," and the couples began playing a bullfight game, the girls waving their red and yellow silk scarves to imitate the *torero* teasing a brave bull. The men charged head-on but always managed to pass safely under the simulated cape, without missing a single *zapateado* step.

Several times during the dance, the music suddenly stopped and someone shouted, "Bomba!" This was the signal for the man to pay a compliment, always ending in a quip that caused general laughter. Two or three of the *bombas* dealt humorously with the *ejidos* and the Partido Socialista, but one in the traditional romantic vein declared: "I'm fascinated by your heavenly eyes! The beauty of your face has won my heart—and if you are not already married, this cock would sing a different tune!"

Felipe had seated me on his right at the banquet table and during the *jarana* described, with his characteristic enthusiasm and flair for vivid word pictures, the meaning and origin of the different steps and the regional forms of folk dancing in other parts of Yucatán.

When I told him that I found the *fiesta* costume of the *señoritas* most attractive, he said: "I hope, Almita, that you will give me the enormous pleasure and do me the great honor of seeing you dressed like one of our pueblo Mestizas before you leave us." Since this was his wish, I assured him, I could certainly try to arrange it.

"Please give no thought to the arrangements," he answered. "You forget that I am the 'arranger' here, and despite what some of the *enemigos* may tell you, I am quite efficient when it comes to details. I'll attend to everything at once—early tomorrow morning. Your stay among us is so short, and there are many things that I want you to see and understand before you return to your frozen North, so that you will never forget us and will want to come back to your tropical *tierra* someday."

Felipe had proposed that instead of going directly back to Mérida, we return by a "roundabout" switch-track route permitting us to enjoy what was bound to be "a glorious sunset," and to pass through a region that we might otherwise miss seeing.

So, sipping iced *limonada* in the comfortable observation car on the trip back to Mérida, the expeditionaries engaged in a general discussion of the historical background of the moving ceremony we had just witnessed at Suma. The well-informed representative of the Agrarian Commission explained that the word *ejido* was derived from the Latin *exitus,* signifying "exit," and originally designated lands of villages in Spain newly created by Royal Decree. Through the Fuero Real, or recapitulation of the Spanish laws of the epoch, the designation had applied as early as 1255. These lands embraced by the *ejidos* could not be appropriated to personal use and could not serve for building purposes. Their main function was to provide a common area for the threshing of wheat and other community agricultural tasks. The area was also a corridor through which cattle were driven to summer pasture. In some cases, the *ejidos* were held in reserve as extra ground for the growth of the village to permit its expansion. The *ejidos* of New Spain adjusted to their Old World antecedents. But across the historical evolution of agrarian reform in Mexico, the word *ejido* has changed not only its ideological significance but its social and economic content as well.

Several others who took part in the improvised roundtable agreed that the Spaniards displaced the natives in the ownership of Mexico's land with the pressure and speed with which they extended the Conquest. The patrimony of the Conquistadores, they pointed out, was constantly enlarged by lands taken from the nobles, the cults of the Indian gods, and the holding of the *capullis,* or clans, without compensation and with no redress on the part of those stripped of their possessions. Right up until the War of Independence, the Spanish Crown engaged in tireless efforts to stop these abuses through laws in favor of the Indians, but with little if any real result.

The first major step after the Conquest in the redistribution of the lands came about through an ordinance of May 26, 1567, on the pretext that in order to achieve the delayed evangelization of the aborigines, it was a necessary to concentrate them in villages. Accordingly, the Marqués de Falces, Viceroy of New Spain, assigned areas for these so-called places of "reduction," or reservations, an arrangement that was known as *fundo real.* Continuing with this policy, Felipe II ordered, in 1573, that the villages, or rather the sections set aside for administrative purposes, should contain water, entrances and exits, and adequate tillable land. There was also a provision for a piece of common land, a league in length, where the Indians could keep their cattle, "without mingling with others of the Spaniards."

The discussion disclosed how even these meager rights—in comparison to pre-Conquest holdings—were taken away from the Indians during the Colonial era and most sweepingly in the Díaz epoch. Around 1905, Díaz ordered a resurvey of 125 million acres (50 million hectares), parceling out the project among twenty-nine companies, not on the usual basis of one-third as payment for the work, but a much larger part, and permitting the companies to buy up the balance at virtually their own prices. An era of speculative land grabbing followed. The Díaz *políticos* were quick to take advantage of this chance for fabulous gains. In any event, less than eight million pesos entered Mexico's treasury for the surrender to private ownership of one-fifth of the national domain. The discrepancies found in old titles and the vagueness of boundary lines supplied the pretext for the voiding of claims. In the confusion, it was the great estate owners, the *latifundistas,*[11] who benefited, and the villages, especially the Indian communities, who were the chief victims.

One of the Yucatecans of our party recalled the notorious legal case of the Indians of the pueblos of Xbohom, Sosichen, and Xpambiha, which was reported in 1909 in the *Revista de Yucatán.*[12] The lands of these pueblos were declared *baldíos*[13] by the court and awarded to Don Olegario Molina, the Díaz Minister of Agriculture who was already Yucatán's largest landowner. All of the inhabitants who over the years had labored to dig wells, plant gardens, and build houses were dispossessed, losing all their spring planting and their means of sustenance for the coming year. The *Revista* article discreetly commented that the *campesinos* had gained nothing from their court action except the right to dismantle their houses and transport them elsewhere within a certain short time limit.

A serious examination of the land problems of the Indians was also simultaneous with the beginning of the 1910 Revolution, when Francisco I. Madero in his "Plan of San Luis Potosí" formally proclaimed among his principles the return of lands taken from the pueblos. Four years earlier, in June 1906, the patriots in exile, headed by Ricardo Flores Magón, who formulated the Program of the Partido Liberal[14] in St. Louis, Missouri, had included the land question among the provisions of the epochal document. Madero stated the urgent need for restoring possession and ownership of their lands to numerous Indian communities in these terms:

> In taking unique advantage of the Law for Common Lands, numerous small owners, in their majority, Indians, have been deprived of their lands, either through a decision of the Developments Department or verdicts of the tribunals of the Republic. Since there is complete justification in a restitution of lands to their former possessors who were despoiled in this arbitrary manner, such dispositions and verdicts are held to be subject to revision, and those who acquired these properties in such an immoral way, or their heirs, will be required to return them to their original owners, to whom they will pay indemnity for damages suffered.

But as Felipe himself, now entering spiritedly into the discussion, stated, the first specific method for agrarian reform found expression in Emiliano Zapata's "Plan de Ayala" of November 28, 1911, calling for a distribution among the landless of a third part of the nation's great estates. He recalled that the first official division of lands during the Revolution took place in Morelos on April 30, 1912, under Zapata's authorization, more than a year before Constitucionalista General Lucio Blanco cut up large estates for the benefit of the poor.[15]

Dr. Morley asked Felipe about his own association with Zapata in the early days of the Revolution. He replied that he had been with the agrarian leader for several years, working mostly in Cuautla and in other towns of Morelos. But realizing that the land distribution program was in the most capable hands in Zapata's territory, he decided to return to his native Yucatán in the hope that he might work there with General Salvador Alvarado in the enforcement of the Agrarian Law of January 6, 1915, promulgated in Veracruz by Venustiano Carranza, then the First Chief of the Constitutionalist Army and head of the Executive Branch of the Mexican Republic.

This law, it was pointed out, was basic to the Mexican Agrarian Law as it then stood, and in synthesis it made these essential provisions: It declared null and void the alienation of communal lands of the Indians, and all obligations, sales, concessions, and evasions realized in disobedience to the laws of June 26, 1856. Authorizing the creation of a national Agrarian Commission in each state and territory and the particular executive committees they would require, it also empowered the military chiefs, previously authorized, to give or restore *ejidos* in an interim capacity to the soliciting villages. Felipe added that the Law of January 6, 1915, had been elevated on February 5, 1917, through Article 27, to the category of Constitutional law, in order to expedite the political constitution of the Republic.

Later, when I asked Felipe to tell me something more about his Zapatista days, he spoke freely and volunteered interesting details. He related how with the first Revolutionary expression of agrarian reform—sounded on November 28, 1911, in Zapata's "Plan de Ayala," as a call for *immediate* expropriation and distribution of a third part of the great estates among the landless—he went to Morelos to join the movement that so closely coincided with his own ideas of social justice . . . By that time, he explained, a whole year had elapsed since Madero in the agrarian plank of the "Plan de San Luis Potosí" had pledged to return to the Indians their illegally confiscated communal holdings. It was Zapata's slogan, "Tierra y Libertad," accompanied by "direct action" to guarantee its translation into reality, that had won his allegiance. In 1912, he added, he joined the Zapatista ranks serving as *proveedor* (purveyor), buying the foods and other supplies for the Liberating Army of the South. With the Zapatista delegation, headed by Antonio Soto y Gama, he arrived at the Hotel Morelos on October 24, 1914, two weeks after the opening of the historic sessions. Jesús Silva Herzog, who, as a young journalist for the newspaper *Redención* of San Luis Potosí, reported that the Zapatistas gave the convention its ideological content. Felipe himself recalled the heated arguments and the convincing discussions of Zapata's Revolutionary principles of agrarian reform. Through the persuasive oratory of Díaz Soto y Gama, who appeared on the rostrum in a *charro* outfit, with a drill *guayabera* and an enormous brimmed straw sombrero, the Zapatista delegation was able to swing the convention members from a virtual worship of Venustiano Carranza to naming General Eulalio Gutiérrez, instead, as Provisional President.

Records on file in the archives of the Ejército Libertador del Sur (the Liberating Army of the South) confirm, with several documents I was later to discover, Felipe's recollections of his Zapatista activities. Among them is a letter written by Felipe in March 1913 to General Emiliano Zapata then in Cuernavaca, in which he manifests his sympathy with the movement to deliver lands to the *campesinos* and his complete agreement with the postulates of the "Plan de Ayala." This document was found in the archives collected in Cuautla by General García in August 1913.

The Liberator Army archives also contain a report on Felipe's interview with Zapata at Milpa Alta of the Federal District in July 1914. During their long conversation, Zapata impressed upon Felipe the urgent necessity of struggling for agrarian ideals in Yucatán, a struggle which Felipe solemnly promised the Caudillo he would carry on to the end.

A third document written in Mexico under a November 1914 date records Felipe's appointment by Zapata as Colonel of Cavalry. Another, bearing a December date of the same year, gives an account of Felipe's interview with Zapata in the General Barracks of Tlaltizapán, Morelos.

Felipe did not mention that he was present in Mexico City when Zapata, Francisco Villa, and General Gutiérrez, as a short-lived triumvirate, watched from the central balcony of the National Palace what Sr. Silva Herzog describes as "the resplendent march of the Division of the North," but Licenciado Arturo Sales Díaz states that he was there at the time. In any case, it was at this period in the capital that Felipe met Sales Díaz, then third judge of the Federal District. Sent to prison for his Carranza affiliations by the government emanating from the Aguascalientes Convention, he gratefully recalls that Felipe personally undertook to secure his liberty and protected him until the Villistas and Zapatistas left the city, a step taken because General Obregón, obeying orders of the First Constitutional Chief, was advancing from Puebla.

Felipe was still in New Orleans, where he was staying with his brother Benjamín when the reactionary *hacendados* sponsored the so-called Separatista movement,[16] supplying money and arms to the adventurer Abel Ortiz Argumedo to head a revolt of secession from Mexico, launched in February 1915. Carranza sent a government force to crush the uprising. In a sanguinary battle at Blanca Flor, many inexperienced young men and boys were killed. The victory won at so great a cost in terms of Yucatecan youth was achieved by General Salvador Alvarado, who arrived in Yucatán on assignment from Carranza to put down the rebellion. In recognition, Alvarado was appointed Operations Chief and State Provisional Governor. Meanwhile, Ortiz Argumedo had absconded with the funds provided by the Separatista *hacendados.*

In connection with the carrying out of the agrarian reform movement in Yucatán, Felipe wrote from New Orleans to his brother Acrelio on July 8, 1915. The letter, in answer to one dated June 24 of the same year, which he had received from his brother praising the administration of the new Governor and military Commander, Salvador Alvarado, is as follows:

> I am happy, dear brother, that you are convinced of the "justice" that is being bestowed by Sr. General Alvarado, of whom, as I see by the Yucatán press, they are making a saint or a little less. I cannot give credit to such bombast because I know from experience that the function of the press in these times when the public liberties are being contested is to muzzle the principal valve of humanity and to suppress it even to the right to think.
>
> But you seem highly satisfied there and, I repeat, I am pleased. I firmly believe that you really are satisfied, since you know how to think and to equate matters so as to give them their just value. With respect to the most honorable enemies of Delio (Moreno Cantón) what they do does not surprise me, because I am convinced that if he were governor, they would also play the toady to him, since this individual does not possess a shred of dignity nor of shame.
>
> Very well then, do you know the meaning of justice?
>
> I suppose now they will begin to treat Indians as equals—will return to them that of which they have miserably robbed them, as had been done in the states that Zapata dominates—Morelos, Guerrero, and Mexico, that the *ejidos* will be given back to the pueblos. . . . I suppose also, dear brother, that the plantings have been left in benefit of the *ayuntamientos*[17] and that by this time they will be receiving compensation for their labor with the *henequén,* which they must transport to those who scrape it—certainly not the *hacendados,* but the real agriculturists, those who plow the earth, sow it, and burn the stubble—the very ones, in short, to whom lands have been distributed in the states I mention.
>
> Also, dear brother, they must have already established the Rationalist Schools to teach the children and the youth the truth about the things they

should know so that they might not be exploited nor exploit others. Also, they must no longer have priests of those religions that, in large measure, have contributed to the enslavement of humanity. And finally, because of what you say, Yucatán must now be enjoying a period of real happiness. And if all that you say is actually the case there, then, with all my soul, I congratulate you and my countrymen. In this event, I shall soon begin to seek the means to return to my native land, because if that which I have pursued for so many years is now being realized, I, too, have the right to enjoy it, since I believe I have suffered more than many others in that state. But unfortunately, realism makes me see that they are not as happy there as one might suppose. There are men who toady and who will always toady while they have authorities to flatter in order that they might exploit their fellow men. By this, I do not mean to say that nothing has been done there. I am informed that Gen. Alvarado has done what he has been able to do in the midst of the horrible corruption in which society lives. In any event, I firmly believe that conditions are better now than in the days of Ávila y Santos.

Soon thereafter, Felipe did find the means to return to Yucatán. He was met at Progreso by Acrelio, who recalls that his brother entrusted him with a small metal box containing one of General Zapata's documents. "Felipe asked me," he said, "to guard it carefully, suggesting that it be hidden in the storage room of our father's wholesale establishment. Destiny decreed that the place made of *huano* palms should burn down and the secret of the box was, of course, lost."

The gold and purple glory of the sunset measured up to Felipe's predictions, and when we motored through the "White City" en route to our respective domiciles, the walls of marble palaces along the Paseo Montejo were still aglow with rose-tinged light.

That evening another *banquete,* followed by an illustrated lecture on Chichén Itzá, in preparation for our weekend visit to the most famous of America's pre-Hispanic capitals—the site of Carnegie's future research—enchantingly occupied us until long after the Cathedral bells struck twelve.

Then, in fitful dreams, I nebulously floated through the night visions of a radiant Maya *fiesta* dress. But for longer hours, as I lay awake in the darkness, the secret intoxication of a newly awakened love was diffused through every fiber of my physical being, charging with ineffable magic each thought and intuitive impulse. Together, mind and heart vibrated with the rapturous discovery that heaven is earthbound, that no promised bliss of any afterlife could surpass the mortal heritage of supreme joy, mine, at this hour, in the here and now.

Early the next morning the *simpática modista,* Sra. Marcelina Pérez, called on me at the Cantón residence, announcing that she had come at the request of the Señor Gobernador to take my measurements for a *traje de Mestiza,* if I found it convenient. She explained that Don Felipe's order called for a beautiful costume of the finest white silk, trimmed with precious old petit point embroidered on ivory satin. She would do her utmost, she said, to make something "especially lovely," and she hoped I would be pleased with the result.

# 9. Motul

Adjusting, it seemed, to some happily preordained plan, the "formal" Friday interview took place in Felipe's native Motul instead of at the Liga Central as scheduled. Calling for me in time to keep my 9:30 appointment, Antonio handed me a note from his idolized *jefe,* in which a change in our program was suggested. The message reminded me that it was a "free day" for the American guests, permitting them to inspect the schools, churches, markets, and the city's historic buildings. Consequently, he, too, had declared a "free day," and it would please him "immeasurably" if I would accompany him to Motul to visit his mother, who had already expressed a desire to know me. If I found this plan "agreeable," he would personally guarantee that I would not miss any of the local points of interest on the day's itinerary of my fellow expeditionaries.

The railroad trip, Felipe explained, would require about three hours—"long enough for *several* interviews." We could dine with his mother—at the same old family home where he spent his boyhood—do a little sightseeing, and return to Mérida in time for the late banquet arranged for the archaeologists and tourists in the foyer of the Teatro Peón Contreras.[1] He added that Profesora Rosa Torre, the dedicated little *regidora* whom I had met at Suma, would join us. Both she and his sister Elvia, who was already in Motul, were slated to speak at an important regional session of the Feminist Leagues there.

I eagerly accepted so promising an invitation. Antonio drove me to the railroad station to see me aboard the special train and went back to the Liga for Felipe and Maestra Rosa. Again I experienced the ecstatic mood of the night's wakeful hours, as Felipe greeted me in a shaft of brilliant sunlight. His tall figure clothed in white linen, his radiant smile, the gleam that flashed from the depths of his "eyes of jade," combined to give credence to a belief current among his Inditos—as I later learned—that he wore a halo. As for myself—despite the archaeological anachronism—I could think of no better metaphor to describe his "resplendent" quality than a gentle, kindly Maya version of the Aztec solar deity Tonatiuh, who discharged the functions of the Celestial Señor and whose daily spectacle in the heavens was so vitally associated—in the religion of Anáhuac—with all terrestrial existence.[2]

With his invariable down-to-the-good-earth approach to all problems, Felipe did not leave me long adrift in the ethereal blue. "Well, here I am, Almita," he announced. "Behold your willing victim! Now you may carry out your threat to ask me many 'many personal questions,' and I'll do my utmost to give honest answers regardless of the great embarrassment this may cause me."

Antonio, who had placed the big red Packard in the freight car ahead for use in Motul, retired with Profesora Rosa to the opposite corner of the observation lounge, where they doubtless exchanged the loving sentiments they held for one another and discussed secret plans for their coming marriage. Felipe cheerfully responded to my journalistic prodding and recalled some incidents of his early home life that served as prelude to my meeting with his mother, Doña Adela Puerto de Carrillo. In our very first conversation during the Kanasín ride, he had described her as a "truly remarkable woman." And now, filial devotion was mingled in his voice with national pride when he spoke of her valor, her profound love of country, the wise counseling she gave to each of the surviving fourteen of her seventeen children. What commanded his deepest admiration, he said, was the fact that besides the enormous responsibility of bearing and rearing a family—exceptionally large *even* for Yucatán—she always managed to find time for impersonal matters beyond the domestic circle, lending thought and effort to the general betterment, keenly alive not only to the interests of her own community but to world problems as well. Those closest to her, he said, regarded her as a "modern-day Roman matron," because of her many noble qualities and civic virtues.

Felipe cited several instances that demonstrated his mother's intense feeling for the common welfare and for the liberty-inspired causes of the Indian people, even though, as he remarked with an amused smile at the rather incongruous idea, she was said to be a descendant of the Conquistador Juan Díaz de Solís. He related that once in the period when, with the help of his brothers, he was organizing Ligas de Resistencia in Yucatán and throughout southeastern Mexico, Doña Adela came in the middle of the night to the rooms of her eight sons, all sleeping in dormitory-like quarters that opened upon the big patio of the Carrillo home. Arousing them by flashing her lantern over each of their beds, she said in stern tones: "What, how can it be that I find ye here sleeping peacefully surrounded by all the creature comforts while your blood brothers, the Maya Quiché, are fighting and dying in a just revolution in Guatemala? Have done with your organizing of *sinvergüenzas*—shameless ones—into Ligas until the sufferings and sacrifices of those other Maya end in victory . . . *¡Váyanse!* . . . Go, all of ye, to Guatemala and join the Revolutionaries in their struggle!" Felipe recalled, too, how on other occasions, Doña Adela, making her nocturnal rounds of the extensive premises with her inseparable lantern, discovered bombs that had been placed in front of the house by the *enemigos*. More than once she had lifted the crude but deadly devices with her bare hands and carried them out of harm's way to the center of the Plaza of Motul.

As I had requested, Felipe began "from the beginning" with his story. He explained that, in the 1880's, Motul offered scant facilities for education above the primary grades. Yet the teachers were so thorough and conscientious that in the few years under their influence, the normally serious child developed a desire and laid the sound foundations for more advanced personal studies. "Basic to all progress of the individual and the state," he observed, "is the sacred role of the *maestro*." In his own case, he added, he would always cherish grateful memories of Prof. José Isabel Manzanilla Medina, the director of the first school he attended, once maintained by the Ayuntamiento of Motul. Later, he was enrolled in another public school, located near the Municipal Palace and directed by Prof. José Rivero. Due to the city's financial deficit and its inability to meet teachers' salaries, the school closed. With his brother Gualberto, he entered the private Catholic School of San Juan Nepomuceno, supported by the parents of the pupils and directed by another conscientious though less stimulating master, Juan de Ancona, who later became a priest. With the replenishment of the Motul treasury, the lay schools were reopened, and Felipe and Gualberto returned to the animating guidance of Prof. Manzanilla Medina. Later, when San Juan Nepomuceno was rebuilt, the three Carrillo brothers, including Eraclio, at that time the youngest, went back to the Catholic institution.

During these school years Felipe, unlike his brothers, rarely assisted in the carpentry and cabinetmaking shop of his father, Don Justiniano Carrillo. He preferred, instead, to work outdoors, and each afternoon when classes were over, he would ride horseback to a small piece of land, about three miles from Motul, which Don Justiniano had recently purchased. Here, he attended to the upkeep and improvement of the place, chopped wood, and watered the ten or twelve head of cattle. In connection with Felipe's care of the cattle, Elvia later recalled an occasion at the *finca* when the generous-hearted Felipe gave away, without permission, a valuable milk cow. Don Justiniano was furious and whipped the unauthorized donor of the family patrimony—one of the very few instances, she would remember, that her normally tolerant father had raised his hand in anger to any of his sons. Felipe took his punishment stoically but with curious prophecy in his words, cried out: "*No me mates, papacito, porque yo voy a inmortalizar tu nombre*—Don't kill me, Papa, because I am going to immortalize your name."

At the period, Felipe related, vanes on windmills were unknown in Yucatán and the water had to be hand-drawn in a bucket from a depth of twelve meters.

These and other chores on his father's *finca* and the neighboring henequen plantations brought him in daily contact with the Indians. Communicating with them in Mayan, which he spoke ever since he could remember, he learned their intimate problems. And even as a child, he could not help but see that the system under which they existed always favored the side of the rich and that the *jefes políticos* were the *caciques,* or chiefs whom the government had placed at the service of the great landowners.

The Motul of Felipe's youth, as later described by his brother Acrelio, was a prosperous city of fifteen thousand inhabitants, connected by a forty-four-kilometer highway with Mérida. Another fine road running north led to the Port of Telchac, where hundreds of families flocked each summer to enjoy its clean, cool beaches. The sumptuous mansions in the residence section indicated the affluence of the *hacendados* who, at the turn of the century, began to realize enormous incomes from the cultivation and exploitation of henequen. Their ostentatious drawing rooms displayed German pianos and elaborate Austrian vitrines filled with precious bibelots. French period furniture and brocaded silk hangings adorned their boudoirs, while domestic services were performed by pretty, attractively costumed young girls. This luxurious way of life was supported by a thriving commerce since, in addition to its agricultural wealth, Motul was the purchasing center for merchants of towns in the surrounding area. Frequent band concerts were held in the central plaza "J. M. Campos," always fragrant with *tulipanes,* roses, or orange trees. In the splendid Circo Teatro Motuleño were held the first bullfights with high-quality *toros* from Piedras Negras and Tepeyahualco. Flamboyant posters imported from Spain announced the *corridas,* which introduced famous toreros, both national and Spanish. Dramatic operatic and musical comedy companies featuring renowned artists appeared in the magnificent Teatro Motul, and the Cine Olympic and the Cine Ideal continuously showed the latest in motion pictures. There were visits also from the celebrated circuses, such as the Chiacini and the Circus Ricardo Bell. And invariably, as Acrelio records, the July *fiestas* and the Carnival "made history."

Motul's *cenote,* which Felipe, with tender recollection, had mentioned on our ride to Kanasín, was known as La Sambola. One of the delights of his boyhood, he told me on another occasion, was provided by its limpid and transparent waters flowing in perpetual coolness beneath a solid piece of curving stone that formed a protecting natural archway.

Listening to Felipe's objective account of how, following his brief schooling, he gained economic independence in his adolescent years, one might detect little connection between the prosaic tasks that occupied him and the meaning his life was destined to hold for the Maya race, the Mexican nation and tomorrow's world. But as the story unfolded, the monotonous routine limited to the physical exertion of lifting and hauling freight or driving mule teams with heavy loads to distant *haciendas* over jungle trails assumed a closer relation to his future apostolic role. No occupation of these youthful years, however humble, I gradually realized, was wasted. Like every square inch of canvas in the masterpiece of some immortal painter, every day of the wearisome period could be assigned its indispensable functioning in the total picture of his fully realized maturity. Each experience emerged finally as necessary and even inevitable for his complete, intimate knowledge, at the grassroots level, of the social and economic problems he would be called upon to solve. Moreover, then, as later, the two motifs were identical. Unchangeably, these remained a relentless personal struggle and a courageous, consistent effort for the relief of the oppressed and helpless.

The homely details of his simple, yet always moving narrative disclosed that upon leaving school, Felipe went to work on the railroad, owned by General Francisco G. Cantón and managed by the latter's son, Licenciado F. Cantón Rosado. Through efficiency and attention to duty, he became, in 1891, conductor of the passenger train that ran between Mérida and the Hacienda Cahuaca, a center for the laborers who had come there to open up the way for the building of the Valladolid road. Throughout most of the several years that he worked as conductor, he also held the position of baggage master, responsible for seeing that all baggage got off at the proper stations.

Only his unusual stamina and endurance enabled him to fill simultaneously the grueling demands of the two jobs. He would leave Cahuaca at seven o'clock in the evening for Motul by a three-wheeled handcar and be back at Cahuaca at four in the morning, leaving again for Mérida after a two-hours' rest.

Out of the money saved from the railroading jobs, he launched a trucking business of his own in Valladolid. With three *carretas*[3] and their corresponding mule teams, he transported sisal hemp and corn to Motul, driving one of the *carretas* himself. He and his two Maya Indian associates made commercial trips to the east and northeast regions of the state, supplying the merchants of Valladolid, Tizimín, and Espita with salt and other provisions. An important feature of this enterprise was the delivery of equipment to isolated *haciendas,* often through tropical forests, and the transporting of henequen back from the plantation warehouses to points of shipment.

It is unlikely that Felipe ever heard of the eighteenth-century United States frontiersman, Johnny Appleseed, who preached from the Old Testament prophets and Swedenborg, planting seeds as he journeyed back and forth across Ohio, and leaving fruit-bearing trees as living memorials of his passage through the wilderness. There was, indeed, wide divergence between the messages of these two New World humanists—one religiously, the other rationalistically inspired. Yet, in the ardent desire of each to improve the condition of his fellow man, they served a common cause. Both made their constant breadwinning wanderings the means of reaching the people, of communicating with them, instructing them—generous-hearted, public-spirited ministrations that have passed into American continental legend. In method, at least, one impression of Felipe at this period brings him close to the Bible-quoting, seed-throwing crusader among Ohio's backwoodsmen. As Mario Negrón Pérez, his friend and Motul townsman, was later to report: "It was not rare to see Felipe standing at the crossroads or in the plaza of some Yucatecan town, while the mules of his *carreta* rested, using the time to translate into Mayan the articles of the Mexican Constitution for the benefit of the Indians who crowded around him, teaching them to know their rights guaranteed by the Magna Charter, but trampled upon by their arrogant masters."

On February 2, 1898, while still in his twenty-third year, Felipe married Isabel Palma of Motul, daughter of a conservative *hacendado.* All members of the Carrillo Puerto family—as Elvia later informed me—refused to attend the wedding. Their absence was a protest against the cruelties of the bride's brother, Pedro Palma, to which they attributed the death, four years earlier, of his wife, the sensitive and talented Enriqueta, eldest of the Carrillo daughters. Elvia, who was then not quite ten years old, remembers how Felipe rushed home in his distress and carried her off in his arms in order to have at least one of his sisters or brothers present at the ceremony.

Before his marriage, Felipe had increased his trucking facilities to five *carretas,* but new family responsibilities required a larger income and he gave up the transportation business to go to Tampico, Tuxpan, and Tabasco, where he purchased mules for resale in Yucatán. This venture did not succeed, and returning to Motul, he resumed the mule team transportation. He carried on this tiresome labor until he met with a serious accident when setting out on a routine trip. Upon recovery, he engaged in a local delivery service, carting merchandise and building material from the railroad depot to stores and construction firms. It was in the course of this enterprise that he put his ideas about "eliminating the boss from the job" into practice by establishing his first systematic cooperative. Each Saturday night in a corner of the Parque José Marín Campos, accounts were settled with his workers and *compañeros* on a profit-sharing basis.

While Felipe reminisced and I diligently took down his every word in shorthand notes, Rosa and Antonio, who were within hearing distance, laughingly cautioned him against "understatement," with the same freedom that they might have shown toward members of their own families. "Don't be too modest, *por favor,*" Rosa said. "Remember that this is a fine chance to let the world know about our Partido and its peerless chief, because Almita is going to write all that you are saying to her in her newspapers."

And now I asked Felipe to tell me the things I most wanted to hear—about those events or incidents that had shaped his intellectual and spiritual development. I wanted to know how and why and when he had become "socially conscious," what had caused his awakening to the need of a different economic and social system, what had sparked his present outlook on man's relation to his fellow man and changed his views on orthodox religion.

"These are big questions, Almita," he commented in reply, "at least for a single sitting. Still, I might summarize the answers to them simply by saying that my 'awakening,' as you call it, came in two dramatic experiences, one in my seventeenth year and the other in my early twenties. While, as I've mentioned, my formal schooling was limited, I had inherited from my parents a love of books and music. We had a family orchestra, you know—in which I played the flute and the saxophone—and from childhood, I was an avid reader. I don't remember the time that I would not travel far to find a good book and spend my last peso to acquire it."

He told me how his chief source of stimulating literature in that period was his friend, the Cura[4] of Valladolid, who possessed not only an excellent library but a wide knowledge of classical music. With picturesque detail, he related that whenever he passed through that fine old city near Yucatán's eastern boundary, he never failed to visit the Rectoría.[5] Like the great Miguel Hidalgo, father of Mexican Independence; the San Juanista patriot-priest Velázquez of Mérida, disseminator of Libertarian doctrines; the famous scientist Padre Alzate, contemporary and eulogist of Benjamin Franklin—all of whose libraries bulged with the works of the French rationalists—the Cura of Valladolid, Felipe explained, had stocked his bookshelves with volumes compiled by the Encyclopedists, radical disciples of Diderot and D'Alembert, who submitted all issues to the analytical glare of the lamp of reason. Although Felipe did not imply it, the Cura must have been clearly aware of his young visitor's superior mind and generous heart when he invited him to browse at pleasure among his books. On one of these happy occasions, to which Felipe assured me he looked forward "with tremendous anticipation," he discovered *Le contrat social,* by Jean-Jacques Rousseau. Fascinated, fired by a new passion as the significant message of the philosopher gradually emerged from the French text, above all, thrilled that the validity of his own intuitions about democracy and government with the consent of the governed had been supported by so discerning a thinker, Felipe read on and on through the night, oblivious to everything but the rewarding if slow task of extracting, one by one, the spiritual building blocks for his new universe from the foreign language of the printed pages. Finally, at dawn, he asked permission of his understanding host to remain there "for a few days" while he studied every enlightening word of Rousseau's epochal revolutionary document.

"I did not leave the Rectoría until two weeks later," Felipe admitted. "And during all that time I was out of the Cura's library barely long enough to eat and to bathe. That experience determined my future conclusions about humanity's most vital problems and, to a large extent, my personal efforts to alleviate some of the worst conditions. At least, it definitely spurred my ambition to remedy the terrible injustices I saw everywhere around me in Yucatán."

The second event in his youth that was to have, he observed, lifetime repercussions in his purpose and action, occurred one Sunday morning on a vast henequen plantation near Chemax, where he stopped to deliver supplies. In front of the administration building, he noted that guards with canes were herding the enslaved male workers who had just emerged from religious services in the *hacienda* chapel into two facing rows, a few feet apart. He thought the men were waiting there for some kind of an inspection, until he was told that a woman who had been late for roll call the previous day without sufficient excuse was about to be punished. Then he heard a female voice, sobbing and shrieking in agonized terror, while a young Maya woman, completely nude, was being dragged into public view at the head of the double line, a point from which she was forced o walk forward between walls formed by men of her own race, as well as Yaquis, Chinese and Koreans. When she sank to the ground in an effort to hide her shame, she was rudely handled by the guards, who shoved her back into a straight path down the long, narrow *vía dolorosa.*

Felipe did not drive his mule team to Motul that day. He remained to plead with the *hacienda* workers, evading the suspicions of the guards by talking to individuals or small groups, arousing them through his impassioned words to a full awareness of the outrage they had just witnessed against their own mothers, wives, and daughters, a revolting offense against all the people of the Mayab. In their ancestral tongue he called upon them to organize secretly, so as to be strong and united for that inevitable moment when they could strike for liberation. At these surreptitious Chemax meetings was born the dream of the Liga de Resistencia—the League of Resistance—realized in and gradually expanding into a powerful Yucatecan federation that was later to penetrate and embrace the six states of southeastern Mexico, claiming the allegiance and defining the faith and hope of exploited millions.

Edesio, one of Felipe's seven younger brothers, met us at the railroad station and escorted us to the Carrillo home, where he lived with his mother and maintained the adjoining wholesale mercantile establishment left by his father. Closely resembling Felipe but with blue-gray eyes instead of "ojos de jade,"[6] the handsome Edesio, with his finely chiseled features, fair complexion and athletic build, would have commanded attention anywhere as a superb specimen of young manhood. I had the impression that he might have creditably substituted for Pantarkos, favorite model of the great Phidias, when he carved out of white Pentellic rock his immortal *Ephebe*—the ideal of Greek youth. Felipe's junior by fifteen years, Edesio's own public career was already well launched. He not only headed the Liga de Resistencia of Motul but had just been elected *alcalde,* or municipal president.

From the moment that Doña Adela greeted us in her high-ceilinged, old-fashioned *sala,*[7] I realized that Felipe had described her with complete accuracy as "a truly remarkable woman." Weighing, apparently, no more than one hundred pounds, and with her soft wavy hair still a glossy black, Doña Adela, despite her seventy-two years, was as agile and as sure of her movements as she was intellectually alert. An innately dignified bearing and a simple, long navy blue taffeta gown with its antique lace *fischu* added illusionary impressiveness to her slight, erect, compact figure. But it was the keen, appraising expression in her dark eyes, flashing through bifocal glasses both worldly and spiritual awareness, that suggested a highly charged current of personal dynamics flowing beneath the containment of poised authority and mellow wisdom. At first sight, I knew that I would love and admire her.

Felipe embraced her warmly and lifted her off the ground as if she were a small child. Closing his eyes, he kissed her forehead as he said to me: "Almita, I want you to know my marvelous *madrecita* and know her very well, because she is entirely *worthy* to be the mother of Felipe Carrillo."

Doña Adela was ready with an answer in the same bantering mood when, lowered from her midair position, she asked us with a feigned expression of disbelief: "Did you all hear what *este gran egoista*—this great egotist—was saying? One might imagine that our Socialist Governor believes himself worthy to be the son of his parents."

Elvia left her Feminist League conference long enough to welcome us. Rosa and Felipe accompanied her back to the session, all agreeing to return in an hour or so with two or three friends for one of Doña Adela's famous home-cooked Motul-style *comidas.*[8]

When we were alone, I said to her: "Señora madre de Felipe,[9] your son is very good to the Indians, but he is a bit stubborn with me. He does not tell me all that I need to know about those days when he was a little boy and a young man here in Motul. But he assures me that you have a wonderful memory and that you will tell me everything. I want to know these details, not out of curiosity, but because I am writing an article about him and his work for one of our national magazines and for various newspapers in the United States."

She graciously consented to tell me "all that she could remember," and I begged her to "begin with the ancestors."

"For that, *niña,*" she replied, "we must go to the Registro Civil[10] in Mérida, but

I can tell you about some of them. My great-grandmother, on my mother's side, was Doña Santos Díaz de Solís of Peto. Her father was born in Spain. Her daughter, my grandmother, was Doña Juana Solís, also of Peto. She married Manuel Puerto of Motul. Ah, she was very fearless, very energetic, and very rich. She owned a silk establishment on the plaza of Motul and, besides, many buildings in the city. My grandfather was a trader and traveled a great deal. They had three sons and one daughter, my mother. When he did not return from his trips within a reasonable time, my grandmother went in search of him. Sometimes her trip would last two or three months, and at that period, one confessed before embarking at Sisal for Havana."

Doña Adela said that her mother, Josefa Puerto, married Domingo Mendiburu, a *trigueño*[11] of Motul. She regretted to tell me that he deserted his wife and their four children, all girls, and ran off to Belize, where he married Lucinda Kelly of England. Fourteen years later he returned and informed the young Adela that he was her father. "*Tal vez*—perhaps" was her laconic reply. In speaking of her girlhood, Doña Adela continued with the family story:

> I was not yet fifteen when I married Justiniano Carrillo. He was thirty-three years old, a military man. His hair was a chestnut shade, and he wore a mustache. His complexion was fair and high colored. His eyes were light hazel and sparkling. His features were very delicate, like my daughter Ernilda's. His father, Felipe Santiago Carrillo, was born in Sotuta and was the owner of a very large merchandise store and a distillery there. He was a very handsome man, fair with blue eyes. Don Justiniano's mother, Josefa Pasos, was born in Tixkokob. When he was fifteen, my husband came to live in Motul with his cousin Condia. For thirteen consecutive years he was a member of the *columna volante*, the flying column. Upon the arrival of Maximilian and Carlotta at Campeche in May 1864, Justiniano, then eighteen years of age, was one of the four young soldiers selected for strength and good appearance to carry the Empress from the prow of the little tender to the shore, carefully lifting her above the waves and placing her on dry land. "Bueno, muchachos . . . Valientes, mis soldados,"[12] she said, in appreciation of their gallant assistance, later rewarding each one with a new uniform and a pair of shoes.

Doña Adela continued:

> Don Justiniano's father, for whom Felipe was named, was a poet. And Don Justiniano himself frequently wrote verses. When he would go to gamble, perhaps with five pesos, he would say to me: "I shall gamble this much for

a diversion." He did all things with calmness and moderation. He would win much more than he lost, but he would stop when he had won. When he returned from a game, he would write in his notebook, "Impressions of a Gambler," in verse. Felipe's uncle, also Felipe Carrillo, was another member of the family who wrote poetry.

I asked Doña Adela if she could locate any of Don Justiniano's verses. There were many in his notebooks, now stored away, she replied, but she thought she could remember one and would recite if for me. It was written while Don Justiniano was *alcalde*—mayor—of Motul and when Felipe was serving for a few months at the Registro Civil. Part of his duties there, she explained, was to burn the bones of the poor who had been disentombed and whose remains were not reclaimed by friends or relatives. One day, Don Justiniano came to see how Felipe was meeting his new responsibilities at the cemetery, and with his cane he turned over the skull of an infant girl, from whose earth-filled eye socket grew a tiny flower. He brought the little skull home, cleaned it and had it put back in the Registro Civil as a scale weight, and then wrote these lines:

¡Bella flor, qué funesta es tu suerte,
que al primer paso que diste
tropezaste con la muerte!
Llevarte es cosa triste,
y dejarte en donde naciste
es dejarte con la muerte.

Beautiful flower, how said is your destiny!
At the beginning of life
you stepped into death.
It's of no use to take you,
but if I leave you here,
I will leave you with death.

Doña Adela resumed her recollections:

Now and then, Don Justiniano would order beer. When they were all seated at the table, he would have some poured in each glass. Jokingly, and always with entire freedom, the boys would ask: "What goes, Papa?—*¿Qué pasa, papá?*"

"Well, I wanted some beer, and I thought perhaps that you would all like to have some, too," he would answer.

Occasionally, he would do the same with a bottle of very sweet wine—*vino de San Juan.* But moderation ruled all his acts, and his sons were models of temperance. As boys, none of them ever went near a saloon. They grew up in a simple home, one without luxury, but there was always plenty and no one ever lacked the things that made for health and average comfort. At all times there were at least twenty persons in our house—fourteen in the family, three nurses, a cook, and a laundress. The bread alone for the evening meal was eighteen pesos daily, and who knows how much more for breakfast. When the baker would come in the morning and place the bread on the table, each child would select *pan dulce, teleras,* or *bolillos*[13] according to his taste. "*Mamacita,* give me mine, now," they would ask, but I would make them wait until the breakfast hour. If Don Justiniano was near, he would gently scold me, saying: 'Let them have some now. For this we are working, you and I—to give the poor little fellows what they need and want." Breakfast was at ten o'clock, dinner at four o'clock, and chocolate was served at six o'clock, and before bedtime, rice and milk, *chiote con miel,*[14] in place of sweets. They broke so many dishes that I had to keep buying new sets constantly. Finally, in desperation, I bought a whole tubful of *jícaras,* and afterwards they ate from *puras jícaras*—their little white gourds.

It was Enriqueta, the oldest of the daughters, who taught them table manners and politeness. She studied to be a teacher at the Colegio Francés in Mérida, but Don Justiniano did not want her to be a *maestra* and she became proficient in bookkeeping.

Doña Adela explained that the education Don Justiniano gave his sons was so special that it was completely out of its epoch, for, in that period in Yucatán, education was based on Catholicism, or had a Catholic influence. She described her husband as a "free thinker, a man dedicated to his work, his family, moderately cultured, and very deeply concerned about the protection of the poor and the laboring class." He was highly esteemed, she said, in the city of Motul and in his native Sotuta, "the city of the great Maya king, Nachi Cocom, to whose family he belonged, fifth in order of direct lineage."

Indicative of his fine sense of justice and his sympathy for the exploited, Doña Adela cited Don Justiniano's attitude upon becoming the owner of a small piece of land. A friend had invited him to visit the site, and he was so pleased with it that he decided to purchase it, having in mind that it would be a good place to cultivate later with the help of Felipe and Gualberto. During transactions in setting boundaries to the property, Don Justiniano, whose liberal views were well known to all, gave the laborers three times more than the price paid in the region for this class of work. The neighbors visited him in a group protesting his action, requesting him not to pay so high a wage to the Indians, arguing that they must not become accustomed to receiving amounts larger than the standard. Don Justiniano answered his friends, stating that the wage seemed to him very reasonable and that it should not, therefore, prejudice their interests.

Doña Adela felt that Don Justiniano's independence of mind as well as his tactfulness were most clearly shown in his frequently expressed opinions in regard to the training of his daughters. When they reached the age of fifteen, they were permitted by custom to attend social affairs, to visit friends, or take part in diversions such as *fiestas* and balls, or religious ceremonies in the public churches. Whenever they were invited to the popular dances, he permitted them to accept with pleasure, since he himself was very fond of this type of recreation. But he had an entirely different attitude toward religious functions. He would plead some excuse to prevent their attendance, saying, for instance, to those extending the invitation that his daughters would not understand the priest since he spoke in Latin and the girls had not studied Latin. To other persons he would answer that he would gladly consent to let his daughters attend a church affair, if they could assure him that there would be a good orchestra. The music, he said, would distract them from an otherwise boring and tiring experience, through their not understanding the maneuvers of the priests. In this way, Doña Adela explained, Don Justiniano managed that his children held no particular grudge against the church nor harbored any love of religion. They were merely indifferent to it.

Doña Adela's account of the family discipline revealed an advanced system for any time or place. As each one of the Carrillo sons reached the age of fifteen, he was regarded as a man. They had no occasion to ask permission of their parents to go out in the evenings and amuse themselves with their friends. Don Justiniano fixed no hours for their return, but it was certain that at ten thirty or eleven o'clock at night all the boys were at home. In his hardware establishment, Don Justiniano never locked up his merchandise or his cash drawer, which were within reach of all of his sons. In the morning after breakfast, each one of them would go to the money boxes and take out a rational amount to spend for fruit and other sweets. No budget was established in the house because of the wide liberty permitted the children. But Doña Adela said that she and Don Justiniano preferred it this way, "which gave us all the sense of working together, parents and children, for our common welfare and happiness."

This liberty allowed Felipe to realize his altruistic nature at an early age. Constantly worrying about Motul's poor children, especially the fatherless boys, with whom he always made friends, from Don Justiniano's store he would supply them with the pencils and the copybooks they could not buy. His innate generosity, as Doña Adela—and later several neighbors who had grown up with him in Motul—related to me, was demonstrated in many ways. They remembered how Felipe used to divide his candies with these poor children and lend them his toys. In playing games, he displayed a sense of fairness and calmly accepted just decisions whether he won or lost.

When Doña Adela's narrative turned to Felipe's adolescence, she described him as a "very restless youth." She recalled that he did not like the idea of staying in the store, but wanted to move about and see the country. He felt sorry that he disappointed his father and used to say to her: "Pobre de mi papá."[15]

Always very manly for his years, Felipe was a tall, handsome lad. As Doña Adela related:

> When only eleven years old, he insisted upon having long trousers. We had our photographs taken that day, his eleventh birthday, in celebration. He would come home with his little jacket filled with wood, asking me to buy it from some Indian. I used to think of him as a *predestinado*—one born to help the helpless. As he grew to manhood, his mind seemed to be occupied almost entirely with the sufferings and problems of the Maya. Don Justiniano would often warn him: "*No es bueno ser redentor*—It is not good to be a redeemer." But Felipe would answer: "I am not working to have them pay me, but for the liberty of these Indians . . . If I come out crucified, I shall not turn back—*Aunque salga crucificado, yo no retrocedo.*" . . . But Don Justiniano would always insist, "The Indians will never thank you for this favor." "*Sin embargo*—nevertheless," Felipe would reply, "I must go on."

On one occasion during his sixteenth year, Felipe, as I later learned, had to acknowledge the validity of his father's warning on the thanklessness of the "redeemer's role." The episode, related by Edmundo Bolio Ontiveros in *De la cuna al paredón,*[16] involved a pretty young contortionist, the daughter of Pancho Quijano, owner of a traveling circus of the same name. During the prolonged stay of the troupe in Motul, Felipe became enamored of the girl, advertised on the billboards as La Niña Elvira. But the romantic youth was horrified at the thought that daily she was compelled to give dangerous and painful exhibitions before a bored public looking for new excitement. Pancho Quijano, always seeking fresh talent and observing the sympathy that existed between his daughter and the athletic youth, encouraged Felipe to learn the "tricks of the trade," personally training him in gymnastic acts on the bar and other spectacular acrobatic feats. The agile and dynamic Felipe proved so apt a pupil that he was invited to accompany the circus as a professional performer to Tixcocob, which he did, without consulting his parents. In consternation, Doña Adela and Don Justiniano, armed with an order from the Chief of Police of Motul for the return of the runaway minor to legal custody, drove to Tixcocob. When they entered the town, about twelve kilometers distant from Motul, they were speechless with amazement when they saw walls and buildings placarded with large posters announcing the debut of a sensational new trapeze artist, the young Felipe Carrillo Puerto of Motul. On presentation of the order from the Motul authorities to those of Tixcocob, Felipe was promptly delivered to his parents. He was truly remorseful, he said, for having caused them so much worry and trouble, but as he explained to them and, afterwards, to his companions, his impulsive act was caused not by the deep affection he felt for "La Niña Elvira," but by his fears for her safety and even for her life when executing her contortions in the circus arena. He had hoped that his devotion, which she seemed to return, might win her away from her "abhorrent sufferings" and, in this way, "redeem" the lovely and unhappy creature from a life of hardship and constant peril.

Doña Adela, looking back over the long period of her life with Don Justiniano, described it as a happy and spiritually rewarding one, despite the inevitable sorrows and loss of three of their young children. "The most treasured memories of our true companionship," she said, "are of those hours when we used to sit in our rocking chairs through the warm evenings, here in our patio. He would read to me while I knitted or sewed little garments for the babies that were on the way. He had a fine voice and enjoyed reading aloud from his favorite books."

A tender wistfulness replaced the sharp, penetrating expression in her appraising eyes as Doña Adela spoke of her husband's final days:

> He was thirty-two when he left the military service and went into the hardware business, here in this building. He kept it with strict attention to every detail—giving much public service besides—until the time of his death eight years ago. When the end came on February 26, 1915, at the age of seventy-eight, after several years of suffering from heart trouble, he was surrounded by all of his children. He died in the arms of Ernilda and the wife of Eraclio. From this very house, our eight sons bore his casket to the cemetery; four of them would carry the body of their beloved father for a while, then would step back, and the four others would take their places. A Motuleño remarked to a visitor as the cortege passed by: "*Dichoso él*—happy man—those are his eight sons!"

The entire city of Motul and many persons in every walk of life from nearby and distant pueblos attended his funeral. He was a friend to hundreds, and his passing was deeply felt in the whole region.

Turning now, at my urging, to Felipe's young manhood, Doña Adela recalled the following episode that caused great commotion in Motul but illumined at the same time her son's almost naive sincerity of spirit, ever in quest of truth: One day, a few months after his marriage, when he was not yet twenty-two years old, Felipe mysteriously disappeared. Isabel sent over to the family home to find out if he was there. Doña Adela assured her that she had not seen him, but that his twenty mules had been left in the patio. Don Justiniano was very grave, even angry, because several serious complications had arisen. The boys who drove the *carretas* went *borrachos.* Two of them were in jail, and he had sent the police to rescue one of them. The inspector inquired of him: "Where are your *compañeros?*"

"They are drunk."

"Where is your *jefe?*"

"*¿Quién sabe?*"[17]

Doña Adela had her suspicions, but she bade the servants search the well in case Felipe had fallen in. Meanwhile Don Justiniano and the brothers had to keep drawing up the water by hand pump to supply the mules. And at eleven o'clock at night, so as not further to arouse Don Justiniano's ire, Doña Adela would quietly slip out to the corral to feed the hungry animals, carrying ten sacks of *maíz*[18] on either shoulder and a stick in her hand to scare them. "Morillo," "Pajarito," "Canela," "Castaña," she would call as she placed their feeding bags over their noses. After five days Felipe presented himself at midnight: "*Buenas noches, mamacita.*"

"*Gran sinvergüenza*—big shameless one—where were you?"

"*Ah, qué lástima*—what a pity—*mamacita.* I never left Motul. I was with my great friend, Father Martín Calderón. He was showing me all of his wonderful books. He took them all down from the shelves for me."

"The *muchachos* are in the jail, drunk."

"Please don't worry, *mamacita.*"

"But I must pacify your father. I'll tell him that you went to a *finca* to look at some mules."

"All right, *mamacita,* but later I must tell him that I went to look at some books. I spent a long while looking for the poem that *papacito* recites:

> Cualquiera hija o criatura de cura o fraile
> que con pastor se casare,
> que tenga por cosa segura,
> que a los cuatro meses pare.
>
> Any servant maid of priest or friar
> who would marry a shepherd
> can be completely sure
> of delivering four months later.

"And for this you left me with twenty mules for five days?"

"But it was very important, *mamacita.* The Cura told me that the Catholic religion means nothing more than an effort to guard the public morals—to serve as a rein for humanity. He proved it all to me with his books."

The program of the morning's session of the regional Feminist Leagues—which Elvia had founded in Motul in 1912, as the first suffrage and equal rights group in the Republic—provided the main theme of table conversation during Doña Adela's delectable dinner. Both Elvia and Rosa and two of their Liga *compañeras* were enthusiastic about the impromptu remarks Felipe had made at his unheralded appearance at the meeting, when he urged the Liga members to make their life-conserving maternal viewpoint articulate on the question of aggressive international war. He had proposed, they reported, a drastic pacifist plan for bringing armed conflict to an end. "You women," he had told them, "have it within your power to change man's thinking on this barbarous system, a survival of the jungle. Within a few months, the insane bloodletting of centuries could be stemmed through the simple expedient of a united ostracism of the military uniform on the part of women. If you really desire a world in which your sons may live their lives without constant fear of being maimed or slaughtered by the sons of other mothers, whom they have never harmed, then you must be courageous enough to reject rather than flatter, as you now do, the men of the military caste who wear it as a symbol of the heroic."

Before we arose from the table, I announced that Doña Adela had given me many interesting facts about the family and especially about Felipe's boyhood. Elvia asked if her mother had told me about his protection of the birds. I replied that with so much to tell in so short a time, some incidents were necessarily omitted, but that I was eager to hear it.

Smilingly, Felipe requested Elvia to defer the "cuento de los pajaritos"[19] and other legends of the "boy marvel of Motul" until we were back on the train with three hours at our disposal. Meanwhile, he asked her permission to relate to me instead an incident in the life of their father—one that was his own constant source of admiration and pride.

In recognition, Felipe related, of Don Justiniano's years of distinguished military service and later civic leadership, President Díaz had him appointed *jefe político*—an enviable post that carried practically unlimited power and emoluments as "boss" of the governors of the six southeastern states. Don Justiniano accepted, but at the end of eight months, he addressed a letter to the dictator in which, after expressing profound gratitude for the honor, he declared: "Since I find, Sir, that my chief duty is to return escaped Maya slaves to their owners, I must, most respectfully, submit my resignation from the high office you have so generously entrusted to me."

As we left the Carrillo home, where the very walls seemed to vibrate with noble impulses and generous feelings—the spiritual residue of lives they had sheltered for more than half a century—Doña Adela promised Felipe that she would come to Mérida in a few days to attend some of his festivities for the Carnegie guests. And as she embraced me affectionately, she voiced the hope that I would find the "memories" she recalled helpful. Meanwhile, she assured me, she would put her mind to the matter, and when we next met in Mérida, she would perhaps have other *recuerdos* and *cuentos*[20] that, for the moment, had escaped her.

When we were again seated in the observation car for the train trip back to Mérida, Elvia informed Felipe that he had better place cotton in his ears because now she was going "to tell Almita some things about him that their mother might have overlooked," especially the tale of how in his childhood he used to rescue the birds. She began to tell the story:

> My brother commenced his lifelong labors for *los caídos*—the fallen—at the age of eight. During the summer months in our torrid heat and long period of drought, the birds all over Yucatán would die by the thousands. Felipe, always the leader of his brothers and playmates, was deeply moved by the sight each morning of scores of dead birds in the patio. He decided to try to prevent it and organized his companions—boys of his own age—into a juvenile "battalion of mercy." As a first step, he set them all to work, gathering twigs with which to build little cages. As the cages were completed, they were placed in the patio with cups of water and bits of food inside. The wickets were left open, and, in this way, as many as two thousand birds found sanctuary each season in the spacious patio during the months of parched earth and stifling, motionless air. As you know, all of Yucatán's rivers flow underground, and when there is no rain, the land becomes bone dry. So, gasping for breath, the tiny creatures would enter the cages and remain there, supplied daily with water and food by Felipe and his helpers for the duration of the summer. But with the first autumn breezes, heralding the end of the terrible heat, Felipe would set the little prisoners at liberty with the words: "*Vayan mis hijos . . . tengo tantos hijos . . . ¡Vayan a su libertad!*—Go, my sons . . . I have so many sons . . . Go to your freedom!"

Elvia concluded "the bird story" with the comment that Felipe at that time reminded her of a "young Saint Francis or even a boy Don Quixote with many Sancho Panzas at his side."

# 10. Conflicts and Amenities

The formal banquet on February 15, 1923, in the Teatro Peón Contreras of Mérida, "offered"—as the engraved invitation announced—"by the Constitutional Governor of the State of Yucatán to the scientists of the Carnegie Institution and the North American tourists," was perhaps the most positive indication of improved relations between the United States and Mexico in more than a decade.

During the long period of pre-atomic-age cold war separating the neighboring peoples that followed the overthrow of the Díaz regime in 1911, bitter enmity was fanned by acts of treachery and violence on both sides of the border. Among the grave offenses inciting the average Mexican to hatred of North Americans, and many even to a desire for revenge, was the ignoble role played by U.S. Ambassador Henry Lane Wilson during the Decena Trágica—the Ten Tragic Days—in mid-February, 1913, culminating with the assassination of President Francisco I. Madero and Vice President José María Pino Suárez at the hands of General Victoriano Huerta, the U.S. Embassy-approved usurper of the supreme power.

From the Mexican side, two atrocities ordered by Pancho Villa and carried out by his chiefs Rafael Castro and Pablo López aroused worldwide indignation. Both of these wanton and ruthless acts were committed, however, without the authorization or prior knowledge of any legally established or constitutional government. The first was the slaying on January 10, 1916, of eighteen foreigners, including fifteen North American employees of a mining company, who, at Santa Isabel Station, were shot after having been forcibly removed from a train en route from Ciudad Juárez to Chihuahua. Only one of the group managed to escape to tell the story of the massacre to a horrified public. The second was an attack on March 9 of the same year on the town of Columbus, New Mexico. Three soldiers were killed, seven of the military and five civilians were wounded, and various commercial establishments were looted and burned before the marauders fled back into Mexican territory.

In both countries other serious grievances widened the rift, some of them rooted, paradoxically, in good intentions. Woodrow Wilson's attempts, for instance, to destroy the power of the traitorous Huerta were obviously planned to help the Mexican people. When the assassin of Madero and Pino Suárez refused to resign after having been given ample opportunity to do so, on April 21, 1914, President Wilson ordered the occupation of Veracruz by United States troops, an act that involved the death of two gallant young defenders, cadets of the Naval Academy. The occupation and blockade, designed solely to oust Huerta—and with no motive of invasion or annexation—had been provoked by an attack on American sailors at Tampico. But its net result was merely to provide the intransigent Carranza with inflammatory material for stoking the fires of Mexican nationalism. Even his once-ardent supporter, Plutarco Elías Calles, pointed this out when in disillusionment he resigned from the Carranza cabinet.

The Veracruz "invasion" picture has recently been given deeper perspective by the American historian Charles Callan Tansill, who describes how the German ship *Ipiranga* delivered arms and ammunitions purchased by Huerta for use against Carranza himself.[1] This shipment, together with another from Germany, was landed at Coatzacoalcos shortly before the usurper fell. Despite the fact that the German arms arrived too late to do Huerta much good, as Isidro Fabela, Carranza's Minister of Foreign Relations, points out in his memoirs, the danger of a "takeover" by Germany or other European powers doing business with Huerta was present and could not be discounted by President Wilson.[2] Yet, in justice to Carranza's stand on principle, it must be said that although his cause would have been greatly benefited by intervention, he insisted unswervingly, as did his followers later, upon Mexico's full rights as a sovereign nation, regardless of internal weaknesses or peril.

In big-business circles however, an unremitting drive for intervention continued throughout the Carranza administration, adding fresh insult to already injured Mexican pride. The agitation, led by groups demanding "protection of American rights," precipitated an investigation by a Congressional Committee, headed by Senator Albert B. Fall, subsequently convicted of bribery in the Teapot Dome scandal.[3] The committee's findings recommended that no Mexican government be recognized unless it exempted Americans from certain provisions of the 1917 Constitution. On Mexico's refusal to accede to these conditions, affecting Constitutional Articles 3, 27, 33, and 127, the committee urged that "a police force consisting of naval and military forces of the United States be sent to Mexico."

In the interim between the outbreak of the Revolution and its consolidation under President Obregón, there had been sporadic efforts at international rapprochement, but these were mainly at the level of conflicting financial interests. Meetings of hard-dealing bankers representing the two governments were called by one group or the other for the purpose of gaining some national advantage, but showed little or no desire to further lasting across-the-border harmony. For the most part, the Americans aimed to recover heavy losses suffered by business between 1910 and 1920 and to fix indemnity for seized properties or the lives of innocent victims sacrificed during the period of lawlessness.

The Mexicans, on the other hand, sought to borrow desperately needed funds for rehabilitation and construction in many fields after the upheaval. This was a difficult task; for while the Obregón Government was daily demonstrating its stability, die-hard elements on both sides of the Rio Grande were vigorously striving to prevent any U.S. assistance or encouragement. Only the perseverance of the able Mexican negotiators and the support of a few staunch American friends, notably Mr. John Glenn, U.S. Consul in Tampico, finally induced the reluctant investors to risk additional capital and make it possible for the infant Revolutionary regime to survive at all. Fortunately, too, organized labor, inspired by its effective leaders—Samuel Gompers, Andrew Furuseth, and William H. Johnston of the Machinists Union—stood firmly by Mexican trade unionism. Continental solidarity and especially close ties with Mexico's workers became a leading issue at the Congress of the Pan-American Federation of Labor[4] held at Laredo in November 1918.

From other sectors, a few American statesmen and authors came passionately to Mexico's defense. These well-informed, peace-loving groups attributed the failure of the financial negotiations to the unjust demands made by Washington as the price of recognition. Despite mounting press criticism in the United States of the harsh policy of Secretary of State Charles E. Hughes, the Harding administration continued to require a treaty in advance of recognition. In public addresses and in widely distributed books and articles, this little band of highly articulate spokesmen reiterated the fact that for the two previous years Mexico had enjoyed a Constitutional, pacific, and progressive government—clearly the most stable since the overthrow of Porfirio Díaz. They maintained that the inflexible attitude of the United States towards the southern Republic was totally unjustified by the current situation.

On July 19, 1922, the withholding of recognition was denounced on the floor of Congress by Senator E. F. Ladd of North Dakota "as an unfortunate departure from our former standards of honorable and just dealings with other nations, both great and small." He declared it to be injurious to the best commercial interests of the United States and Mexico, even though "it may be advantageous to certain corporations and individuals in this country and elsewhere."

In his brilliant plea, bristling with challenging statistics, Senator Ladd argued that the withholding of recognition made it impossible for the Mexican government to borrow funds needed for the reestablishment of transportation, commerce, and agriculture, and that it "offered encouragement to certain sinister interests on the northern side of the border which have meddled unhappily in Mexico's internal affairs in the past and were showing an evident desire to do so again." The clear-sighted statesman pointed out that "last, but by no means least, it postponed the industrial and agricultural development of Mexico, which otherwise would speedily become one of the best customers of the United States and restore a languishing foreign commerce by huge purchases, furnishing orders to our idle factories and giving employment to our jobless workers."

Officials and financiers of both countries, however, were equally eager to adjust Mexico's national debt. While the Obregón administration had honorably assumed the old fiscal obligation — sometimes illegally incurred — it was endeavoring and eventually did succeed in achieving a considerable reduction of the astronomical sum demanded by the international creditors to more realistic figures. For, as a result of the millions of dollars borrowed during the dictatorship from foreign treasuries and private sources on promissory notes — in many cases providing for the payment of amounts far greater than those actually advanced — the national debt that burdened the sorely impoverished Mexican people was, at the period, one of the largest quotas per capita in the entire world.

Preceding by ninety days the celebrated Bucareli Conference opening in Mexico City on May 14, 1923, and with recognition of Mexico by the United States still eight months off, Felipe's banquet to the Carnegie expeditionaries reflected an epoch of deepened understanding, respect and confidence — one of closer human and social relations between the two countries. No antagonism or controversy impinged upon the festive mood of this cordial "goodwill" event. The happy, officially sponsored gathering, unclouded by any suspicion or skepticism, ushered in a new season that promised a changed and decidedly more agreeable political climate.

Neither the Socialist State of Yucatán nor the distinguished Carnegie Institution had hidden axes to grind. Under the universal aegis of science, the affair had been inspired by an earnest desire to collaborate in the impersonal task of penetrating the mystery of a remarkable autochthonous New World culture. Here, Mexicans and North Americans were meeting in a fraternal spirit to map out ways and means for retrieving knowledge of the common continental inheritance. The things that had long separated them — memories of aggressive invasions, nefarious land-grabbing, ideological feuds, treason and bloodshed — were all blotted out, at least for this interlude, in the realization of their mutual stake in a larger and unifying issue. It was an issue that equally concerned Governor Felipe Carrillo Puerto, descendant of Nachi Cocom, Lord of Sotuta, last defender of Maya sovereignty, and the scholars from the United States, dedicated seekers after historic truth. There seemed to be full awareness that only through joint action *now* would it be possible to salvage and preserve for the future the coherent evidence of Yucatán's splendid ancient civilization, key to the great American continental story—the precious endowment of both Republics.

These and similar elevated sentiments conveyed in toasts and responses—limited to nonalcoholic *refrescos*—passed during the convivial evening between the Yucatecan elite and the North American scientists in Spanish, Mayan, and English. Dr. Spinden, who was fluent in all three languages, replying to the introduction by the local archaeological society's president, assured the gathering that he and his fellow investigators from the United States had come to Yucatán with the hope of discharging a debt dating from the very inception of their national independence. For five-eighths of his country's vast agricultural wealth—the greatest in all human history—could be directly traced, he pointed out, to the intuitive knowledge and to the painstaking experimentation over millennia by the Maya race in southeastern Mexico and Guatemala.

It was Maya initiative and patient toil, he explained, that had made possible the present high living standards of the American people and established the world supremacy of their economy. Maya-produced nutritive edibles unknown to man's diet before the discovery of the Americas included many of the major crops not only of the United States but also of modern agriculture everywhere. Indigenous Middle American farmers had more than doubled Europe's food supply. Maya ingenuity and systematic labor, he added, had contributed to contemporary fare numerous products today regarded as table essentials. Among them he cited potatoes, corn, tomatoes, beans, avocado, pepper, squash, other fibrous vegetables, the papaya, and a variety of spices and berries. The list, in fact, was so lengthy, Dr. Spinden observed, that one really wondered what pre-Columbian Europe ate.

I was seated on Felipe's right at the long fruit- and flower-laden table. This was the honored place I had occupied since our very first public appearance together, and the arrangement was apparently accepted as protocol. When Felipe arose to greet his guests, all eyes, as usual, were focused upon him, and I realized that I was sharing his limelight. I was tranquilly conscious that the collective gaze not only was embracing me but was taking detailed note of my personal appearance. My French blue satin dinner gown, my simple, classic hairdo, and my every movement were under close and, I sensed, approving scrutiny.

In his brief remarks, Felipe commented on Dr. Spinden's broad knowledge of Yucatán's pre-Conquest production, laughingly declaring that he would place the Peabody Museum savant in nomination for the post of Minister of Agriculture as soon as the Maya Renaissance restored the race to its former prestige and political power. Then, outlining the next day's program, he announced that the morning and afternoon hours would be devoted to general sightseeing in Mérida—the Maya city of T'Ho[5]—which, he said, was already a thousand years old when the Spaniards arrived in Yucatán. But he hoped that we would not all be so completely fascinated by the various delights of La Ciudad Blanca that we would forget to be at our respective domiciles before eleven o'clock, since we were scheduled to board the train at midnight for Chichén Itzá. This, he explained, would be the main event of our trip, the real start of the promising archaeological adventure that had brought so many eminent scholars to the "Land of the Pheasant and the Deer." The railroad would take us as far as the little pueblo of Dzitas, some 240 kilometers from Mérida. At that point, automobiles would be waiting for us, and in caravan formation we would drive for another 56 kilometers over the almost-completed new highway to the very base of El Castillo—the great pyramid at the heart of the ritual center of the ancient capital of the "Holy and Learned Itzáes." The members of our expedition would be the first to use it, thus inaugurating what he hoped might prove to be a line of more-direct communication between the past and present. But the Dzitas road, he explained, was only the initial step in a statewide network, soon to be realized and eventually connecting all of Yucatán's principal archaeological sites. The large-scale program, however, had been designed for other purposes besides scientific investigation and tourism. His own concern, he frankly admitted, was mainly the Maya Indian. For, while facilitating the scholar in his discovery of temples and palaces more important, perhaps, than those already in sight, the new roads would still make the Maya himself the chief beneficiary. With access to all the marvelous structures bequeathed him by his ancestors, it would be less difficult, he was convinced, to awaken pride in racial capacity and stimulate ambition and effort for personal achievement.

As Felipe had assured us at the banquet, there was indeed much for the Yucatalogists to see in Mérida—much which was poignantly related to the story of Chichén Itzá. And the most dramatic link with the valor of the descendants of the "Holy and Learned Men at the Mouth of the Great Well" was Mérida's most famous building, La Casa de los Montejo. At the invitation of its owner and occupant, the aristocratic Señor Don Álvaro Regil, an heir of the Montejo family, I toured the palatial dwelling with a group that included the *esposos* Barry and the white-haired Mrs. William James, an active member of the local archaeological society and for many years a prominent North American resident of Yucatán. The elaborate structure, erected in 1549, is a monument both to Spanish Conquest and to the gallant autochthonous spirit. In 1543, when El Adelantado Montejo[6] finally succeeded in making Yucatán a vassal province of Spain, as his chief, Hernán Cortés, had done a few years earlier at Tenochtitlán,[7] he attempted to establish the seat of his government at Chichén Itzá. But the Itzáes so bitterly resisted the desecration of their sacred city that he was forced to evacuate and retreat to T'Ho, then the capital of the province of Cehpech.

Montejo's defeat at Chichén Itzá, however, did not prevent him from gloating in pompous sculpture over his victories elsewhere in the peninsula. On the profusely adorned walls of his palace, constructed of stones taken from the pre-Columbian buildings and reworked by native artisans with the wooden mallets and nephrite chisels used by the ancient temple builders, he portrayed his costly triumph, achieved only after sixteen years of sanguinary struggle. On either side of the wide balcony, placed high on the intricately carved, age-mellowed façade, stands a heroic-sized figure of a bearded and helmeted Spanish soldier clad in full armor and carrying a fifteenth-century halberd. The two stern-visaged warriors are shown pitilessly trampling with mailed feet on the necks of conquered and weeping natives. Between them, on an enormous shield, is emblazoned, in deep relief, the heraldic insignia of Francisco Montejo, Captain General of Yucatán.

That night, according to schedule, the expeditionaries were rounded up from hotels and private dwellings by the hospitality committee and driven to the train for our midnight departure, Antonio calling for me at the Cantón residence as usual. Felipe had courteously given Vera Barry and me his personal compartment and had remained, as we later found out, in the observation car for most of the night, discussing with Dr. Morley and Ingeniero José Reygadas Vértiz, representative of the Mexican Department of Archaeology, details of state and federal collaboration in the exploration project. The brilliant, penetrating Yucatecan sunlight made sleep impossible after dawn, and everyone appeared in the dining car for a six o'clock breakfast. Unlike their Yucatecan hosts—who were notoriously early risers—most of the Americans seemed to be in a tropical daze until after the flavorful Xalapa coffee, *pan dulce,* and delicious *guacamole*—creamed avocado—had restored some of the animated optimism of the official banquet. Gradually, stimulating conversation enlivened the atmosphere as, for the second time in an exciting week, we sped past monotonous miles of planted sisal towards Maya ruins. The visit to Chichén Itzá, we all understood, was in the nature of a preliminary survey. There would be no definite decisions until after the recommendations had been turned in to Washington, probably in late autumn. But at this point no member of the party imagined any occurrence that could hinder the realization of Carnegie's proposed long-range project.

Over a broad, white undeviating clearance, channeled straight down the middle of a dark, compact expanse of brush, I rode beside the jubilant Felipe in the rear seat of a Fordinga driven by the equally jubilant Antonio. With us was Felipe's favorite brother, the dark-eyed, brown-haired Benjamín, who, though fourteen years his junior, seemed closer to him in tastes and in general outlook than the older ones I had met. Benjamín was accompanied by his bride of a few months, the vivacious English-speaking Pilar Díaz Bolio, daughter of long-established and socially prominent residents of Mérida. Polished of man-

*The omnipresent "Fordinga," a modified Ford Model T.*

ner, with a certain streamlined "young man of the world" personality, Benjamín, like his sister Elvia, suggested Spanish rather than Maya ancestry. The twelfth son of the Carrillo family, he was the only one to embrace a military career. Upon completing preparatory school, he pursued his studies at the Military College of Chapultepec, finishing with the grade of Second Lieutenant. In February 1914, following what he had referred to in a treasured letter his mother later read to me, as his "baptism of fire" during campaigns in the Territory of Tepic,[8] he was raised to the rank of Captain in the 22nd Regiment for personal bravery. While in the capital he was appointed administrator of the public abattoir at Tacubaya and was elected representative to the National Chamber of Deputies. Upon returning to Yucatán, he became a member of the local Congress, Secretary of the Liga Central de Resistencia, and Chief of the State Agency of Purchases.

Occasionally, Felipe would leave the car to check on the progress of the caravan, comprising some twelve Fordingas in each of which rode two or three Americans escorted by state or federal officials or members of the local archaeological society. In a few sections, the road ahead, he explained, would not be entirely finished for another four or five months, but with careful driving it was easily passable for lightweight automobiles. With vivid and amusing detail, he recalled the old mode of travel to the Chichén Itzá ruins. He described how the brave tourists, if alone, would stretch out full-length in a strange contraption that outwardly resembled an old-fashioned delivery wagon hung on heavy leather springs swung between a pair of big high wheels. The occupant was supposed to find comfort on a mattress filled with tree cotton placed over a network of cords.

When there were two or three passengers, they sat crosswise. The rickety vehicle known as a *volan coche* was drawn, according to the load, by either three or five mules. One of the animals was placed between the short twin bars, and the other two or four, on either side or in front of him. All were attached to the *volan* by a rope harness without the customary iron or strap that enabled the mules to back up or hold back, and on downgrades they would have to keep ahead of the *volan* or fall under the wheels. Sitting on the edge of the mattress at the front of the vehicle, the driver swung his long whip, shook his rope reins, shouted the order "Váyanse," and the mules started off at a gallop. If he were lucky and the *volan* were not overturned and wrecked, for six painful hours the helpless traveler was jolted over numerous rough spots and bounced upon his theoretically protective pad, trying, at the same time, to avoid being lashed from both sides of the narrow trail by protruding branches.

"But that's all in the past now, like the *hacienda* floggings of our Inditos," Felipe said with keen satisfaction. "By July, the last layer of macadam will be laid, and the motoring time between Dzitas and Chichén Itzá will be cut to less than half an hour. Yes, I have already set mid-July as our deadline. We are planning a splendid festival—a reunion of thousands of Maya from all over the peninsula—the first in centuries.

Then, taking my hand, he added with feigned solemnity: "And remember,

*The caravan on the road to Chichén Itzá, 1923.*

Almita, no matter to what part of the globe your capitalist newspaper sends you, the Socialist State of Yucatán will expect your honorable presence at this historic event. In fact, here and now, in my official capacity, I command your attendance, and Pilar, Benjamín, and Antonio are my witnesses."

Responsive to his humorous mood, all three signaled with raised hands their approval of the executive order, and with the utmost sincerity, I assured them that I would do my best to obey instructions. I was indeed hoping in the depths of my heart that I might somehow arrange to return for the crowning moment in Felipe's lifelong effort to revive the spirit of the Mayab. Yet the usually reliable inner voice kept reminding me that July was a long way off.

My diary entry written at midnight on February 16, 1923, recording with youthful exuberance that first trip to Chichén Itzá, evokes an atmosphere of all-pervading magic. The gaiety of our laughter, the felicitous expressions of mutual admiration, voicing our happiness in one another's company, seem now to re-echo from sound waves endlessly vibrating through infinite space. The poetically phrased diary notes that attempted to convey the day's thoughts and impressions summon out of the conserving ether wordless but equally imperishable impulses and emotions. The adoration in Benjamín's gaze as he constantly kept looking back from the driver's seat at his radiant Pilar, my own ecstatic delight in the secret knowledge of Felipe's impassioned need of me—these, and other events that transpired in the silence, again leap flamelike into consciousness with all their nascent intensity.

But the enchanted hour on the Dzitas road seemed to flash by with the speed of light, leaving no hint in its dazzling passage of another hour already darkly forming in the unseeable, onrushing future. Within our charmed circle, dual ringed by magnetic attraction of mind and heart, there entered no premonition of the anguish that would soon crush our mirth, of the abysmal despair destined, before another February claimed its place in the succession of months, to engulf the lives and forever shatter the dreams of four people in love.

# 11. City of the Learned Itzáes

For nearly a kilometer, the pyramid marking the terminal point of our journey was plainly visible. There was not a turn or a hillock along the flat limestone surface of the land to obstruct our view of El Castillo's[1] mighty bulk. As we neared the grandiose structure, Felipe's extraordinary eyes glowed with the pride born of personal accomplishment. He had not only planned the road, which he sentimentally called *sacbeob*—a raised stone highway that connected the ancient Maya cities—but had assisted in its actual building. Both Maestra Rosa and Manuel Cirerol had told me how, during the past months, their tireless leader would often slip quietly out of Mérida to be found hours later on the job, with rolled-up shirtsleeves, working and perspiring in the intense heat. His white linen jacket and his broad-brimmed "Governor's Stetson" hat hung on some nearby bush, he would be swinging away with a pickaxe, helping to break rock or, with a shovel, clearing the jungle of deeply imbedded roots the tractors had missed.

At sight of Felipe, the four Indian musicians of the native stringed orchestra came forward in single file to greet him with a lively air, playing as they walked what was probably a Maya equivalent of "Hail to the Chief." Warmly saluting them and his many Liga *compañeros* present, he asked me to remain beside him with Pilar and Benjamín to await the arrival of the caravan. When the last car had pulled up and the expedition members and the Yucatecan officials were assembled at the spot of the brief, informal ceremony, the State Band that had preceded us from Mérida struck up Mexico's stirring National Anthem.

Looking around me I could read in the faces of my countrymen—undemonstrative savants and eager, romantic tourists alike—that they, too, were gripped by deep emotion and were thinking perhaps in Felipe's humanistic rather than in their own archaeological terms about the true significance of the occasion. All stood, at least, in respectful silence, as though participating in some solemn religious rite. And tears filled other eyes besides my own when Felipe cut the white ribbon to signal what he ardently believed would initiate a new era for his ancestral race.

*El Castillo at Chichén Itzá, from a photo in Alma Reed's collection.*

*Carrillo Puerto inaugurates part of his new highway from Mérida to Chichén Itzá, from a photo the governor sent to Reed by post.*

*(left) Scaling the heights of El Castillo.*

*(below) Alma and Felipe in the company of other "Yucatologists" beside the Pórtico de los Tigres at Chichén Itzá.*

From the lofty heights of the great "Castillo" behind us, many centuries were looking down from celebrated monuments of antiquity upon men who had invoked the glorious past at other times and places. The more famous of these predecessors, history records, came as conquerors to impose with armed might their will upon vanquished peoples and subject them to the despotism of their respective dynasties. How different, it occurred to me, was Felipe's role, as he stood that day in the shadow of Chichén Itzá's majestic pyramid—an ambassador of brotherhood. Dispensing hope and courage, he had come as another redeemer to the ancient shrine of the American Messiah, Kukulcán, with a pledge to heal the wounds inflicted by men of the sword and the lash—to break the fetters of ignorance and superstition that, despite political liberation, still held the Maya in spiritual and economic bondage.

Felipe himself eloquently stated his purpose in the few simple words he addressed to the Maya Indians who surrounded him. "I have opened this road," he said, speaking in their own tongue, "so that you may come here to contemplate the grandeur of your fathers, confident that inspired by them you also will aspire to be great."

To the simultaneous and, at moments, cacophonous accompaniment of the two very different musical groups, we all surged into the vast quadrangle. There, Mr. Edward H. Thompson, owner of the Hacienda Chichén Itzá—comprising an area bordering both sides of the highway, running two miles from north to south and one and a half miles from east to west, the site on which the major ruins were located—embraced Felipe as an old comrade and cordially welcomed the visitors to what for over thirty-eight years had been virtually his personal domain. The day marked both a beginning and the end of an era for the veteran New England explorer. It foreshadowed the termination of his life of toil among the ruins, of intensive study of the inhabitants of the region, descendants of the builders of this once magnificent and still impressive Maya capital. Don Eduardo, as he was affectionately known throughout Yucatán, not only had conducted extraordinary explorations in *cenotes* and in the sepulchers of the priestly dead, making such valuable discoveries as the inscribed and dated tablet of the Initial Series, but had become an authority on almost every phase of the Maya culture: the native habits and customs, language, history, folklore, and religion. And now, after decades of patient but fruitful waiting, the emissaries of a powerful, richly endowed institution from his own country had arrived at last to take over his lonely, one-man task of guarding the vestiges of Chichén Itzá's splendor against total destruction by natural forces and man's vandalism.

With an agility and enthusiasm that belied his years, Don Eduardo guided us over the crumbling remains of temples and palaces, relating, as we approached the various structures, the legends associated with them and interpreting the symbolism of their lavishly adorned walls and columns. The scientists, meanwhile, directed their attention to the object of their immediate interest, the zone designated in previous planning for their first exploration. This was a huge elevated area, resembling a chain of hills that was known to contain, beneath a covering of tropical brush, quantities of collapsed material and a series of long colonnades around a great open plaza some four and a half acres in extent. This site was believed to have been the marketplace of the once heavily populated metropolis.

But all that any of us could see then of the now completely excavated and beautifully restored Temple of the Warriors with its Court of the Thousand Columns was an inch or two of masonry emerging here and there above the dense mass of tangled growth. Dr. Morley and the members of his exploring staff, however, seemed pleased that the jungle had swallowed up the enormous architectural complex. They explained that the lush vegetation had doubtless served as a protective blanket for whatever bas-relief carving or hieroglyphic inscriptions might remain on the columns, which they judged to be from eight to nine feet in height.

Looking over that rambling, irregular mass of shrub-covered earth and rubble on the first day of the Carnegie Preliminary Survey, who could have foreseen with what rhythmic grandeur would emerge during the ensuing two decades the vast ensemble of pyramids, colonnaded halls, massive platforms, terraced buildings, and exquisitely sculptured colonnades? Or who could have predicted that in temples buried under earlier temples archaeology would discover such precious objects as the celebrated turquoise mosaic plaque later evaluated by Dr. Morley himself as an outstanding example of the finest development of ancient indigenous art? Or who could have guessed then, nearly forty years before Dr. Jorge Acosta completed his exploration and restoration of the pyramids of Quetzalcóatl at Tula on the Mexican plateau that the Temple of the Warriors imbedded in this unprepossessing mound would divulge the long-held secret of the identity of the real builders of Chichén Itzá as we know it today?

For it was only in the 1960–1961 season that the true provenance of the tenth-century invaders of the Maya capital was revealed. And it was the bas-relief figures of the columns forming the portico of the Temple of the Warriors, identical with those of the portico of Tula's Quetzalcóatl Pyramid, that told the story. In all details—features, attire, headdress, weapons, adornments—these sensitive warrior portraits coincided perfectly. A second most convincing similarity was the placing of a pillar at opposite ends of the ninth step of a broad staircase in both structures. These analogous architectonic elements unequivocally supported Dr. Acosta's discovery that it was the Toltecs of Tula and not the Teotihuacanos, as previously believed, who were responsible for the non-Maya influence of this sacred city of the New Empire.

Many other elements of Toltec origin from the Mexican plateau, as Dr. Alberto Ruz Lhuillier was later to indicate, were integrated with the buildings of Chichén Itzá. Among them were columns in the form of feathered serpents, abutments against the side slope at the base of the temples, the use of a merlon on the roofs, human sculpture of the "Atlantean" type, standard-bearers, the Chac-Mool, intertwined serpents on balustrades, drawings of tigers and eagles devouring hearts. But none served to pinpoint Tula as the source of Toltec cultural penetration in the capital of the Itzáes more precisely than the bas-relief portraits and the ninth-step pillars of the Temple of the Warriors.

Anticipating by many years some of the attention-rousing tactics of the contemporary Yucatecan tourist guide, Don Eduardo brought to high pitch the dramatic interest of what for most of us was a first view of Chichén Itzá's imposing monuments. He stood, for instance, at the north end of the Ball Court—the largest in the entire Maya area—and asked us to stand at the opposite end. Then, speaking in a normal voice, he demonstrated its perfect acoustics. For at a distance of 450 feet, we could clearly hear his every word and even the sound of a coin that he dropped upon the limestone.

Leaving the Carnegie explorers to puzzle over methods of attack to be used in their proposed colossal excavations, Felipe joined us in the Ball Court. Don Eduardo greeted his timely arrival with an invitation for him to assume the role of guide. "I'm going to ask our sports-loving Governor to tell you," he said, "exactly what happened here. Better than myself, he knows how the ancient Maya played *juego de pelota,* or *tlachtli,*[2] as they called it in the old days. He's an authority, too, on the modern and far less strenuous version of *tlachtli*—not only Yucatan's greatest baseball 'fan' but rapidly making 'fans' of us all. Just recently, Governor Carrillo organized and equipped baseball teams in every part of the state. He's even apt to revive *tlachtli* after the new road is officially opened."

"That may happen someday," Felipe answered, "but before it does, our new generation of Maya youth will need a lot of hard discipline." Then, illustrating the points of the ritualistic game with lively gestures and swift movements, he explained that it was played with the object of driving a rubber ball through the small openings of stone rings still in place on each of the two parallel walls forming the sides of the court, approximately twenty-eight feet above ground level. He never ceased marveling, he said, at how the Maya players of the rival teams, using only their elbows, knees, and hips in striking the ball, sometimes succeeded in reaching the winning goal. This, he felt, was such a tremendously difficult feat that it seemed only a fair reward that the victors be permitted to go among the spectators and take all the costly feather mosaic cloaks they could carry away with them.

Felipe assisted me up the steep climb of El Castillo's principal stairway, and for a moment we stood in silence, looking out over the uninhabited city as it slept in the morning sun. When he spoke, it was to tell me how happy I had made him by my quick response to the beauty created by Yucatan's ancient peoples. "I was certain from the very first moment," he said, "that you, too, would deeply feel the importance of preserving what remains of it for the future."

I knew that Felipe, like myself, had read the provocative works of Dr. Augustus Le Plongeon, whose theories, rejected as bizarre in his own day, have steadily acquired repute with scholars and a growing public acceptance, due to the fact that the so-called Diffusionists daily gain ground in their controversy with the Independent Inventionists regarding the enigma of Maya origin. And I felt that his thoughts, like my own, were directed in thanksgiving at the promise inherent in the Carnegie Expedition. At least, we were both sure that the presence of the North American scientists offered some hope of arresting the decay and the disintegration encountered a half century earlier by the French savant, Dr. Le Plongeon, in the abandoned Maya capital—neglect which he pictured in his challenging book, *Queen Moo and the Egyptian Sphinx:*[3]

> The temples of the Maya sages are in ruins, slowly but surely crumbling to dust, gnawed by the relentless tooth of time; and what is worse, recklessly destroyed by the iconoclastic hand of ignorance and avarice. Sanctuaries have become the abode of bats, swallows, and serpents. Lairs of the wild beasts of the forests, they are not only deserted, but shunned by human beings, who stand in awe of them. Where now are the sages who used to assemble within their sacred precincts to delve into the mysteries of creation, to wrest her secrets from the bosom of Mother Nature? Do their spirits still hover there, as the natives assert? Purified from all earthly defilement, have they been reabsorbed in the great ocean of intelligence as Buddhists would have us believe? Are they enjoying the perfect repose of Nirvana, waiting to be summoned to begin another cycle of mundane existence in more advanced planetary worlds than ours?

When we were joined by the *esposos* Barry and other expeditionaries, Vera asked Felipe his opinion about the purpose of the enormous structure. "I believe—contrary to Diego de Landa—" he replied, "that this was not a temple to Kukulcán, but one dedicated to the worship of the sun. And who can conceive of a more logical or a more indispensable deity or a more munificent benefactor of mankind?" He explained that this theory was strengthened by the measurements of the pyramid itself. He pointed out that the four stairways of 91 steps each, plus the step to the upper platform on which we stood, totaled 365, corresponding to the number of days of the solar year. Moreover, in the nine terraced bodies are contained fifty-two panels, equal to the years of the Toltec cycle. Still further support for the pyramid's identification with worship of the sun was to be found, Felipe believed, in the fact that the nine terraced steps gave a total of eighteen sections on each of the four sides when divided by its stairway, corresponding to the eighteen months of the Maya calendar year.

The existence beneath El Castillo of an earlier pyramid of lesser dimensions but similar design was unknown at the time. More than a decade later, the discovery was made by a member of our own party and provided one of the real sensations of modern Mexican archaeology. While working with the National Institute of Anthropology,[4] Manuel Cirerol, who had been Felipe's friend and English interpreter and the treasurer of the Liga Central, after penetrating the structure from the east side, found in the sanctuary of the hidden temple a remarkable throne in the form of a life-sized jaguar. The spots of its vermilion coat are represented by incrusted jade discs, the eyes are balls of the rarest quality of jade, and the fangs are of flint.

Leaving Felipe to conduct the rest of our archaeological tour, Don Eduardo returned to his residence, the nearby Hacienda House, to supervise arrangements for his numerous luncheon guests. He urged us to visit the Sacred Cenote before the sun was much higher and said that he would expect us at one o'clock for *tamales motuleños*[5] prepared especially in Felipe's honor.

By an ancient causeway three hundred yards north of the ceremonial center and in a direct line with the base of El Castillo, we reached the great sacrificial well of the Holy and Learned Itzáes. Most of the expeditionaries were familiar with the sinister legends associated with this enormous symmetrically rounded mouth of a subterranean river some ninety feet below. These legends had been recorded by Bishop Diego de Landa in 1566, and the French translation of his work by Brasseur de Bourbourg made the story of the Sacred Cenote available to the general public, concerning which the Spanish Friar had written:

> From the court in front of these theaters (at Chichén Itzá) runs a wide and handsome roadway as far as the Well, which is about two stone's throws off. Into this Well they have had and still have the custom of throwing men alive as a sacrifice to their gods in time of drought, and they believed they would not die, though they never saw them again. They also threw into it many other things like precious stones and things they prized, and so if this country had possessed gold it would be this Well that would have the greater part of it, so great is the devotion the Indians show for it.

De Landa's account of the lurid Cenote Sagrado tradition stirred our eager curiosity, but even in its physical aspect the well was a strangely eerie spectacle. Its white walls uniformly lined in stratified patterns suggested a gaping wound, a livid gash in the heart of the dark forest encircling its rim. Yet still more exciting were the vague rumors that Don Eduardo himself had actually descended into the yawning water-pit and recovered quantities of ancient Maya treasure. We were warned, however, by the Peabody Museum representatives that this was a very "touchy" subject with Don Eduardo and, consequently, when we arrived at Hacienda House, where he warmly received us, there was a discreet silence on the veteran explorer's subaqueous research.

*Alma and Felipe accompanied by archaeologists and Yucatologists at a luncheon hosted by Sir Edward Thompson at his hacienda at Chichén Itzá. Alma's face—and engaging smile—may be admired on the left (seventh seat, front to back).*

Don Eduardo's *tamales motuleños* did credit to Felipe's native Motul and the iced *limonada* proved to be the ideal beverage after the morning's exertion in the tropical heat. Following luncheon most of the party rested on the broad terrace of the rambling old Colonial-style mansion, built, its owner informed us, on the foundations of the original structure, which dated from 1681. I used the *siesta* hour to transpose my stenographic notes into copy for cables I would send to the *Times* on my return to Mérida and for the record I carefully kept of impressions and of Felipe's words. While I was writing, Don Eduardo seated himself near me and complimented me on my "attention to duty" when the "other ladies were idly swinging in hammocks." After questioning me about my newspaper work and my previous experience in archaeological reporting, he said: "You remind me so much of a girl I knew long ago in West Falmouth. She was also quite a student and had very large blue eyes like your own." Then, lowering his voice and moving his chair closer to mine, he asked if I would like to have an exclusive story on "the greatest archaeological adventure of the New World." I assured him that I would indeed appreciate the chance of being the first to tell the public about so important an event. "Well," he continued, "you will have that chance, but not today. I do not wish to talk before these Carnegie and Peabody people. You must come here again within the next few days—and alone. I am sure that

Don Felipe will arrange for your return. I've observed that he's anxious to do anything you may ask, just to please you." Explaining that the archeological adventure he referred to concerned the Sacred Cenote, Don Eduardo said that he would relate his interesting and significant experiences there only on condition I promised to quote him verbatim. "Much is involved," he added, "in the way my story is handled, because it is somewhat in the nature of a confession. Yet the facts must come out someday, and I'd rather 'confess' to a pretty and ambitious young journalist like yourself, especially since I find you so *simpática.*"

I thanked him for his trust in me and promised to give a factual report of his *cenote* "adventures" in a feature article that I would write for the *Sunday Times Magazine.* He requested me to keep the matter "strictly confidential" meanwhile and warned me that a secret so closely guarded for forty years was now in danger of leaking out, particularly when there was new interest in Yucatán and when there were "many scholars around" who were connected with rival institutions. "One group," he said, "is in possession of some of the facts but has good reason to keep them out of newspapers. The other group would like to give my story the widest possible publicity."

Refreshed and rested, we were now ready to tour the ruins south of El Castillo, among them some of the oldest in Chichén Itzá. Fortunately, Dr. Spinden, who was then preparing his erudite paper on the reduction of Maya dates for the Peabody Museum, accompanied us to the most spectacular building of the southern group, the Astronomical Observatory, known as El Caracol. Seen from a distance, this large elevated structure-in-the-round, rising upon three graduated rectangular platforms surmounted by a massive tower some 50 feet in height, dramatically dominated several kilometers of level land. On closer view, its commanding contours even gained in impressiveness through such striking elements as two encircling galleries and a grand stairway leading to a parapet—20 feet high and 220 feet in length—adorned with stone censers in the form of human heads. A few of the more enterprising "Yucatologists" ascended the interior stairs, winding around a solid center, snail-like—as the Spanish word *caracol* signifies—to a chamber that served as an observatory for the Maya astronomers.

Dr. Spinden explained that the small openings in the thick walls pointed to the cardinal directions and to other prominent positions in the celestial geography. The affable scholar—prematurely gray-haired but with the ruddy complexion of a schoolboy—said that the observatory was inevitably associated in his mind with America's Unknown Scientist who, in the seventh century B.C., so admirably conceived and patiently completed the first piece of systematic science anywhere in the world. "It was this 'Great Unknown,'" he assured us, "a thinker worthy of ranking with Buddha and Zoroaster, who solved the tangle of discordant lunar months, planetary cycles and tropical years by his invention of the

*Alma and Felipe explore the ruins of Chichén Itzá and appear to be almost holding hands.*

so-called Central American Time Machine. This feat Dr. Spinden regarded as all the more remarkable since the Maya astronomer's observations "were carried out by the very tools of thought which he himself had created for his work."

The southern section of Chichén Itzá contains a group of important and very old buildings, but our narrow schedule on that first visit limited us to four. One was the Nunnery and Annex, with its western façade solidly adorned from base to cornice with masks of the Rain God in an early Maya style called Chenes. The next, to the southeast, was the heavenly ornamented building known as the Iglesia, or Church. Of the classic period, this structure is outstanding because of its profusely decorated façade and the mask of Tlaloc, whose hooked nose extends from the corners, a feature that brought out the full battery of tourist cameras. Our third stop was at the greatly admired Chichán-Chob, or Red House, also belonging to the classic period and notable for its flying façade and roof comb—or *crestería*—forming a latticed wall.

But the temple that intrigued us most and certainly attracted Felipe's deepest interest was the Akab-Dzib, believed to be the most ancient structure in the entire Maya capital. Composed of various superimpositions and additions, it received its name—meaning "House of the Obscure Writing" or "Writing in the Dark"—from a sculptured lintel on a doorway of the inner chamber at the south end. According to the interpretation of one of the local archaeologists, the carving represented a priest seated on a throne contemplating hieroglyphic inscriptions on a vase or vessel containing incense.

Dr. Le Plongeon, a recognized authority on the hieroglyphs of Egypt, Saba, Sumeria, Mesopotamia, and other biblical lands, maintained that the "awful, tenebrous record" referred to the submergence of a continent in the waters of the Atlantic Ocean, Yucatán forming its western extension and Africa on the east. The savant believed that this was the same dreadful cataclysm described by Plato from the narrative of Solon, who, in turn, had received the account from the Egyptian priests Psenophis and Sonchis. Several Maya records, notably that of the Troano Manuscript—one of the three existing Maya codices—fixes the date of the catastrophe as "the year *Kan,* on the eleventh *Muluc* of the month *Zac,*" and states: "There occurred terrible earthquakes which continued without interruption until the thirteenth *Chuen.*" The account relates that it was then that the "country of the Hills of Mud, the land of Mu, was sacrificed. Been twice upheaved, it suddenly disappeared during the night, the basin continually shaken by volcanic forces. These caused the confined land to sink and rise several times and in various places. . . . At last, the surface gave way and the ten countries were torn asunder and scattered in fragments, unable to withstand the force of the seismic convulsions. They sank with their sixty-four million inhabitants, 8,060 years before the writing of this book."

Dr. Le Plongeon claimed that the date of the submergence became a new starting point for the chronological computations of Maya historians. From it, they began a new era and reckoned the epochs of their history as the Christians do from the birth of Christ and the Mohammedans from the Hegira, or flight of Mohammed from Mecca.

As we stood in the unlighted inner chamber, the possibility of truth in these traditions was argued by the scientists and the tourists. Dr. Merriam, a confirmed Independent Inventionist, treated the "Lost Atlantis" theories lightly and even with disdain. "Why is it necessary," he asked, "to connect resemblances between such widely separated cultures as the Maya and the Egyptian? Were not the lands where both flourished of about the same elevation, the same climatic conditions? And were not the human beings who lived and created in the two places physically identical from head to foot? Doesn't it seem logical that their reactions to similar natural conditions might have been about the same?" Endorsing Dr. Merriam's stand, an expeditionary—also a devotee of the Independent Inventionist School—quoted Sir James Fraser, author of the *Golden Bough,*[6] who assumed the extremist view that parallel developments grow spontaneously out of human nature as a result of psychic unity between all men wherever found.

Felipe listened attentively but took no part in our discussion. Yet, despite his silence, it was clear that he favored the Diffusionists and did not wholly reject the idea of a submerged Atlantic Continent—an idea that seemed to trouble him. This was the first occasion I had noticed how swiftly his face changed its usual relaxed expression for one of tense preoccupation. The smile that, as Dr. Ernest Gruening wrote at the time, "could win a child's faith or rivet the hearts of a vast multitude" was suddenly replaced by a strangely disturbed, puzzled look—the look of one completely absorbed in search of an answer he knew would forever elude him. Somehow, his mood recalled to mind words he had spoken during our very first conversation. He had told me on the road to Kanasín of his travels "over the length and breadth of the Mayab on foot and on horseback, through the Yucatán, into the wilds of Campeche, Tabasco, Quintana Roo, and the forest jungles of Chiapas, *hasta* Guatemala," and how, standing before the majestic monuments in the silent and deserted cities, "wondering and wondering," he had tried to penetrate the age-old mystery that might draw him closer to his "blood brother, the Maya."

While Antonio held up a flashlight, Felipe carefully studied Akab-Dzib's lintel bas-relief, still as intact as it must have been on the day it came from the sculptor's hands. Many times before, he had seen these carvings and, doubtless, with his poet-friend Luis Rosado Vega, who, in his ode "Chichén Itzá," refers to "Dismal Akab-Dzib, where all is silence and dread." But, never, perhaps, had he witnessed such scholarly concentration on the theory that the "obscure inscription" recorded humanity's supreme disaster. Incredulously, he seemed to be asking himself: "Does the solution to the Maya enigma lie, then, in these legends of a terrible cataclysm? Could this very thing not happen again?" An ardent worshipper of Nature—personified in his public utterances and in our intimate talks as the bountiful dispenser of the multifarious gifts of the Good Earth—he appeared, for the moment, unable to reconcile his hopeful outlook and Pantheistic Faith with the ominous "handwriting on the wall." It could have been my own lively imagination, but I thought he had grown pale in his visible depression at the frightful picture our quotations from Le Plongeon and the Maya codices had evoked. In his sensitivity and his enormous love for people—for the helpless and the afflicted everywhere—the possibility that the Great Universal Mother of the warm, generous heart had, in mad fury, destroyed millions of Maya ancestors, causing the last survivors to seek shelter on the fringe of the submerged continent, seemed to weigh upon his spirit like some evil portent.

With less vivacity but with more knowledge of the ancient Maya than they could claim upon arrival at Chichén Itzá's celebrated ceremonial center, the expeditionaries walked back to the spot where the Fordingas awaited and, in the deepening twilight, retraced the new Dzitas road to board the train for Mérida.

# 12. *Ritmos del Mayab*

Sightseeing in and out of Mérida continued at an uninterrupted pace, but as the close of the first half of the expedition's stay in Yucatán approached, many points of archaeological and historical interest still remained on our schedule. For greater convenience and the saving of limited time, the hospitality committee invited those official guests housed in private residences to change to the leading centrally located hotels. At Felipe's suggestion, I was assigned to the Hotel Imperial, facing on the small plaza of La Tercera Orden[1] and only a short distance from my almost daily objectives, the García Rejón Library and the Yucatán State University.

The massive walnut furniture of my spacious, high-ceilinged room was the same, the manager proudly informed me, used by President Porfirio Díaz when he occupied the suite and one adjoining mine on his visit to Yucatán for the celebration of Mexico's Independence Centennial. Among the more spectacular notes in the ponderous mid-Victorian scheme was an enormous mirror with a hand-carved wooden frame that extended almost the full length of the wall. Another was the elevated four-poster bed, also of heavily carved walnut and draped with a voluminous muslin canopy. Adding to the pompous atmosphere was the huge sunken Roman bath set in an elaborately patterned tile floor—a perfect symbol of the grandiose inefficiency that appealed to the taste of the typical Díaz regime oligarch.

But there was little likelihood that a reputation for conservative elegance had wholly determined Felipe's choice of the Hotel Imperial for the final days of my Yucatecan sojourn. I soon guessed—what he later cheerfully confessed—that he had selected the old stone building because its corner location afforded the ideal setting for serenades. Below my second-story *balcón* around two o'clock each morning, his favorite *cantante,* Alfonso, whose tall, slim figure and soulful dark eyes recalled the traditional troubadours of Spanish chivalry, could be seen with the three short, rotund *muchachos* of his quartette, strumming guitars and singing the lovely *canciones* of Ricardo Palmerín, Guty Cárdenas, and other local composers, with an occasional plaintive song in Mayan. I knew that Felipe was always somewhere in the background, hovering on one side or the other of the convenient corner. Out of the serenaders' range of vision and following the course prescribed in amatory literature, I would muster up the courage to drop a rose from my window, like any romantic maid of sixteenth-century Castile—or twentieth-century Mérida.

My favorite *serenata* was "Las golondrinas," by the poet Rosado Vega, for which Palmerín had written the hauntingly tender music. The theme itself, reminiscent of Bécquer's famous poem of the same name, which I had already memorized, conveyed with poignant simplicity the cosmic truth that all cycles are destined to close . . . "The swallows that came, bathed in light, in youth's fair morning" and "like its loves and its dreams, disappeared with winter's dark clouds." The words fascinated me because of their ominous if imagined relation—in my strange forebodings—to the life pattern of someone dear to me—or could it have been my *own?*

Another serenade, "Mi guitarra," in which the same two sensitive Yucatecan artists united their talents, seemed to speak to me with Felipe's voice. Both the music and the exquisite lyric had recaptured and translated into sweet lingering cadences the ineffable sadness that enveloped his and their native land. And long after Alfonso and his *muchachos* had vanished into the night and Felipe had retrieved the rose that I hoped would spell out the unspoken words that were in my heart, the final stanza remained with me as his personal message:

> The profound silence rends with nameless sorrow
> My *canto* of love,
> Listen, Alma *mía,* hear my guitar
> That with me sings and weeps my Song.

I was fascinated by the Maya songs with which the *cantantes,* strumming monorhythmic guitar accompaniments, would usually conclude their serenades. Mayan, I realized, was Felipe's favorite language, and although Spanish was spoken in his paternal home, he had acquired the ancient Indian tongue in early childhood and continued to use it throughout his public life. With obvious pride, he had mentioned the fact to me and with equal pride had also related how, following the Conquest, the people of the Mayab preserved the purity of their ancestral idiom from the disfigurement that occurred throughout centuries of hybridization in other areas of their folk culture. Mayan not only was the language of the grandfathers of the grandfathers of the founders of Uxmal and Chichén Itzá, he explained, but was the one in which, from unknown ages, the creators of the race and their first offspring expressed themselves.

While I found some of the Mayan words rather harsh or rasping, their sounds always vibrated for me with haunting overtones, suggesting remote times and vague, far-off places. As Prof. Esteban Durán Rosada was later to observe, the tones and inflections of Mayan speech were like "winds from the sea blowing through a conch shell." My own impressions were further confirmed by the Yucatecan scholar who noted that the Maya songs strangely evoked the mood and images of that vanished yesterday when, in the same land, the Maya would gather on moonlit nights beside cool *cenotes* or under fronds of the *ceiba* tree, while their bards, to the monotonous chords of *zacatanes* and *tunkules,*[2] recounted venerable legends and fantastic tales of *xtabayes*—sirens who waded along *sacbeob,* the white roads of Mayab, to lure the guileless wayfarer to his doom.

During our very first conversations, I discovered Felipe's almost passionate desire to perpetuate the Mayan tongue. As I surmised, his crusading interest aimed primarily to provide the non-Spanish-speaking bulk of Yucatán's population with a defensive weapon in the struggle to win and maintain control of their own civic affairs. One of the many ways I soon learned in which he demonstrated his crusading spirit was his sponsorship of the *Dictionary of Motul.* Shortly before our meeting, he had commissioned his friend, the eminent North American historian and etymologist Dr. William E. Gates, to prepare the monumental work in English and an amplified Spanish translation. Previously, Dr. Gates, who had made a lifelong study of Mayan linguistic problems and was a recognized authority on Mayan glyphs, had translated into English, Bishop de Landa's *Las Cosas de Yucatán.* He was also the author of several interpretative treatises on the codices, among them, *Codex Maya-Tzental-Pérez,* published in 1910 by the Peabody Museum of Harvard University.

There were many elements in the Mayan language—Felipe assured me—that vividly reflected the Maya temperament and character. He explained that the Maya seldom affirms categorically and that rarely does he compromise himself by asserting that something is good or valuable unless he has given the matter mature reflection. This attitude of permanent doubt, he pointed out, was imbedded in the language as *bey ulale,* implying deeper meaning than the Spanish *así será*—"perhaps so," or "thus it could be."[3] While *bey ulale* may appear to be a synonym of obedience or resignation, it is, in reality, an expression of irony that provokes a mysterious inner smile—one that never reaches the lips of the Maya. On the other hand, the negative *ma*—"no"—is constantly and emphatically heard. In the picturesque definition that Professor Durán Rosado has given to the word *ma* is the "thorny cuirass that protects the flower of Maya sentiment, jealously guarded by the racial atavism." The Maya will say "no" even when he is consumed with desire to say "yes," faithful to the hermetic withdraw of the race. It was this same hermetic withdraw to which Felipe had made implied reference on our memorable ride to Kanasín—the spiritual ailment at the core of racial consciousness he was attempting to probe and heal with psychological therapy. The Maya's regard for his age-old language, Felipe was convinced, was one kind of stimulus that might help transform a "sad" people into a happy one, awakening in them the capacity to feel both pride and joy, to respond more quickly to "yes" than to "no" after so long a period of humiliation, sorrow and skepticism.

Shortly after my arrival at the Hotel Imperial, Antonio appeared one morning, bearing a basket full of gay *tulipanes* and a large cardboard box that contained my eagerly awaited *fiesta* dress. With it came a gold filigree rosary and a crucifix to complete the beautiful costume. In a note attached to the flowers, Felipe asked me when I would receive the photographer Badia for my portrait as "una guapa Mestiza de Yucatán."[4]

Meanwhile, he hoped that I would be free to visit the new Archaeological Museum, of which his friend, the poet Rosado Vega, was the director, and afterwards to join them both at luncheon. I had met Don Luis at the expedition receptions, but I wanted to know him better because of my growing admiration for his poetry, legends, and songs. Just a few days before, I had received as Felipe's first gift to me, a two-volume set of the poet's collected works, one titled *Libro de ensueño y dolor (Book of Reverie and Pain)* and the other, *Alma y sangre (Soul and Blood).*

In the heart of the city at the ancient church of San Juan de Dios, we found Don Luis supervising the adaptation of the building to its new role as an archaeological museum. An additional nave to accommodate the already large and daily augmented collection destined for public display was also under construction. In his vigorous forties, of medium build but appearing shorter than his actual height alongside Felipe, Don Luis—his eyes aglow with zealous enthusiasm behind their thick bifocals—led us around the atrium and through hidden corners of the old temple to the sacristy, where the prize items of different types of ancient objects were temporarily stored. It was clear that his was a labor of love and that his poet's nature was wholeheartedly responding to the cultural undertaking that Felipe had astutely entrusted to him.

Although in close touch with the entire museum project in his ambition to have it all completed before the formal opening of the new Chichén Itzá Highway in July, Felipe received a pleasant surprise when Don Luis triumphantly uncovered several remarkable pieces he had collected during the week while everyone was occupied with the Carnegie Expedition tours. The newly acquired lot included a Chac-Mool, two large figures—a warrior and a goddess—masks of Tlaloc, and other treasures that formerly would have been shipped to the National Museum of Anthropology in the Mexican capital. It was moving to watch these modern-minded sons of the Mayab reverently handling and even affection-

*Reed in Mérida, photographed by Badia in her traditional Maya costume, known as a* traje de mestiza, *given to her by an enamored Felipe Carrillo Puerto in the fall of 1923.*

ately caressing the vessels and artifacts their ancestors had fashioned in a spirit of religious devotion and left as an artistic legacy to unborn generations.

Eager to have me fully appreciate the significance and the broad scope of the Museum's educational program that he and Felipe had together devised, Don Luis spoke rapidly, stressing his points with characteristic gestures. Usually, there was a picaresque flavor to his words, in striking contrast to the gentle romanticism of his verses. "Socialists," he explained, winking at Felipe, "are invariably unorthodox. Consequently, here in this Socialist State our Museum will not fol-

*Reed appears on the cover of the periodical* El Agricultor, *wearing the same outfit as well as her gold filigree rosary, also a gift from Felipe.*

low the standard routine but will introduce activities aimed to give a fresh meaning to the ceramics and sculptured stones we exhibit." Among the innovations, he cited models of Yucatán's principal monuments that were then being built by skilled native craftsmen, bibliographies containing special reference to the diverse theories of Maya origin already in preparation, and recently organized classes for the study of the ancient codices and other historic documents relating to the Maya. A very important aspect of the educational program, he pointed out, and one that bore directly on the present economic reality, was the launching of a campaign to promote Maya stylization in art and architectural works. All these factors, Don Luis believed, formed an ensemble that would synthesize Felipe's various efforts and advance his underlying purpose and social objectives, which were to stir and activate among the patient, long-suffering Maya Indians subconscious memories of Yucatán's epic aboriginal race.

Felipe was not the only one to be pleasantly surprised that day by Don Luis. As we left the Archaeological Museum and drove to a little *fonda*[5] with a tropical setting off the Paseo de Montejo—one that Felipe said he could highly recommend for its excellent *pollo p'bil* and my favorite *sorbetes*—the poet revealed that he also had a surprise in store for me. "I hope that you will find my surprise to your liking," he began. "It is a song—composed with *cariño*[6] and admiration. From the moment we met, I knew that I must write a song to you. But I can claim only half the credit for the result of my impulse. You see, I was not alone in my decision. No sooner had the idea occurred to me than our great good friend here, Don Felipe, conceived the very same idea. In the name of our long *compañerismo*,[7] he begged me to write and dedicate to you "the real masterpiece" of my career. He gave me the title for it—"La Peregrina"—and during these days, when he has unburdened to me his thoughts and his feelings about you, he has even unconsciously provided me with many of the sentiments and phrases. So now, Señorita Alma, you are to be 'La Peregrina,' and soon our lyric will have its musical accompaniment."

"Yes, *very* soon," Felipe added, beaming at the prospect. "Palmerín, Yucatán's greatest composer, is already at work on the music. You know some of his other songs—'Mi guitarra,' 'El rosal enfermo,' 'Las golondrinas,' which Alfonso has played for you. But I feel that Palmerín will surpass himself with *your* song."

The moment we were seated at our table on the *fonda*'s palm-enclosed terrace, I begged Don Luis to recite the words of my song. Some of the nostalgic nuances of Alfonso's minor-keyed serenades were in his deep-throated voice as he read the lines of "La Peregrina" from a handwritten page. When he finished he presented the manuscript to me, bowing low in a gesture of Quixotic Spanish gallantry. I glanced over the phrases extolling my eyes "claros y divinos,"[8] my "empurpled lips," "engaging smile," and "beauty as radiant as the sun," and as any young woman might have felt under similar circumstances, I was profoundly pleased that a poet whose work delighted me should have pictured me in such glowing terms. Yet despite the compliments and the flattering metaphors, the song itself did not make me happy. I wondered why the lovely sentiments aroused no joyous response in my heart, and why, instead, they left me saddened. Soon I realized that their suggestion of unsatisfied longing, the implied prophesy of separation, the emphasis on the vast distances between the "virginal snows" of my own "Northern land" and the "palmeras," the "perfumed nectar of the flowers" of Felipe's "tierra tropical," evoked the sorrow experienced at parting forever with the dearly beloved one . . . I could easily have wept—although I managed to smile—when I grasped the resignation in the words of unfulfillment, stressed in the closing lines with Felipe's reiterated appeal: "do not forget, do not forget my land, do not forget, do not forget my love."

That night, I went with Felipe and Don Luis to the modest home of Ricardo Palmerín in a poor neighborhood on the outskirts of Mérida. In a cool, moonlit garden beneath blossoming orange trees, Felipe and I sat on a bench before the open door of the composer's sparsely furnished little studio. Inside, Palmerín was playing a small upright piano while Don Luis stood near him, listening intently to the various musical phrases as they rippled off the keyboard in swift melodic succession. But not one of the many beautiful strains impressed the sensitive ears of the two judges as the "inevitable" theme of "La Peregrina." The short, heavyset musician, whose placid countenance, tranquil poise, and trim black mustache seemed to type him as a physician or a member of the legal profession, rather than as a master weaver of the gossamer fabric of ethereal sound, cheerfully accepted the unfavorable verdict. He assured us that the right mood and rhythm were soon bound to come to him. He asked us to return, and Felipe said that we would do so within the week.

My second trip to Chichén Itzá to hear Don Eduardo's "confession" on his Sacred Cenote exploits was combined with Felipe's regular Thursday Agrarian Program. Leaving Mérida by early train, we rode together to Dzitas, where I was met by one of the faithful Fordingas and again driven over the new highway to the old Maya capital while Felipe went on to a pueblo some fifty kilometers beyond. He would call for me that same afternoon, following the land partition, at the Thompson Hacienda House, and we would return by railroad to Mérida. He realized, he said, that there was a full day ahead, but if I still felt in the mood, we would make another night call with Don Luis at Palmerín's home.

En route to Dzitas there was little opportunity to resume my interview with Felipe covering his background, now behind schedule, since it did not include the first years of his public life. Discussions with the agrarian officials over details that had to be worked out before the day's *ejidos* ceremonies occupied most of the journey, but he "solemnly promised" to talk "only with Almita" on the homeward trip.

# 13. Well of Sacrifice

Upon my arrival at Chichén Itzá, Don Eduardo announced that he was fully prepared with all the facts of "America's greatest archaeological adventure" for my *New York Times Magazine* article. But mere facts, he warned, were not enough. If I were to tell his story as it should be told, it was essential that *I feel* the tragedy repeatedly enacted at this place in those remote days. He said that he would try to make *me* feel the ancient tragedy so that I might convey how his response to the human values involved with the Maya ritualistic sacrifice had originally impelled him to risk the terrible hazards of a descent into the Sacred Well. I agreed with him that feeling was a vital element in effective journalism or, for that matter, in any form of communication. And so, with wide-eyed eagerness, I followed every word of the aging explorer's narrative as it summoned a lovely young phantom out of the *cenote*'s depths.

Don Eduardo's natural flair for atmospheric "buildup" and the creation of dramatic setting would have done justice to a professional stage director. He approached his strange tale by leading me from El Castillo along the three-hundred-yard macadamized causeway to the sinister, brackish pool I had seen for the first time earlier in the week. On the way, he pictured, with the aid of descriptive movements and swift changes of facial expression, a maiden of flawless beauty who has emerged from the sanctuary that crowns the mighty pyramid. Even a mole on her cheek, he observed, would have disqualified her for the exalted public mission toward which her entire education and spiritual training had been directed. She wears a bridal wreath of white flowers, as the black masked priests escort her from the sculptured chamber. To the beating of the death drum, the shrill screeching of a reed whistle, and the mocking notes of a high-pitched flute, she descends the imposing stairway. Below, in the shadow of the vast monument, await other priests and a company of nobles in stately procession. Trembling and helpless, the maiden joins them in their march along the sacred road. They pause at the *cenote*'s edge. The ominous music increases in volume as, unresisting, she is lifted to the granite platform supporting the little temple. The nobles and priests form a line around the pool's circular rim. Their voices are raised in loud supplication. At a signal they throw their precious jewels, treasured ornaments, and vessels of smoking incense into the pale green water. Then comes the moment of appeasement—the moment of supreme sacrifice to the offended deity. A priest chants while another tears the clapper from a tiny copper bell that the maiden wears around her neck. To the Maya, the act signifies death. The mystic bride has been mercifully drugged with *balché,*[1] the sacred nectar. Her whole life has been a preparation for this hour. She believes that her symbolic marriage to Chac—the Water God—in the depths of the Great Well is the sole means of saving her people from present or impending disaster. She believes, too, that the *cenote* is only the door to immortal happiness. But the urge to live and love is stronger than drug or faith, and a shriek of despair may pierce the forest as she is hurled headlong into the yawning water pit.

As we sat on the stone platform of the temple that projected out a foot or two from the rim of the *cenote,* Don Eduardo explained that this cruel ritual was performed whenever pestilence, famine or military defeat threatened the Itzáes. Invariably the spectators waited a while for the return of the beautiful victim, assured that such a miracle would mean an immediate answer to their prayers. It is said that once or twice a maiden did return.

The legendary tale finished, Don Eduardo told me the equally dramatic story of how he had translated the tradition of the Sacrificial Well into historic fact; how, after years of lonely labor, he proved that the Sacred Cenote was the place of human sacrifice as reported by Bishop Diego de Landa in his sixteenth-century book *Relación de las Cosas de Yucatán,* as well as by Fray Diego López de Cogolludo and other chroniclers.

"The mysterious, dismal aspect of the *cenote,*" Don Eduardo began, "impressed me as much as its tradition of human offerings to the gods. For years I experienced a growing belief in the accuracy of the Spanish historians, although they made it clear that they were reporting merely from hearsay the dreadful religious rites practiced here until the Conquest.

"But my own intuitions," he continued, "on the close association of the Maya religious conceptions with physical Nature was a strong factor in my decision to search for proof of human sacrifice in the *cenote*'s murky depths. If human beings were actually consigned to a watery grave in Yucatán to avert the anger or win the favor of a deity, I reasoned that this would be the logical place of their doom. I had seen the *cenote* under all conditions—in the soft glow of sunrise, at brilliant noonday, in the silver moonlight, and always there was the suggestion of solemnity, mystery, and tragedy."

But when he decided to verify the *cenote* legends, Don Eduardo related, obstacles on all sides confronted him. His faith met with ridicule from the layman

*The back of this photograph reads: "Governor Carrillo and members of the Carnegie Expedition beside the Sacred Cenote. I'm fourth from left, front row, with large hat."*

and discouragement from the scientist. The scholarly W. H. Holmes, visiting Chichén Itzá in 1895, wrote of the plan: "There has been some talk of exploring the bottom of this *cenote* with the expectation of securing works of art or other treasures. But the task is a most formidable one and will require the erection of strong windlasses and an efficient dredging apparatus. It is doubtful if promised results warrant the expenditure necessary for carrying out the work in a thorough manner."

Don Eduardo said that he had been in perfect agreement with Holmes that the task was indeed a formidable one, especially since the money for the "strong windlasses" and "efficient dredging apparatus" was not available. The *cenote* measures 165 feet in diameter. The limestone wall drops an average 60 feet from the tree-fringed rim to the surface of the pool. And beneath approximately 33 feet of water is a mud bed 30 feet deep. Unable to find the proper support for his extensive enterprise, Don Eduardo recalled how he decided to pursue less costly research methods. He learned the diver's art from a Greek sponge diver, and night after night he descended in his diving suit only to have his inexperience meet with accident. In many instances, he narrowly escaped death.

Don Eduardo had but slight precedent for his exploit. Years later historians brought to light the fact that the only person known previously to have dived into the Sacred Well and live to tell about it was Hunac Ceel, who became ruler of Mayapán as a result. Many doubted the claim of Richard Halliburton, the popular travel writer, that he, on two occasions, had also done so.

The legends held that in addition to the sacrifice of the maidens, victims were sometimes thrown into the Well at dawn to receive messages from the Rain God, Yum Chac. If they lived until noon they were rescued and asked to reveal the message that had been given them regarding the rain for the coming year. This happened so rarely that survivors were signally honored after emergence from the Sacred Cenote, as was the case of Hunac Ceel of Chichén Itzá.

One night, Don Eduardo related, his perseverance was rewarded by the discovery of human bones, which proved to be those of a girl between twelve and sixteen years of age. This success sharpened his enthusiasm, and finally, by sheer force of determination, he won the interest and aid of a wealthy North American. By 1903, a simple dredging apparatus had been purchased and installed. Soon thereafter, the work was well under way, the cranes being operated by hand power of the Indians. Almost from the start the dredging yielded results. Again, human bones—among them those of young girls—were brought to the surface to support the theory of sacrifice. Gradually, precious pre-Colombian objects began to make their appearance in the scooped-up silt. The assortment included jade, gold, copper, ebony, balls of *copal,* obsidian, knives, weapons ornamented with turquoise mosaics, and even fragments of hitherto unknown weaves. All this treasure, Don Eduardo admitted to me, was then in the Peabody Museum, having been sent there via the U.S. consular mail pouch as, over the years, he recovered it from the *cenote* during his diving operations.

"And now you know the whole story," he said as we arose to turn away from the Sacred Cenote and its somber traditions towards the ancient causeway. "It is a confession that has to be made sooner or later. And since life is so uncertain, I have waited long enough." Again, I thanked him for his confidence in me and assured him that my first-run account of his extraordinary discoveries would surely further my ambitions to succeed as an archaeological reporter.

In the flaming sunset Felipe called for me, as arranged, at the Thompson Hacienda House. He was followed by several worshipping Maya, who remained a short distance from the terrace while we chatted and took our leave of Don Eduardo. As we walked toward Chichén Itzá's ceremonial center, where Antonio waited at the wheel of the Fordinga, the Inditos trailed behind us until Felipe beckoned them to join us and, shyly, they approached. Addressing each one by name, he introduced me as "La Indita Blanca, Pixan Halal"—Alma Reed, the white Indian girl. I greeted them in the few Mayan phrases I had learned and took their timidly extended hands. Their approving smiles seemed to welcome me as a member of their ancient tribe. In words that Felipe translated, their young spokesman returned my greeting and said: "Remain with us, lovely Pixan Halal, but if you must leave us now, may your absence be only a short one."

The little group encircled us while we stood for a few moments to enjoy the spectacle of changing light on the colossal symbol of Maya ancestral grandeur. From its broad base to its surmounting sanctuary, the monument was flooded with a golden glow that obliterated the melancholy scene so vividly reconstructed in Don Eduardo's dramatic narrative. The image of the doomed maiden, descending the great stairway between rows of black-masked priests to the ominous beating of the death drum receded, and another that supremely projected love and compassion took its place in my vision of the Mayab. A few of the older men pressed close enough to Felipe to touch gently with affectionate respect the hem of his white linen jacket or the tops of his black leather riding boots. To each of these inarticulate *humildes,*[2] the mere fact of his presence obviously brought comfort and reassurance. I recalled how Mr. Hart had earlier depicted him as "towering above his 'Inditos'—truly a god among them." This was now my impression of the relationship he bore to the exploited peoples of his land. Such a relationship explained why the Greek Euripides exalted heroic humanity over the divinity of the arrogant, vengeful deities. And I was aware, too, that this sunset hour in the capital of the "Holy Men beside the Sacred Well" would immutably shape the course of my deepest, most intimate recognition of all that mattered in my personal life. For it was the hour when I first realized that I could ask no fulfillment of self more complete than the privilege of adoring Felipe for all the days that remained—of working beside him in his Messianic labor, serving him while he fought to win for Earth's helpless ones their long-withheld right to beauty, dignity, and creative joy. And even then I knew with the total knowing that overwhelms the senses like some mighty tidal wave of prophetic discernment that whatever the future might hold for us, my own destiny was now inevitably united with that of a Maya savior.

That night I wanted to share with my diary the feelings that had gripped me in the shadow of Chichén Itzá's immense pyramid. But the words to describe my awakening to the unimagined possibilities of consciousness eluded the usually cooperative fountain pen. Like some sudden fugitive solar ray that can be captured in passing only by the most highly sensitized film, the radiant energy that pervaded my spirit defied the inept process of written analysis. Frustrated, finally I gave up the attempt. Instead, under the date of February 22, 1923, as a postscript to notes covering Thompson's Sacred Cenote "confession"—until that time one of the two most sensational events in my young journalistic career—I recorded in a brief sentence the emotional experience that was to embrace life's most magical memory: "Love, beyond my every hope or dream, comes to me at last!"

Yet the words that could have expressed what I felt about Felipe in that hour of my heart's decision were eventually written. A year later, the perceptive Dr. Ernest Gruening, historian and North American statesman, wrote in tribute to his friend, Felipe Carrillo Puerto: "Like a great comet he came out of age-long darkness, lifting men's eyes and hearts, a fiery token of cycles reaching into the vast unknown, a vision unforgettable. He was a cosmic figure. He linked in his single person the far-flung epic of the great American race and the undying epic of man's quest for freedom."

# 14. The Arena

We were alone on the observation platform of the Mérida-bound train. Felipe's right arm, which had become a symbol of protection throughout Yucatán, rested reassuringly across the back of my chair as it swayed with the movement of the speeding car.

Deep emotions were still responding to the spell of the Chichén Itzá sunset, and I would have preferred to sit silently beside him, watching the unruly lock of hair that had fascinated me from our first meeting, as it played in the wind over his ample forehead. But I could not escape the haunting thought that our remaining hours together were numbered. Prompted by some driving sense of obligation, I felt that I must learn everything possible about the course of his life from the very beginning. Thorough knowledge of his motives, his acts and aims, seemed of the utmost urgency not only because of my own intense desire to understand him completely as a man, but because of a crusading spirit that longed to bring to the awareness of current and perhaps future readers facts that would acquaint them with his true significance as a public figure.

With little enthusiasm, however, at the prospect of disturbing with historic data a blissful mood wholly immersed in the "beauty that was in passing," and emotionally aloof at the moment at the things of yesterday and tomorrow, I nevertheless produced my reporter's pencil and notebook. Felipe himself observed my determined move with a look of disappointment. This was the first occasion that we had not shared with a crowd or at least with a third person. His voice betrayed resentment as he said: "I would rather, of course, talk about *you* . . . Less than a week now remains for me to convince you that you should stay here with us or quickly return to Yucatán. You have no children to care for and you are not married to your capitalist newspapers. Why won't you consider a 'new life'—one that I feel will bring you deeper satisfaction and even a more rapid literary success than your present occupations?"

Suggesting that I write books on archaeology, Felipe added: "There is so much to be learned today about our Maya and the other advanced races of ancient

Mexico. This is the golden hour for getting at the truth about the long-buried past. While taking part in this great adventure of rediscovery, you would, at the same time, be able to satisfy your own love of humanity by working with us in the causes that I know are your very own." I promised to give my most serious thought to his words but I reminded him that as a former journalist he could understand how, with my present commitments, "time was of the essence," and I begged him to resume the story of his entry into Yucatán's political arena where he left off on our unfinished interview.

"Very well, Almita, you win. If it will make you happy, I'll do my best, now and always, as you doubtless already know."

Felipe's chronological outline of events was related with directness and characteristic modesty. At points where his modesty of understatement left the narrative incomplete, I have amplified it with details gleaned from subsequent conversations with his mother, Doña Adela, Elvia, Acrelio, Benjamín, and Gualberto Carrillo and the recollections of family friends. From each source came fresh testimony to support the ineludible fact that Felipe's entire youth was lived under conditions of ceaseless struggle, sacrifice, and constant peril in pursuit of the single goal of achieving for his helpless people the substance of their social needs and impulses.

Reports published in the newspapers of the period document much of the challenging story, which opened with mention of his first prison sentence, served while he was still an adolescent. He had defied, he explained, the proprietor of a large henequen plantation who had ordered a passageway closed to the Indians because they had dared to reclaim their rights to communal lands. After delivering an impassioned speech, the teenage crusader resolutely tore down the barriers that blocked traffic.

In 1906, around the time of the crucial strikes of the Río Blanco Textile Mill workers and the Cananea copper miners, Felipe began publication of a weekly paper, *El Heraldo de Motul,* an organ aimed at the uprooting of the intolerable *enganchado,* or company store, system, which John Kenneth Turner was soon to call to the attention of the English-speaking world through his exposé, *Barbarous Mexico.* During this period, Felipe was also correspondent for *La Revista de Mérida.* In both papers, he vigorously denounced the evil practices on the *haciendas* and the flagrant disregard by their owners of the laws of the nation.

Talk of silencing the fearless young journalist was so common in Motul that Don Justiniano was persistently pleading with him to be on his guard against paid assassins. But Felipe, refusing to heed his father's warnings, would answer: "*No, papacito, tú en cada individuo ves a un enemigo mío*—No, dear Papa, it is not so. In each person you behold my enemy."

Opposition of the guilty slaveholders to his public stand was intensified with the formation in Mérida during 1907 of the Independent Electoral Center, an agency that launched the candidacy of Delio Moreno Cantón for the governorship of Yucatán. Felipe became the ardent supporter of the gifted poet, courageous editor, and champion of democratic methods. To further the campaign, he organized the liberal elements of the Motul region. His leadership in the Centro Electoral Independiente[1] in its fight against the humorously titled Partido Demócrata[2] was, obviously, a mere farcical declaration of principles, since Molina, one of the richest men in the Republic and the most powerful and ruthless *latifundista* in Yucatán, could laugh at the popular vote as a means of obtaining his reelection. But the array of political and financial forces enjoying government protection failed to weaken Felipe's efforts for reform. To that end, he created the Centro Obrero Motuleño.[3] Through this organization, dedicated to the intellectual and material improvement of the local wage earners, he spread the gospel of human and civil rights and even finally succeeded in establishing a fine library for the benefit of the members.

Meanwhile, in order to promote the liberal Morenista[4] program, Felipe enlisted able collaborators in his forthright and incorruptible periodical *El Heraldo*, among them, Prof. Pedro Pérez Miranda and Dr. Manuel Amézquita. The Central American contributors included Dr. Silvio Salas and Don Mariano Tovar. Other well-known writers whose columns added distinction to *El Heraldo* were Don Luis Librado Montesinos of Tampico and Don Salvador Martínez Alomja of Campeche, then residing in Motul. To meet the accusations against the ruling *políticos* and monopolists, an opposition paper, *La Gaceta de la Costa*,[5] was founded by the government clique. And as charges and countercharges incited passionate polemics and fanned the already explosive situation, the local officials, bent on defeating Moreno Cantón and fearful of his reform measures, caused Felipe's arrest and detention. The trumped-up indictment was based on the "abuse of the Chief of the Public Ministry, Manuel Palma Cervera," ex-director of *La Gaceta de la Costa*, who also happened to be the nephew of the *jefe político*. Through the latter's absolute power, Felipe was consigned to the Penitenciaría Juárez[6] in Mérida on the plea that his accuser lived in that city.

Commenting on the "unusual course of justice" pursued by the Public Ministry, the *Revista de Mérida* stated: "Sr. Carrillo for his honesty and the independence of his character is highly esteemed by the society of Motul, which is pained to witness the unjust proceedings against him. Nevertheless, with the President of the Republic, who holds that we 'must have faith in justice,' we are certain that Sr. Carrillo will soon again breathe the air of liberty."

After spending twenty days in the Penitentiary, Felipe was freed and cleared of the charges, the same journal announcing his vindication in the following note: "Yesterday afternoon, Sr. Don Felipe Carrillo was the object of a warm reception from his many friends upon his arrival at Motul after suffering unjust incarceration. The railroad station was crowded with admirers and well-wishers."

In connection with this incident, Felipe's generous spirit and tolerant nature, his willingness to overlook injuries and forgive those who had harmed him, is shown in an anecdote related by his brother Acrelio. Upon learning that Manuel Palma Cervera, who had maliciously caused his imprisonment, was gravely ill, Felipe, to the amazement of the Palma Cervera family, visited the sick man. He recalled their old friendship, explaining that he thoroughly understood the devious machinations of politics, which had ruptured but not destroyed their years of neighborly relationship.

With the spread of the movement in favor of Francisco I. Madero for President there emerged after 1908 a new challenge to Felipe's idealism and boundless energy. During this period he attended and called secret meetings, often at his own home, protesting the failure of Díaz to relinquish the presidency in accordance with the promise made in the James Creelman interview published by *Pearson's Magazine* in March 1908. His opposition to the "Reelectionists," headed in Yucatán at the time by the interim Governor, Enrique Muñoz Aristegui, became increasingly vigorous as the 1910 expiration date of the dictator's thirty-three-year-old tenure of office and eighth term approached. When it became known that the hated Sonora Governor Ramón Corral—who had masterminded the cruel deportation of thousands of Yaqui Indians to Yucatán for slavery on the *haciendas*—was selected as the vice presidential candidate, Felipe's outspoken condemnation of the choice brought severe reprisals. With local rebels against the Díaz despotism, including Carlos R. Menéndez, the Yucatecan journalist, Felipe was again jailed. In an attempt to silence his popular voice, the *políticos* held him incommunicado—but aided by loyal followers he managed to wage an effective propaganda campaign from behind prison walls. And soon after his release he engaged intensified efforts on behalf on the Anti-Reelection and other political campaigns, some of which frequently took him to Valladolid, a center of restlessness and of incipient collective resistance.

An incident recalled by Sr. Rafael Quintal of Motul, who had known Felipe since his first railroading period in 1891 and had occasionally acted as his substitute during vacations or leaves of absence, is eloquent on the "human" methods of approaching problems, which helped him win the faith and support of Yucatán's dispossessed thousands. Sr. Quintal relates that he was with Felipe in Valladolid when he spoke from a platform to an Indian gathering. As he was finishing his talk, an old Indio, literally in rags, shoeless, and with a tattered sombrero, said to him: "Listen, Chanzul (young gentleman), in other days there came to us another like you. He told us that he wanted to do on the *fincas* the things that you now want to do . . . But he never accomplished . . . Never."

Felipe replied: "Don Fulano (Mr. So-and-so) spoke thus to you . . . What do you say?"

"I say that he never accomplished . . . And I say now, let the Maya rise up. And I am going to tell them to go to Mérida to urge others to do the same. I am ninety-six. I am very poor. I have only my grandson."

"Why so poor?" asked Felipe. "Why have you no clothes? Why are you without shoes, *camisa,* and *calzones?*"

"There are no pesos for us . . . anywhere!"

"Is there someone here who can make the clothes you need? If so, I shall buy the white cloth and get a hat and cloak for you . . . But help me make conditions better for all. Help me with your fellow townsmen that *I* may accomplish . . . Here are thirty pesos. Keep them in case you fall sick."

A few weeks later Felipe returned. The old Indio, wearing shoes and hat and his new outfit, was on hand to greet him: "Come on," he shouted to his Maya companions . . . "Here is Chanzul." And addressing Felipe, he said: "In Valladolid, we are bathed in joy, because you have come back to accomplish!"

But the hour for Felipe's greatest accomplishment had not yet struck. He was destined to struggle for another five years before the hopes he held out to Valladolid's Indians in 1910 could be realized with their deliverance from slavery on the *fincas* and from the abject poverty that was their lot when too old and feeble to toil for their heartless masters. And Valladolid was to witness much shedding of blood and tears before the chains that bound the Mayab to degradation were broken.

Felipe is generally recognized as the intellectual director of what has been called "la primera chispa de la revolución social" (the first spark of the Social Revolution) — an uprising of the workers in Valladolid on June 4, 1910. As a conductor and baggage master on Yucatán's railroads and as an organizer of labor during the years preceding the rebellion, he took advantage of his frequent stopovers at Valladolid to enlist Maderistas[7] and to disseminate Revolutionary ideas through persuasive arguments at underground meetings. When the rebellion, in which fifteen hundred *campesinos* took part, finally broke out, a wave of consternation swept the state and nation, already tense with expectancy of startling events. Federal troops were rushed to the scene, but it was some days before the rebels abandoned possession of the city. The three principal chiefs — Maximiliano R. Bonilla, Atilano Albertos, and José Kantún — were captured and, on June 25, shot by a firing squad in the patio of the church of San Roque de Valladolid. Two other leaders of the thwarted armed movement escaped. One of them, Miguel Ruz Ponce, took refuge in the Quintana Roo jungles. Marrying the daughter of the native *cacique,* he returned to Yucatán after the fall of Díaz. The other leader, Claudio Alcocer, was later assassinated.

In his book, *Mi vida revolucionaria,*[8] Félix Palavicini, Mexican intellectual and publisher of *El Universal,*[9] records that Don Francisco I. Madero once declared in an interview: "If there is a Social Revolution in Mexico, it will commence in Yucatán." His prophetic words were fulfilled to the letter, as Antonio Bustillos Carrillo points out, when the Revolution, which the Apostle of Democracy[10] himself headed, actually did originate in Yucatán, sparked five months earlier at Valladolid by Felipe Carrillo Puerto.

Felipe once told me that he had served a total of seven years on five different occasions in Yucatán's prisons on charges growing out of political activities. A natural target for the embattled enemies of social renovation, he evidently avoided additional years of incarceration and possibly death by escaping to the United States immediately after the Valladolid uprising in which the rebels were virtually annihilated. Different accounts of what actually occurred in the summer of 1910 leave a hiatus in the verified record of this crucial period. A frequently published version is that when Felipe crossed the border, he personally contacted Madero, who in early October had broken jail in San Luis Potosí and, disguised as a laborer, reached safety in Texas. According to Edmundo Bolio, Felipe went directly to New York, where he worked on the docks as a longshoreman. Contrary to some accounts, it is the opinion of Professor Bolio, who was a close friend and, later, director of the cultural programs of the Liga Central, that Felipe did not meet Samuel S. Gompers, President of the American Federation of Labor, during this or any of his three visits to the United States.

Professor Bolio informed me that his friendship with Felipe dated from 1909 when, as a young schoolteacher from Izamal, he was invited to Motul by Gualberto Salazar, *jefe político,* to attend a reunion in his home. Salazar had expected that the learned Maestro, an authority on Mayan language, history, and legend, would speak in laudatory terms of his administration. But when Felipe produced the record showing that the same Salazar was an enemy, not the friend of the Maya Indians, Professor Bolio, instead of praising, publicly rebuked him. A fistfight was prevented only by the interference of the other guests. But knowing that the Maestro was in danger, Felipe hid him before dawn in his *carreta,* well concealed beneath sacks of cattle fodder. Then, driving off to Temax, he placed his new friend on the train for Mérida.

Whatever Felipe's associations north of the border after Valladolid, his absence from Mexico could not have been longer than three months. On September 13, 1910, we find him in San Luis Potosí as one of the two delegates from Yucatán to the Third Congress of Periodistas de Prensa de los Estados.[11] The other delegate, Carlos R. Menéndez, discloses in his book, *Ninety Years of Yucatecan History (1821–1910),*[12] that together they presented a motion that, "in the midst of great applause, was approved by acclamation." The motion called for the sending of two urgent telegrams, one directed to the President of the Republic, General Porfirio Díaz, and the second to Governor Muñoz Aristegui of Yucatán. "By unanimous accord," the message read, "this Congress respectfully asks that liberty be granted to the political prisoners who languish in the Castle of San Juan de Ulúa and in the penitentiary of Mérida, respectively, imploring you that at sunrise of the Centennial not a single Mexican will be in prison because of his political convictions." As a postscript to the reproduced telegram, Sr. Menéndez commented that neither President Díaz nor Governor Muñoz Aristegui took the trouble to answer the Congress. At the time, five thousand Madero sympathizers were in Mexican prisons.

From his own passing references to his movements following San Luis Potosí and from the detailed accounts of several of his associates in that ominous period, I learned that Felipe, before returning to Yucatán, went to Belize to supply himself with arms for the struggle he anticipated. But during a brief stay at Champotón on the Campeche Coast, he learned of the swift succession of Mexican events in the last week of May 1911. The series of happenings—the most sensational perhaps to occur up to that time in any single week of the nation's modern history, began on May 24, when Porfirio Díaz reluctantly submitted his resignation as President. On May 26, Francisco de la Barra, a member of the Díaz cabinet and former Ambassador to the United States, assumed the interim presidency. On the same day, the insurgent leader, Madero, issued a manifesto calling upon the citizenry to recognize the interim government of de la Barra, stating: "He is entirely with us." Finally, on May 31, amid shouts of "Death to the dictator," the eighty-two-year-old Díaz, "respecting the will of the people," sailed away from Veracruz into European exile, thus confirming the triumph of the Madero-led Revolution.

Going at once to Mérida and then to Motul, Felipe placed himself at the head of the partisans of Delio Moreno Cantón, who, for the second time, had been nominated for Governor of the Centro Electoral Independiente. Opposing him was Licenciado José María Pino Suárez, also an independent and editor of the liberal paper *El Peninsular*. Pino Suárez sought the aid of Madero and tried through various inducements to win Felipe over to his side. But aware that the trust and hopes of the *campesinos* and *obreros*[13] had been wisely placed in their long-tested defender, Felipe indignantly rejected the offers, preferring, as he said, to lose with Moreno Cantón. Madero himself had suggested to Pino Suárez in a letter dated August 15, 1909, that he supported Moreno Cantón for Governor in "exchange for the aid of all his elements for the National Anti-Reelectionist campaign of the next year." Felipe's own unswerving faith in Moreno Cantón was obviously shared by Madero, whose decision in the matter was prompted, however, by political expediency rather than personal conviction. As Stanley Robert Ross observed in his biography, *Francisco I. Madero:*[14]

> Although he believed that the long-range objective would be served best by the candidacy of Moreno Cantón, he revealed his respect for local wishes

by withholding endorsement until after the state convention had been held. The government was not concerned about the preference of the people. Governor Enrique Muñoz Arístegui was reelected. Madero could then point to events in Morelos, Sinaloa, and Yucatán as proof that Díaz would not promote a truly democratic government by himself.

In answer to my question concerning the man who shared Madero's tragic fate, Felipe related that Pino Suárez had come as a youth from his native Tabasco to Yucatán, where both as a lawyer and as a journalist he had defended Maya workers on the *haciendas* and, "as a poet, had fanned the Revolutionary flame." In June 1909 when Madero visited Mérida, entering the Yucatecan capital amid a tremendous ovation, Pino Suárez was one of the six persons to welcome him at the Progreso docks. Throughout the following year, up until the eve of the "rigged" elections, Pino Suárez organized Anti-Reelectionist groups in Tabasco, Campeche, and Yucatán, but during the election period, both he and Delio Moreno Cantón were forced into hiding. In the name of the Revolutionary Army, Pino Suárez signed the Treaty of Ciudad Juárez on May 20, 1911, calling for the resignations of President Díaz and Ramón Corral before the end of the month. The Treaty also provided that Francisco León de la Barra, Secretary of Foreign Relations, be named as President Pro Tem of the Republic and that he issue a call for national elections. During the interim presidency of de la Barra, Pino Suárez served as Yucatán's Governor.

With Madero's election on October 15, 1911, as Constitutional President, he was able, with his immense influence as a national idol, to swing the nominating convention of the Progressive Constitutional Party to the side of Pino Suárez, despite the greater popularity of the opposition candidate, Dr. Francisco Vázquez Gómez. A single eulogistic speech had tipped the indecisive balance between the contenders to his favorite. The act was interpreted by many staunch Revolutionaries of the period—and I gathered from Felipe's tone in discussing the incident that he was among them—as clear "imposition." Their judgment has been sustained by several eyewitness historians, including Jesús Silva Herzog, who contend that Madero's vigorous support of Pino Suárez brought about the alienation of numerous sympathizers of the President-Elect and marked the beginning of the decline of his bright political star.

A radiant bed of *amapolas*[15] alongside the railroad track interrupted my note taking. At a passing glimpse of the vermilion blossoms glowing flamelike amid the dull stretch of tawny shrub, Felipe exclaimed: "*Mira, Almita, ¡qué preciosas!*—Look, Almita, how lovely! You must have a few of them!" I wondered how this poetic impulse might be realized, but I soon learned when, stepping inside to the far end of the parlor car, Felipe aroused the dozing Antonio and handed him an order for the engineer. In answer to the message a workman appeared, and Felipe asked to have the train slowly backed up for a kilometer or two. When we reached the poppies, he got out and gathered a bouquet of the flowers. The episode made an enduring impression on me, for it dramatically illustrated a rational attitude towards the Machine and its role as the servant rather than the master of man. It also indicated a philosophy that held beauty to be an essential element of life. But the all-pervading magic evoked by the lyrical interlude of the *amapolas* faded abruptly when Felipe resumed his narrative. For it was then—and he was the first to inform me—that I learned of the tragedy that overshadowed the years of his young manhood.

"It is not easy, Almita, for me to tell you," he began, "something that sooner or later you will have to know about me. Just a few years after my entrance into public life, I killed a man. It was an act of self-defense. I was fired upon by a political enemy, one who had been paid by rich and powerful opponents to get rid of me, but who for a long time had posed as a family friend. His name was Néstor Arjonilla. And since you insist upon probing into the past of a Socialist leader, I feel, in fairness, you should know all of the circumstances."

Felipe then related that he was on his way to the Motul railroad station on July 16, 1911, to await the arrival of the newspapers for which he was local correspondent and agent. Arjonilla approached him to complain about some severe criticisms of the city officials that had appeared in the Mérida press. Felipe replied that if the reports were signed by the correspondent, he had sent them. Insults followed, and Arjonilla boasted that Motul was supporting José María Pino Suárez instead of Felipe's close friend and journalistic collaborator, Delio Moreno Cantón. Explaining that the bitterness had erupted at the height of the struggle between the two vice presidential candidates, Felipe said that Moreno Cantón, with whom he had been associated in reform movements since 1906, was the popular choice, while Pino Suárez had been imposed by Madero.

In the heat of the argument, Arjonilla struck with such violent force that Felipe doubled under the surprise blow, and his assailant, taking advantage of a momentarily stunned condition, fired at close range, burning a hole in his coat sleeve. "When I saw him preparing to fire a second time," Felipe continued, "I realized that to save my life, I must return the shot. Most certainly, I did not aim to kill, merely to disarm my attacker. The bullet penetrated the left forearm near the wrist, but unfortunately, it traveled in such a strange course that it lodged in his heart." Other details of Arjonilla's unsuccessful attempt to eliminate Felipe from the political scene were recorded in Motul's annals and preserved in the collective memory. Later, I was to learn the whole story and its aftermath chiefly through Don Efraín Palma Castro. He had accompanied Felipe to the railroad station and had, in fact, warned him that there could be truth in the street rumors. Living in the Yucatán until his death in 1958, Don Efraín used to relate how Felipe, after the fatal encounter, went immediately to his father's store and announced: "*Papacito, sucedió lo que teniá que suceder: Creo que maté a Arjonilla porque lo ví tendido en el Parque José María Campos*—Dear Papa, what had to happen, has happened: I believe that I have killed Arjonilla, for I saw him stretched out in the Parque José María Campos." Don Justiniano, who had also previously warned his son against Arjonilla's murderous intentions because of certain incidents that had aroused his suspicions, now counseled him to go alone to police headquarters and surrender to the authorities.

There was one detail, however, that Felipe himself recalled with the pride invariably reflected in his voice and eyes whenever he spoke of his parents. He said that after he had given himself up and was held in the case, his father went to the plaza where the shooting had occurred and where a large crowd had gathered around Arjonilla's body. Going among the people, Don Justiniano boldly addressed those whom he recognized as the instigators of the murder plot. In defiant tones that everyone present could hear, he said: "If you have another bull, I have more bullfighters. One is now a prisoner because of your iniquity, but I have others who are ready. Just tell me who has been chosen as the next bull so that I may give orders to another *torero*." "There were not many men in those days," Felipe observed, "who, like my father, dared to confront the wealthy landowners and the slavish officials protected by ruthless Porfirista[16] power."

A tyrannical local *cacique*, controlled by the *jefe político*, sentenced Felipe to a long prison term. But after serving more than a year instead of the seventy-two hours decreed by law for homicide in self-defense, the verdict was reversed because of "legal defects," affirming that Felipe had killed in the act of saving his own life. The testimony submitted at the rehearing revealed that the same *jefe político* who had used his potent influence with the court also demanded that the eyewitness, Sr. Palma Castro, make a declaration in favor in Arjonilla, describing him as "an honest worker" and observing that "Felipe had the attack coming to him." But Sr. Palma Castro remained firm, stating that he could testify only to the truth and to what he had seen.

Despite the court decision absolving Felipe of guilt, it was clear to me then, as he recounted the details of the case and on later occasions, that Arjonilla's death at his hands remained an ineradicable cause of profound regret. His abhorrence of violence that apparently grew with the years became at last so firmly rooted that he even refused to take part in the killing of animals for sport. With the look of one still shaken by a dread experience, he related how he had once joined a group of friends on a western Yucatán safari when a huge antlered deer suddenly appeared on the crest of a hill. He aimed, and the magnificent stag fell helpless at his feet, its great brown eyes seeming to plead with him for mercy. The sight filled him with such deep remorse that he determined on the spot to make this his last appearance as a huntsman.

A period of intensive physical and mental labor followed Felipe's acquittal in the Arjonilla case. Retiring to his father's *finca,* "Akim Kek," near the pueblo of Uci, he chopped wood and engaged in other heavy farmwork. His free hours were devoted to completing and editing his translation of the Mexican Constitution into Mayan and to acquainting non-Spanish-speaking Indian groups with the document's guarantees of human and civil rights. As part of his defiant resumption of his "field work," he organized the hitherto voiceless masses, forming them into coherent and articulate units in the various areas. In reality, it was his insistence upon making thousands of Yucatecan slaves aware of their illegal bondage that had in the first place aroused the hostility of the *hacendados* and led to the hiring of Arjonilla for the carrying out of their sinister plans. For the most part, Felipe's narrative was confined to the main turning points along the rough and perilous road to his future political leadership. At the time, I lacked sufficient information to frame questions that might stir the memories of other dramatic experiences in his twenties, among them a period of captivity in Mexico's southeastern jungles.

It was not, in fact, until he became Governor—when as one of his first official acts he invited General Mai, venerable high chief of the Quintana Roo Maya, to visit Mérida as an honored state guest—that the story of his kidnapping more than a decade earlier by the same *cacique* was generally known in Yucatán. For motivating the warm welcome and the round of colorful festivities that greeted the arrival of the long-haired, befeathered and ring-nosed aboriginal ruler—as vividly described to me by Elvia and Maestra Rosa, both of whom assisted in the royal reception program—was the following background: A few years after his marriage, Felipe mysteriously disappeared, failing to return from one of his occasional trips to Belize, where he traded farm implements, arms, and miscellaneous merchandise for *chicle*[17] produced by the natives of the interior. At the time, he was in charge of the post office located in his own home, fronting on the Motul Plaza. After weeks and months had passed without word from him, Isabel was appointed as his substitute. The family had long since given up hope of his return, even mourning him as dead, when suddenly, unannounced, and to the joyous surprise of all, Felipe appeared. Heavier by several kilos than when he left Motul, his darkly tanned skin contrasting curiously with his shoulder-length blond hair and full beard, he explained that on his homeward journey he had been captured and, in the depths of the Quintana Roo jungles, held prisoner by a group of Maya Indians. There he was required to serve as their interpreter and instructor and to organize their commerce in *chicle,* hardwood, and other forest products. In numerous ways they demonstrated their absolute confidence that he would protect the tribal interests in dealing with the sharp Belize traders. But while they trusted him completely in the conduct of their business affairs and treated him with every consideration, he was closely guarded day and night to prevent escape or communication with the outside world. Aided by his own thorough knowledge of the Mayan language, he taught General Mai to speak Spanish and gradually worked out a sound basis for barter and financial negotiations. Then, one morning, amid expressions of profound gratitude from the chief and the assembled tribesmen, Felipe was released and ceremoniously escorted back to the edge of civilization. In discussing his long absence with members of his family and his intimates, he did not seem to regret the "lost" period of his captivity. He assured them that his months of sharing the daily lives of the people of the tropical *selva*[18] had given him a firsthand knowledge of their good characters and their serious problems that he could have gained in no other way. He was deeply sorry, he said, to have caused everyone anxiety and fear for his safety, but he felt that the strange adventure would serve him as an invaluable guide in his plans for ending the isolation of millions of Mexico's Indians.

The White City's mingled mass of buildings assumed gracious contours in the pallid moonlight, enveloping impartially Vice-Regal façades and nondescript storefronts in a soft luminosity of shadow. Structural crudities and disharmonies vanished, and even the tragic memories imbedded in the stones of Mérida's old churches and palaces were forgotten as Antonio drove us from the railroad station to the open-air Nevería Colón, the popular ice cream parlor that faced the Parque de las Armas.[19] Despite the gaiety of the evening promenaders and the bright street illumination, everything seemed to be part of a mystical backdrop for the reenactment of situations summoned by Felipe's narrative from the ever receding realm of "that which *was* but can never cease *having been.*"

During the three-hour ride from Dzitas, he had outlined determinative events and activities of his stern apprenticeship, revealing to me unimagined facets of his integral character. There was no need now for words as we lingered over our *guanábana sorbetes* or just wonderingly gazed at each other, oblivious of onlookers who gathered, as they invariably did, whenever we appeared together in a public place. Taking the longest and somewhat roundabout route across the central plaza as he escorted me to the foyer of the Hotel Imperial, Felipe, in a serious mood, suddenly paused and said: "This has been an important day in my life, Almita. I want you to know that I no longer feel lonely . . . or alone!"

I eluded his sincerity with a defensive impersonal reply. The day was also an important one in my life, I assured him, since it had shown me how consistent and courageous a Mexican youth could be in his struggles for a happier, saner world.

There were many other thoughts besides my awareness of his true greatness as a leader that I longed to convey to him then. Yet I sadly realized that if these deeply personal things were ever to be said, it must be at some distant future hour. How intensely at that moment I wanted him to know that he represented for me all possible beautiful relationships of life between man and woman—father, brother, friend, comrade, lover, teacher, guide, and symbol of the ultimate realization of self!

But when he impulsively pressed both my hands to his heart as he said, "*Hasta mañana*—until tomorrow," I smothered the impulse to shatter the foolish restraints of my conformist code. Instead, I locked the unspoken words "*Te quiero*—I love you" in the recesses of my consciousness, sharing them only with my private diary later that night.

# 15. Flowers of Stone

A visit to the Cave of Loltún some one hundred miles south of Mérida was the most exciting event of the expedition's final week in Yucatán. The trip had been proposed by several of the scientific investigators not only because Loltún—Mayan for "Cave of the Stone Flower"—was regarded as an outstanding natural wonder of southeastern Mexico, but also for its archaeological possibilities, since it was said to conceal within its forbidding depths ceramics of an important Maya cultural phase known as the Tzakol. Corresponding to a period of the Old Empire, the Tzakol stage, according to Dr. Morley, witnessed in the course of its Early, Middle, and Late phases (A.D. 317 to 633), major architectural developments, including the appearance of stone monuments and corbelled roof vaultings.

Felipe welcomed the suggestion of the scholars with enthusiasm but warned them that the journey was not an easy one. He said that he had learned much about the cave's marvels from his own visits there, sometimes in the company of his friend Don Eduardo, who was more familiar, perhaps, with Loltún's geologic structure and archaeology than anyone in Yucatán. As far back as 1888, the intrepid explorer, then in his adventuresome youth, had conducted a Peabody Museum party through the cavern's hidden tunnels and chambers, recording his observations and discoveries in the 1897 volume of the Harvard University Memoirs.[1]

At Felipe's suggestion and by group acclamation, Don Eduardo was named Director General of the tour, and at dawn, three days before our departure for New York, we started out from Mérida by railroad for a trip of some four and a half hours. The route led due south for about fifty miles and at Nuna swerved into the Low Hill, or Puuc, country, stretching for the same distance in a southwesterly direction. We left the train at Oxkutzcab, where Felipe and his guests were warmly greeted by the *presidente municipal,* the full membership of the local Liga, and scores of schoolchildren, all to the accompaniment of spirited music from a native stringed orchestra. At the station, the Feministas, attired for the occasion in colorful embroidered *huipiles* stood against a background of their massed triangular red banners, behind long tables, dispensing hospitality in the form of assorted fruits and cool beverages. After a few words of official welcome and Felipe's response, both spoken in Mayan, Oxkutzcab's entire population, preceded by musicians, escorted us to the several waiting *plataformas*—iron-wheeled flatcars drawn by mules over the railroad tracks. For the comfort of the *norteamericanos,* mattresses had been very considerably laid on the *plataformas*—vehicles ordinarily used to transport henequen from the *haciendas* along the line—and we all settled down for another hour's ride in the optimistic mood that envelops the start of a novel and exciting group adventure.

While grateful for small favors, the expeditionaries kept good-naturedly bemoaning the fact that the mattresses were not "bigger and better and in more generous supply," as we were jounced and jolted over the bumpy roadbed beyond Oxkutzcab. Occasionally, the monotony of the bleak, tawny landscape, stretching to the limit of vision in a phalanx of calcareous hills, was varied with a humble thatch-roofed dwelling. And in one of the few planted areas in a narrow valley, stood a small chapel, La Ermita, dedicated to the Virgin María del Pilar.

On the final lap of the journey we stopped at a weather-beaten house that functioned as the government caretaker's lodge, an inn for the accommodation of the rare tourist who remained overnight in the region, and a station for the guides. Here, we were met by a group of *chicleros*[2] from the state of Campeche who, as a sort of "auxiliary corps," were awaiting our arrival there.

Felipe warmly greeted Nacho, leader of the *chiclero* group, as an old *compañero* and introduced him to the archaeologists as "un buen colaborador."[3] From a chain around Nacho's neck was suspended a small camera that had been given to him, Felipe explained, by the Partido Socialista del Sureste for the purpose of photographing unknown Maya ruins concealed in the lush vegetation of the *chicle*-producing region, the dense Campeche forests. Other *chicleros* of proven intelligence were also given little cameras. For the delivery of each negative of an undiscovered or unexplored structure or site, they received a bonus of fifty pesos. "This method of locating zones for future study," Felipe said, "saves the government time and money. And no less important, it creates for these poor exploited Indians, whose brief annual working periods are filled with hazards, deeper pride in the achievements of their Maya ancestors." Felipe pointed out to us why the *chiclero*'s life was so pathetically short. The fact was due not only to the wild animals, reptiles, and poisonous insects of the jungle, but to falling trees. Frequently the *chicleros* cut too deeply into the trunk of the tall sapodillas that yield the white sap for the manufacture of chewing gum to supply a large international market. When this happens, the tree topples to earth carrying with it the *chiclero* to serious injury and often to death. He disclosed that the *chicleros* of Yucatán, Campeche, and Quintana Roo had recently organized themselves into a *sindicato*[4] and that the Liga de Resistencia was preparing a series of demands upon the employers that would protect them and their families against industry-caused liability or fatal accident.

As Director General, Don Eduardo proved to be an authoritative, stimulating, and entertaining guide, his quips and reminiscent yarns often making us forget that we were being bounced over the rough roadbed in primitive conveyances. As we approached Loltún's deeply shadowed mouth, guarded by what appeared to be a defensive barricade of heavy boulders, he related experiences of his first research project in Yucatán. "Our purpose at that time," he explained, "was to sound the cave's hitherto unknown depths and to photograph its moss-covered walls where, in some remote era, man had carved strange figures and mystic symbols." Recalling his earliest impressions of Loltún, the explorer remarked: "It was like entering an enormous tomb—truly like a place of the dead."

I could fully appreciate Don Eduardo's descriptive powers only after I myself had descended by rugged stone steps to the damp, chalky floor. For here, if anywhere on earth, could one visualize the netherworld, the dismal abode of disembodied spirits, as pictured in the Stygian myths and the sixth book of Virgil's *Aeneid.* As I glanced into the black overhead spaces—which opened, Don Eduardo assured us, upon still larger and more awesome chambers, pierced here and there with patches of light that seemed as distinct as stars in the night sky—I was filled with admiration for our scholarly guide's vivid and accurate reporting.

Amid Loltún's inescapable associations with death, the members of our party moved very slowly along a narrow ledge in single file. The Indians, clad in white cotton *camisas,* lighted our way with candle flares while another group, carrying ropes and tackle for emergency use, formed a rear guard. The mingled sounds of Maya, Spanish, and English voices echoed through the vast silence, to evoke the eerie suggestion of the futile moaning of lost souls. Through long corridors that connected grottoes that might have been planned for human habitation, Felipe guided my steps until we emerged into a high-domed gallery hung with stalactites of varying lengths and colors. Some of the more massive forms were a dull gray or stained with a reddish brown—rust coated by centuries of dripping water. Others, of delicate shape, were spotless white, their crystalline tips sparkling like multifaceted brilliants in the glare of the candles.

In what at first seemed to be a prospect of unrelieved gloom, we discovered other beautiful objects fashioned by Nature's artistry. Leading us to a passage between two of the chambers, Don Eduardo pointed out his personal selection as "the prize exhibit in Loltún's vast subterranean museum." This object, as he poetically described it, quoting from his memoirs, was "a cylindrical pedestal of white stalmite of fluted walls and base, the rounded crown of the column resembling the tightly closed petals of a snow-white blossom. At its center is a cavity like a chalice, half-shielded by a transparent limestone veil." He explained that while not a single drop entered the chalice from the cavern's roof, it was always filled with cold, clear water, which, as we could see, overflowed down the sides of the pedestal. The curious phenomenon was the result of an interior reservoir and a natural siphon within the walls.

The spectacle and the magnitude of the Cave of Loltún, believed to extend for miles beneath Quintana Roo's limestone cap, entirely captivated the imagination of the Yucatalogists. Its fascination for the scientists, however, was centered in the traces of ancient man and his handiwork for which the cavern served as a depositary. Don Eduardo had himself located numerous signs of prehistoric occupation, notably, deep layers of broken pottery. There were also the *haltunes*—or water troughs—hollowed out of boulders and placed where they received water that percolated, drop by drop, through the roof openings. He also called our attention to a broad band of hieroglyphs carved on a smooth section of vertical wall near the entrance. Moss had grown over the inscriptions, but they were still visible. The archaeologists interpreted certain rock carvings as the conventional design for mummies but conceded that no proof had been found as yet to indicate that America's pre-Columbian races interred their dead in the Egyptian manner.

Curiously enough, it was during this erudite discussion of "mummy" symbols that we were abruptly plunged into total darkness. The several candle flares were simultaneously extinguished, and at the moment no one knew why. In the confusion, the obvious cause—a strong air current blowing through some overhead opening—could not be immediately verified. The bolder of the Indian workers ran to escape from some nameless terror; others stood as though petrified with fear. Murmurs that grew in volume to loud wailing reverberated through the uncharted spaces. Clearly, these Maya had accepted the sudden failure of the light as a sign of impending disaster. Tales of similar panics at archaeological sites where native laborers believed that their old deities still possess the power to destroy those who desecrate their altars are plentiful in the travel books of all lands. Most of the expeditionaries were probably thinking of incidents of this kind. My own thoughts wandered off to the Valley of the Kings, at distant Luxor, where the violators of Tut-Ankh-Amen's tomb met with fated vengeance in fulfillment of Pharaoh's far-reaching curse.

The Indians of the Loltún region were known to hold the cave in superstitious dread, and except when acting as guides to inspectors or tourists, they rarely visit it and then only in groups. It is not illogical that in the mysterious blackout they should read evil omens, a supernatural warning that their worst fears were about to be realized. The inflammable situation threatened to leap completely out of control when someone shrieked: "*Estamos perdidos*—We are lost . . . We cannot find the trail . . ." In the rising commotion, Don Eduardo's slightly nasal voice, pleading in Mayan for calmness, was barely audible. When the pleas went unheeded, Felipe assumed the Director General's role, and with the shock effect of an earthshaking blast, he thundered commands in his ancestral tongue. Almost instantly the howling ceased and every Maya present stood at rigid attention. Fortunately, Felipe was prepared with an electric flashlight. Wielding it as though it were an imperial scepter, he swiftly passed its glare back and forth across the faces of the demoralized "auxiliary corps," while his stentorian voice continued to resound with accelerated power and tempo. His commands were answered with immediate action. The candle bearers came forward to relight their flares from matches supplied by the expeditionaries. Nacho, with two of his men, went off with Don Eduardo in search of our "lost trail." I sensed an indefinable mystical quality in the silent speed and precision with which all orders were carried out. It occurred to me that implicit obedience of the Inditos might be less a result of their fear of Felipe's official authority than recognition of Maya tribal leadership inherent in his royal Sotuta lineage. After some moments of uncomfortable suspense, Nacho returned to announce that Don Eduardo had located the passage from which we had inadvertently strayed in the confusing maze of chambers and tunnels.

When, to the infinite relief of the party's most seasoned explorers, we finally emerged into the radiant sunlight, the reinstated Director General assured us that in all their long friendship he had never known Don Felipe to be in so "autocratic" a mood. While the directives aimed at getting us out of the cave in the shortest possible time were clear and to the point, Don Eduardo said that Felipe used language so vehement and accompanied with such "awful imprecations of all the gods of the Maya pantheon" that his words would hardly bear English translation, especially "in the presence of ladies." The Inditos were evidently stunned by this unsuspected side of the personality of their kindly, generous-hearted Big Brother "H'pil," as they called him. They now realized he was capable, when the occasion required, of giving a superb imitation of a formidable, outraged deity. The archaeologists, too, appeared startled by the display of imperious wrath from their mild-mannered, gracious host. Vera Barry later reported that she overheard Dr. Merriam remark: "Governor Carrillo knows how to assert his ancient kingship and his modern political sagacity—and both with constructive results. His is a potent brand, and they certainly feared it more than the darkness."

During the return trip to Mérida, Felipe, with his usual composure and in amiable mood, exchanged witty observations with his guests over the "rigors of the journey, which, through circumstances out of my control and with the best intentions, I have caused you all to endure, because we lack roads and electrification." But some good, he assured us, would come out of the day's discomfort and perils, even though "the belated benefits might be of small consolation to the present greatly inconvenienced company." He explained that as a result of our experiences, he had decided to project and to build at once a direct highway to Loltún and to equip the grotto with special illumination. "When Nature has staged such an extraordinary spectacle, it is our duty to make it easier and safer for everyone to enjoy it."

# 16. Civil Liberties

Upon their return late at night from the strenuous and rather disturbing Loltún trip, the expeditionaries unanimously decided to rearrange the scheduled itinerary in favor of needed relaxation and the leisure for eleventh-hour gift shopping in Mérida. The "free day" removed my preoccupation about how I was going to complete the frequently interrupted interview with Felipe before we left Yucatán. I realized that many local matters, which had been postponed because of the time and attention he had so generously devoted to the entertainment of his American guests, must now demand his presence at the Liga Central. Taking the initiative, I suggested that we continue our conversations there during intervals between his official duties. This would positively be my last chance to victimize him with "personal questions," I assured him, although my motives in again wishing to visit the Liga were not "purely journalistic." I frankly confessed to harboring "an ulterior aim and a suppressed desire." The latter, I explained, was to strengthen and to fix fast forever my cherished memory-image of him "in action," formed on the afternoon of our first meeting while I watched him ministering with paternal solicitude to the appeals of his Indito suppliants.

At the professional level, I realized that my report on his public career lacked an important chapter—an account of those years following his association with Zapata and his return from Morelos to Yucatán, until after his elevation to the governorship.

Felipe expressed hearty approval of the idea, finding, he said, "the romantic motive involved especially appealing." He continued, "It will save time and talk that could be very profitably used for themes more worthy than my unhappy past and perhaps, I venture to hope, for the discussion of our mutual happier future." Besides, at the Liga, he added, there was a complete collection of the Partido Socialista publications, so that whatever information he neglected to give me about his public record, I could find in the *folletos*.[1]

Alfonso called for me the next morning at eight, and when we arrived at the Liga, the large upstairs assembly room was half-filled with Indian and Mestizo petitioners. Many others, I learned, had already come and gone, since, according to his usual custom, Felipe was at his desk before seven o'clock. Smiling radiantly, he arose at our entrance and ushered me to a seat a step below the slightly elevated platform he occupied. A table with a typewriter had been placed for my use, and a number of brochures and pamphlets arranged according to subject matter were at hand. Two or three of the booklets referred to the work of the Congresses of Motul and Izamal. Others contained reports of state-sponsored education, the feminist movement, birth control, temperance campaigns, prison reform, land distribution, and general progressive legislation enacted by the Socialist Government. He excused himself momentarily from a group of *maestros* and schoolboys, seeking a baseball field in their pueblo, to call my attention to the more "useful" booklets for my immediate reading. Selecting a small volume from the table, he recommended it as a "good synthesis," the authoritative work of his *estimado compañero*[2] Juan Rico, published only recently and titled *La huelga de junio*.[3] He said that it was clearly and concisely written, but whatever points seemed obscure he would clarify for me later.

I read with the keenest interest Juan Rico's outline of the proceedings of the Workers Congresses of Motul and Izamal. As Felipe was careful to point out, these two historic assemblies were the culminating events in a long succession of efforts to achieve labor movement cohesion and solidarity. They were destined also to define unequivocally the future course and the major content of his own political action. Although the Leagues of Resistance, as he had related to me in the story of his entrance into political life, had been organized years earlier in various communities of the peninsula, it was not until 1917 that the different local units were consolidated and their diverse programs for the attainment of a better life for the bulk of Yucatán's population coordinated. As the author of *La huelga de junio* had reported, almost an entire year was spent in preparation, but on the morning of March 29, 1918, there assembled, with poetic fitness, in Felipe's native city of Motul, 144 delegates to Mexico's First Congress of Workers. Nominated by Enrique Jiménez of the Liga of Izamal, Felipe was elected President. Named to serve with him as members of the directorate were Bartolomé García of Mérida, Vice President, and Gonzalo Ruz of Valladolid, Secretary.

Significantly, the first theme on the Congress agenda concerned the cultivation of products of the soil—not only henequen but, as Felipe was vigorously to advocate for the rest of his days, the production of cereals, tubers, dye plants, orchard fruits, berries, sugarcane, and all the plants grown in the home regions of the individual delegates. From this first session resulted conclusions and decisions that were to reverberate through the succeeding years in Mexico's agrarian movement and organizations of agricultural workers.

Among the accepted provisions at the Motul Congress was one calling for the rejection of routine agricultural methods that yield "a minimum result for the maximum of labor." Instead, scientific methods for intensive production were urged in the cultivation of corn and other cereals that serve as the basis for general nutrition. To facilitate this end, the Ligas were required to possess two hectares of land as local experiment stations where the members could assist in the practice of intensive farming and learn how to avoid plant diseases. Conferences on these subjects were to be called periodically. The Ligas were to be held responsible for the training of the workers in the experimental field in order to achieve the specified ends — an increase of farming lands, the renovation of soil, a saving of energy, and a maximum of production and profit.

The Congress provided for education along economic lines through the Ligas, which were to be converted into *cooperativas de consumo* — production cooperatives — so that "in this manner will be attained the goal envisioned by Socialism, namely, that there may be 'neither exploiters nor exploited.'" It was pointed out that *cooperativas de consumo* had failed in most places and especially in the Yucatán Peninsula for two well-known reasons: lack of administrative ability and, secondly, lack of honesty on the part of those entrusted with directing them. Heading the committee drafting the proposals on cooperatives was one of Felipe's most reliable and devoted supporters, Sr. Franco Aguilar of Motul. Serving on the same committee was Roberto Haberman, a Romanian Socialist known as a "professional atheist," who had injected himself into Mexico's Revolutionary affairs, for the purpose, as many believed — and as Felipe ultimately realized — of his personal aggrandizement. He was the confidant and international "legman" for Calles, through whom Felipe had met him, and was sometimes accepted as a sincere Socialist and a loyal friend of the workers. I met him in Mexico City before coming to Yucatán and distrusted him at sight, a first impression that was later to be strengthened by revelations made to me in New York by Mr. Harry Weinberg, the generous volunteer attorney who handled the defense of the imprisoned pacifist Ricardo Flores Magón, a cause for which large sums were contributed by labor organizations and individuals in the United States and Mexico and deposited with Haberman as treasurer.

In approving the plan of the formation of the Liga night schools, it was pointed out to the Congress that ignorance of the larger part of the citizenry of the states was not only a weakness but also a grave political and economic danger. The complete slavery into which the worker had been plunged was vividly pictured. Now that he had acquired, through severe struggle, his rights as a citizen, he must take the next step, which was to seek adequate means to emerge from his ignorance and make himself a conscious individual so that he would not again be dragged along by the reactionary current that constantly tried to persecute him. The educational provision stressed the urgency for the worker to acquire the rudiments of social organization and the economic sciences. The curriculum of the night schools was clearly indicated as preeminently Socialist, "discarding all that foments the prejudice encountered in the books and the living voice of official teachers that until now have come to be a hindrance and an obstacle for the recovery of the proletariat." A stated aim was "to make known to the people that political liberty is a myth if it does not rest upon economic liberty." Another aim was to awaken, "under a simple regimen, the soul of adults to the truth, making them aware of their oppressors." The object of the night school was defined as "not primarily to teach the workers to read but rather to show them how to draw conclusions from their reading as to their social condition."

The resolutions adopted by the committee stipulated that the "adult night schools should confront with the truth all the errors that materially and morally have enslaved the people." The recommended curriculum consisted of the Spanish language, arithmetic, natural sciences, and "ideas that would lead to the collective rehabilitation."

When discussions arose as to the best ways of forming treasuries to support schools, Felipe, who, with Agustín Franco and Esteban Andrade, was a member of the investigating committee, suggested that "a good and safe rule was to be guided by experience." In this regard, he stated that he could point with pride to the *campesinos* of Espita, who, in order to collect funds for their association, decided to cultivate one thousand *mecates*[4] of land. "I believe," he said, "that if the members of the other Ligas would do likewise, they would very soon possess the common fund they aim to create. We should have in mind that the treasuries of the Ligas are the pooled result of efforts of all the workers and thus, as each Liga member regularly contributes five or ten pesos for the formation of a common fund, we should be disposed to give four or five hours of work each month, dedicating the entire product to the enrichment of the treasuries. This method is not only more representative but can improve the operations."

In addition to the nine scheduled themes considered at the Motul Congress, the delegates at the closing session discussed ideas related to the collective welfare. Among them were the suppression of the sale of intoxicating liquors; the use of marijuana, which Florencio Ávila Castillo declared was spreading "like a plague"; and other poisonous drugs. One of the more controversial subjects informally debated was the prohibition of religious worship, a proposal made by the brilliant and fiery Elena Torres, later a national feminist leader of the Mexican capital. When the delegate, Ávila Castillo, reminded *compañera* Torres that the general Constitution of the Republic granted liberty of worship, she answered: "It is true that we cannot act contrary to the Constitution, but I believe that it is possible to eliminate ostentatious worship. It would be easy for the government to eliminate, for instance, the clanging of the church bells, calling people to mass and to other religious ceremonies. Since they are Catholics, they should attend ceremonies quietly in the same way as Protestants and those belonging to other religions observe their respective rituals."

Before his election as Constitutional Governor, Felipe had twice served as Chief Executive of the State of Yucatán. Both periods occurred during the incumbency of his close friend and Socialist collaborator Governor Carlos Castro Morales, head of the Railroad Workers' Syndicate of Motul. The first interim period lasted only four days, between September 5 and 9, 1918, while Sr. Castro Morales was in Mexico City. It has been claimed that the Governor carried back with him to Mérida an order from Carranza to expel Felipe from the country because of his radical pro-labor activities. In any case, such an order could not have come as too severe a blow or much of a hardship, since Felipe had long desired to visit the United States. His object was to contact Socialists there and to let them know of the Party's achievements in Yucatán. A deeper reason, perhaps, and one that he had mentioned to me when I asked him about this particular trip, was his need to rid himself of a sense of loneliness and isolation and to share in a community of interests with his spiritual brothers. He longed to experience, he said, the comforting assurance that the cause he had so ardently espoused was a universal one in which all men could join in fraternal cooperation, working together for a world free from aggressive wars, rivalry for power, and riches at the expense of the "inarticulate ones." On this and other occasions when Felipe discussed Socialism, I inevitably associated his personal concept of the political system with the "gentle" type as envisioned by the young Clement Attlee,[5] who left his home of wealth and ease to live down in London's Limehouse slums, from which he wrote his compassionate poems, among them my favorite, which begins, "How shall they work tomorrow, who have no bread today?"

But voluntarily or otherwise, shortly before the close of World War I, with the Armistice of November 11, 1918, Felipe found himself in Manhattan. His arrival there coincided with the terroristic climax of one of the most repressive developments in recent American history—the infamous "Palmer Raids."[6]

Only vague references or no mention at all of Felipe's unscheduled move appeared in the little books and pamphlets stacked on my typewriter desk at the Liga Central. But his own reminiscences when I questioned him about the particular trip and my later conversations in Mexico City with Sr. Jorge Rodríguez, who had acted as English interpreter throughout the New York visit, supply many colorful, often amusing details. Felipe's dramatic experiences in the Great City not only illumine facets of his magnetic personality but vividly highlight the acute fear and suspicion that gripped the United States immediately after the end of the international conflict, the rigid restrictions that mocked Constitutional guarantees of privacy and individual liberty, and foreshadowed the reactionary McCarthy-McCarran legislation.

At the time, Sr. Rodríguez was secretary to Dr. Álvaro Torre Díaz, general manager of the Comisión Reguladora del Mercado de Henequén,[7] with offices on 120 Broadway. As a member of the local Chamber of Deputies, a former interim Governor, and the president of the state's leading political party, Felipe was already regarded as Yucatán's most prominent and influential citizen and, accordingly, was shown the attentions due to his status by the state-controlled henequen interests. Sr. Rodríguez, who was delegated to act not only as interpreter but as Felipe's full-time guide, recalls that the New York atmosphere of the period was charged with the hostility bred of suppression, the ever-tightening censorship of the spoken and printed word arousing strong resentment among intellectuals and progressive, spirited youth. But the incipient hope of a new order was also in ferment. It was a hope sharpened by the success of the Russian Revolution, the vain efforts to thwart its advance by the international capitalism working through England and Vladivostok, despite such measures as the devaluation of the Russian currency, nonrecognition, and complete diplomatic ostracism.

Up until that year, the Socialist ideal had not taken political root in any part of the world except Mexico. In New York, Party members were even forbidden to carry the customary red cards, and the organizations were compelled to change them to pink. Probably unaware of the true situation, Felipe spoke freely about the advantage of Socialism and predicted its ultimate triumph. He expressed great eagerness to meet with the various groups because he felt that he had something encouraging to tell them, considering himself the bearer of welcome news about what the Party had accomplished in Yucatán. When he finally met the leaders of the American movement, they all voiced tremendous surprise at the Yucatecan achievements—the divorce laws, labor code, birth control clinics, feminist "liberation," distribution of lands to the workers and the well-organized Ligas de Resistencia. In their enthusiasm, they at once invited him to lecture at different centers, among them, the Rand School of Social Science. In his direct, persuasive manner, Felipe, speaking in Spanish, described the Socialist gains, and judging from the riotous applause he evoked, his message evidently lost little of its emotional impact through the expert translation of Sr. Rodríguez.

In discussing the transformation that had taken place in Yucatán in the short space of a few years, he told how, during the Díaz regime, men and women were enslaved on the *haciendas* and publicly whipped for minor infractions at the whim of the *mayordomos*. He described, too, the changes in the attitude of entire populations, the new dignity and self-assurance the people had acquired through cooperative ownership of lands by those who worked on them, with resulting material progress throughout the state. Sr. Rodríguez spoke of Felipe's reception everywhere as "nothing short of sensational," stating that he was a "real hero" to his audience, for he showed them what miracles Socialism was capable of performing.

On the morning following a "monster mass meeting" in the Bronx Theatre, the New York daily *World* reported that Felipe had caused so much excitement that people were leaning out of their windows on either side of the street to see what the "big uproar" was about.

Felipe himself had once unconsciously indicated to me that his appearances at the Rand School, the Bronx Theatre, and other Manhattan centers must have indeed caused a "big uproar," when he casually remarked: "The next time I go to your country, Almita, I shall take with me many handkerchiefs and a supply of neckties."

"And why all the excess baggage?" I asked.

"*Porque me robaron . . . a pedacitos . . . como recuerdos*—Because they robbed me of them and tore off little pieces for souvenirs."

But while Felipe's New York reception demonstrated popular admiration for the man and his cause, both were considered to be highly suspect and even dangerous in the eyes of the dozen or more policemen who kept armed vigil outside the various meeting halls where Felipe lectured. Ever at his side, Sr. Rodríguez was asked as they emerged from the Bronx Theatre: "Are you Bolsheviks?"

"No, we are Mexicans . . . If you want to find out about us go to the Reguladora offices. We have eight lawyers there to answer your questions."

The impressive Lower Broadway address and the size of the Reguladora legal staff had their calming effect on the guardians of public safety, and the two "aliens" were permitted to depart by taxi instead of the "paddy wagon." Gradually, as Sr. Rodríguez recalled, Felipe became aware of the risks he was running and toward the end of his stay took care to assure his audiences that the North American concept of Mexico was a myth.

Felipe was particularly anxious to meet Morris Hillquit, the brilliant Russian-born Socialist lawyer and author who grew up in Manhattan's East Side. Hillquit was confined to a tuberculosis sanitarium on Lake Saranac, which, with the entire northern part of the state, was under the ice and heavy snows of a very severe winter. But, with Sr. Rodríguez, Felipe visited the staunch veteran of many labor battles, who in the period between 1904 and 1933, the year of his death, was Socialism's most authoritative spokesman at international conferences. For an entire afternoon, Sr. Rodríguez relates, the two leaders held a heartwarming session, exchanging the advances made by the workers through the Socialist Government in Yucatán. A week later, on the date he was scheduled to leave for Yucatán, Felipe went to the Ward Line pier, accompanied by his faithful interpreter. But before the sailing hour, complications and delays were encountered at the U.S. Customs office, in line with the rigid surveillance of the "comings and goings of all foreigners," imposed by Attorney General Mitchell A. Palmer. Brusquely shoved to one side by two detectives, Felipe and Sr. Rodríguez were informed theirs was "a federal case." After pulling out all the drawers of Felipe's wardrobe trunk, the "Palmer raiders" announced in triumphal tones they had found what they were "looking for." The "revelation" consisted of a thousand small bright red satin banners stamped in gold with the words "Liga de Resistencia—Partido Socialista del Sureste." Felipe had ordered them made to his design at a badge-and-emblem shop and was proudly taking them back to Yucatán for distribution among the Ligas as a souvenir of his New York trip. With the vainglorious strut of heroes who have made some momentous discovery in the nick of time to save the nation from catastrophe, the investigators cleared a space on the wharf and carefully laid out the little red banners in rows, for all the world to behold. Then, while a guard stood by the "incriminating exhibits of Mexican subversion," Felipe was taken inside and searched for further evidence of the "plot" conceived in the rampant imagination of the two enterprising sleuths.

There was some blundering talk about holding him, but again Sr. Rodríguez came to the rescue. He explained Felipe's official position, hinting at the "Washington influence" of the powerful Reguladora with which he himself was associated and at the Commission's eight-manned legal battery ready to come to his countryman's defense. Just a minute before the liner's gangplank was lifted, the detectives decided to allow Felipe to go aboard with a practically empty trunk. Meanwhile, the thousand gilt-stamped scarlet banners were carried by the winds in all directions, drifting like a swirling shower of leaves out to sea or back towards the multimillion-dollar towers of Wall Street. With a typical Mexican sense of the dramatic, Sr. Rodríguez assured me that he would not be at all surprised if some of the "evidence" had not finally been borne over the bay as far as Bedloe's Island, perhaps to become impaled on the bronze tongues of the flame leaping from freedom's torch, upraised by the Goddess of Liberty.

# 17. Social Justice

At three o'clock on the sultry afternoon, Felipe, appearing a trifle weary but cheerful of mood and voice announced that "man must eat and, incidentally, *las mujeres*—the ladies." Clearing his desk, he added that both of us had fully earned "our daily bread." I agreed that he, at least, was fully entitled, by any labor code, to take time out from exacting demands of the presidency of the Partido Socialista del Sureste for a leisurely *comida* and that, speaking for myself, I was entirely satisfied with my morning's work. Between numerous phone calls, for several hours, he had been continuously hearing and disposing of petitions, requests, and applications covering a wide range of human needs and desires—and had been doing so even before my arrival at the Liga—always with patience and courtesy. To one of my own countrymen, a melancholy-eyed Spanish-speaking professor from Chicago, he had given detailed information on the proposed state divorce law as it would affect foreigners. For a Montreal merchant, he had clarified complicated data on henequen shipments to Canada. For scores of native petitioners—most of them Inditos in white cotton *camisas* and *huaraches,* he had explained how they must go about the organization of local Ligas, agrarian committees, experimental farms, and adult evening classes. With personally signed recommendations, he had arranged on the spot for Maya mothers in embroidered *huipiles* and dark *rebozos* to enroll children of unusual aptitudes in special technical schools where they might learn trades and professions. Other mothers who complained to him—speaking with greater frankness than they might have shown to their parochial "father confessors"—that they were already overburdened with large families, he directed to the newly opened birth control clinics.

Amid the vestiges of faded Porfiriana[1] elegance, I dined with Felipe at the Gran Hotel where the owner, Sr. Rafael Gamboa, a veteran Socialist crusader affectionately known as Ravechol, personally supervised the service of a typically Motuleña *comida,* specially prepared, he announced, in honor of "el Sr. Gobernador y la encantadora periodista Almita—the Governor and the charming journalist

Almita." My efforts to divert our table conversation back to the issues presented in Juan Rico's reports on the Workers Congresses met with swift defeat. Gently, but resolutely thwarting what he called my "inveterate journalistic preoccupations," Felipe assured me there would be plenty of time on the long voyage to New York to study carefully all the little informative *folletos* that Antonio had collected at the Liga and delivered to my Hotel Imperial suite. "At the moment," he insisted, "I'm less interested in past events, however noble they may be, than in future plans—beginning with a delightful plan for this very evening, unfortunately your *last* one among us, at least for a while."

He proposed that we again pay a visit to Ricardo Palmerín to find out how the music for "Peregrina" was progressing. Accompanied by Don Luis, he would call for me around nine o'clock, immediately after his scheduled conference with the Carnegie archaeologists to conclude arrangements for the Chichén Itzá permit. No plan for the evening could have been more appealing, since I was eager to hear the melody to which my lovely song would be sung before I left Yucatán.

For several days I had been considering the idea of writing at some future date Felipe's biography, not as a magazine article but as a well-documented book. From what I already knew and sensed about his ideological position, social attitudes, political program, and aims, I believed that his life story held significance for the reader not only in Mexico but everywhere. And as I worked on the hotel terrace through the cool sunset hours before our meeting appointment, taking notes and organizing the voluminous material that defined the major achievements of his public career up to that time, the idea of the biography assumed decisive form. One could hardly read the record without becoming aware of the universal implications of Felipe's undeviating redeemer's role or his consistent vigilance for the worldwide welfare of the common man.

The most desultory statistical survey of Felipe's efforts and accomplishments demonstrated his total dedication to fundamental causes, all designed to lift humanity to higher levels of collective thought and action. It was evident, at least, that he had lost no opportunity to contribute to the welfare of the state, the nation, and humanity as a whole throughout the years of his political maturity. He achieved major reforms even during periods of delegated authority.

Prior to his election as Constitutional Governor, Felipe had twice been called upon to serve as the state's Chief Executive. On both occasions, Don Carlos Castro Morales, Socialist railroad worker and labor organizer, was the incumbent. The first period of Felipe's occupancy of the gubernatorial office lasted only four days, from September 5 to 9, 1918. Between November 11 and December 24 of the same year, Felipe, the presiding deputy of the local congress, was Acting Governor during a prolonged visit of Sr. Castro Morales to the national capital. It was in this later *pro tempore* forty-one-day period, at the Twenty-fifth Constitutional Congress, that on December 16 he promulgated one of Mexico's earliest regulations of a radical character dealing with labor. Known as the Código de Trabajo del Estado de Yucatán,[2] it prohibited all work on Sunday in commercial houses, factories, and shops and established an eight-hour maximum and a six-hour ordinary working day. Differing from the 1916 Código Laboral[3] of General Alvarado, Felipe's Código de Trabajo authorized strikes and recognized the right of free association or union organization for collective bargaining.

Often referred to as the "most advanced Socialist legislation on earth," the Código de Trabajo is based on the principles that work is free to all, that everyone should work and live on the proceeds of such labor, and that no one has the right to exploit the workers. The text adds that all workers have the right to unite in defense of their personal and common interests, forming Ligas de Resistencia or other similar associations.

The code also insists that contracts between the employer, known as the *patrón,* and the workers, designated as *obreros,* must be in writing and that no contract is valid for more than a year. When prices of common necessities rise or when, for whatever reason, the cost of living increases, the worker may demand a revision of his wages. A Central Conciliation and Arbitrations Board is authorized to fix a percentage of the profits of the business in which the worker will at all times share. All disputes between employer and employee must be referred to this Board, whose decisions will be final.

The Código recognizes the validity of contracts made between workers of either sex of eighteen years or more, but persons between the ages of fifteen and eighteen must secure the consent of their parents or guardians or, failing these, of the mayor of the town in which they live. The usual considerations under which a contract between employer and worker is made are recognized, but a special paragraph provides that if the employer should cease to operate his business without justifiable cause, the government may step in and run it in order "to avoid losses to the worker."

Many of the measures since adopted by the most advanced social security systems in the United States and elsewhere are contained in Felipe's Labor Code. Among them are full pay for the worker in case of accident or illness contracted on the job and half pay during illnesses directly traceable to his employment. In the case of death by accident or illness contracted at work, if in the employ of his *patrón* for more than one year, he will be paid his full salary during illness. In case of death, his funeral expenses will be paid, and his next of kin will receive a year's salary.

Stipulations regulating the employment of women require that an employee about to become a mother rest at home two months prior to and two months immediately following her confinement. Upon her return to work, she shall have two periods of an hour each, free from work, in which to nurse her child. Minimum salaries were fixed by the local Ligas under direction of the Liga Central in Mérida. Double pay was required for all extra work.

As a member of the Federal Chamber of Deputies, to which he was elected in July 1919, Felipe fought at the national level for the right of labor organizations to strike. His initiative as reported in the *Diario Oficial*[4] of September 18 of the same year (no. 15, page 12) is as follows:

> Citizen Felipe Carrillo, president of the Ligas de Resistencia of the Partido Socialista de Yucatán, sends from the city of Mérida a telegram in which, in the aforementioned Ligas, he asks this Honorable Cámara[5] not to approve the amendments to Article 123 of the Constitution calling for the restriction of the right to strike and the substitution of Arbitration Tribunals formed by a Special Tribunal of the Statute Labor Law (Fuero del Trabajo) with irrevocable decisions.
>
> The undersigned have examined the said petition and, finding it according to legal regulations, feel honored to submit to the deliberations of this Honorable Cámara the following economic resolution *(acuerdo económico):*
>
> The telegram of Citizen F. Carrillo should be delivered to the united commissions of Labor and Previsión Social.[6]
>
> *Sala de comisiones. Cámara de Diputados*[7] . . . Sept. 17, 1919. Signatures: Manuel Andrade, José P. Saldaña.
>
> The resolution was put to discussion but no one was willing to discuss it. When submitted to a vote, it was approved.

In opposition to the presidential candidacy of Ingeniero Ignacio Bonillas, the leaders of the Partido Laborista[8] under the slogan of "For Justice and Democracy" held their first convention in Zacatecas, where the then stalwart "Obregonista"[9] General Enrique Estrada occupied the Governor's Palace. Felipe was among the forty-four delegates who met at the Calderón Theater in Zacatecas City early in March 1920. The group included the Generals J. D. Ramírez Garrido, Jesús M. Garza, Francisco R. Serrano, Licenciado Emilio Portes Gil, and Luis N. Morones, who was President of the CROM, and members of its Central Committee.

Meanwhile the Socialist cause in Yucatán and those who led and supported it were destined to pass through a prolonged reign of terror before a Second Congress of Workers could assemble in conformity with the schedule fixed at Motul. Socialist hostility to the imposition by Venustiano Carranza of the unpopular Ingeniero Ignacio Bonillas as his successor to the presidency of the Republic brought on a persecution of the "dissidents," which did not end until late 1920.

Colonel Isaías Zamarripa, Chief of Operations, was given a free hand by Carranza to crush the opposition, and he burned and killed with barbaric ferocity. The agitation became so acute and the disorder so general that Governor Castro Morales went to the capital to intercede with the President and refused to return to Mérida while Zamarripa continued his orgy of violence. Hundreds were killed, their homes destroyed. The Ligas were broken up, the buildings burned, and their meager, laboriously accumulated funds confiscated.

Felipe and the more prominent Socialist leaders barely escaped with their lives; several of them were not so fortunate. Only through the intervention of General Obregón, who became President on December 1, 1920, were the murders and the destruction halted. At the height of the Zamarripa persecutions, instigated and abetted by reactionaries who paraded under the name of "Liberals," Doña Adela called together her sons and said to them: "Do not go out. Do not walk along the streets, exposing yourselves to the savagery of the Liberals. But if you are ever unfortunate enough to fall into their hands, kill, or defend yourselves until they kill you. I would rather have you dead than try to mend your broken backs."

The maternal admonition of this extraordinary Yucatecan woman was spoken in the great ancient tradition of the valorous autochthonous American race. Native chroniclers tell us that when a warrior youth left his home for battle, his mother, standing at the door of their dwelling, would, by age-old custom, deliver to him his shield with these words of farewell: "Return to me *with* it—or *on* it!"

The elections of July 1921, designating Felipe, candidate of the Partido Socialista, as Governor of Yucatán for a term of four years took place, according to all reports and to quote the local press, "with notable animation, but without sanguinary clashes." By an overwhelming margin Felipe emerged as the popular choice in what Dr. Ernest R. Gruening, an on-the-ground witness, describes as "one of the first thoroughly square elections ever held in Mexico." Forced for the first time to resort to democratic methods, the *hacendados* complained that their candidate was not getting a fair hearing from the Indians. Felipe, as the historian-statesman relates, at once hired a special train at his own expense, turned it over to his opponent, and issued a proclamation urging all to give his rival "the fullest attention." The election results showed 60,765 votes for Felipe against 4,048 for the candidate of the *hacendados* and 621 for a third candidate. The entire Socialist legislature of fifteen deputies was likewise elected.

In conformity with Article 49 of the Constitution of Yucatán, the Governor-Elect, upon taking the oath of office, was required to pronounce certain words in connection with the inaugural act. At the special session of the State Congress held at ten o'clock on the morning of February 1, 1922, Deputy Ariosto Castellanos Cárdenas, who, as President of the Congress, administered the oath, presented Felipe with the prescribed text, which he read, with the addition of a few significant words of his own. After promising "to guard and have guarded the political Constitution of the United States of Mexico, the particular state of Yucatán, and the laws that emanate from them and loyally and patriotically to discharge the office of Governor, which the people have conferred upon me, seeking in all welfare and prosperity of the Union and of the State," he concluded with another promise—one that did not appear in the formal oath. To the amazement and great satisfaction of all present, he added: "I equally promise to fulfill and have fulfilled the principles postulated at the Congresses of Workers of Motul and Izamal, and if I do not do so, may the Nation and the State take action against me."

Then, from the balcony of the Government Palace, Felipe, speaking in Mayan, addressed the enormous throng as follows:

> *Compañeros:*
>
> For all workers this should be a day of rejoicing and of deep satisfaction, because today there has been realized one of the great dreams of the Partido Socialista del Sureste. Because here are united all true Socialists who have come to celebrate the triumph of our cause, the cause for which we have so long struggled. In our hearts, we should feel profound gratitude, because today we have ended the era of Socialist propaganda and the era of work begins, and because from today we can make a start at realizing that for which so long a time our enemies have impeded; because, from today, we shall give ourselves no rest in our eagerness to do something in direct benefit of the laboring majority.
>
> *Compañeros:*
>
> The moment has arrived to demonstrate to the Señores[10] that we know how to govern, that we, *not* they, are the builders. It is necessary that we tell them that without workers this sumptuous cathedral would not exist; that without the workers this palace would not exist; and without the workers we would not have this lovely plaza where all may come for rest and to enjoy the aroma of flowers. And finally, we must remind them that without the workers would not exist the railroads, the automobiles, the carriages; in short, without the worker, nothing that is useful to man would exist.
>
> It is necessary also that we tell the "all-powerful" ones that we are fully aware that labor came before capital; we must make them understand that those who produce everything have the right to possess all that exists, instead of the old way, where the minority always absorbed everything without exerting the least effort.
>
> Now that the glorious and legitimate triumph of the Partido Socialista

del Sureste has been achieved, now that the people have elected me to govern them, we shall show to these Señores that we are not thieves or assassins as they have always claimed, that we do not come to this palace to rob the public funds, that we are not here to deceive the workers, but that we are here resolved to give them true tranquility and authentic well-being.

*Compañeros:*

The government has much before it, and it is necessary to see that our plans materialize. Roads must be opened for the traffic of all kinds of vehicles. Many schools must be founded. How many schools must be established so that your children and yourselves learn to read and write and, above all, that you learn Spanish and can give validity to all your rights! All the wilderness of Yucatán remains to be planted. We shall plant as much as we can. We shall plant henequen that produces great wealth so that this wealth may reach the hands of the people who have the indisputable right to enjoy it.

I repeat, the land belongs to you . . . You were born here, and here you grew up; here you have passed your lives, bent over in the fields, cutting sisal leaves for the owner, who has possessed himself of the soil.

But you will retrieve your rights in accordance with the new laws, which recognize these legitimate rights. And since the land belongs to you, and since you are the ones who work it, the crops, the production, naturally, also belong to you.

All this, *compañeros,* you know, and if you have not realized until today that everything belongs to the proletariat, it is because you yourselves have contributed to the delay, by wasting your time in the saloons and in sleeping.

You will be directly responsible for not learning to read and write, for not knowing the Constitution of the Republic and of the State, for not making the men you elevate to public office fulfill their obligations. You must demand of these same officials that they carry out the agreements reached in the Congresses of Motul and of Izamal.

Felipe personally commented on the tranquility and order of the elections in a letter written on the stationery of the Liga Central to General Francisco J. Mújica, Governor of Michoacán, under date of November 21, 1921, and reading as follows:

My very distinguished and dear friend:

The Partido Socialista del Sureste won the last elections held in the state and, in the course of the democratic decision, gave proofs of laudable patriotism and political solidarity. There were no scandals or sanguinary clashes. The serenity that dominated in the contest brings great irritation to the reactionaries—those who do not know against whom to fire their cannons of insult and falsehood. Scarcely were the elections over, relieving me of "politics," than I placed my thoughts at a higher level, intensified my efforts in the good direction of the social struggle, and directed to all the Socialists the circular that I herewith enclose, that you may study it and tell me what you think about it since, for me, your judgment is of real value, having as I do that highest concept of your culture and talent. Your firmness in sustaining radical ideals in this rich land, but in which still survive memories of Munguía[11] to obscure the emblem of Ocampo,[12] is a source of pride for all your co-religionists. It is necessary to struggle constantly without losing heart on the journey. With my profound wishes for your personal happiness, and once more recalling my affection, I remain your friend,

Felipe Carrillo Puerto.

A factor in the enforced postponement of the Izamal Congress had been the burning, at Zamarripa's order, of the archives of the Liga Central. The delegates, however, finally convened in the Teatro Izamal on August 15, 1921, under the chairmanship of Governor-Elect Felipe Carrillo Puerto. The Congress agenda consisted of fourteen points, most of them concerned with determining adequate ways and means for raising the workers' living standard, achieving higher social and cultural levels for the masses, and measures for financing the educational and other communal projects of the Ligas. Typical of the conclusions reached by the Congress were those of "Theme Five," dealing with civic ideals, reported as follows by the committee over which Dr. Louis Torregrosso presided: "Virtue, education, union, economy, hygiene, love, respect for woman, order, sacrifice, and courage are the complex of precepts that, engraved in the minds of the worker, will lead to the road of liberation for which we are struggling."

Cultural matters were considered in "Theme Nine," calling for the support and patronage of the fine arts, especially music, singing, dance, and cinema as "molders of the generous spirit of the masses, which must be activated."

"Theme Thirteen," concerning social questions, exhorted the Ligas de Resistencia to support with enthusiasm and true love the Feminist Leagues, whose noble and elevated principles would lead to the integral emancipation of woman: "With emancipation will emerge wives and mothers who, within the spirit of liberty and justice, will shape the incipient consciousness of the children that have been entrusted to them and, later, to the well-performed labor of the teachers."

In its long-range effect on the course of Mexico's political future, the most significant proposal, perhaps, to come before the Izamal Congress was "Theme

Fourteen." The last on the agenda, it submitted this question: "Should the Partido Socialista del Sureste and the Agrario de Campeche[13] unite themselves with the Third International of Moscow?"

All of the other thirteen propositions had been accepted by the delegates with several conclusions, in a few cases with as many as ten. "Theme Fourteen," alone, was rejected with but a single—*única*—conclusion by the reporting committee, headed by Juan Rico. The decision read: "The Partido Socialista del Sureste and El Agrario de Campèche will not ally themselves with the Third International of Moscow, while declaring that they may be emphatically in agreement with the step it has taken for the social transformation of the universe."

Thus, as has been pointed out by the historian Prof. Antonio Bustillos Carrillo, who since 1909 had played an active role on Yucatán's Revolutionary scene, the Workers Congress of Izamal laid the basis for a new and superior political orientation by definitely repudiating Moscow's repeated invitations to Yucatán's Socialist movement to align itself with the Third Communist International. As directing head and the most influential single voice of the Congress, Felipe assumed this unequivocal stand against the communizing of a Mexican state, even though—years earlier with scores of Mexico's young radical idealists—he had been a member of the Continental Bureau of the First International. The total effect of the Izamal Congress was to reinforce and improve thoroughly democratic and evolutionary Socialist doctrines of a distinctly Mexican origin and character. With Campeche, Quintana Roo, and Yucatán, the Congress created, subject to a Federal Council, a Federation of Parties of the Southeast, with a fundamental desire to achieve a glorious unity along ethnic, revolutionary, and traditional lines. No aim could have been more logical or even basically nationalistic, since these regions of the Republic shared the same history and their people were descended from the same race, who for unknown centuries had lived under cloudless skies between the same tropical forests and the immemorial azure sea.

In effect, as Prof. Bustillos Carrillo maintains, the Workers Congress of Izamal did no more than to evoke those distant times of the New Maya Empire when the people in its jurisdiction created the Confederation of Mayapán, a pact of race and of blood, of juridical and political standards, to defend the liberty altered by the invading Toltecs.[14] And this same base served for the formation of the Federation of Central American States, pursuing unity of a people in defense of its autonomy and its independence when trampled underfoot by the hosts of Cristóbal de Olid, Pedro de Alvarado, and Francisco de Garay.[15]

Yucatán's Socialism, as he further points out, never adopted Communist practices. Always a party of the state, it never secretly worked in the cells of the Communist International or in the Mexican Communist Party. Politically, it was maintained within the National Revolutionary Party, and its posture was invariably clear, urgent, and definite. Over the years, its influence may be traced through the transformations of the NRP[16] into the political party and the Confederación Sindical[17] until, as a sector, it entered Mexico's dominant political organization, the Party of Revolutionary Institutions, known as the PRI.[18] With the latter have been incorporated some of the outstanding features of the Partido Socialista del Sureste.

For the third time in two weeks I found myself with Felipe and the poet Luis Rosada Vega in the orange-scented, moonlit garden of Ricardo Palmerín. As on our previous visits there, the gifted and very modest Yucatecan composer, after greeting us with a few simple words of welcome, went at once to his small, weather-beaten upright piano. But with an artist's typical penchant for dramatic climax, he prepared us gradually for the pleasant surprise he was certain he had in store for us. Lightly gliding over the yellow keyboard, his sensitive fingers produced several themes in Yucatán's romantic tradition — one to which he had himself made many contributions. Felipe, seated beside me before the open door of the humble studio living room, listened with critical ear to the tentative accompaniments for my song, "Peregrina," but his silence and his cheerless expression plainly indicated disappointment.

Suddenly, a glow of excitement flared in his jade green eyes — the passionate response of his own trained musicianship — when Palmerín, with an abrupt change of mood and tempo, played a completely different kind of melody. "Now, here at last, my friends, I think we may have *something,*" the Maestro announced with a confident and slightly roguish smile. Again and again, with occasional variations, he repeated the throbbing notes of the opening motif, as though to reassure his fascinated audience of three that, unlike the famous "Lort Chord," the lovely strains would not drift out, irretrievably, into the cosmic ether.

"Keep on playing, *hombre, por favor,* keep on playing," Felipe pleaded with him. Then, impulsively, he ran into the studio and, bodily lifting the short, plump Maestro from the piano bench, warmly embraced him. "*Sí, sí, querido, compañero mío* — Yes, yes, my dear *compañero,*" he exclaimed, "you, indeed, *have* something here — something very beautiful, something really marvelous! This is what my heart has been waiting to hear!"

Voicing his own profound satisfaction and gratitude, Don Luis, who, all the while, had been standing behind the composer, also congratulated him with a fervent *abrazo.*[19] He assured Palmerín that his music had already made articulate all the elusive shades of feeling that he wished to express in "Peregrina" but which mere words were powerless to convey. With Felipe, the poet strongly urged that the work be finished without delay so that an orchestration might be started at the earliest possible moment.

I, too, was deeply aware that Palmerín had presented to us the "inevitable" melody for the poet's moving lyric. For even then, as the first measures of the composition frilled the perfumed stillness of the tropical night with their poignant burden of longing, enveloped in recurrent overtones—strangely seeming to foreshadow some imminent nameless sorrow—I felt that Palmerín had recaptured much more than the pain of the individual soul at parting from the dearly beloved one. I realized then, as I have ever since that enchanted hour in his little garden, that the composer had caught in the magic web of sound, woven of ecstatic harmonies and evocative minor nuances, vibrations that penetrated the unutterable age-old tragedy of the Mayab. His sweet, sad rhythms, born of a creative impulse rooted in some remote yesterday, stirred me to a new consciousness of the portentous mystery that still hovers over the Yucatecan earth. They revealed to me, too, Palmerín's racial pride in the brilliant culture that had once flourished on his ancestral soil, his congenital if unrecognized grief over the disappearance forever of all this ancient splendor—grief that echoed from his musical idiom like a sob of anguish.

The next day at noon, February 28, 1923, the American scientists and the Yucatalogists assembled at the Mérida Electric Railway Station to bid an unwilling farewell to the White City. Individually and in groups they thanked Felipe for his magnificent hospitality and directed appreciative sentiments to the good people and the great state he represented for having made possible their memorable experience. They assured him that they would come back in the not too distant future to the fascinating land they were so regretfully about to leave. During the forty-five-minute train ride to Progreso, Felipe and I sat together, both of us glibly exchanging across-the-aisle pleasantries with our fellow passengers. Only a few words of personal import passed between us—Felipe's expressions of pain at my leaving, my own emphatic promises to return soon. Yet our nearness and the occasional meeting of our hands served to communicate in the silence all the unspoken thoughts that were clamoring for a voice in the few precious moments that remained to us. Thus were conveyed our intimate emotions at separating, our mutual adoration, our unfulfilled desires, our faith in a predestined need for each other and an ordained relationship. Felipe's face revealed his feelings of depression, and only with effort I managed to hold back my own tears. But from a verse written long ago by Sir Phillip Sidney and curiously recalled from my college course in Elizabethan Literature, I gleaned a little consolation. In any event, all the way to the Ward Line dock, my mind kept repeating the old English poet's concept of supreme realization in the life of the woman who could confidently say: "My true love hath my heart, and I have his."

I already *knew* that I could say as much—shouting, singing it from the housetops—without fear of contradiction!

# 18. Homeward Journey

During the homeward voyage, conversation among the passengers of the Ward liner *Mexico* differed radically in tone from the tirades spearheaded by the reactionary Yucatecan *hacendados* who, less than a month earlier, had sailed with us on the same vessel between New York and Progreso. To the general relief, the more loquacious and vehement of Governor Carrillo's political enemies, with the exception of Sr. Luis G. Molina, had remained in their *patria chica* permanently or on extended vacations from their adopted northern land. Sr. Molina himself, I soon learned, had left Mérida only with the greatest reluctance, since the main objective of his return to his native city was to court the Governor's young golden-haired daughter, Gelitzli, whom he had known during her attendance at a Long Island academy for girls. His criticisms of the "Red Idol with the Eyes of Jade," as he previously referred to the man he now selected as his future father-in-law, were milder and less frequent. Everyone missed the *esposos* Barry, who left Mérida on a tour of the Republic a day or two before our departure. Dr. Morley had also remained in Yucatán to work out exploration details with Felipe and Don Eduardo Thompson.

The archaeologists and tourist members of the Carnegie Expedition, eager to share their common exciting experiences and enjoy the new friendships formed during their Yucatán adventure, grouped themselves at adjoining tables in the dining *sala*. Across the boards at mealtime, the scholars exchanged theories or made predictions of significant discoveries in the majestic Maya capital they had so recently surveyed and which they planned to explore the following season. To my intense delight, however, many of their discussions began or ended in expressions of esteem for Felipe as a sincere, able, and dedicated public servant and a vigorous promoter of the arts and sciences. It was clear that these distinguished representatives of Middle American research from my own country regarded him as an official on whom they could depend for moral support and practical assistance in their contemplated long-range program. As I listened to their eulogies of the leader whose image had become my radiant emblem of life's fulfillment,

I even experienced a certain pride of having my intuitions and intellectual convictions verified by such authoritative male judgment.

Placed between Dr. John C. Merriam, Carnegie Institution president, and Dr. Marshall H. Saville, director of the Museum of the American Indian (Heye Foundation), at the dinner table, I absorbed ideas and conclusions resulting from their years of investigation among Maya ruins in various regions of southeastern Mexico and Central America. Seated opposite was the senior member of the party, General William Barclay Parsons, who headed the Carnegie Board of Trustees. A man of striking appearance, tall and of commanding bearing, his fine aristocratic features, graying hair, and meticulously trimmed Vandyke, suggested the model for a builder of railroads and international bridges. His very articulate admiration of Felipe found a fervent response in my intimate thoughts and emotions, for as he had done from the moment of their first meeting in the offices of the Liga Central, he continued to comment that "Governor Carrillo was the handsomest man he had seen in all his worldwide travels."

A theme that on several occasions elicited incredulous or witty comment and even sighs of regret was the story of how the United States, through its own volition, lost the proffered chance of owning Yucatán's pre-Colombian cities as well as the state's multimillion-dollar henequen industry.

Little-known facts dealing with this dramatic period of Mexican history emerged at dinner-hour and deck-side meetings of the expeditionaries, most of whom were well informed on all phases of the nation's remote and recent past. It was explained that preceding the crisis of 1848, the people of Yucatán had become disgusted with the prolonged chaos. During the dictatorship of Santa Anna, when the self-styled "serene Highness" occupied the Presidential Palace between his periods of exile, their state was abandoned by whatever still functioned of the federal authority. Governor Santiago Méndez, who had moved his capital from Mérida to Maxcanú, was hard-pressed by the mass uprising of Maya rebels in vengeance against their white and Mestizo oppressors. The radical rebellion, known as the Caste War, began in 1847 and reached its peak of terror with the total collapse and rout of government forces at Valladolid on March 25, 1848. Before the struggle had run its sanguinary course, leaving both sides exhausted in resources and fighting spirit, more than half of the population of the Yucatán Peninsula had been killed or put to flight, and the Maya rebels had all but succeeded in driving their former masters—the Ladinos, or "crafty ones"—into the sea.

With the fall of Valladolid, Governor Santiago Méndez, in his desperation, sent identical letters to the three powers closely linked with Yucatán's political situation. These were the United States, which, at the time—the period of the 1847–1848 Mexican-American War—maintained a blockade of Yucatán; Great Britain, whose Admiral in Jamaica was in control of the Belize gunrunners; and

Spain, with Antillean possessions and a triple bond of language, religion, and tradition with Yucatán's ruling class.

From each of the three nations, Governor Méndez asked for "powerful and effective help," offering the first to respond to his call "complete domination and sovereignty over Yucatán," thus following a Spanish precedent set by the legendary Count Don Julián, whom historians claimed avenged a personal insult by inviting the Moors into Spain. To further the negotiations, Governor Méndez sent his son-in-law, the young historian and liberal intellectual Justo Sierra, as a special envoy in Washington. Sierra offered Yucatán's neutrality in the Mexican-American conflict in exchange for the lifting of the tariff on shipments of goods moving between Ciudad del Carmen in Campeche and Yucatán.

President Polk granted this concession, but in addressing Congress, he rejected the idea of United States domination of Yucatán and invoked the Monroe Doctrine against any European power that might accept the Méndez offer. When the so-called Yucatán Bill came to vote, his stand was supported by the senators from the slave-owning Deep South, who opposed annexation of the territory on the grounds that it was populated by a "colored race."

In wistful notes, one of the archaeologists, commenting on the historic incident, remarked: "Just imagine, if our Senate had only seized this marvelous opportunity, we might have had the world's greatest ancient ruins right in our own backyard!" Bemoaning the loss to the United States from the financial standpoint, an International Harvester representative who had joined our group explained that the American farmer was entirely dependent for the binding of his grain crop upon Yucatán's sisal hemp production. He quoted figures to show how American ownership of Yucatán's "green gold" would have boosted by astronomical sums the national economy during the previous half century.

In all of its lurid details, Yucatán's Caste War continued to be a popular topic with the history-conscious expeditionaries. Discussions of the conflict that had left such deep scars upon the "Land of the Pheasant and the Deer"[1] revealed that after Washington had spurned the Méndez annexation offer, peace by negotiation between the Yucatecan Government and Jacinto Pat, the most influential of the native chiefs, allegedly of Irish descent, was achieved through a "New Declaration of Independence." The document called for the end of three centuries of exploitation and enslavement of the Maya. It included a provision that canceled all the debts incurred by Indian workers on the *haciendas,* anticipating President Álvaro Obregón's legislation to the same effect by some seventy years.

But the uneasy peace won by the treaty was short-lived, and it was only after another eight years of bitter struggle involving incredible cruelties, widespread destruction, broken agreements, and provoked rivalry between the two rebel leaders, Jacinto Pat and Cecilio Chi—both of whom, as Felipe had informed me at Kanasín, were commemorated by the central monument in the plaza—that the

Caste War officially ended. This was in 1855, although repercussions continued in sporadic hostilities until 1912.

Meanwhile, the New Declaration of Independence had long since become a dead letter. The Ladinos had recognized it only as an expedient to gain time in their determination to subjugate and control the indigenous people, keeping them enslaved through the old "service for debt" system while they produced vast wealth to support the *hacendados'* generally sybarite way of life. To accomplish these ends, the "crafty ones" relied mainly upon the Machiavellian technique of dividing Maya loyalties, attempting especially to stir enmity between Jacinto Pat and Cecilio Chi. Acts of vengeance against peaceful Maya were resumed by the whites, who revoked the civil rights of the Indios. In retaliation, the Mazehual,[2] as the rebels were called, declared a war of total extermination, burning villages and crops. Atrocities mounted on both sides, and in the midst of the havoc the Bishop of the Tekax District, alarmed at the destruction of religious objects and threat to the churches, preached that "Divine Justice" would be directed against those who tolerated the growth of secularism. To his warning, a group of Maya chiefs gathered at Tabi replied: "It is only now that you remember that there is a True God? You were always recommending the name of God to us and you never believed in His Name."

Eventually, both Ladinos and Mazehuales in their common exhaustion ended a fight in which military victory eluded both camps. And lacking real leaders until the appearance among them of Felipe Carrillo Puerto some forty years later, the Maya were again maneuvered into servitude on the *haciendas.* This time the rich and powerful landowners joined in unholy alliance with the unscrupulous *jefes políticos* and trapped them in a peonage more rigid and degrading than the one they had struggled so desperately to uproot.

Many who refused to return to the *haciendas* sought refuge in the southern and eastern forests of the peninsula. Faced with hunger—for during the Caste War, agriculture except in the west had been neglected—the remnants of an entire people migrated, while thousands of others were sold as slaves in the Cuban markets by the Governor Miguel Barbachano. The strong protests that flared in the Mexican press forced him to order the trade to stop, and he sent the Indios to Veracruz instead. But the refugees who managed to survive the hardships of the long trek settled in Quintana Roo at a place called Chan Santa Cruz, about fifteen miles inland from Asunción Bay and twice that distance southwest of Tulum's famous ruined citadel overlooking the Caribbean. There, in the heart of the tropical jungle, they established a religious center around a cult known as Cruzob, the Mayan word for "cross." In this mystic society they hoped to find spiritual solace and relief from insupportable physical burdens. Their symbol and fetish was a "speaking cross," manipulated by a priestly ventriloquist concealed in the floor of the huge thatched church. His voice, purporting to be that of the True God, uttered counsels and commands that directed the lives of the faithful.

During those scholarly deck-side excursions into Yucatán's tragic past, who would have ventured to predict that the courageous rationalist then guiding Maya youth away from the withering grip of atavic superstitious fears to the emancipation of a humanist philosophy, and whose political and social action was aimed at the eradication of religious fanaticism, would one day give his name to the town that harbored the shrine of the "speaking cross"? Yet, in keeping with the flagrant irony that accompanies almost every chapter of Mexican history, this strange thing happened. Today Chan Santa Cruz, long the holy place and high seat of Cruzob worship, with its crude deceptions and weird perversions of Catholic ritual—boasting an electrically lighted plaza and sharing its now undercover devotees with the Maryknoll missionaries, due to what the Mazehual define as Ladino infiltration—is known as El Pueblo de Felipe Carrillo Puerto.

But long before a proud, defiant remnant of the Mayab was to honor Felipe by renaming its venerated jungle refuge in his memory, the Mazehual who remained on the agricultural lands were destined to endure several other agonizing decades. The melancholy sequence of late eighteenth-century events as narrated by the Manhattan-bound historians aboard the *Mexico* revealed that with the destruction of its cornfields, the chief source of sustenance, and the sugar plantations, pivot of the state's economy, Yucatán faced virtual ruin. The imminent danger of total collapse would be averted only by a lucrative crop that could be grown on the barren, rocky soil of the vast *latifundista* estates of the peninsula's northwestern region. Henequen was the answer, and it proved to be an auspicious moment for the production of Yucatán's sturdy fiber, since new needs and multiple uses were created with the dawn of the period of rapidly expanding industrial development everywhere in the world. Before long, the *hacendados* were holding what amounted to a global sisal hemp monopoly. As profits soared, they would purchase greater political power, enabling them to tighten their grip upon the courts, with the correspondingly weakened capacity of the Indios to win or even seek legal redress of injustices. Impoverished, frustrated, and helpless, they suffered beatings, insult, and inhuman hours of forced labor, ever at the mercy of merciless *mayordomos,* conditions that were first brought to my attention through John Kenneth Turner's fully documented, epoch-making book, *Barbarous Mexico.*

Some of the more conservative Yucatalogists of our party found it difficult to believe that such practices as the scholars described could have existed anywhere on the American continent in the twentieth century. But the Austrian woman psychiatrist, who during her Yucatán sojourn had avidly gathered information on the history and social patterns of the Maya, observed, as one of the most tragic chapters of the Caste War story unfolded: "These terrible things have really happened in our time. And isn't it better that we face the truth? How else can we appreciate what that great man, Governor Carrillo, has done and is now doing for his people?"

The *Mexico*'s twenty-four-hour stopover at Havana had been long enough for me to learn that unfriendly rumors preceded our arrival at the pearl of Antilles. Not only did the reactionary press, naturally antagonistic to Felipe's Socialist program, disparage the state-sponsored plans for the Carnegie exploration at Chichén Itzá, but Governor Carrillo was showing "marked attentions to the young and beautiful *New York Times* correspondent Alma Reed." Felipe's discreet gift to me of the gold filigree rosary was mentioned in such inflated terms that the reader might assume it to be at least an emerald necklace or a diamond bracelet. The "news" item greatly amused several members of our party who were themselves taking back to their wives and daughters replicas of my rosary, a typical souvenir of Yucatán's distinctive popular arts.

Our brief stay in Havana allowed time also for the sending of a cable to the *Times* editor, stating that Edward H. Thompson, former United States Consul in Yucatán, had given me an account of his explorations at Chichén Itzá's Sacred Cenote. I had been careful not to mention his "confession" to any of the archaeologists, fearing that somehow the secret so closely guarded for a quarter of a century might leak out before the publication of the *Sunday Magazine* feature article.

The cable brought an eager "star" reporter to interview me upon my landing at Brooklyn's Ward Line pier on the morning of March 5, 1923. He requested "details" on the spot, but I explained that I had solemnly promised Mr. Thompson to write his story just as he had given it to me and that it would even be necessary for me to make certain investigations before I wrote anything further under my byline. I telephoned this decision to Mr. Ochs immediately upon arrival at the Hotel Waldorf-Astoria, explaining that the veteran explorer's narrative might well be a "tall tale" or "a madman's dream," the imaginary adventure of the "science" fictionist. I reminded the already famous publisher how he taught me that accuracy was journalism's first essential, and he laughingly admitted that his words had been meticulously heeded. Arrangements were soon made with the Mexican Consulate General to have my friend Sr. Roberto Casas Alatriste, then in New York on an official mission, and a young woman in the consular service accompany me within the week to Cambridge. Sr. Casas Alatriste, I knew, could represent his government as a qualified witness to verify that the half ton of ancient Maya treasure recovered from the Sacred Well was, as Don Eduardo had claimed, still preserved in the Peabody Museum.

# 19. Mexican Crusade in Manhattan

A cablegram from Felipe greeted my arrival at the Hotel Waldorf-Astoria. With an intensity of delight seldom experienced before or since, I read it again and again, lingering over words that conveyed to me the thrilling reassurance of his devotion. "Almita," the message ran, "I anxiously await notice of your safety. You have left my heart overwhelmed . . . I love you deeply. All my thoughts are at your side . . . Felipe."

My profound emotion was stirred by his ardor, filling me with an overwhelming desire to board the next southbound passenger ship. But my first hours in Manhattan after a month's absence afforded little time to indulge in romantic daydreams. Numerous duties in connection with work and social obligation demanded immediate attention. There were consultations with the *Times* editors, telephone and personal calls from friends who had eagerly awaited my return, among them the husky-voiced charmer who had seen me off to Yucatán and who now, by comparison with Felipe, had lost his allure. There were, too, meetings at the Mexican Consul General's office to arrange for a visit to the Peabody Museum with Señor Casas Alatriste and the young lady secretary connected with the Ministry of Foreign Relations then on vacation in New York. Since Mr. Ochs was anxious to have my article on Don Eduardo Thompson's Sacred Cenote exploits as soon as possible, the Cambridge trip was scheduled for the third day after my arrival. The diary entry showing that a few of my precious hours were spent downtown in the selection of a "guaranteed" noiseless typewriter indicated my determination to work into the late-night hours, free from the fear of disturbing other hotel guests.

Armed with the "confession"—parts of which Don Eduardo had signed—we arrived at the Peabody Museum, and not finding the salvaged material on public display, we asked permission to inspect it. None too willingly, and only after considerable delay and argument, were we led to an upper-floor storage room where, in rows of glass-covered cases, we found the enormous collection exactly as the discoverer had described it to me. My signed article detailing the story behind the Museum's possession of the archaeological objects appeared in the *New York Times Sunday Magazine* of April 4, 1923, under the headline, "The Well of the Maya's Human Sacrifice," the opening paragraphs reading as follows:

> Within the year, the Peabody Museum of Harvard University will announce officially the finding of the Maya treasure at the bottom of the Sacred Well at Chichén Itzá.
>
> The discovery, although admitted to be the most important in the history of American archaeology, has been a carefully guarded secret for over two decades. Exactly how much light it will throw upon one of civilization's most obscure paths is a question that must remain unanswered until Prof. A. M. Tozzer and Dr. Herbert J. Spinden publish their erudite commentary. For the present, we know only that a quantity of precious material and an astonishingly weird romance have been reclaimed from the ever-receding past.
>
> But there is the romance that science pursues, and there is the one lived in the pursuit! And the 'unofficial' announcement of the recovery of human bones, gold ornaments, and objects of jade, copper, and wood from the depths of the Sacred Well, or "El Cenote de los Sacrificios," involves a worthy sequel to the strange story that the world had forgotten.

I then related in detail the account given to me by Don Eduardo when I interviewed him in Yucatán, wording the article as tactfully as I knew how, fully aware that the revelations it contained could provoke an international incident. The day following its appearance I was asked by the editor of the *New York World* to rewrite the article for his paper. On April 22, the *World* published it as a front-page Sunday feature under an eight-column headline that read: "Thompson's own story of his discoveries in Yucatán," illustrated with the three photographs I had supplied.

Several newspapers and magazines in the United States and Europe requested amplified versions of the sensational Chichén Itzá exploit, and for months I was kept busy writing and lecturing on the subject. Almost immediately, there were other repercussions from Don Eduardo's "confession." Some of them were felt not only in New England's halls of learning but in the United States Congress and in the Mexican courts. In less than sixty days after the disclosures—which, due to Mr. Thompson's status as American Consul in Yucatán, had created a scandal—the government of Mexico, demanding return of the whole collection of ancient objects or an indemnity of two million dollars, instituted a lawsuit against the Peabody Museum.

Meanwhile, I had received Felipe's first letter, dated March 10. But when it was delivered to me at the hotel desk, what should have been pure elation was tempered with a mild sense of shock. I noticed, or, at least, my self-consciousness imagined—as a result, doubtless, of the Ward Line captain's chilly reaction to the Havana newspaper item—that the mail clerk had handed it to me only after a lifted-eyebrow scrutiny of the envelope, addressed in red ink. I fully realized that this circumstance at the period might easily have aroused suspicion, especially in the ultraconservative precincts of the Waldorf-Astoria. It was on our memorable ride to Kanasín that I had gently warned Felipe about the unpopularity in my country of *tinta roja* (red ink), impressing upon him that its use, except on balance sheets, was interpreted as indicating Leftist affiliations. In jesting words but with a serious intent I had assured him that I would always have an infallible clue to his identity, regardless of how he signed his letters. Red ink, I explained, was strictly taboo in the personal correspondence of my other men friends. It occurred to me that the suspect nature of my "foreign communication" might be highlighted in the mind of the mail clerk by the emblem of the Partido Socialista del Sureste, an embossed globe in screaming vermilion encircled by the clasped hands of universal brotherhood at the upper corner of the envelope. And certainly not designed to allay the worst fears of super-patrioteers, there appeared beneath the symbolic globe of solidarity the slogan of the Liga de Resistencia: "Tierra y Libertad—Land and Liberty." Little did I then surmise that these same words were soon destined to become the most revered of my private vocabulary. In Yucatán, the red ink of the Socialist insignia had not only seemed to me perfectly natural but even inevitable among a people so recently redeemed from the hunger, exploitation, and slavery that had flourished for decades under the guise of a democratic system. In economically thriving Manhattan, however, barely emerged from the Bolshevist witch-hunting era of the Palmer Raids, both the Partido's favorite color and its official slogan could be construed by the "one hundred percenter" fanatics as subversive or as a sign of involvement in some movement to overthrow the government. Stranger accusations had been made against loyal American citizens in the not too distant past.

But all my naive fears and misgivings dissolved of their own futility soon after opening Felipe's letter. The red ink of its two closely spaced typed pages even impressed me as a much more appropriate color than blue or black or brown to convey his human longing for love and companionship and his affirmation of life's most radiant possibilities in adventures of the mind and sprit. Written in answer to the note I had mailed to him from Havana, the letter read:

> Unforgettable Alma: I am thinking with great intensity on the sympathy that already exists between us. But taking into consideration your public life and the work you are doing in the New York press, I sometimes think that

you cannot care for me nor believe in the love that we, as Latins, passionately feel for the woman we adore. From the day I met you until the moment I write you this letter, you live perpetually in my mind. I am tremendously desperate to see you, and the only things that give a little consolation are your photographs and the lock of your hair that you left with me. I do not know when I shall see you again, but I conform myself with loving you until who knows what future date.

Recently, I visited the caves of Calcehtok, of which I send you photographs. We passed through all the galleries, and as we entered them, I felt that you were always at my side. The caves are marvelously adorned with Nature's art and are even more beautiful than those of Loltún. In one of the galleries through which we managed to pass by creeping along, we encountered a stalagmite, which the Indians, with much justice, call Lacichpanxinan, meaning "the Beautiful Lady." But these, our poor *compañeros,* are greatly mistaken, because the statue that I see represented in my Pixan Halal[1] is so much lovelier that I remain in ecstasy much of the time, regarding her with my soul and with a desire that is very sure of itself.

When we left Calcehtok, we went to the ruins of Oxkintok, where we came upon the extraordinary hill Za Tun Zat, which means "labyrinth." Here, one enters through a door and must leave in a crouching position by another, that is, if the guide knows the terrain perfectly. Many comments have been written on this hill, especially by Ingeniero Reygadas who believes it to be a vast sepulcher of the Maya. The construction, however, of the galleries does not seem to indicate that it had served this purpose but, rather, was a place of vigilance or of inspection for all those who wished to belong to the religion of the inhabitants of Oxcintok or dwell in the community and who, before being accepted, must pass severe initiation tests, as in the epoch of Masonry. We took a photograph of an almost completely ruined building, and I am enclosing a copy of it. Later, we visited a very beautiful grotto with a huge single *sala* in which, according to the natives, the Maya held their *fiestas.* The place is so enormous that one can readily believe that it accommodated, as they claim, thousands of guests.

How many times during these trips do I think of my lovely Alma and how many times do I find my soul in New York while my body is in this land suffering annoyances, even to a crash of my automobile that broke my arm. It happened when my tranquility had completely evaporated and my thoughts had traveled to you with tormenting doubts that this little city holds, as you said in your letter, your sentiments or that you remember our promises of love. I send you various photographs already colored to bring out your true loveliness, for surely it is your mission on this earth to go forward with your intellect and your beauty.

> Receive my endearments and my wish that you do not delay in answering me, and in your delicious Spanish . . . I do not sign this letter by hand because it is only three days since I broke my arm.

In the signature typed by his secretary, Felipe had used his Mayan name, H'pil Zutilché. On the ride to Kanasín he said he would sometimes sign his letters "H'pil," since that was the name by which his Inditos knew him and he wanted me to become accustomed to it.

Upon my return from Cambridge, Mr. Ochs phoned, requesting that I see him on a matter of "great importance." At our meeting, he complimented me both on the Mexican and Carnegie Expedition coverage and then, broaching the real purpose of the interview, said: "If what you have been writing for the *Times* in the past months on the performance and aims of the Obregón Government is factual, and I do not in the least doubt the absolute veracity of your material, I am seriously considering editorial support for the recognition of Mexico by the United States. The real proof of President Obregón's intentions will be found in the 1923 budget to be released publicly on September 1. But we could save time in bringing about normal relations between the two governments if we were to have the budget figures now. The figures will show where the emphasis lies, since we could know what amounts are appropriated for educational and cultural activities and those allocated to armament and military purposes."

The publisher assured me that he knew of my contacts with the top Mexican officials, laughingly commenting that he heard I "had led the grand march with President Obregón at the American Legion's Armistice Day Ball." But what he regarded as even more important at the moment, he explained, was my friendship with the members of the technical committee then in New York to prepare the documents necessary for the operation of the terms of the so-called De la Huerta–Lamont Agreement. I was aware that through this agreement the obligations contracted by the usurper General Victoriano Huerta were rejected as having no binding force upon the Mexican government, but all other debts were, including those representing notes signed for larger amounts than the sums collected and saddled upon the Mexican people during the Díaz dictatorship, to create a per capita national debt for fifteen million Mexicans that was one of the world's highest. The technical committee, headed by my friend Sr. Roberto Casas Alatriste, whom I had first met on the trip to Yucatán with the Carnegie Expedition, included the prominent banker Sr. Elías de Lima, Licenciado Miguel Palacios Macedo, and Sr. Olallo Rubio, secretary.

Instantly recognizing the importance of such influential journalistic support for Washington's recognition of Mexico, I at once advised Sr. Casas Alatriste of the suggestions made to me by Mr. Ochs. The brilliant and patriotic young economist, to whom the great Wall Street firm of J. P. Morgan Co., through its director, Thomas W. Lamont, had made tempting offers for his services, communicated with Chapultepec[2] and received the budget statistics Mr. Ochs had requested. The article favoring recognition of the Obregón Government appeared as the leading *Times* editorial on April 29, 1923. Occupying four half-page columns under the caption, "Mexico's Budget Indicates Progress," the editorial read as follows:

> A significant statement of Mexico's aims and policies made by the present Government has just reached the world through the publication of the Federal Budget for 1923. More forcibly than the eloquence of official proclamation, the plain figures tell where President Obregón's Administration is placing its emphasis. The fact that this budget is the first in a decade to fulfill all the constitutional requirements points to a new era in Mexico's financial scheme of things, with certain effects of internal strengthening and improved international relations.
>
> The budget for the current year is the first one issued by the legislative power on behalf of the Mexican people since the Madero Congress of 1912. If one excepts the unrecognized legislation of Provisional President Victoriano Huerta, the public funds of Mexico, from that time until last January, were created and used at the will of the President, acting under "facultades extraordinarias en Hacienda" (extraordinary powers in the treasury).
>
> This unchecked control of the national purse strings was tenaciously held by Carranza throughout his regime, on the plea of "unsettled conditions." Even after the restoration of the constitutional government, the "First Chief" did not permit the Cámara de Diputados (House of Representatives) to exercise its vital constitutional right, in spite of the long and bitter struggle of the "Obregonistas."
>
> But there was a prompt surrender of "facultades extraordinarias" by President Obregón, as soon as the financial reorganization of the country had been perfected under his Minister of Finance, Adolfo de la Huerta. This act, indicative of official sincerity and national stability, made possible the first budget backed by the Mexican people.
>
> Economy is its keynote. Compared with the budget of 1922, there is a total decrease of 10 percent. The amount provided for last year's Federal expenses was 383,658,608 pesos. For this year the budget totals 347,006,719 pesos, showing a savings of 36,651,889. But the reduction gains its real significance from the fact that 11,470,000 applies to the wiping out of national obligations, and that 30,000,000 pesos of this amount appears as a new item, being Mexico's first payment of her international debt, according to the De la Huerta–Lamont Agreement of June 16, 1922. Already 21,000,000

pesos of the payment has been deposited with the international committee of bankers, whose conferences in this city with the Mexican financial commission have just come to a close. In Mexico's movement to pay back her foreign loans lies the fulfillment of the promises made by President Obregón in his message to the people of the United States, on June 26, 1921:

> We have stated repeatedly that Mexico would not repudiate any just obligations. We have always paid our debts: we always will pay our debts. We have seen a loan of $20,000,000 received in 1824 changed magically into a debt of more than $100,000,000. We have seen Maximilian sign off an obligation of $40,000,000 in return for a loan of $20,000,000. We have seen Miramón, the counter-revolutionist, sign a note for $15,000,000 in return for a loan of $750,000. Yet not once, even under these outrageous burdens, have we ever advanced the idea of repudiation.

Throughout the Revolution we stated repeatedly that Mexico would meet every just obligation without evasion. It is a promise that will be kept to the letter. Even now we are planning the machinery that will settle all claims in accordance with the principles laid down by international law.

An attempt to make satisfactory settlement of complicated problems and claims growing out of the chaos of revolution is revealed in other divisions of the *deuda pública* (public debt appropriation). There is a provision, for instance, of 1,300,000 pesos for the redemption of bonds from Federal civil employees, who, during the Carranza days, were forced to accept these securities for 25 percent of their monthly salaries. Last year 2,827,618 pesos were paid to these bondholders, and this year's payment will practically cancel the debt.

Conforming to the law of January 1, 1920, 800,000 pesos have been set aside as interest on the "Agrarian Debt." The acknowledgement of indebtedness by the payment of interest to the former owners of these vast nonproductive estates, which are now being divided among small farmers or converted into cooperative colonies, answers the charge of "confiscation" raised against Mexico's agrarian program, even though it be an admitted impossibility to make immediate payment on the principal.

There is a provision of 4,000,000 pesos for interest on the "recognized" debt to the banks taken over during the period of the Carranza Revolution, and just as significant in backing up President Obregón's assurance that "Mexico does not mean to ignore established rights, but shall honestly and justly act by others," is the item of 50,000 pesos for the "full settlement with the holders of the National Gold Certificates, which were placed against the deposits made in paper money," in accordance with the decree of the Carranza de facto Government in 1916.

In step with progressive legislation in the United States, 500,000 pesos of the "public debt" appropriation is destined for teachers' pensions. There is a total of 4,000,000 pesos for the pensioning of retired civil Government employees, military officers and soldiers, railway employees, and of the dependents of those who died in any of these branches of the public service.

The 1923 budget strikingly demonstrates Mexico's harmony with the present world ideals, by its substantial decrease in army and navy appropriations. Independently, and without the pressure of participation in the League of Nations or the Pan-American Union, Mexico is reducing her armament. There will be 30,000,000 pesos less spent on her program of national defense this year than last. Throughout the Obregón Administration, armed forces have been gradually eliminated as a continuation of the policy initiated by Acting President de la Huerta in 1920. Between January 1, 1922, and January 1, 1923, about 10,000 men were discharged from the army ranks. But the most drastic "dropping" of Generals and soldiers in Mexican history was an event of the past ninety days.

Aside from the economy involved, and its evidence of forward vision, the 15,000 (pesos) decrease in military funds tends to prove that the Mexican Government is no longer sustained by the force of bayonets but by the will of the people. It is the best test of internal security and order since the overthrow of the Díaz autocracy.

The sum of 52,362,903 pesos, or about 15 percent of the entire budget for 1923, is allotted to public education. Here is an increase over the 1922 amount of 2,436,187 pesos. The addition helps to provide for two important movements—Indian education and the campaign against illiteracy. Since the first of the year, 3,000 new resident rural teachers have been appointed. The staff of *maestros misioneros* (missionary teachers) has been enlarged to 650. They speak the native dialects, and their work is to establish schools and "agricultural" classes in the most isolated pueblos, in an effort to lift the Indians from their centuries of ignorance and exploitation.

Eloquent of Mexico's attempt at child welfare is the item of 320,000 pesos for "breakfasts for children of the public schools." The Government's desire to foster better international understanding through education appears in the following appropriations: 300,000 pesos for "scholarships for Mexican boys in foreign countries"; 300,000 pesos for the "interchange of teachers and pupils between Mexico and foreign countries, and to pay the salaries of foreign teachers"; and 120,000 pesos for "scholarships for sixty boys of Central America in the Mexican schools."

> There is a decrease of 128,763 pesos in the amount to be expended this year on Mexico's archaeological program, but an analysis of the figures shows important work accomplished for science and plans for new excavations, which will add to the world's knowledge of vanished peoples. There are between 800 and 900 archaeological sections in the Republic, but the larger part of the 1922 appropriation for the Department of Anthropology was devoted to the exploration of the city of Teotihuacán, about twenty-five miles from the capital. Last year saw the completion of an undertaking that resulted in the uncovering of two distinct civilizations and the conservation of the Pyramid of the Sun, as well as other structures of the region. The 1923 budget provides 50,000 pesos for a "study of the ethnological zone of Oaxaca," with its famous ruins of Mitla and Monte Albán, and another 50,000 pesos for the preservation and investigation of the Maya architecture of Yucatán and Chiapas.
>
> Mexico will carry out these large projects "in the event that there is money enough in the treasury." Her present achievements and immediate undertakings, as shown by her latest budget, suggest the performance of a national miracle. For, contrary to all theories of government, Mexico is existing today without national credit and under financial "boycott" at a time when every established institution has been overturned and the old order completely demolished. If figures talk, the 1923 budget tells its own story of Mexico's solution of her problems and of her placating of the impatience of an impoverished people with a diminished armed force, and of her willingness to take her place among the advanced nations of the world.

The Mexican press reacted to the editorial with gratified amazement. The leading dailies of the capital commented on the hopeful outlook for recognition created by the support of the powerful *New York Times.* The cabled report of *El Heraldo* was headed: "An Eloquent Indicator of Mexico's Progress," while *El Universal* hailed the "extensive article as a study of the actual present Federal Budget, clearly indicating a new era of order and prosperity."

On the day after its publication, I received a call from the editor of the *New York Journal,* requesting an interview. When we met at his Gold Street offices, he informed me that he was aware that I had obtained the advance Mexican budget figures for the *Times* editorial, and stated that Mr. William Randolph Hearst was also considering support for U.S. recognition of Mexico through its nationwide chain of newspapers. He asked me if I would write a series of ten stories, highlighting different aspects of the constructive program of the Obregón regime. He explained that since my own byline was associated with the *Times,* the articles would have to be signed by what I understood was the fictitious name of "C. B.

Travis" and bear a Mexico City dateline. Only too eager to help in bringing about friendly relations between my own country and the land that had already won my affection and esteem, I consented. The first of the syndicated series appeared on May 11, 1923, in three columns with a boxed headline, "Mexico's 1923 Budget Proves Government Is Finally Stable." An italicized introductory note read: "This is the first of a series of highly important articles on present conditions in Mexico, with special reference to the question of the stability and the integrity of the present government. The fact that the special envoys of the United States government left Washington Sunday for Mexico City to reach an agreement is evidence of the fact that recognition of Mexico is expected soon."

The cables filed from New York and Washington by the Mexican correspondents bordered on disbelief. Most of them seemed at a loss to understand why the hard-hitting Hearst syndicate suddenly, and without warning, had made so complete a change in its obstructionist policy toward the Revolutionary Government. One of the Mexico City dailies, trying to analyze the reversal of the traditional Hearst attitude, asked with a note of skepticism: "What's Behind it All?"

Only a small group of Manhattan crusaders for Mexican recognition could be quite sure that the motivating factor in the sensational journalistic development was the ancient phenomenon of the "handwriting on the wall."

# 20. Platonic Love

Among the social events that relieved my full-day concentration on the journalistic telling of the contemporary Mexican story, none gave me greater pleasure and satisfaction than the Costume Ball held in early March by the New York Actors' Group—forerunner of Equity. It was inevitable that I appear on this very special occasion as a Mestiza of Yucatán, wearing the exquisitely embroidered, heavily lace-trimmed *fiesta* dress Felipe had designed and presented to me and which had become the most treasured ensemble of my wardrobe. The one hundred or more guests at the glittering affair included such stage celebrities as the Barrymores, Ruth Chatterton, Blanche Bates, and other distinguished characters of the theater world, all of them disguised as familiar characters of history or legend, ranging from the pirate Jean Laffite to Marco Polo and Helen of Troy. When, to my amazement, the jury awarded me the first prize for the "most beautiful, authentic, and original" costume, I felt that I was sharing honors with Felipe, knowing his profound pride in the folk art of his beloved Yucatecan *tierra* and recalling his admiration for the colorful native garments worn by the *señoritas* we met at the pueblo celebrations.

In several of Felipe's letters, which continued to arrive with each Ward Line boat, he mentioned the Actors' Ball. In one dated April 1, he writes: "You have told me nothing about the *fiesta* in which you were to take part wearing your Mestiza dress. Have you forgotten your promise? Are you so considerate that you fear my ardor will be a torment? I beg of you, tell me something, tell me about your triumphs that on one hand bring me joy and, on the other, cause me pain never experienced." But in a letter written later that day—in answer of my own, which had been evidently delayed reaching him, he deplored that he could not have been present at this "tribute to Pixan Halal and the Raza Maya[1] by the artists of a great city." In another, written the same week, he observed that it is "difficult to believe that what happened to me has not happened to your countrymen, when they saw you in all your natural charm in your Mestiza dress. I am filled with sadness, fearing that after this Fantasía Ball of the Actors' Society, you may cease writing to me. But patience! Finally, I shall know from your own lips all that you have offered to relate to me regarding the event."

Throughout April, May, and June, Felipe's letters—frequently two or three at a time—arrived weekly via the Mexico-Cuba mail. With rare exceptions, each morning also found a cablegram waiting for me in Box 393 at the Waldorf-Astoria reception desk. Among the cables, one dated April 17 announced the discovery at Chichén Itzá by the artist Miguel Ángel Fernández of a "new *chac-mool*, different in attitude from the well-known type and measuring one hundred and fifty centimeters."

Almost invariably, Felipe's messages conveyed his longing for my presence in Yucatán. His letter dated April 7 stated:

> As much as I would desire it, I do not presume now to ask you to spend your life at my side. But I beg of you, come for some days—at least for a month—and if you feel that you cannot remain longer, return to your feverish Manhattan where no one knows his neighbor, where one passes unperceived, where humanity does not exist, yet where people live, where they work and prosper and there they die. It is possible that I may go to New York, but this cannot be as soon as I wish, a fact that causes me still greater sorrow. My presence in this state is indispensable since if I were not here, we might have to lament some incidents that could develop within the Partido Socialista itself.

What visions of "joy, dim descried" were evoked by Felipe's mere suggestion of spending my life at his side! How eagerly I would have sailed back to Yucatán and to him, if I could have been certain that our emotional tensions, nourished through separation and affectionate and almost daily communication by letter or wire, would permit the continuance of the Platonic relationship of the brief Carnegie expeditionary period. Yet, whatever the situation, I realized that in Mérida we would both be exposed to the insinuations and slander of the ever-active political enemies. At the moment, the safeguarding of Felipe's prestige and the forward impact of his most cherished values—those goals, as he once assured me, that gave him "no peace until they were won"—seemed to lie in flight from temptation. Falling back upon my disciplines, I decided to go abroad—to put thousands of miles between myself and the alluring proximity of the Ward Line pier. I even made serious efforts to do so, requesting Mr. Ochs to assign me to Constantinople to cover the story of Kemal Pascha. At that time, the Revolutionary leader was struggling to modernize Turkey. He had already succeeded in abolishing the anachronistic Caliphate and in liberating the women of his country from feudal customs. The genial *Times* publisher promised to consider the matter and give me an early reply. In late May, I received his negative answer. But significantly, instead of bitter disappointment, I secretly experienced a thrill of exaltation when, in refusing my request, he announced: "We already have plenty of good reporters in the Near Eastern sector, capable of handling Atatürk as well as those veiled ladies along the Bosphorus. But we are depending upon you for feature coverage of Mexico. You know everyone down there, and besides, you were a party to committing the *Times* to Washington's recognition of the Obregón Government, an issue that may come up any day now." He suggested that I prepare to return to Mexico City at the end of June or early July. He would give me a list, he said, of key officials whom he wished me to interview, among them President Obregón, General Calles, and Licenciado José Vasconcelos. Despite my avowed rationalist views, I was not yet entirely liberated from esoteric concepts that had lingered from my youthful Theosophist and Rosicrucian association. The decision of Mr. Ochs was accepted, as a result, somewhat in the nature of a call from well-disposed Destiny, drawing me back sooner or later to Yucatán. I found a certain moral satisfaction, however, in the conviction that I had sincerely tried to evade the mystic summons.

As the letters conveying his desperate desire to see me continued to arrive, I kept asking myself: "Where will all this lead?" The answer eluded me, but of one thing I was virtually certain. Despite my strong impulse to be near Felipe and his own impassioned pleading, I felt that I would not, *must* not, return at once to Yucatán, unless I were definitely sent there to fill some journalistic mission. My resolve was based not only in an individual sense of the fitness of things but in an even more compelling urge—my profound solicitude for the unhindered progress of Felipe's significant public service. The cause for which he struggled and sacrificed for so many years—the cause of human well-being—was also of deep personal concern to me. Almost as far back as I could remember, I had been involved, emotionally at least, in "crusades." Ever since grammar school days when I would win the annual prize for "elocution," I had been articulate in various "uplift" and social betterment movements, following the example set by my idealist father. Among those enlisting my spirited juvenile loyalty and occasional "speech making" were racial equality, single tax, minimum wage, Indian independence, Irish freedom, abolition of capital punishment, and rights for women. While my hair was still hanging in braids, I became known as the "Girl Campaigner" to the members of the College Equal Suffrage League, headed by my intimate friend and "Big Sister" guide, the courageous Charlotte Anita Whitney.[2] A photograph of the period shows me in a street parade, crowned and robed as the Goddess of Justice, enthroned upon an elaborate float and holding aloft the scales that had tipped in favor of equal political and economic opportunity for the women of all nations. My earliest envisioned career was that of social service, and up until the previous autumn when I left San Francisco for my first Mexican visit, I had pursued welfare work through a daily newspaper column devoted exclusively to obtaining aid for those in trouble or in want. In view of these girlhood activities in congenital interests and a "reformist" temperament, it was natural that I should instantly recognize in Felipe a most effective champion of the identical causes that claimed my youthful enthusiasm. I was convinced that the theater of his compassionate action at the social, labor, and cultural levels was a universal one and that Yucatán, as he once assured me, was only his "laboratory."

A few days before Mr. Ochs had sealed my fate—as I mentally referred to his reassigning me to Mexico for the summer of 1923—I disclosed my travel plans to Felipe. I felt it was more considerate to prepare him for the possibility of the Near Eastern trip than suddenly to announce such unpleasant news. His reply left me deeply disturbed, for I knew he could not penetrate my motives. In fact, he had attributed them to indifference when he wrote:

> I am plunged into melancholy since I see that instead of wishing to come closer to me, you are each day going farther away. Now it appears that you are not even thinking of coming back to Yucatán, but of going to Europe to work there and send articles to the journals for which you are a correspondent, while your poor Dragoncito remains here alone and, as I have done until today, hoping for the return of the blue-eyed Dragoncita[3] who cares only for her newspapers. I am truly very sad, Almita, because you have left such a great emptiness in my heart. Never could I have imagined that I would be so desperately in love with anyone as I am with you. In your letter you say that love makes for happiness. But for me the contrary has resulted, since the love I feel for you makes me an unhappy man, knowing that you are so far away from me and that each day you wish to widen the distance between us.

In the same letter, he asked: "Have you not also felt something of the great love that I keep in my soul for you?" And he added: "Mine is not a sentiment of carnal desire. What I feel for you is a sentiment of spiritual longing. Just to see your eyes, to hear your voice, to look at your face, to feel you near me, to sense the perfume of your breath. Together, all these things would convert existence for me into a life of inexpressible delight."

It was with tremendous relief that I was able to tell him of the adverse direction of Mr. Ochs in regard to the proposed interviews with Kemal Pascha and my acceptance of the counter proposal that I write feature articles for the *Times* from July through September in Mexico. Assuming that the Mexican visits would include Yucatán, Felipe wrote in reply:

> Eventually, with difficulty, we will succeed inaugurating, on the 14th and 15th of July, the Chichén Itzá Highway. With all my heart I invite you to this event and I beg you to make every effort to attend and to stay some days with us. Have no fears! I shall be just the same as I was the first time I saw you. I'll not do anything against your ideas, and you may be sure that you will continue being for me the same little star I looked at from afar the night I broke my arm. And when you are here, near to me, I will think of you as that same little star, to which I dare not come closer because of sentimental differences.

In this letter Felipe also commented on one of my observations concerning the similarity of his Casa del Niño[4] program to the ideas of the Greek Plato who advocated state responsibility for the care and education of children:

> It is true that we have in mind some of Plato's ideas, but we have not copied them. Only by intuition are we implanting them. I have read Plato's *Republic,* but it is also true that those ideas came to me not for having read this classic work. They came independently because of the many mothers, divorced and married, who have asked my help for their children. They are the ones who have made me understand the urgent need for creating this benefic institution. Here we aim to provide a real home for the neglected or abandoned children of those men without courage or conscience, so that these little ones may develop normally and receive an education instead of facing a life of misery and uselessness.
>
> Our program is based on simple justice because these children are not the ones to be blamed for their situation. They did not come into life of their own free will. Such are the considerations that have induced me to create the Casa del Niño, and we are now working to build a fine establishment and do whatever is necessary to instill a more humane if less orthodox code of morals. In a few days I shall send you other new initiatives with which we are now occupied on behalf of society in general, but especially for the proletariat, who are in the greatest need. From these legislative proposals you will understand that we are working not only at the material level but with our best efforts for our ideals, in order to improve the condition of the humble ones and the helpless children.
>
> I have sent you all the photographs you requested in your little letter, and I hope that you will never forget that your requests for me are commands that I obey as if they came from my beloved mother.
>
> I ask you, out of whatever affection you may have for me, that you write me in Spanish. I shall then be happy in the certainty that nobody except

> myself will read your precious letters. I ask also that you do not fail to send me a wire in case you are coming to Mexico. And now, I will say "good-bye," wishing you success in all your worthy undertakings and with all my soul deeply wanting to see you and kiss you. (Signed, H'pil)

A cable published in the *New York Times* of April 4 announced that the State Legislature of Yucatán had ratified an amendment granting divorce on the solicitude of "only one party, without cause."

The report sent from Mérida, dated the previous day and bearing the caption "Easy Divorce Easier in New Yucatán Law," read:

> Amendments which will ease further the easiest divorce law on the American continent went into effect today in the Mexican State of Yucatán. The new legislation, ratified by the Socialist Governor, Felipe Carrillo, provides that a decree of divorce may be demanded and obtained on the simple application before a duly authorized Justice of the Peace, by both husband and wife or by only one of them.
>
> Rules governing the divorces of persons married outside the State and outside the territory of the Mexican Republic are also fixed by the new legislation. One month's residence in the State is necessary for foreigners before a divorce application will be heard. Proof of the validity of a marriage celebrated outside the territory of the nation among foreigners, in accordance with the laws of the country in which it was celebrated, must be filed with the office of the Registrar, together with proof of the required residence in the State of Yucatán, before divorce will be granted.
>
> In all cases where there are children, a certificate of marriage must be accompanied by a "protest of trust" containing the age, names, and present custody of the children of the union to be dissolved.
>
> In the wording of Yucatán's civil code, "divorce is of three classes—voluntary, or the mutual agreement of the parties; contested divorce, with cause; and contested divorce without cause."
>
> The last named class of divorce is granted upon the simple application of the interested party to proper judicial authority but is obtained only after a month's trial at reconciliation.
>
> If the applicant for a divorce with cause fails to establish the necessary grounds, the action will in no way prejudice a second action which may be made on an application "without cause."
>
> Women who apply for divorce with cause and establish grounds are not to pay court and attorney fees.
>
> All children, legal and illegal, in Yucatán must be supported by their fathers, although the custody belongs to the mother until the child is eight years of age. The child may then choose between the parents.

A few days later I received a printed copy of the amendment with the official legislative record, enclosed in one of Felipe's letters.

Obviously, the way was now clear for Felipe to terminate his own marriage. Yet the fact did not suggest any valid reason for rejoicing. I was still haunted by the hobgoblin of "what people would say" about him. Despite the documented sequence of events, proving that Felipe had contemplated the amendment months before my arrival in Yucatán, there were many, I was aware, who, with reference to myself, would suspect his motives in giving legal force to a "one party, without cause," divorce application. I fully realized that his influence as a pathfinder for his generation would be weakened by such charges of personal interest, however unfounded.

The fact that the amendment had been proposed before I appeared on the Yucatecan scene was, opportunely for my peace of mind, confirmed by an article in the *Outlook Magazine* of January 23, which I discovered by chance in my library research. The author, Mary Turner Mason, after making an on-the-ground survey of Felipe's new laws, had written: "Other Socialist Government reforms in prospect are easier marriage and divorce laws and the legitimizing of all children, a child born out of wedlock taking the father's name and sharing in all inheritance legally with the children of the man's legal wife. It is said that at present (1922) 30 percent of the children of all Yucatán and 45 percent of the children of Mérida are illegitimate."

Further reassurance came from my ever-reliable diary in which I had recorded that in the very first days of our acquaintance Felipe had informed me that he was planning to make the word *bastardo*—illegitimate—when applied to any person in Yucatán born of unmarried parents, an offense punishable by imprisonment.

Yet that I might become the unwitting cause of retarding or perhaps even nullifying his rare contribution was my ever-present fear, almost to the point of obsession. And I reasoned that in an immediate return to Yucatán, I would be running just such a risk.

Certainly, it was common knowledge throughout Yucatán that for three years before I even heard of Felipe's existence, he had been completely separated from Sra. Carrillo and that during all that period he had maintained a home for her in Havana, where she was currently residing. All Yucatán knew also that throughout his governorship Doña Adela, his distinguished mother, had acted as his official hostess. But in the eyes of the Mexican law, Felipe was still a married man. And it was doubtful if the moral truth about his marital status would reach that vast "outside" public to which his great regenerative and educational program was ultimately aimed.

Meanwhile, until the position of everyone involved was clarified, the logical if difficult course for me was to silence the voice of my heart and maintain what must have appeared to Felipe to be an attitude of romantically detached admiration. For the first time I understood what the poets meant when they sang of a love that was strong enough to leave love alone. Yet, an intuition of a destined "belonging" did not desert me. I continued to trust that our pale hope of mutual happiness would one day be transmitted into radiant reality in an honest, unequivocal stand before the world on our right to be inseparably together.

Before saluting Wall Street's sky-piercing towers in a less romantic farewell than these symbols of centralized financial might have evoked from me four months earlier, I cabled Felipe that I was about to sail—on that date, July 5—for Mexico.

# 21. Foreboding Moments

Two young Mexican officials—an economist of the Technical Committee for the Adjudication of the National Debt and a member of the New York Consular staff—who together had courteously filled the four-month interim between my visits to their country with dinner and theater parties, diplomatic receptions, concerts, and other social functions, accompanied me aboard the Ward liner *Yucatán,* when, on July 5, it sailed from Manhattan Pier, both promising to greet me *pronto* in "ol' Tenochtitlán." The ship, which had a long record of Cuban and Mexican service, looked as though it had weathered a severe hurricane. Captain Blackadder, at whose right I was seated at luncheon, apologized for his vessel's "battered condition," explaining that there had not been time between his New York arrival and departure schedule to repair the damage caused by a "rampaging band of *chicleros*" while they were being transported through Caribbean waters after their season's work in the sapodilla forests of Quintana Roo. The spirited Scotch veteran of tropical seas gave us a vivid picture of how the "jungle men had run amuck, whacking off with sticks and machetes virtually every object that protruded from wall or ceiling." In order to provide light during the dinner hour, a crew of electricians was feverishly working to reinstall dangling fixtures.

The *Yucatán* was docked at Havana only between dawn and sunset, but I went ashore in the early morning, escorted by a middle-aged New England bachelor who for some years had been a banker in Manila and was visiting Latin America for the first time. After collecting and sending our respective cables and letters at the local Ward Line office, we made the rounds of the popular tourist attractions, many of which I had investigated on my recent longer stay in Havana, but adding a tour of Morro Castle and Cabaña Fortress to the February itinerary. From the moment we left New York Harbor, my new acquaintance, who in his conservative outlook and his rigid regard for the "American way of life" and its political status quo could have modeled for the original "Boston Brahmin," had singled me out for special deck-side attentions. We passed many hours in pleasant "bookish" conversation that revealed his alert, observing mind and, despite his Puritanical code, a kindly, sympathetic spirit. His romantic interest and even his serious intentions were disclosed quite unexpectedly, with a proposal of marriage during our drive along the *malecón* to the Vedado and Marianao and back again to port. He could assure me, he said, of his lifelong devotion and a worthy home of my choosing "in our own country." He was prepared, if I were to accept him, to sever his Philippine business connections so as to be free to travel, a "constructive diversion," he noted, that I apparently enjoyed. In response to his sincerity, I replied that while I was fully aware of the compliment he had paid me, I had no desire at present to give up a mode of life that entirely satisfied me. The poignant experience, however, more clearly than any other of the period, served to highlight for me how radical a change my preference in male companionship had undergone since my contact with Mexico. A year earlier, it occurred to me, I might have considered the challenge of transforming into love my high esteem for this refined, sensitive, personable, and obviously lonely suitor who shared my Anglo-American traditions and whose moral standards and mental perspective represented familiar ancestral patterns. I still continued to admire the stalwart and stabilizing values of my inheritance, but now they held far less appeal for me than the more profound emotional and spiritual motivations I had so recently discovered in the impulsive and warmly human Latin temperament. I recognized that Dr. Herbert J. Spinden had correctly if unknowingly analyzed the psychological change when, in presenting me with a copy of his book on Maya time correlation, he had written above his autograph: "To my friend, Alma Reed, who has tasted of the tropics and found the flavor *good.*"

Upon my return to the ship, Captain Blackadder informed me that he had just received orders from "Yucatán's highest authority" to take "very special" care of me, adding that he had already found this an easy and agreeable responsibility. He had made the announcement in the presence of my visibly mystified escort, but I did not feel it necessary to explain. That evening, the new British Consul in Mérida and his two London friends who were on holiday for a Campeche jungle safari gave a party in the captain's quarters, inviting as their guests a young Mexican couple, an attractive Los Angeles widow, and myself. The next morning, the New England banker expressed his disapproval of the English hosts, describing them as "rather frivolous companions for so serious a young lady." Serene in the blissful confidence that within twenty-four hours I would again look upon Felipe's face, I merely smiled in answer. But if I had spoken, I would have said that no male fellow passenger—whether as frivolous as Punchinello or as solemn as Jeremiah—could offer the most ephemeral rivalry to the noble masculine image that dominated my consciousness, an image that completely fulfilled my dreams of perfection.

And now, as the long-anticipated moment neared, I found myself in a state of delicious excitement. Attired for the occasion in an attractive costume—a pale blue organdy gown and a picture hat of the same shade—I hurried through breakfast and shortly after sunrise went out on deck, followed by my puzzled admirer. Eager to watch the departure of the shore-to-ship tender from the Progreso wharf, five miles distant, I had borrowed the captain's binoculars. Soon I imagined I saw Felipe's tall athletic figure vaguely discerned against the cabin of the little boat, as with ribbons of white foam it streaked the expanse of turquoise water between us. But my elation vanished with the realization that it was all illusion—a figment of my wishful thinking. Felipe was not aboard the speeding tender, although he had wired me on June 28 that with Don Eduardo Thompson he would meet me aboard the steamer at Progreso. I felt crushed and even humiliated when none of his friends or assistants appeared in sight. But disappointment gave way to anxiety as I continued to wonder what could have prevented his coming. Both emotions, however, were of short duration. For as soon as the *cargador*[1] Gómez, whom I had met on my previous trip, leaped over the liner's deck rail, he announced that Felipe was sending out his own launch with a reception committee, headed by Manuel Cirerol and carrying a stringed orchestra. As it approached, Felipe's musicians, each wearing a bright silk scarf and sash, were strumming their guitars and singing "Peregrina." The orchestration of my lovely song had not yet been completed, but I remembered the opening theme from that enchanted evening in Ricardo Palmerín's little garden. And now, hearing the words and the melody together for the first time, was almost as thrilling an experience as the second time, when, a few months later—and again at sea—the musical accompaniment reached me in its exquisite finished form, at midnight, in my cabin aboard the storm-tossed cruiser *Jalisco.* In a few minutes, Felipe's motorboat drew up alongside the *Yucatán,* its gaily festooned arches of *bugambilia* and *tulipán* daubing with a spot of radiance the *Yucatán*'s tarnished white hull. After a cordial *abrazo,*[2] Manuel presented me with a huge bouquet of red roses. "These are from His Majesty," he said, laughingly adding, "as though you had to be told." Escorting the "Prime Minister"—as Felipe and I often referred to Manuel—was the lively red-haired Louis Crossette, personal representative of the U.S. Secretary of Agriculture, Herbert Hoover. The affable Californian had been sent to Mérida to work out a direct-bargaining arrangement between the henequen cooperatives of the Partido Socialista del Sureste and the Grange organizations of the United States. At the time, the vast majority of North American farmers were dependent upon Yucatán's sisal hemp for the binding of their grain crops.

In his role of "Prime Minister," Manuel, aided and abetted by the persuasive Crossette, kept urging me to "jump ship" and give Felipe the "infinite joy of seeing me at Chichén Itzá on the Maya day of days." But when he realized that arguments were futile, he handed me as "a token of defeat" a letter from Felipe in which he expressed his "deep pain" at being unable to welcome me at Progreso because of "moral commitments to the Inditos who were arriving hourly by the hundreds from every part of Yucatán." He knew I would understand his position, as he would understand that I, too, had good reasons for not accompanying Manuel to Mérida. His letter closed with the exciting announcement that he would arrive in Mexico City the following week, sailing Wednesday on the *Esperanza,* and with the glowing promise to "spend a long time" with me there.

Manuel also delivered to me an envelope bulging with carefully handwritten pages from the veteran explorer Edward H. Thompson and a bound volume gold-engraved with my name, containing all the laws enacted by the Socialist Government of Yucatán. Manuel's vivid descriptions of the preparations for the historic assembly at Chichén Itzá provided me with colorful material for cables, which he sent for me from Mérida to the *New York Times* and the United Press. In my radioed message to Felipe, I congratulated him on his epochal achievement and assured him that I would eagerly await his arrival in the capital.

Captain Blackadder, whom the British Consul and his friends had toasted before disembarking as "that jolly old Scot off the Clyde," took advantage of the presence of the serenading *guitarristas* to declare a *fiesta* of his own in celebration of Felipe's completion of the highway to the ancient Maya capital. Right up until the anchor was lifted, he dispensed liquid hospitality while the musicians charmed the passengers with their repertoire of tender Yucatecan songs.

To the delight and information of everyone on board, Manuel contributed, in his perfectly good English, an outline of the meaning and objectives of the Chichén Itzá celebration. He explained that in addition to dedicating the new highway, Governor Carrillo was using the occasion to make his people conscious—and proudly conscious—of their noble cultural heritage and to bring together from the most isolated pueblos Indians who had never before looked upon the architectural magnificence created by their gifted forebears. The Maya—some ninety thousand of them—Manuel said, would remain for several days in their ancient ancestral capital as Governor Carrillo's guests, during which period he would try to impress them with their duty to build a new civilization upon the solid foundations of their racial achievements over the past millennia.

Two restless, impatient days and three nights were occupied in the run between Progreso and Veracruz where, after brief port formalities, I boarded the early Mexico-bound train. To the chagrin of the unfailingly attentive New England banker, I accepted a Pullman seat beside Sr. Tomás Castellanos Acevedo, *gerente*[3] of the Reguladora Henequenera Exportadora de Yucatán, whom I had met at Carnegie Expedition social affairs. His appointment as head of the henequen industry had been criticized by some of the Partido Socialista members on the grounds that the *hacendado* belonged to the *clase aristocrática.* But Felipe defended his choice with the answer that it would have been difficult in the entire state to duplicate the experience of Castellanos, known as *el financiero,*[4] in the production and marketing of henequen. He pointed out that during the current crisis period Yucatán's most urgent need was for a man of proven ability to handle efficiently the business upon which the economy of Yucatán was dependent.

On my previous Mexican visit, I had traveled to the heights beyond the Oaxaca Valley into Tehuantepec, and on several occasions I had joined the missionary teachers in their trips by truck and ambulance to the isolated pueblos of Morelos hidden among the crags of the *mil cumbres.*[5] But now, as we gradually ascended to higher levels, Mexico's true scenic grandeur unfolded with dramatic impact. I was making the daylight train trip between the Gulf Coast and the Altiplano[6] for the first time and it was only now that I could fully appreciate the passion of the average Mexican for his native soil, as well as the country's magnetic appeal for the many foreigners who came as tourists and remained as permanent residents.

Assuming the attitude of a host who proudly displays his treasured possessions to a new guest, Don Tomás indicated the chief points of interest along the route as we passed over miles of tropical luxuriance. But in less than an hour or two later, in striking contrast to the radiant *tierra caliente*[7] with its rich coffee plantations and gardens hailed as the "orchid collector's paradise," we entered a temperate zone where the railroad tracks were bordered by dark pine forests. About midway on the journey appeared the flourishing industrial cities of Córdoba and Orizaba, the latter near the base of the towering peak of the same name. Dominating the landscape from almost every angle, the stark white of its symmetric bulk was silhouetted against an azure sky, like a Japanese painter's concept of the Sacred Fujiyama.

But throughout all our rapturous gazing from train windows, I did not lose sight of the more personal implications of my chance encounter with Don Tomás. I was conscious that the shrewd success-minded financier had not invited me to sit beside him during the twelve-hour ride for the purpose of exchanging impressions on the grandiose Mexican landscape. He was far more interested, as I soon gathered, in learning my views on immediate ways and means of spreading, in the United States and Europe, information on Yucatán, its natural resources, business opportunities, and unique tourist attractions. In discussing the publicity outlook, I suggested a Yucatecan celebration of Washington's recognition of Mexico, which now seemed imminent. He urged me to call this and other forms of promotion that occurred to me to Felipe's attention, and I promised him that I would do so. I rather suspected that in view of all the gossip and the rumors then current in Mérida, he might easily believe I could exert an influence upon Felipe's future thought and action. At least it might be useful for his own political purposes merely to know my opinions on various controversial public issues.

Unlike my first arrival in the capital seven months earlier, there was no reception committee bearing huge bouquets and birdcages on hand to greet me, when at sunset, the train pulled into the Buenavista railroad station. However, Don Tomás and the New England banker together handled the baggage details, and both escorted me to the Hotel Regis. When I entered the lobby, the room clerk, the elevator operator, and the bellboys gave me a warm welcome, and evidently someone notified the press. Reporters from the leading dailies were soon asking for interviews, and on the following day a very flattering article carrying my photograph appeared in *El Universal.* The announcement brought several visitors—the distinguished Sr. Don Elías de Lima, who had been the Consulate for the Technical Committee for the National Debt Adjustment; his son, Clarence, with his lovely young wife, Carlota, daughter of the former Minister of Foreign Relations Ignacio Mariscal; and her blonde sister, Mrs. Arthur Constantine, whose husband, the Hearst syndicate representative, was the most prominent North American newspaperman in Mexico. Bon and Aimee Rovzar, with their usual heartwarming responsiveness, and Dr. Jorge Enciso, director of restorations and preservation of the nation's artistic and historic monuments, were among friends who welcomed me and made me feel that my return was a real "homecoming."

But as I soon discovered, the Regis management was strangely lacking in cordiality in contrast to the very friendly attitude displayed the previous December when an assistant manager had been sent to the station with flowers to see me off for San Francisco. I was at a loss to understand the reason for the completely different attitude. It was somewhat of a shock, as my diary records, to be greeted by Manager Montes at our first meeting after my arrival with the curious question: "Returning to Yucatán?" especially when his voice carried vaguely unpleasant inflections and supercilious undertones. There were other disagreeable changes. The atmosphere of the lobby that had formerly seemed a proper place to receive callers now repelled me. The armchairs and the cushioned benches were occupied day and night by unmistakable adventurers and confidence men, mostly Americans. They were often in conversation with the uniformed Mexican Army officers, while a frequent participant in the international huddles was Joe de Courcy, ex–lightweight pugilist from Chicago and the present staff reporter for the *New York Times* in Mexico. I sensed something so unwholesome in the air that I even noted my dismal impressions of the "change" in my diary. Yet I could not have guessed that this same group of lobby loungers was plotting treason that would so vitally affect my own life, under the pay and direction of Rodolfo Montes, owner and manager of the Hotel Regis and chief publicity agent for Adolfo de la Huerta.

When the de la Huerta revolution broke out in the early part of December 1923, Felipe was giving enthusiastic attention to the details of his program. He was in high spirits. Things were going well; there was no interference on the part of the Chief Executive with the ever-broadening measures that were being taken for the people's welfare. Hostility of the dispossessed *hacendados* could not be overlooked, but they were held in check and did not dare move against the new way of life, where the slave of former years was now a proud citizen, participating in government and enjoying the fruits of his labors.

Rumors of unrest throughout the country had reached the southeastern states but, for the most part, were not taken very seriously. After years of active warfare, Obregón now seemed well entrenched in political office, and it appeared that he was supported by the populace. Still, 1923 had been a time of endless disagreements, perhaps only natural among men who were seeking to stabilize the government after thirty years of dictatorship and the subsequent upheaval. Several quickly formed parties were struggling for power, and now that Obregón's term was drawing to a close, ambitious individuals were casting sidelong glances at the presidency. The main reason, eventually, for disaffection of some of his former supporters was Obregón's backing of Plutarco Elías Calles, formerly Governor of Sonora, as the next presidential candidate.

Adolfo de la Huerta, an ex-café singer, former Governor of Sonora, and in that crucial year of 1923 Secretary of Hacienda[8] in the cabinet of Obregón, had been interim president after the assassination of Carranza, and the taste for supreme office remained in his blood. Under Obregón he had been diplomatic representative of Mexico in the United States and had wrestled with a tough and relentless policy that threatened to make a nervous wreck of him. He was especially upset by the Bucareli Agreement, whereby, for the price of recognition, Mexico was forced to concede certain economic rights to its powerful neighbor. When he entered Obregón's cabinet, he was in such a state of doubts and fears that he became easy prey to politicians who felt they could use him for their own ends. Among these were Jorge Prieto Laurens and Rafael Zubarán Capmany.

These men had at first been vociferous advocates of Calles, enfolding his image with brotherly love. Prieto Laurens had said: "Calles is the symbol of revolution." And in the summer of 1923, de la Huerta spoke at a big meeting of the Cooperative Party to this effect: "For no reason will I betray the brother of my soul, General Calles."

But the situation changed when Calles took no steps to uphold Prieto Laurens in a dispute over the governorship of San Luis Potosí, to which the latter contended he was duly elected. De la Huerta supported the Prieto Laurens claim and took it up with Obregón, who said it was a matter for that state to decide. De la Huerta flew into a rage and threatened to resign as Secretary of Hacienda. Obregón did not try to stop him. On September 24 he did resign and openly declared himself an enemy of Calles. At the Cooperative Party Convention on November 23 he accepted the candidacy for President.

By the end of November de la Huerta was sure, rightly or wrongly, that on two occasions he had escaped assassination. He felt that certain death lay ahead if he remained in Mexico City. According to Alfonso Taracena, in *La verdadera revolución mexicana (1923–24)*,[9] on December 4 he was told his residence was to be ransacked for arms. He hid in the house of a friend. At two o'clock in the morning a spokesman for General Guadalupe Sánchez, in command at Veracruz, invited him urgently to go to that port, as he had learned of a plot to assassinate him that day in Mexico City. He hid in a house in Villa Guadalupe, waiting for the night train to Veracruz. With him were Zubarán Capmany and Prieto Laurens to bolster up the spirits of the panic-stricken Sonoran.

On December 5 the train arrived in Veracruz, the crew having torn up the rails behind them. De la Huerta and his friends were welcomed by General Guadalupe Sánchez, and by evening the rebellion was installed. From his hotel in Veracruz, de la Huerta praised President Obregón as a man of talent who, if he would curb his hatreds and his passions, "could be considered as a true superman." His friends were appalled by these words. Prieto Laurens said: "We are in Veracruz because we have no security in Mexico." A call was immediately sent out to the five southeastern states to join the revolution. The navy, stationed in the harbor of Veracruz, submitted to the rebel commander, Guadalupe Sánchez, as did the army in that area.

On December 7 de la Huerta issued a manifesto in which the government of General Álvaro Obregón was no longer recognized. The President was accused of tyrannical acts, among them the violation of states' rights and of enforcing support for the candidacy of Plutarco Elías Calles. Obregón answered with a strong statement on behalf of the Constitution and called attention to the loyalty and discipline of the national army. De la Huerta shrank from the thought of bloodshed. When Xalapa was taken, he ordered that no prisoners should be killed. High-ranking military men were to be allowed to walk about freely. Zubarán, Prieto Laurens, and others believed him to be absolutely crazy.

During this time many generals, eventually more than a hundred, were rising throughout the country. De la Huerta was named as supreme chief of the revolution. He went into a panic and claimed he didn't know anything about a revolution. Alonzo Capetillo, in *Rebellion without a Head*,[10] says that de la Huerta had none of the qualities of a leader but would fly into emotional rages in a crisis.

His suspicion of others—especially of General Antonio Villarreal, who was of presidential timber and was also a rebel because of his hatred of Calles, responsible for the death in 1918 of his very good friend, Lázaro Gutiérrez de Lara—created one split after another. But Puebla was temporarily taken by Villarreal, and through urgent necessity, agents were sent to the United States to buy arms, a move that was quickly frustrated by Samuel Gompers and the labor unions. Through the Pan-American Federation of Labor, American workers upheld the legal government in Mexico, and along the docks they refused to load arms and supplies for the de la Huerta uprising.

When Felipe, as Governor of Yucatán, received the invitation that was practically an order to rebel, he acted both in his role as Chief Executive of the State and as head of the Socialist Party of the Southeast. Declaring his allegiance to the legal federal government, he ordered the organization of all military forces. He sent Manuel Cirerol Sansores to the United States to buy arms. The Comisión Exportadora supplied 200,000 pesos. His plan was for every man to have a rifle so that the Leagues of Resistance might defend themselves against the greed and brutality of reaction. Later, in a letter he wrote to me:

> . . . and in the midst of this bloody and desperate activity, you were always in my imagination, adored of my soul. If you knew how much I wish that you were at my side! Only because I love this country so much, with all my heart, I will not abandon it. It is an injustice to involve men in war for personal and egoistic concerns, such as I now have. I feel that I was not born for these times, nor for this land full of ambitious and inhuman people . . .

Eulalio Gutiérrez, former interim President, launched from Saltillo a manifesto condemning Guadalupe Sánchez and Enrique Estrada, a leading rebel. He called on all soldiers of the Republic to remain loyal to General Obregón.

On December 12, at eight o'clock in the morning, the presidents of the Leagues of Resistance in Mérida and nearby pueblos held a meeting. Felipe had government funds moved from the Bank of Lacaud to the General Treasury. He had an inventory made of powder, dynamite, etc., in the stores and gave instructions that they should not be sold without an order from top authorities. At eleven a.m. he and some of his friends went to the railway station to dispatch troops to aid Campeche under Colonel Robinson, in whom he had complete confidence. Robinson was chief of the garrison in Mérida; like Felipe, he refused to support the rebels. In another letter to me, Felipe explained:

> Your house is like a barracks; a group of friends are with me here, and a small force of police is on guard in case anything happens; at this moment we do not have confidence in anyone, because even the least of men may

> have a friend who is a traitor parading as a socialist, who is only with us to spy on us, especially the so-called military men, so that we don't know from one minute to the next who is going to stab us in the back . . .

Colonel Robinson had taken the place of Lieutenant Valle, who was now on the side of the rebels. As the Colonel and his contingent left for the Campeche train, there were many *¡vivas!* for Felipe and Obregón. But what lay ahead was uncertain. For one thing, the attitude of Colonel Durazo, chief of military operations in Campeche, was ambiguous. Xavier Marín Alfaro, who was with Felipe, tells what happened in an *Excélsior* article, published on December 20, 1962:

> The train left and we were all convinced of the loyalty of the soldiers to the federal government. Accompanying Felipe Carrillo Puerto, we went to the offices of the Socialist Party, where a telegraph office was installed, in order to learn the news and find out what progress the military advance troops were making in Campeche, as the security of the government depended on them.
>
> In the pueblo of Uman, eight kilometers from the city of Mérida, we learned that the train had been detained and that the troops got off in order to buy *aguardiente*.[11] That was where treason started.

Colonel Robinson could not control the situation. The soldiers started shouting *¡vivas!* for Guadalupe Sánchez and Adolfo de la Huerta. Felipe and his friends were at lunch in Felipe's house when a telegram arrived from Robinson, telling what had happened. Again Robinson telegraphed, advising that Felipe should go by ship to buy arms. Then Robinson was taken prisoner. The men did not finish their lunch. They went at once to the center, where they found out that merchants were robbing the Lacaud Bank. Then they went to the railway station, where Felipe ordered a train to be made ready. At the station they met a large group of peasants carrying shotguns. They were from the pueblo of Kanasín and were led by the president of the League, Entimio Ek, who addressed the Governor in the indigenous language: "Don't go, Felipe. Stay with us. We'll fight those wicked men. We'll make them turn their backs."

Felipe answered him in the same idiom. He and his friends were merely going to hide, he said, as the wicked men had good arms and much blood would be spilled. And he promised to come back with arms and defeat them. In his mind his plans were developing. First he would go to his native village of Motul. He and his brothers would arrange to get the ship that was on its way to the east coast to pick up supplies. Once in the United States, he knew he could count on the labor unions there. At the very moment that he talked to Entimio Ek, his enemies were robbing the offices of the Socialist Party. Alfredo Ponce, one of the proprietors of the Yucatán Brewery, who was nicknamed "Little Rabbit," organized a demonstration with automobiles; on one of them was fastened the triangular banner of the Socialist Party of the Southeast. It was being dragged derisively through the streets of the city until it fell into rags.

Felipe knew beyond any doubt that the Church and the once powerful *hacendados* of the henequen plantations were backing the Guadalupe Sánchez–de la Huerta rebellion in Yucatán. It was their opportunity to repossess the lands and again establish conditions of actual slavery. They had moved with great speed, taking advantage of the surprise element. The garrison in Mérida, notably the 18th Battalion, had been taken over by General Hermenegildo Rodríguez; Juan Ricárdez Broca had usurped the governorship. The revolt was spreading rapidly. The army of Guadalupe Sánchez took Orizaba, Córdoba, and Xalapa. Maycotte, Zone Commander in Oaxaca, rushed to the capital and received 200,000 pesos from Obregón to defend the government. He then joined the rebels.

At three o'clock that day, December 12, the train left for Motul, where it arrived an hour later. At the station were three hundred men under Felipe's brother Edesio, who was municipal president. They were armed with shotguns and rifles. A train carrying Constitutional police under Benjamín Carrillo followed. Most of the men seemed very much upset, but Felipe maintained his usual serenity. He conferred with Edesio, who said he could raise five thousand men, but they needed ammunition to go into action.

By telephone Felipe was informed that a military train was in pursuit. He ordered a "wild" locomotive sent toward Mérida. Being loaded with dynamite, it blew up between Motul and Chacabal, thereby cutting off means of communication. It was about five in the afternoon when the two trains went on to Cansahcab. There was no excitement at this place, only the usual peddlers of food. The agent of the Hacienda of Temax delivered some funds to Benjamín Carrillo. Then the two trains went on toward Tunkas. In Temax Felipe had advised anyone who wanted to leave the train to mingle with the populace for greater security. But only two or three did this; the others chose to stay with Felipe.

The two trains arrived in Tunkas a little after six that evening. Here the Governor asked for municipal funds, obtaining the grand total of nine pesos and a few centavos. Benjamín Carrillo and Captain Rafael Urquía explained to the police that they should stay in Tunkas, as it was not possible for everyone to go to Cuyo. They were well armed. But the body of police threatened to kill Felipe if he did not pay them, so he had to use the funds gathered in the little towns, along with what Xavier Marín supplied. The police train was ordered back to Mérida, while Felipe's train went on to Dzitas. There they were fed by the authorities, after which they proceeded toward Tizimín. Felipe told his group that in a month they would return. In Espita they halted, not knowing which road to take or just what to do in their critical economic situation.

Finally their train arrived in Tizimín with the following persons:[12]

Felipe Carrillo Puerto
Benjamín Carrillo Puerto
Edesio Carrillo Puerto
Wilfrido Carrillo Puerto
Licenciado Manuel Berzunza
Capitán Rafael Urquía
Officer Marciano Barrientos
Officer Fernando Mendoza
Officer Julián Ramírez
Adjutant Antonio Cortés
Cecilio Lázaro
Daniel Valerio
Pedro Ruiz

At the station in Tizimín the travelers were met by a delegation of Socialists, with horses for the journey to Cuyo. Edesio went on foot to Sucopó, not waiting for horses; he made the trip alone. Valerio, Lázaro, and Cortés decided to stay in Tizimín and go into hiding. Later these men, with guarantees promised by Ricárdez Broca, rebel military commander of the state, handed themselves over to Manuel Bates. Antonio Cortés was not detained and took passage to Mérida.

The goal was now El Cuyo, eighty kilometers from Tizimín. José Duarte, a schoolteacher and writer, transcribed the events that followed less than a month after they happened. On the morning of the 13th he was teaching in his little school when Eligio Rosado Alonzo came to see him. He was general contractor for the extraction of *chicle* and the cutting of wood for the Cuyo Company. He asked Duarte to give a group of strangers some breakfast. Duarte ordered the breakfast prepared immediately. No one in the district knew of the de la Huerta revolution.

"Chato,"[13] as Duarte was called, and his friend carried the half-cooked breakfast to a place called Moctezuma. In Canimuc they were overcome with surprise on recognizing Felipe Carrillo Puerto and his friends—nine in number, all well armed. Felipe asked Chato and Eligio to step aside a moment and inquired if anyone had come from Cuyo, explaining that they wanted to leave the country and return with arms and ammunition. He said they had destroyed telephone lines and railroad tracks. "But," he added, "my government is one of construction, not destruction. I hope you will not put obstacles in our way."

Felipe asked that Chato and Eligio go with them through the *chicle* country so as not to excite suspicion.

Duarte, realizing the tensity of the situation, extended himself to be merry in an effort to put them in a lighter mood. He was touched to see how avidly they ate the poor breakfast. He kept up his bantering while Felipe struggled with a tough chicken leg. He writes: "If he had fought with it an instant longer, I would have torn it apart with my pistol." It was second nature to express himself in verse, and he made lively impromptu poems about the breakfast. Even Wilfrido and Berzunza, both in low spirits, applauded him.

With Duarte and Rosado, they started out at noon to Solferino and San Eusebio. From Canimuc to El Crucero the distance was sixteen kilometers. The latter was the territorial dividing point between Yucatán and Quintana Roo. During the ride a branch caught Chato in the right eye and on the ear, so that both organs swelled up. They all teased him, even the serious Berzunza.

In this way—laughing, joking, and reciting verses—they arrived at El Crucero. They stopped at a small hut and were invited to have coffee. Felipe displayed his genuine love for the natives and explained to Berzunza why he had to protect and defend these people.

"Look," he exclaimed, "how happy these comrades are here in the mountains! They have their shotguns to get food and to defend themselves against fierce animals. And at this moment," looking at his watch, which indicated 4:00 p.m., "they are through working and are resting to be ready for tomorrow's labors. No, there is no race more worthy of protection than the Indian. In him there is no falsehood; he does not know the perfidy of what is called civilization. I could live happily among them, far from the ingratitude of the men of society." Berzunza, who was used to city life, said: "Not I, Felipe."

When it was time to go on, Felipe thanked and embraced the workers. At five o'clock they arrived in Solferino, where they stayed for half an hour. While the others rested, Felipe, his brothers, and Berzunza had a consultation. Felipe said: "I think we should go directly to Havana. There we can get funds and develop our plans more freely for our prompt return." Berzunza thought they should go to Belize: "There we'll have fewer stumbling blocks than in Havana."

Edesio was for hiding in the mountains. Benjamín favored Sayo Obispo or a safe place near there. They could send an emissary to the Governor of Quintana Roo, who was loyal to Obregón.

"Let's go to Ingenio[14] San Eusebio," said Felipe, "and then we'll come to a decision. It's safer there."

At half past five, they started off. The distance was only twelve kilometers, but the road was up and down. They arrived at half past six. Through Eligio Rosada, an evening meal was served, and they ate like wolves. The tortillas were like leather, but Edesio said: "When one is hungry, there isn't any bad bread."

Then they went to bed, some in hammocks and some on the ground. Wilfrido and Capitán Urquía stood guard. Immediately there was a plague of gnats and mosquitoes. The only one who slept was Berzunza, who for three nights had had no sleep.

Chato gave up and got behind some sacks of maize, but the situation was no better. His right eye was swollen shut. Before long Felipe, unable to sleep because of the plague of insects, joined him and burst out laughing. "Chato, you look like Cyclops! No, you look like a Maya idol. You should be in a museum."

Then, apparently familiar with Chato's poetry and plays, Felipe asked him to recite some of his verse. Benjamín joined them, and soon the others came. In this manner, with poetry and conversation, they passed several hours.

One of the officers had gone to Chikila to find out about a boat. When he returned, they all sat at a table and had coffee. Someone called out: "They're coming!" Every man ran for his gun. But it was a false alarm.

At two o'clock that morning Felipe gave orders to prepare to go to Chikila. Eligio furnished two canvas coverings, quilts, and some food supplies.

On that day, December 14, at 12:30 p.m., they arrived at Chikila, which was not far from Ingenio San Eusebio and was on the seashore in the neighborhood of the port of Holbox. At the wharf was the motorboat *Manuelita*, property of the Cuyo Company. They found this boat to have motor trouble. It could not be used without being repaired by a mechanic. The only mechanic was Pepé Padrón, and he was in Río Lagarto getting drunk. Pedro Ruiz, who knew something about machinery and was also a seaman, began tinkering with the boat while the others sat on the wharf, waiting. Finally Ruíz said it was impossible to make it go.

There was another motorboat tied up at the wharf. After saying good-bye to Chato and Eligio, Felipe and his friends took their departure, along with two boatmen. Felipe gave all the money he had left, also his gold watch, to pay these boatmen. They went toward the Río Turbio, which the boatmen said was a safe place. But these two men had somehow been contacted by persons hostile to Felipe and slipped away. It was very likely that they had been hired to damage the machinery of the *Manuelita.* The refugees were left on a beach in a strong, bitter wind, without funds, without any resources whatsoever.

It was hard to decide what to do next. Finally Felipe sent Berzunza on his way to see a certain harbor pilot who would hide them in the mountains, from whence they would go to Santa Cruz or Guatemala. When Berzunza passed through the *finca* of Chikila, he was seen by an old caretaker, who telegraphed about him to Solferino. When the lawyer arrived at the *hacienda,* he was arrested by the commissary, who had previously armed *chicle* workers and solicited aid from the agent of El Cuyo to capture him. Four dayworkers, armed, conducted Berzunza to Tizimín, which he entered on foot at three o'clock in the morning. He was taken to the house of Manuel Bates, military commander, who turned him over to Ricárdez Broca.

Felipe and his companions remained in Río Turbio, waiting for Berzunza. Finally they decided to return to Chikila and try to find out what had happened. A gale was blowing, delaying the arrival of the *C. C. Wehrum,* the ship from Tampa, Florida, that was expected to call at Chikila to pick up lumber. The circumstance of violent weather was to prove fatal to the fugitives. In order to get to Chikila they made use of a motorboat, *El Salvamento.* But the wind, lack of skill on the part of the navigators, and possibly impaired machinery on the part of the enemy hirelings swung them toward Holbox, where they ran aground on a sandbank.

It was apparent that the enemy was keeping track of every move they made. Captain José Cortés was sent with twenty-eight soldiers to El Cuyo. On December 21 they were finally captured and lodged in the public jail of Tizimín.

At ten o'clock that night a military train arrived. Fernando Mendoza, Daniel Valerio, and Cecilio Lázaro were taken to Mérida. At 10:45 a train under Captain Cortés left with the other prisoners. On December 23, two days before Christmas, they were taken to Juárez Penitentiary and placed under lock and key.

# 22. Martyrdom and Infamy

The train that bore the captives to prison had stopped en route in Felipe's hometown of Motul. Here his brothers Acrelio and Audomaro were seized and taken along with the others. It was obvious that the rebel leaders, backed by the henequen planters and the Church, intended to immobilize the entire Carrillo family. But when the train was unloaded in the rear of the O'Horan Hospital, both young men managed to escape. They were later recaptured and placed in cells.

Hermenegildo Rodríguez, in control of the army barracks in Mérida, and Ricárdez Broca, who was now political dictator, were conducting themselves with the cynical insolence of easy victory. The Socialist State had not been geared for war and hatred, but for peace and brotherhood. The indigenous masses were loyal and ready to fight to the death with machetes and whatever guns they could muster, but there was definitely a shortage of ammunition. On the other hand, scores of shopkeepers, clerks, and civil servants were crawling before the traitors, who had the arms. In the federal capital, more than one deputy who represented Yucatán in the Congress showed open delight over the counterrevolution. Secret meetings were held and plans laid for remunerative posts in the government now led once more by the old ruling classes.

In this month of December the forces of rebellion were winning several military engagements. Although jealousy and suspicion had penetrated the leadership of the rebel forces, dissension had not visibly sprouted. With stolen government funds in their possession, the insurgents were hopefully expecting the country to rise against Obregón and were confidently awaiting shipments of arms from the United States and Europe. If they were aware of Roberto Haberman's mission from CROM to Samuel Gompers, to prevent military supplies from being loaded by North American dockworkers for the de la Huerta armies, they did not measure this circumstance as one of the factors that proved a powerful weapon against them.

On December 24, the day after the incarcerations, Cristóbal Carrillo prepared to go to the penitentiary with a satchel that Doña Adela Puerto had sent to her sons. A man named Barbosa hurried to some rebel officers, saying that the satchel probably contained documents. Three officials went to the house of Pastor Campos, where they found Cristóbal. They examined the contents of the satchel and discovered only clothing.

When he learned of the arrests, the journalist Carlos R. Menéndez, an intimate friend of Felipe, immediately telegraphed Adolfo de la Huerta in Veracruz, asking him to take action at once to protect the lives of these men. Roque Armando Sosa Ferreyro (*Excélsior*, January 4, 1954) has said that the telegram of Menéndez was the only plea made to de la Huerta to save Felipe's life. The rebel leader sent word to Ricárdez Broca to grant *garantías*[1] to his prisoners and dispatch them to the Port of Veracruz. Ricárdez Broca promised to comply but claimed there was no means of transport. De la Huerta sent Licenciado Arce Correa from Veracruz, and the lawyer arrived in Mérida on December 26, having been a passenger on the Norwegian ship *Fritzoe* to Progreso. He conferred without delay with Ricárdez Broca, who promised to carry out the instructions of de la Huerta, asking only that the *Fritzoe* be placed under his orders as Governor and military commander of the state. He told Arce Correa that he could talk with Felipe if one of his own officials were present. The conversation was brief. Arce said later that Felipe was in a melancholy mood, although he listened with interest when assured that he and his friends would soon be in Veracruz.

The historian John W. F. Dulles, in *Yesterday in Mexico*,[2] states that Felipe called a lawyer to his cell, saying that he was willing to pay 100,000 pesos for freedom. The lawyer wanted a check on a United States bank for his services and then went to see Ricárdez Broca. To quote Dulles: "In the Government Palace Ricárdez Broca stipulated that the 100,000 pesos be turned over precisely when the liberating papers were signed, adding that this amount was applicable to Felipe Carrillo Puerto alone and that an additional ten thousand pesos would be required for each of his jailed companions."

Gustavo Arce Correa, an emissary of de la Huerta, interviewed Ricárdez Broca in an effort to forestall criminal action. The other lawyer, says Dulles, "decided to depart at once for the United States to collect his legal fee before his client might meet his death." Arce saw Felipe again, and this time found him "confident, optimistic, without fear of the future."

Eligio Erosa, secretary of Felipe, had been locked up in the penitentiary several days before the others had been captured. When Felipe saw his friend, he told him in the Mayan language: "Send a message to Mrs. James, telling her to write a letter to Alma, to my Alma."

Erosa wrote a letter to Mrs. James and gave it to Major Palomo, but his office was accused of connivance with the prisoners and he was dismissed. His superiors took the letter, and it was never mailed.

In the meantime, soldiers would gather outside Felipe's cell, mocking and insulting him. The sadistic command sent mariachis to stand in front of his cell and play "Peregrina" over and over, reveling in the acute anguish of their victim.

The last time Arce was in Felipe's cell was on the day Felipe asked Erosa to send the letter to Mrs. James. The official aide of Ricárdez Broca was present. Ricárdez Broca had asked Arce to arrange for the money to be paid. There was the sum of 80,000 pesos in care of the Henequen Commission in New York, but they would not release this sum without a written order from Felipe Carrillo Puerto. Felipe said these funds belonged to the Henequen Commission, operating under his legal government. He said that he had never soiled his hands with another's money.

Ricárdez Broca promised Arce that Felipe would be sent to Veracruz in the *Fritzoe* on January 2.

On December 29 Felipe was walking down the corridor with soldiers escorting him, on his way to take a bath. As he approached Erosa's cell, Erosa gave the soldiers some cigars, and the men allowed Felipe to talk very briefly with him. Felipe said: "I know my brothers and I are going to be taken to Veracruz. After that I am sure you will have more freedom, so when that happens, send this letter to Alma. As soon as I am free, I will go to San Francisco, California, and marry her immediately. I'll tell you when I'm ready to go, so you can go too. In the meantime, send this letter as soon as possible." Then Felipe put his arms through the bars, embraced Erosa, and kissed him on the forehead.

The letter, in an ordinary envelope, was in a book, *La venta de Indios*,[3] which the author, Carlos R. Menéndez, had given Felipe as a present. Erosa took the letter out of the book, and afraid to be searched, he nailed it under his bed. Then he was obliged to move to another cell and had no chance to retrieve the letter. Sometime later, when he returned to the cell, the letter was missing, and he found out that Major Fernández had taken it.

When Licenciado Arce Correa made a final attempt to have another interview with Ricárdez Broca, the latter was not to be found either at the Grand Hotel, where he was living, or in the Governor's Palace or in the chief's office in the garrison. It was clear that he was hiding from the commissioner of de la Huerta while the plans of the reactionaries of Yucatán were being worked out in detail.

It soon became evident, as reported by José R. Juanes, intimate friend of both Felipe and Arce Correa, that a Council of War was being held in Juárez Penitentiary. This was confirmed by Licenciado Salazar Arjona, whose brother was being held in the prison. It was also learned that Felipe's offices had been rifled, and various telegrams, documents, and circulars were seized. This material was used by Hermenegildo Rodríguez, Ricárdez Broca, and other conspirators in a dismal effort to build up a case against the legitimate government of Yucatán. On the order of Rodríguez, at ten o'clock in the morning of January 2, Felipe and his companions were taken from their cells and brought into a large room south of the rotunda, where the members of the so-called Council of War were gathered. This Council was made up as follows: President, Lieutenant Colonel Juan Israel Aguirre; First Vocal, Lieutenant Colonel Rafael P. Zamorano; Second Vocal, Lieutenant Colonel Vicente Fontana, who functioned as secretary; Substitutes, Colonel Ángel González, Lieutenant Colonel Álvaro C. Hernández, and Major Luis Ramírez; Military Instructing Judge, Hernán López Trujillo; Agent of the Public Ministry, Licenciado Domingo Berny Diego; Secretary of the Tribunal, Samuel Jiménez.

Later, Acrelio Carrillo wrote an account of what he could learn on that tragic day as to what went on in the corridor of his cell block. At various intervals there passed by, one by one, Felipe, his three brothers, and their companions. Acrelio noted with surprise that during the day they did not return to their cells, and he spoke of this to his brother Audomaro through the wall that separated them.

What happened in that sinister chamber before the Council of War is the clearest evidence that with Felipe in their clutches his enemies had no intention of letting him go to Veracruz or of conducting a fair trial. Hernán López Trujillo, who as Juez Instructor[4] was forced to be present, has left a moving account of the day's proceedings. He says that Rodríguez was at the prison the whole day, and Ricárdez Broca was present much of the time. No one was allowed to leave, not even the waiters who served the midday meal.

The Council was installed, with Lieutenant Colonel Israel Aguirre in the lectern. The prosecution displayed a circular, without proven identity. Trujillo stated that it was the only document placed in evidence. It read: "This Government (purportedly Felipe's) knows today that enemies of the present general government of the Nation are laboring with intrigues, declarations, etc., in favor of the rebels de la Huerta and Sánchez. Any person, in whatever condition he may be found, is to be shot immediately, since enemies are to be treated that way."

Trujillo and some other officials, who had only a feeling of great friendship toward Felipe, tried to excuse themselves and get away, but were sharply warned that they ran the risk of meeting the same fate as those who were being judged.

Recalling what went on that day, Trujillo wrote in a state of intense emotion:

> When Lieutenant Colonel Aguirre sent for Felipe Carrillo Puerto to examine him, the shock was extreme, and I felt my strength fail me. If I had been ordered to speak I could not have said a word.
>
> Felipe Carrillo Puerto was conducted into the presence of the Council and was questioned by Aguirre. Before any question was asked, Don Felipe commenced to protest with complete integrity against the Council that was trying him. He said that if he had committed any crime, there were legislative bodies that should judge him and not a Council of War, which was

only for military personnel, and he was a civilian. President Aguirre said he should reply to the questions.

Felipe denied all the charges. When Secretary Fontana read the telegram in which he purportedly answered the municipal presidents of the state, ordering them to shoot anyone who was not a friend of the Socialist Government, he denied these also.

Other questions were asked him. Among them were these:

"On what authority did you order the director of the Banco Nacional to hand over the funds to that institution? (It seems that they were referring to the funds of the Banque Française.)

Felipe answered that this was done on the advice of Enrique Manero, who believed that the funds should be placed for safety in the General Treasury.

"Why were the same orders given to the director of the post office?"

Felipe answered that he had given no such orders.

"Why was the shooting of Muna ordered?"

He had ordered no shooting.

"What duties did you discharge in the state?"

"I did not discharge any except that of Constitutional Governor of the State."

"What political activity did you carry out at the same time?"

"I carried out nothing except that of president of the Central League of Resistance."

One by one the others were examined. All denied the charges with the exception of Lázaro and Valerio. According to Trujillo, they admitted the crimes but claimed they were ordered by the Inspector of Police, Wilfrido Carrillo. Wilfrido denied this.

The gruesome performance that was called a trial went on all day and most of the night. Licenciado Hermilio Guzmán, agent of the Public Ministry of the rebel government, formulated conclusions against the accused, making an exception in the case of Licenciado Berzunza, who he said was his friend. But Berzunza rejected the exception. He said that whatever the decision was against Felipe and his comrades, he was equally involved.

Vicente Coy[5] was given the privilege of an exception, to which he agreed.

After the hypocrisy of the "trial," the Council pretended to deliberate a verdict. Finally by a unanimous vote, a vote of terrorized men, capital punishment was decreed for Felipe, Benjamín, Edesio, and Wilfrido Carrillo Puerto and for Licenciado Manuel Berzunza, Mariano Barrientos, Rafael Urquía, Pedro Ruiz, Francisco Tejeda, and also Julián Ramírez, judged for complicity with the twelve men and with the Governor for the crimes that had been imputed.

Edmundo Bolio, a friend and close associate of Felipe, has written about this criminally tragic episode of Mexican history. He says that Lieutenant Colonel

Israel Aguirre, President of the Council of War, and Major Ignacio L. Zamorano and Lieutenant Colonel Vicente Fontana dictated the sentences.

During the time the confrontations were going on, Ricárdez Broca, now Governor in Felipe's place, noted that neither the lawyer López Vales nor Hernán López Trujillo were to be found in their places. He located them and said that if they wanted to hide their faces, they should say so. This was an outright threat. They returned to their designated chairs.

After the death sentence was passed, Major Zamorano warned Trujillo against any defense of the condemned men. The Assessor, the Defender, and the Public Minister were likewise warned. Said Trujillo: "We tried to communicate with someone in the street as to what was happening, but they watched us so closely that it was impossible to do so . . . There were so many threats made against us that the Defense, which is always very full and covers a wide range, was threatened and obliged to adhere to the petition of the Public Minister."

When the men were returned to their cells, Felipe's two brothers Acrelio and Audomaro were still awake and listening, not knowing what had taken place. At about four o'clock in the morning (they guessed the time), they heard soldiers call out names one by one, after each name using a string of curses and insolent words. The two boys somehow managed to cling to the belief that Felipe and the others were being taken out to be placed on board a ship for Veracruz.

It was at exactly 4:30 a.m., January 3, that the thirteen condemned men were summoned by armed guards. On their arrival at Cell No. 13 a mistake was made, and Fernando Mendoza was taken out of No. 14, Cell No. 13 being empty. Mendoza was recognized by one of the guards, who cried out: "Not this one! The other man has escaped!"

Ruiz, in Cell No. 13, had broken the lock and was hiding in another cell. He was soon discovered and brutally dragged into the corridor.

The account by Trujillo of what followed is vivid and extremely harrowing:

> When I thought that everything was ended (at the trial) and that I might go to my home, Colonel Hermenegildo Rodríguez,[6] who was the person most involved in all that happened, ordered me to be present at the executions. All the entreaties and pleas I made to this man were not enough to convince him that I should not be present at the shooting. I tried to make him see that these were my friends . . . it was all useless. Taking me by the arm, he put me in one of the automobiles of the garrison. The same thing happened to Dr. Guzmán Jr., who was told that he had to certify the death of the culprits.

The prisoners were taken out of the penitentiary, bound together two by two and forced into two waiting trucks. The automobiles led the way. When they had left the cells, Felipe saw that his brother Benjamín was on the verge of collapse. He turned to the unhappy soldiers and said: "Men, don't grieve for me, but for my little brothers."

The trucks halted before the east entrance to the cemetery. The iron doors were found locked. A chauffeur leaped over the wall to advise the caretaker. There was a delay of a quarter of an hour; then the gates were flung open, and the trucks entered, followed by the automobiles.

They halted before the wall where the men were to be executed. The terribly overwrought Trujillo moved a little distance away. "I did not want to be present at that savagery," he wrote. "From where I was I could hear Antonio Cortés and Pedro Ruiz saying that they were innocent. One discharge silenced their voices."

Felipe was in the first group of seven men. The others were in three groups, two men in each one. The lawyer Berzunza asked to be shot alone. The request was not granted. Captain Urquía protested that he died innocent of any crime. Benjamín Carrillo embraced his brother Wilfrido and asked the guard to shoot him through his heart. Wilfrido said: "How will they tell this to our mother?"

Felipe remained silent. He had passed beyond any show of emotion into a tremendous quietude.

Benjamín Carrillo spoke to the firing squad, begging them not to shoot him in the face, but in the chest.

"Wilfrido Carrillo and Francisco Tejeda were the two last," wrote Trujillo. "When they were brought to the square where the bodies lay, Wilfrido begged to speak to me. I was called. Wilfrido stretched out his hand with great feeling. On his face, wasted by suffering, I could tell he wanted to say something to me privately."

But there were officers listening, and he said only: "I beg you to go to my house and take leave in my name of my mother and brothers." He and Trujillo shook hands.

After the murders, the corpse of Felipe rested against the wall. On his left was Rafael Urquía, and on his right Mariano Barrientos, who was disfigured by a bullet that tore his face. The corpse of Wilfrido Carrillo fell across that of his brother Benjamín.

Back in the penitentiary, Acrelio Carrillo heard many sounds of men coming and going. These were the troops who had returned from fulfilling their bloody mission. Acrelio in his cell heard one soldier say: "This is the end of Socialism!" Another said: "Poor, poor little Don Felipe!" He was crying as he said this, and he fired his rifle. Another exclaimed: "Oh, this has been barbarous!" Because of this remark the soldier was killed. It was immediately published in the papers that he had been accidentally shot by one of his fellows at the penitentiary.

One soldier, seeing another weep for Felipe, told him roughly: "What are you crying for? You are not his widow!"

Finally an officer, seeing so many soldiers overcome by grief, shouted: "Go to the kitchen or far away from here to cry or whatever you want to do! Don't create a scandal. Don't you see that here in prison are members of the family of Don Felipe? You are only making more bitter the hours of their imprisonment and their grief."

That morning the mother of the Carrillo Puerto brothers went to the Director General of the Civil Register and asked for permission to place the bodies of her sons in their coffins so that they might be seen in the depository. With her were relatives and friends. The Director refused to give his consent, saying that the bodies were at the disposition of Ricárdez Broca. The men who had accompanied Doña Adela interviewed Ricárdez Broca, and he refused to give permission, saying that the bodies were at the disposition of General Hermenegildo Rodríguez. So the men went to him, and he also refused.

All the petitioners resolved to wait in the cemetery until the interment was ordered. Rodríguez decreed this to be at three o'clock that afternoon. Friends and relatives of the assassinated men placed shrouds on their bodies. The burial took place at six o'clock.[7]

# 23. Never Forgotten

Ricárdez Broca had been present in the cemetery from 7:30 to 8:00 a.m. when the corpses were in the depository. He entered to look at them and gave instructions to administrator Alfonso Baqueño to place names on each body and to turn them over to Rodríguez. Inside the depository was stationed Lieutenant Colonel Zamorano,[1] who played the watchdog all day, observing and noting down every person who entered the place. From time to time he communicated with the headquarters of the garrison. Close to the telephone in the office of the depository a lieutenant was stationed. When Zamorano spoke, he made everyone leave the room.

On January 4, Enrique Manero, head of the Finance Commission in the legal government of Yucatán, who was in New York as an emissary of Felipe for the purchase of arms, sent the following message to President Obregón:

> After having exhausted, as Don Santana Almada knows, as many recourses and arguments as is humanly possible to obtain the liberation of Felipe Carrillo Puerto, I was finally informed that he had been villainously assassinated along with his companions. It is strongly recommended that in the name of the nation an anathema of opprobrium be launched against the greatest assassins and traitors who have ever brought shame to our country.
>
> Respectfully,
> Enrique Manero

On January 5, the following appeared on the first page of every daily in Mexico:

> The assassination of Felipe Carrillo Puerto brings grief to the homes of the proletariat and many thousands of humble beings, who on receiving the news will feel the sincere tears of sorrow rolling down their cheeks.
>
> Don Adolfo de la Huerta will realize the enormity of his crime when he receives the furious protests that the workers of the whole world will launch at him for the assassination of Felipe Carrillo Puerto.

> The generous blood of Felipe Carrillo Puerto is the testimony of the apostasy of de la Huerta. From now on, neither he nor his followers may succeed in any way whatever in falsifying the truth through denying the origin and purpose of his movement.
>
> A. Obregón

Ramon P. de Negri, sub-secretary of Agriculture and *Fomento,* published a statement in the press: "The assassination of Felipe Carrillo, apart from the crime itself, is a grave injury to the cause of the proletariat. . . . Carrillo Puerto united a powerful dynamic and an overflowing sincerity with conversion into reality of the luminous doctrine of emancipation that today sustains and will sustain to the very last the workers of Yucatán." He said the day was at hand when the infamous rule of the *hacendados* would be gone forever, due to the stupendous force of Felipe Carrillo Puerto. Reaction had intervened, but, he said, the immolation of Felipe would cost his assassins dearly. Just now there was black crepe on every banner of the laboring classes in the world.

There were many other written protests, including one from Calles, who later, on visiting Yucatán, showed a cynical indifference to the fate of the Carrillo Puerto family. One of the finest tributes to Felipe was made by Ernest Gruening, today a United States Senator from Alaska. In an article in *The Nation,* he said: "Thus perished the most enlightened, the most courageous, the most lovable man in Mexico. Her tragic history of blood and tears has offered no nobler, no sweeter figure as a sacrifice to human freedom."

Workers in Mexico held a convention and proposed reprisals against the murderers. Hostility at home and abroad against the assassins was so outspoken that the arrogant Ricárdez Broca became frightened and wanted to place the blame on someone else. He wrote to Adolfo de la Huerta that one of the intellectual instigators was Dr. Adolfo Ferrer.

Adolfo de la Huerta disclaimed any responsibility for what happened. Hadn't he sent his emissary, Gustavo Arce Correa, to Mérida to arrange for transport of the captives in safety to Veracruz? But he insisted that Ricárdez Broca was innocent of any complication in the murders, and at his instigation Ricárdez Broca was promoted to a generalship and made Provisional Governor of Yucatán, a position he had already usurped. De la Huerta put all the blame on Rodríguez.

It is to be noted, however, that Trujillo, who was present during all the so-called trials, had heard Ricárdez Broca demand the death penalty in the case of Licenciado Berzunza, and he certainly did not show by word or deed that he was against the execution of the others. After the debacle of the revolution, Ricárdez Broca fled from Yucatán, some say to Honduras, where he committed suicide, although others claimed that he was killed for his involvement in Felipe's death, and from still another source it is said (without proof) that he went into hiding and years later was among the living.

Till the end of the chaotic rebellion, a state of terrorism existed in Yucatán. Dora Carrillo, Felipe's sister, arrived in New Orleans on April 5. She had traveled in disguise on the steamer *Elena Valdez.* She said: "My mother, my two brothers, and my sisters are still hiding in Mérida. Of course we could not hide together with the soldiers looking for us."

The early months of 1924 saw the "rebellion without a head" on the downgrade, in spite of a few military victories. The incentives that led to the uprising of so many generals and political figures were for the most part personal grievances and were not of a nature to stir the masses into insurrection. The trade union movement in Mexico, young and spirited, had been deeply agitated by the events in Yucatán. With the support of the Pan-American Federation of Labor, the unions of Mexico and the United States played a leading role in bringing about the defeat of the de la Huerta revolution.

In his carefully documented treatise, *Samuel Gompers and the Pan-American Federation of Labor,*[2] published by Duke University Press, Sinclair Snow, Ph.D., has reviewed the activities of labor at this critical time. Two days after the revolt began, CROM Secretary Ricardo Treviño appealed to Gompers as Chairman of the PAFL[3] for aid in preventing shipment of the arms to the rebels. A similar appeal was made by Luis Morones.

To quote Sinclair Snow: "The reply of the leaders of the PAFL was prompt and unequivocal. . . . They declared that the Obregón government was the best government Mexico had ever had."

Samuel Gompers, president of the American Federation of Labor, was friendly toward Mexican wage earners; when a young man he had worked beside Mexicans in cigar factories. He had watched the development of the revolution against Porfirio Díaz with interest and had protested to the United States government against the persecution of the dictator's enemies. Through contact with the writer and trade unionist John Murray, he had become one of the chief architects in building the PAFL and was now forthright in his condemnation of de la Huerta and his friends.

Morones, as stated previously, had sent Roberto Haberman to the United States as his personal agent and general representative of Mexican labor. Haberman conferred with Gompers, who wrote to Secretary of State Hughes that he had been reliably informed about de la Huerta receiving arms from some illegal source in the Unites States. Gompers then set about enlisting the support of American labor for Obregón. He appealed especially to workers in the transportation and freight-hauling industries. He said that the purpose of the rebellion in Mexico was to set that country back a decade or more into darkness. An emissary was sent to Texas ports to investigate the possibility of arms being smuggled through to the rebels. Gompers also appealed to European labor through the International Federation of Trade Unions, which promised cooperation.

Ironically, two of the most ardent members of the PAFL in former months, both with excellent progressive reputations, were now fighting on the side of de la Huerta. These men were Salvador Alvarado and Antonio Villarreal. Once a political prisoner in the United States and a friend of Samuel Gompers, Villarreal now wrote an emotional letter to the labor chief, attacking Calles and attempting to win sympathy for de la Huerta. His efforts were in vain.

Late in February, Gompers asked Secretary of State Hughes to look into the case of the family and political associates of Felipe Carrillo Puerto, who were in danger of losing their lives at the hands of *delahuertistas.* The persons about whom Gompers was concerned included three members of the Yucatán Legislature who had supported Obregón. They were all women: Elvia Carrillo, sister of Felipe; Betty Paniche de Ponce; Raquel Dzib y Cirerol. Undersecretary of State William Phillips replied for Hughes that inasmuch as the persons named by Gompers were "naturals" of Yucatán, the United States could not intervene.

The vigilance of the transportation and waterfront unions was effective. The action of these North American workers was a deadly setback to the revolution. The International Federation reported that there had been no arms shipments to the rebels from Europe. However, this was not entirely accurate, as the statement of Howard S. Phillips, quoted below, reveals. For many years Mr. Phillips has been editor and publisher of *Mexican Life.* In 1923 he had gone to Mexico as a journalist. He covered the de la Huerta uprising for the *Chicago Daily News.* His comments on what he saw in the Port of Progreso, Yucatán, are now being published for the first time. He has kept silent all these years because, as an Englishman, he did not wish to involve his native land in such a conspiracy. This is his statement:

> When I came to Mexico in May of 1923, President Álvaro Obregón was menaced by a counter rebellion, inspired by the Church and the *hacendados,* the former opposing the enforcement of the 1917 Federal Constitution regulations regarding legal ownership of Church property and elimination of non-Mexican clergy. At that time Calles was the leader of the agrarian movement and of the CROM labor organization. In Yucatán, Calles' organization was the Socialist Party of the Southeast. His antagonism toward clericalism and the *hacendados* won him a host of enemies.
>
> The chosen leader of the counterrevolution was Adolfo de la Huerta, a would-be opera singer who had been rewarded for his aid in overthrow-

ing V. Carranza by a brief period as Provisional President. He was backed by the reaction for presidency following Obregón's term. But Obregón was backing Calles.

The Bucareli Conferences, carried out by Obregón's suggestion and aimed at a resumption of diplomatic relations between the U.S. and Mexico, served as a pretext for de la Huerta's rebellion. The agreement which ensued from these conferences was essentially a tacit horse trade, whereby U.S. recognition and support of the Obregón-Calles regime was given quid pro quo in return for a settlement of the claims of U.S. landowners and a verbal understanding that Mexico would not apply the 1917 Constitution as a means of curtailing the activities of American-owned oil companies.

Regarded by reactionary Mexicans as a sacrifice of national sovereignty, the Bucareli Agreement served as a *casus belli.* Jorge Prieto Laurens, a leader of such Mexicans and a corrupt politician, offered Calles the support of his party in return for the governorship of San Luis Potosí. Calles refused.

In December of the same year, Prieto Laurens persuaded de la Huerta to leave secretly for Veracruz and launch an armed rebellion with the backing of General Guadalupe Sánchez, the Veracruz Zone Commander. Two days later, General Enrique Estrada, Zone Commander of Jalisco, joined the rebellion. The rebels had 23,000 troops on the line, as against 34,000 under loyalist officers. In the following days, of the 508 generals in the Mexican Army, 102 joined the rebellion. De la Huerta, who had been Secretary of the Treasury, looted the treasury of all its cash before he left.

The revolt, which began in Veracruz and Jalisco, spread rapidly. Guadalupe Sánchez's men marched up from the Veracruz coast all the way to Puebla, occupying Xalapa, Córdoba, and Orizaba. He was defeated by forces commanded by Juan Andreu Almazán at Esperanza and retreated to Veracruz. After three months of hard fighting, the rebellion was crushed, and most of its leaders were caught and shot. De la Huerta, Enrique Estrada, Prieto Laurens, and other instigators had found sanctuary in the United States and, during the administration of Lázaro Cárdenas, were permitted to return to Mexico.

Having eyewitnessed some aspects of this rebellion, I recall some details of certain significance. When de la Huerta looted the treasury and went to Veracruz, the Huasteca Petroleum Company (subsidiary of Standard Oil) immediately offered to advance 50 million pesos to Obregón's government against future taxes. A man by the name of Rodolfo Montes, owner of the Regis Hotel and high official for the El Águila Petroleum Company (subsidiary of Royal Dutch Shell), on the other hand, was involved with de la Huerta's conspiracy, apparently backing up the rebellion. This was because

El Águila represented the prerogatives extended in the Bucareli Agreement to the American oil companies, contrary to the interests of the British-owned. (Montes left Mexico when the rebellion collapsed, sold the Hotel Regis, and built an office structure in Los Angeles, California, known as the Montes Building.)

The U.S. government helped the Obregón government with arms and ammunition, establishing an embargo on such shipments to the rebels. De la Huerta, however, received some arms by way of Belize, British Honduras. It was therefore imperative for him to keep the route—Belize, Mérida, Yucatán, Veracruz—open. This, I believe, was the reason why the governor of Yucatán, who remained loyal to Obregón, was killed.

In the local *barrios alambre*[4] set up by Guadalupe Sánchez's men, witness saw men handle brand-new Vickers machine guns that had never been fired.

J. de Courcy filed a phony story about Mexico City being bombarded by rebel planes. He was detained and expelled from Mexico by the government.

By the end of February there was no longer any great danger from the rebels. Two months after the start of the uprising the Port of Veracruz was evacuated. Some of the generals joined the federals. De la Huerta and his contingent in Veracruz went to Frontera, Tabasco. On February 15, Veracruz was open to international traffic. In an effort to raise money, the rebels were trying to export *chicle* and drugs.

Alonzo Capetillo, in *Rebellion without a Head,* reports that de la Huerta felt he was going insane and, in a state of great excitement, said as much to General Cándido Aguilar. He confessed to Aguilar that he intended to go to the United States. When Aguilar tried to dissuade him, he screamed: "I can't do anything more! So much intrigue! I'll be more useful there than here." He left Mexico on the 11th or 12th of March. In New York he named two supreme chiefs, Alvarado and Aguilar. Demoralization was making great inroads through betrayal and fear. Desertions were continuous, and there was very little to eat.

Alvarado, who had gone to the United States to purchase arms, returned in April. At the end of May, he was shot by rebels while encamped in Tabasco.

De la Huerta went to Hollywood, where for many years he taught singing to motion picture stars.

No one who was connected with the murder of Felipe Carrillo Puerto and his companions was ever able to live the infamy down.[5]

# NOTES

FOREWORD

1. The newspaper's social section.

INTRODUCTION

*All translations of original Spanish texts are my own unless otherwise indicated.*

1. For more information about Elvia Carrillo Puerto and her feminist organization, see Monique J. Lemaître's biography entitled *Elvia Carrillo Puerto: La monja roja del Mayab* (Mexico City: Ediciones Castillo, 1998).
2. His Mayan-speaking countrymen called him by his indigenous name, H'pil Zutilché, or simply *yaax ich,* meaning "green eyes."
3. "La Peregrina" was originally a *danza* (also known as a *habanera*), the name of a traditional Cuban dance and the rhythm that accompanies it. Today "La Peregrina" is regularly performed as a bolero, a genre of Mexican popular music developed in the 1930's and 1940's.
4. Although several versions of "La Peregrina" are in circulation, the following is my transcription of Luis Rosado Vega's handwritten original published in the Mexico City magazine *Impacto,* no. 1359:

*The Pilgrim*

Pilgrim of clear and divine eyes
and cheeks aflame with a rosy tinge,
pilgrim of the red lips
and radiant hair like the sun.

Pilgrim who left your own land,
the pine trees and the virginal snow,
and came to find refuge in my palm groves,
under the sky of my land, my tropical land . . .

5. Ishbel Ross, *Ladies of the Press: The Story of Women in Journalism by an Insider* (New York: Harper and Brothers, 1936), 26. See Ross's book for more information about female journalists of this time.
6. "The House of the People."
7. "Idolized Alma."
8. Although documentary evidence is scarce, it is quite probable that this paramour was none other than Katherine Anne Porter. According to her biographer Joan Givner, Porter met Carrillo Puerto soon after arriving in Mexico in 1920, and he "took her rowing on the lake in Chapultepec Park and to the Salón México, where he taught her all the latest dance steps." Joan Givner, *Katherine Anne Porter: A Life* (New York: Simon and Schuster, 1982), 151.
9. "Girl reporter."
10. This is a literal translation of her name into Mayan: "Alma" (soul) as "Pixan," and "Reed" as "Halal."
11. "Lovely little girl."

12. Quoted in Thomas F. Walsh, *Katherine Anne Porter and Mexico: The Illusion of Eden* (Austin: University of Texas Press, 1992), 147.

13. Some of the information pertaining to Alma Reed's New York residence was taken from Antoinette May's informative biography entitled *Passionate Pilgrim: The Extraordinary Life of Alma Reed* (New York: Paragon House, 1993), 211–243.

14. Alma Reed, *Orozco* (New York: Oxford University Press, 1956), 10.

15. Cited in Delpar, 35.

16. Here it should be pointed out that Orozco's widow, Margarita Valladares, strongly opposed the idea that Reed—to whom she curiously refers as an anthropologist—might have helped her husband as much as she apparently did. In an appendix to the second edition of Orozco's *Autobiografía* (Mexico City: Ediciones Era, 1970), Valladares states: "The material solitude, not spiritual solitude, in which Orozco lived, and his lack of dissimulation regarding an unfavorable economic situation were elements that, in her book, Mrs. Reed interpreted erroneously, thus creating an almost pitiful image in which modesty signifies something more than a simple lack of possessions and where solitude represents despair. It is a known style of certain writers who, by employing tasteless devices, thus attempt to manipulate the sensibility of the reader who is least given to easy emotions. If she had found Orozco in a penthouse on Fifth Avenue, Mrs. Reed's book wouldn't have a basis, as her object was to suggest, without ever saying so, that Orozco let himself be led by the hand in a most docile manner in order to achieve success" (111).

17. José Clemente Orozco, *Cartas a Margarita, 1921–1949*, with introduction and notes by Tatiana Herrero Orozco (Mexico City: Ediciones Era, 1987), 117.

18. Valladares comments on this matter: "When Mrs. Reed believed, with good reason, that the dealers would be interested in what was for them the exotic, in this case the Mexican Revolution, her criteria were more commercial than artistic. A painting of Pancho Villa would fetch more money than a reproduction of the Queens Bridge. . . . [Orozco] hadn't gone to Manhattan to create long-distance folklore. Because of this, he preferred to request that I send him his works of the type that were requested for his first exhibitions in Delphic Studios" (in Orozco, *Autobiografía*, 112).

19. Orozco, *Cartas*, 122.

20. Reed, *Orozco*, 5.

21. Orozco, *Cartas*, 122.

22. Orozco, *Autobiografía*, 88. For her part, his widow points out: "[Orozco] accepted the invitations made by Mrs. Reed to come into contact with a strange and heterogeneous society, and later would paint portraits of Eva Sikelianos and Julia Peterkin. . . . Only in this way should one interpret the fact that he accompanied the American writer at Delphic Studios or any similar event" (in ibid., 112).

23. Quoted in Orozco, *Cartas*, 130.

24. May, *Passionate Pilgrim*, 223.

25. Alejandro Anreus, *The Years in New York* (Albuquerque: University of New Mexico Press, 2001). Here I should point out that while his is an engaging story of Orozco's formative years in New York, Anreus rather cavalierly attacks Antoinette May's biography of Reed because it is "filled with inconsistencies and errors and too reliant on Reed's own 1956 biography of Orozco" (149 n. 14). Unfortunately the author of *Orozco in Gringoland* commits two fundamental errors in chapter two, entitled "Gringoland." He states: "Alma Reed died in Mexico in 1961" (36), but she passed away on November 20, 1966. Anreus also confuses Frances Toor, creator and editor of the bilingual journal *Mexican Folkways,*

with Frances Flynn Paine, a promoter of Mexican art in New York during this period (28).

26. Anreus, *Orozco in Gringoland*, 30. Curiously, Orozco's wife received a very different version: "The exhibitions in that gallery confounded the critics. The scenes of the executed by firing squad, those killed by hanging, had nothing to do next to less tormenting New York prints. Which was the true Orozco? The confusion is the natural consequence of the fact that Mrs. Reed unsuccessfully tried to 'lead' Orozco towards a show window in which the tragedy of our revolution was reduced to 'Mexican curios' and that Orozco, on his part, nobly and tenaciously pursued other desires" (in Orozco, *Autobiografía*, 112).

27. Orozco, *Cartas*, 136.

28. Quoted in ibid., 137.

29. Regarding this aspect of Alma's contribution to her husband's U.S. career, Valladares de Orozco is more generous: "Doubtless the North American anthropologist [*sic*] could rightly document objectively that part which in all justice corresponded to Orozco's activities in that epoch. Essentially, the gallery she established under the name Delphic Studios was very useful for Orozco, as it gave him a place to exhibit and, of course, to sell and ameliorate his economic situation. At the beginning there was a rift between the two, because Mrs. Reed hoped that Orozco would produce works of the same kind as those he had realized in Mexico, that is, revolutionary scenes, Mexican landscapes, etc., but he felt the urgency to renovate through the stimuli of his [new] environment" (in Orozco, *Autobiografía*, 111–112).

30. Antonieta Rivas Mercado was the daughter of Antonio Rivas Mercado, chief architect during Porfirio Diaz's three-decade "reign" as President of Mexico. Overcome by personal problems, she committed suicide in 1931 in the Cathedral of Notre Dame in Paris with a pistol belonging to José Vasconcelos, whom she had supported during his presidential campaign and with whom she was romantically involved.

31. In another letter to Rodríguez Lozano dated Wednesday, November 30, 1929, Rivas Mercado develops the same theme: "Alma has goodwill but no brains; a North American vice, sentimental and false, and Clemente is dreadful and believes he has a right to opine because he is a genius." Antonieta Rivas Mercado, *Obras completas de Antonieta Rivas Mercado*, ed. Schneider, Lecturas Mexicanas 93 (Mexico City: Secretaría de Educación Pública, 1987), 406.

32. Ibid., 391.

33. In a letter dated November 17, 1929, Antonieta Rivas Mercado makes her own—albeit unkind—assessment of Alma's physical and mental attributes: "Alma Reed, fair, blonde, with pretty rose-colored skin, voluminous blonde hair, a melancholic smile (memory of Carrillo Puerto) that slides down the edge of her lips, endlessly approves with her head like those Chinese porcelain dolls that say: yes, yes, yes" (ibid., 396).

34. Thomas Hart Benton, *An American in Art: A Professional and Technical Autobiography* (Lawrence: University Press of Kansas, 1969), 61.

35. Ione Robinson, *A Wall to Paint On* (New York: A. P. Dutton and Co., 1946), 150–151.

36. According to Orozco's widow, "The initiative for Orozco to decorate the refectory of Pomona College, in Claremont, California, came from José Pijoan, at the time professor of art history in that institution, and from Jorge Juan Crespo de la Serna. Both were perfectly aware of my husband's prior work. For Mrs. Reed, the Pomona mural became a new and unexpected promotion for sales. She had

completely assumed the gallery's financial administration, which Orozco viewed benevolently, because from his perspective it simply relieved him of something for which he had never been prepared" (in Orozco, *Autobiografía,* 112). In a letter to Guatemalan art historian Luis Cardoza y Aragón, Orozco complains about Reed's questionable administration of his work: "I have tried in every conceivable way to get Mrs. Reed to return my works, but I have never been able to. She does with them what she pleases; she exhibits them without my consent and with no right. What kind of control can I have under these circumstances?" (ibid., 113).

37. Benton, *An American in Art,* 62.

38. Alma M. Reed, *José Clemente Orozco* (New York: Delphic Studios, 1932), i.

39. According to biographer Antoinette May, Reed divorced her husband when she discovered that he was having an affair with her best friend (17). However, in a Mexican travelogue, curiously titled *The Pig in the Barber Shop* (Boston: Little, Brown, 1958), H. Allen Smith claims to have interviewed Reed in the mid-1950's and documents her version of the events that led to the couple's separation, including those mentioned in my text (93). Whatever the truth may be, it does seem odd that Reed would abandon her ailing husband if not for some overriding circumstance.

40. In her fascinating biography entitled *Anita Brenner: A Mind of Her Own* (Austin: University of Texas Press, 1998), Susannah J. Glusker states: "Anita showed [Orozco's] work to many people, among them, Alma Reed, John Reed's sister. At that time, Alma Reed was prominent in a salon sponsored by Madame Siquilianos [*sic*], a wealthy patron of the arts" (50). Given the circumstances of her own life as detailed in this introduction, Alma Reed is in no way related to John Reed, the author of *Insurgent Mexico.*

41. Mary Tudor, or Bloody Mary, was officially known as Mary I (1516–1558). The daughter of Henry VIII and Katherine of Aragon, Mary I was queen of England from 1553 to 1558.

42. Richard Posner, interview with the editor, October 2001.

43. Rosa Lie Johansson, interview with the editor, May 2004. Ms. Johansson died in August 2004, and many objects once belonging to Alma Reed were left in her Mexico City apartment upon her death. I immediately contacted officials from the Swedish Embassy and formally requested that they be donated to a local museum. Happily, in March 2005, I was notified by officials from Mexico's Museo Nacional de Historia that Johansson's nieces had donated a large quantity of their aunt's estate to the museum. Consequently, museum officials are planning to organize an exhibition of this fascinating collection, which includes clothing—Reed's signature hats, veils, and other accoutrements—as well as paintings, photos, and files once belonging to her.

44. "The Aquatic Sports and Exploration Club of Mexico."

45. Quoted from Joe Nash's unpublished memoirs, which he kindly let me borrow.

46. In a revealing FBI office memorandum dated February 3, 1956, sent to the director of the organization by the special agent in charge (SAC) in Houston, Texas, his informant, a Mrs. De Puy, reported under the category of "Peculiarities" regarding the subject in question that "in some instances Reed will appear wearing a long black dress, gilded shoes and big cocktail hat at 9:00 a.m."

47. I deduce this date from the information provided by Antoinette May in her biography of Reed (241–242).

48. May, *Passionate Pilgrim,* 243.

49. The obituary that appeared in the *New York Times* on November 21, 1966, states that Reed died of a heart ailment.

I have not been able to confirm this report and thus rely on firsthand testimony provided by Richard Posner and Joe Nash.

50. Joe Nash, unpublished memoirs.

51. Orozco, *Cartas,* 141.

### OUTLINE OF BOOK

1. The systems of debt-peonage employed by owners of the great sisal plantations of Yucatán, in which laborers were paid not in cash but in vouchers that could be redeemed only on the premises. The Spanish term *enganchado* (meaning "hooked" or "snagged") refers to the fact that any debts incurred by laborers with the local store or cantina prohibited them from abandoning the plantation. These debts were also inheritable, thus creating a de facto slavery, which could span generations. One of Carrillo Puerto's main goals was the revocation of this inhumane practice.

2. An individual of mixed European and indigenous ancestry. Mestizos make up the majority of Mexico's population.

3. Carrillo Puerto employs this term consistently to define those who through lack of education and social mobility were unable to express their opinions or raise complaints. Literally, *inarticulado* means "inarticulate."

4. The Alliance for Resistance established local alliances (or leagues) in even the smallest hamlets throughout the Yucatán Peninsula. Representatives from the Liga Central (Central Alliance) and the Socialist Party in Mérida maintained close contacts with all of these leagues. They were utilized, among other things, for conducting local and state elections. The Liga Central was located in the Casa del Pueblo in Mérida, and delegates from distant Ligas would arrive to present complaints and petitions.

5. The monetary units here are assumed to be pesos.

6. Literally, "political boss"; a local functionary of the Díaz dictatorship also referred to as "municipal president."

7. All ellipsis points are reproduced as they appear in Reed's original manuscript and do not indicate an omission of material by me.

### CHAPTER ONE

1. "Fatherland."

2. The *científicos,* a group of political advisers to Mexican dictator Porfirio Díaz (1830–1915), practiced the philosophy developed by Auguste Comte (1798–1857), founder of the positivist school and considered the father of modern sociology. According to Comte, the only form of knowledge comes from the study of facts and the relationships between different phenomena.

3. *Henequén,* or henequen, is the Spanish equivalent of sisal (hemp), the most important cash crop of the Yucatán Peninsula. Its importance diminished only with the introduction of synthetic fibers in the mid-twentieth century.

### CHAPTER TWO

1. "Patria chica" refers to Yucatán, their "small homeland."

2. John Kenneth Turner, *Barbarous Mexico* (Chicago: C. H. Kerr and Co., 1911).

3. According to the ancient Greeks, Ultima Thule was the most distant unknown land. *Última tule* is also the title of a collection of essays written by Mexican writer and intellectual Alfonso Reyes (1889–1959) and published in 1942.

### CHAPTER THREE

1. "Boardwalk."

2. "The girl journalist."

3. Venustiano Carranza (1859–1920), a Mexican general, was senator during the administration of Porfirio Díaz and later governor of the state of Coahuila. After the assassination of the constitu-

tional president Francisco I. Madero in 1913, he organized and directed a revolution, acting as the first commander of the Constitutional Army and defeating Victoriano Huerta in 1914. Carranza became president of Mexico in 1917, and that same year he promulgated the Mexican Constitution, which is still in use today. He was assassinated in 1920 during a counterrevolution headed by Álvaro Obregón.

4. "CROM" is the acronym of the Comité Revolucionario de Obreros Mexicanos (Revolutionary Committee of Mexican Laborers), founded at the Third National Workers Congress in Saltillo, in which Luis N. Morones was elected general secretary. The organization adopted various anarchist tendencies, among them a call for "direct action."

5. The Renovators were supporters of Venustiano Carranza, leader of the Constitutionalist Army, who in December 1916 convoked the Mexican Congress and instituted a series of reforms to the Constitution of 1857. The changes were promulgated on February 5, 1917, and responded to the new social reality of Mexico. Among other things, the new Constitution ratified a system of direct elections and prohibited reelection. It also guaranteed freedom of religion and free nonreligious education as well as an eight-hour workday.

6. Tracts of communal land owned in common by local villagers and considered to be a hallmark of the Mexican Revolution.

7. Reed is referring to the *"brigadas rurales"* (rural brigades) set up by Mexico's secretary of education under Obregón, José Vasconsuelos. The latter organized the first literacy campaign in Mexico's history.

8. "Development and Agriculture."

9. Rafael López (1873–1943), born in the state of Guanajuato, was the author of several volumes of poetry, including *La bestia del oro y otros poemas* (1941). Reed takes certain liberties when she translates the title of this work, which should be "The Golden Beast." In referring to López as "Jaliscience" (from the state of Jalisco), she also errs regarding López's birthplace.

10. *Cronistas* were the chroniclers, or historians, who documented Mexico's history from pre-Columbian and colonial times to the present. Here Reed is referring to the Spanish chroniclers in particular, whose works were well known during the colonial period of New Spain.

11. "Comrades."

12. *The Population of the Valley of Teotihuacán.*

13. The pseudonym of Gerardo Murillo, respected Mexican painter, writer, and authority on volcanoes. He changed his name to "Atl" (Nahuatl for "water") as a gesture to pre-Hispanic civilization, which he most admired.

14. The former monastery La Merced.

15. In Mexican Spanish, a *peladito* or *pelado* is a person of the lower socioeconomic classes who often demonstrates his or her misery by begging or dramatizing their wretchedness in public. A metate is a stone for grinding corn into cornmeal, which are normally made of *tezontle,* a volcanic stone common in and around the Valley of Mexico.

16. Pulque is an alcoholic beverage extracted from the maguey cactus and popular—especially with the lower classes—from pre-Hispanic times well into the twentieth century. A *pulquería* is a tavern that serves pulque.

17. In Mexico, a *licenciado* is a lawyer, but the term can also designate someone with a university degree.

18. Francisco I. Madero (1873–1913) founded the National Anti-Reelectionist Party in 1910, opposed to the thirty-year dictatorship of Porfirio Díaz. At the beginning of the Mexican Revolution, Madero was named provisional president, and in November 1911 he tri-

umphed in the national elections. In 1913 he was deposed and assassinated by an antirevolutionary movement headed by Victoriano Huerta.

19. The Partido Liberal Mexicano was the major political organization of those who supported the Mexican Revolution, calling for the overthrow of Porfirio Díaz. This party was organized during the Congreso Liberal, which met in San Luis Potosí in February 1901.

20. On the Noche Triste (literally "Sad Night") of June 30, 1520, the Spanish invaders, led by Hernán Cortés, were forced to evacuate the Aztec capital of Tenochtitlán. The retreat occurred after the slaughter of many Aztecs during a religious ceremony, which provoked a local uprising. Because many Spanish soldiers were also killed, they christened it the "Sad Night."

21. The "Plan of San Luis Potosí" was the document that would eventually trigger the beginning of the Mexican Revolution and the collapse of Porfirio Díaz's long dictatorship. It was drafted by Francisco I. Madero in 1910 and called for a national uprising against Díaz on November 20, 1910.

22. Reed is probably recalling this statement of Jefferson's: "Who would voluntarily choose not to have the right to vote, decide to purchase government propaganda handouts instead of independent newspapers, prefer government to worker-controlled unions, opt for land to be owned by the state instead of those who till it, want government repression of religious liberty, a single political party instead of a free choice, a rigid cultural orthodoxy instead of democratic tolerance and diversity?"

### CHAPTER FOUR

1. Reed is referring to Gerardo Machado (1871–1939), president of Cuba from 1925 to 1933. Originally a businessman, he became a presidential candidate in 1924 and took advantage of resurgent nationalism of the era. Machado's campaign for national regeneration initially received wide support, but he was ultimately ousted from the presidency after a period of violence against demonstrators, which eventually led to a military takeover.

2. A ñáñigo is an adept of the Abakuá secret society, which has its origins in the Ngbe and Ekpe secret societies of the Calabar region of Nigeria (their names mean "leopard man"). The first lodge, Efik Butón, was founded in 1836.

3. "Tuntún de pasa y grifería" is also the title of a book of poetry by Puerto Rican author Luis Palés Matos and published in 1937. Palés was one of the founders of the *negrista* movement in Latin American poetry, particularly that of the Caribbean.

4. *Son* is a form of Cuban music that originated in the second half of the nineteenth century, probably in the eastern province of Oriente. The *son* combines the structure of a Spanish *canción* with African rhythms brought by slaves, especially those of Yoruba origins. Reed appears to refer to the lyrics of such songs, which were first published in these journals. She is probably thinking of the work of celebrated Cuban poet Nicolás Guillén, whose poems were often published in magazines and literary reviews. However, such poems were not available in English translation until after her initial visit to Cuba.

5. A *finca* is an estate or rural property, much smaller in acreage than a typical hacienda of the time and often located in regions where tobacco, sugar, and coffee are produced.

6. The name given by Bartolomé de las Casas (who transcribed Columbus's diary) to the ancestors of the Taino Indians who originally met Columbus. They were located in the eastern part of Cuba, now known as Oriente Province.

7. Fray Bartolomé de las Casas was probably the first priest ordained in the

New World, and he dedicated his entire life to the protection of native communities in the Caribbean and other parts of the Spanish colonies. Besides the *Brief Account,* las Casas is the author of a number of other works, including the voluminous *Historia de las Indias (History of the Indies).*

8. The *encomienda* was a colonial Spanish system whereby conquistadors were awarded large tracts of land and their local inhabitants in return for service provided to the Crown. The inhabitants were enslaved on their own lands, and the conquistadors' only responsibility was to Christianize them. Needless to say, this system led to endless abuse of the native population.

9. "Welcome."

10. "The Socialist Party of the Southeast" was the official name adopted by the Yucatecan Socialist Party at the beginning of 1921. In April of that same year, this party elected Felipe Carrillo Puerto as its gubernatorial candidate.

11. "Palace of Government."

12. Literally, "little Indians"; the affectionate way Carrillo Puerto would refer to the native inhabitants.

CHAPTER FIVE

1. "Personal assistant."

2. "The White City," as Mérida is still known today.

3. *Naa* is the Mayan word for the traditional thatched-roof hut still used by the inhabitants of Yucatán.

4. "Melancholic verses."

5. "Little old lady."

6. "Dreamer."

7. "Poor little things."

8. The *mayordomo* was the principal steward of the hacienda.

9. Benito Juárez (1806–1872) was elected president of Mexico in 1858. At that time he enacted the Laws of Reform (Leyes de la Reforma), which, among other things, nationalized Church property. In 1861 he suspended payment on Mexico's national debt, which led to the intervention of France and the imposition of Maximilian of Hapsburg as emperor, while Juárez directed national resistance from the U.S. border. Under pressure from the United States, Napoleon III of France withdrew his troops from Mexico, whereby Maximilian was summarily captured, judged, and executed (1867). Juárez then reentered Mexico City and was reelected to the presidency from 1867 to 1871. Melchor Ocampo (1814–1861) was a Mexican writer and politician who served as governor to Michoacán and, after the Ayutla Revolution (1855), was named minister of foreign relations. He presided over the Constitutional Congress in 1856 and under Juárez was secretary of the treasury. After the victory of the liberals in Calpulalpan, he was apprehended by a conservative group and executed.

10. "Benemérito" (literally "worthy or deserving") is the sobriquet of Benito Juárez.

11. "Enemies."

12. *Camisas* are shirts, and *paja* is straw.

13. *Milpa,* the Nahuatl word for a cultivated field (normally a cornfield), is employed commonly throughout Mexico today.

14. A cenote is a deep, circular sinkhole found in the Yucatán, a product of numerous underground rivers that undercut what is essentially a limestone shelf. For the ancient Maya the cenotes were sacred wells where human sacrifices were at times performed and offerings made.

15. The flamboyant, or *flamboyán,* is a tropical tree with dazzling red blossoms, widespread in the Yucatán.

16. "Commission of Exportation."

17. "Teacher."

18. Literally, "de-fanaticizing." This educational process was developed by

Carrillo Puerto's government in order to extirpate long-standing beliefs and even superstitions that were a detriment to the development of a modern enlightened society.

CHAPTER SIX

1. "It's getting late."

2. Oswald Spengler, author of the important and influential work *The Decline of the West,* viewed cultures as "organic" in the sense that they normally follow a life pattern, one he compares by analogy to seasons.

3. The Mayab is the ancient and modern region of the Maya, extending from the Yucatán Peninsula well into Central America.

4. Reed is referring to the Comisión Reguladora Henequenera Exportadora de Yucatán (Henequen Market Regulating Commission), founded on January 10, 1912, to ensure the value of this important cash crop and to regularize its market price. According to the *Enciclopedia yucatanense,* "its founding constituted the first socialist stone laid in the henequen industry."

5. "Ink shops."

6. "Struggles."

7. "Vulture."

8. "Pure Maya legends and poetry."

CHAPTER SEVEN

1. Originally published in London by R. H. Porter (1896–1902), this was the first comprehensive survey of Maya archaeology and appeared in six volumes with many illustrations, some in color.

2. Augustus Le Plongeon (1825–1908) was born on the island of Jersey, one of the Channel Islands, and later studied in Paris. He was a true renaissance man of his time, having worked as a surveyor in San Francisco during the California gold rush. In 1851 he moved back to England, where he studied photography, returning to San Francisco several years later to open a photo studio. He then traveled to Lima, Peru, where he set up another studio. In 1873 he married Alice Dixon, and the couple sailed for Yucatán, where they remained for twelve years. He was the first to excavate the ruins of Chichén Itzá and applied his photographic talents to the documentation of said ruins, taking more than five hundred pictures of them. His magnum opus—synoptically entitled *Sacred Mysteries among the Mayas and the Quiches, 11,500 Years Ago: Their Relation to the Sacred Mysteries of Egypt, Greece, Chaldea, and India; Freemasonry in Times Anterior to the Temple of Solomon*—was first published in New York by R. Macoy in 1886.

3. A Chac-Mool is a reclining male figure sculpted in stone, with a hole carved in his chest, which apparently was used to hold the hearts of sacrificial victims. Indeed, the discovery of these figures in Tula and Chichén suggests a close relationship between the two sites, possibly indicating a Toltec invasion of the Yucatán Peninsula during the classical period.

4. "Tlaloc" is the Mesoamerican name of an ancient fertility god associated with water and rain. His name is Chac in the Maya region.

5. "Kukulcán" is the name of the plumed serpent, the Maya god of creation, whose name is Quetzalcóatl in the Mesoamerican pantheon.

6. Alfred Marston Tozzer (1877–1954) was a groundbreaking anthropologist who first studied the Maya in 1902 as a Traveling Fellow of the Archaeological Institution of America. For the following three years he worked as an ethnological student among the Maya in the jungles of Chiapas and Campeche. In 1905 Tozzer began teaching anthropology at Harvard. Among other works, he is the author of *A Comparative Study of the Mayas and the*

*Lacandones,* published in 1907 by Macmillan. He also translated and edited Diego de Landa's *Relación de las cosas de Yucatán.* For his part, Charles Etienne, Abbé Brasseur de Bourbourg (1814–1874), first traveled to Mexico in 1848 as chaplain of the French Legation. He later visited the Isthmus of Tehuantepec as well as Chiapas, and in 1864 he became attached to the French scientific mission to Mexico, but due to Maximilian's execution, he was forced to return to France. Above all, Brasseur de Bourbourg was a tireless student of Indian culture and civilization, whose controversial theories attempted to trace the relationships between Americans and Asians, as well as to establish a connection between the Old World and the New in pre-Columbian times. His publications include *Histoire des nations civilisées du Mexique et de l'Amérique-Centrale* (Paris, 1857–1859, 4 vols.), as well as that of the "Manuscrit Troano" (Paris, 1869–1870).

7. "The agreeable Barry couple."

8. "Chenes" is the name of an architectural style developed by the Maya of the Yucatán in the late classical period, characterized by large masks that serve as doorways to temples. The Maya of the western Yucatán Peninsula developed the Puuc style during the classical period (sixth through tenth centuries), and its crowning achievement was the city of Uxmal.

9. In his work entitled *Incidents of Travel in Yucatán* (New York: Harper and Brothers, 1868), John L. Stephens mentions this lintel and how it was removed from its original structure. However, I can find no mention of its tragic fate upon arrival in New York City.

10. *Chicozapote* is the name of a tree native to Mexico and Central America and bearing sweet yellow fruits. The sap of this tree, also known as the sapodilla tree, produces a latex gum known as *chicle,* from which chewing gum was originally made.

### CHAPTER EIGHT

1. The *camisa* and *calzones* constituted—up to the mid-twentieth century—the traditional dress of indigenous Mexicans, normally made of a white cotton cloth called *manta.* The *presidente municipal* is the *jefe político,* or local political boss.

2. The "War of the Castes" lasted fifty-four years and reached its peak of violence between 1847 and 1851. It began as an Indian uprising, caused by the terrible conditions endured on the sisal haciendas, but soon became widespread. It was during this period that Yucatán offered its sovereignty to Spain, England, and the United States in exchange for arms and resources in order to defeat the rebelling Maya.

3. A *huipil* is the embroidered blouse still worn by many indigenous women of Mexico.

4. The Spanish equivalent of "town councilwoman."

5. The Cámara Agrícola (Chamber of Agriculture) was founded in 1906 to defend the price of henequen and to promote improvements of this industry.

6. In reality, the author is referring to Article 2, Section 2, of the Mexican Constitution of 1857. Article 1 states: "The Mexican nation recognizes that the rights of man are the basis and objective of social institutions. Consequently, it is declared that all laws and authorities of the nation must respect and sustain the guarantees provided by the constitution."

7. The monetary units here are assumed to be pesos.

8. Again, it is assumed that the monetary units are pesos.

9. The Ministro de Gobernación is Mexico's equivalent to the secretary of the interior.

10. "Business."

11. The owner of a large tract of land, known in Latin America as a *latifundio.*

12. The *Revista de Yucatán,* directed by Carlos R. Menéndez, was an independent newspaper published in 1912–1915 and 1918–1926.

13. *Baldíos* are uncultivated lands and, according to Mexican law, may be confiscated by the government and sold to another party who promises to cultivate them.

14. "Liberal Party."

15. Colonel Lucio Blanco Fuentes, who had supported Madero for election and later Carranza, took the town of Matamoros, Tamaulipas, in June 1913 after defeating federal troops. On August 30 of that year he expropriated lands belonging to Félix Díaz, nephew of Porfirio Díaz, and distributed it to local peasants.

16. Over the years, Yucatán has attempted to cede from Mexico on several occasions. This first occurred during the Caste War and has been a topic of political debate well into the twentieth century. Because of its unique history, the region is often referred to as the Sister Republic of Yucatán.

17. *Ayuntamientos* are the municipal governments of towns and villages in Mexico.

### CHAPTER NINE

1. "The Peón Contreras Theater."

2. The "Valley of Anáhuac" refers to the geological setting from which the Aztecs ruled during the time of their empire and comprises the plateau between the Eastern and Western Sierras Madres.

3. A *carreta* is a narrow cart or wagon.

4. "Priest."

5. In this case, "Rectoría" refers to the home of the parish priest.

6. "Eyes of jade."

7. "Living room."

8. "Meals."

9. A polite form of address; literally, "Mrs. Mother of Felipe."

10. The Civil Registry, where births, deaths, marriages, and baptisms were documented.

11. Literally, "wheat-colored." Here *trigueño* refers to the color of Felipe's grandfather's hair, which was black or brown.

12. "Good, boys. My valiant soldiers."

13. "Sweet breads, rolls, or buns."

14. Possibly a reference to *achiote,* the Nahuatl term for *k'uxub,* a shiny seed that, when ground, produces a reddish paste used for coloring in Yucatecan dishes, as the Spanish would use saffron.

15. "My poor father."

16. Eduardo Bolio Ontiveros, *De la cuna al paredón: Anecdotario de la vida, muerte, y gloria de Felipe Carrillo Puerto (From the Cradle to the Execution Wall: Anecdotes of the Life, Death, and Glory of Felipe Carrillo Puerto)* (Mérida: Talleres Gráficos y Editoral Zamná, 1973).

17. Here *jefe,* or chief, refers to Felipe, for he was these men's boss. Don Justiniano's answer is "Who knows?"

18. "Maize."

19. "Story of the little birds."

20. "Recollections and stories."

### CHAPTER TEN

1. Charles Callan Tansill, *America Goes to War* (Boston: Little Brown and Co., 1938).

2. Isidro Fabela, *Historia diplomática de la revolución mexicana,* 2 vols. (Mexico City: Fondo de Cultura Económica, 1958–1959).

3. The Teapot Dome was an oil reserve scandal that began during the administration of President Warren G. Harding. In 1922, Albert B. Fall, U.S. secretary of the interior, leased the Teapot Dome oil fields to Harry F. Sinclair without competitive bidding. These operations became the subject of a Senate investigation led by

Thomas Walsh. Fall was later indicted for conspiracy and for accepting bribes. The oil fields were restored to the U.S. government through a Supreme Court decision in 1927.

4. The Pan-American Federation of Labor (PAFL) was an organization conceived by Samuel Gompers, head of the AFL during WWI, as an instrument for dominating the Latin American labor movement.

5. T'Ho was the original name of the pre-Hispanic Maya city renamed Mérida by the Spanish.

6. "Adelantado Montejo" was the title of Spanish conquistador Francisco Montejo (1479–1553), who took part in the Cortés expedition and was later captain general of Yucatán and the island of Cozumel.

7. The pre-Hispanic (Aztec) name for modern-day Mexico City.

8. Tepic is now the capital of the western Mexican state of Nayarit.

### CHAPTER ELEVEN

1. "El Castillo," or "the Castle," is the name given to the largest pyramidal complex of Chichén Itzá. Some experts believe that it could be the burial place of the mythical leader Quetzalcóatl Topiltzin, who, after being exiled from his native Tula, traveled with a band of followers to Yucatán. There he was worshipped as Kukulkán before sailing east on a raft of fire-serpents, promising to return in the year Ce Acatl, which coincided with the year the Spanish arrived on the Gulf coast (1519). It has been argued that the native inhabitants considered Cortés himself as the returning Quetzalcóatl, thus undermining any defense of their lands.

2. *Juego de pelota* and *tlachtli* refer to a ritualistic pre-Hispanic ball game, a practice that links all cultures of Mesoamerica. Many theories exist as to exactly how it was played, but its importance may be gleaned from the presence of ball courts in numerous pre-Columbian sites: Monte Albán, Chichén Itzá, El Tajín, and others.

3. Augustus Le Plongeon, *Queen Moo and the Egyptian Sphinx* (New York, 1896).

4. Mexico's Instituto Nacional de Antropología e Historia was founded in 1939 during the presidency of Lázaro Cárdenas. Evidently, Reed is referring to a prior governmental bureau.

5. Tamales prepared in the style of Motul.

6. James G. Fraser, *The Golden Bough: A Study in Comparative Religion* (New York and London: Macmillan, 1894).

### CHAPTER TWELVE

*The chapter's title means "Rhythms of the Mayab."*

1. "The Third Order" refers to a branch of the Franciscans that encompasses people from all walks of life.

2. A *zacatán* is a drum made from a hollowed-tree trunk covered with jaguar skin and is played with one's fingers. A *tunkul* is essentially a dual-toned xylophone. It is played with two sticks that have one end covered with rubber.

3. Reed is apparently mistranslating the meaning of "Así será," which is "Thus it *will* be."

4. Literally, "a good-looking mixed-race woman of Yucatán."

5. "Eatery."

6. "Affection."

7. "Comradeship."

8. "Clear and divine."

### CHAPTER THIRTEEN

1. *Balché* is the name of a pre-Hispanic beverage composed of water, honey, and the roots or bark of a tree *(Lonchocarpus longistylus)*. Its consumption was prohibited by royal decree during the colonial period.

2. Literally, "humble ones."

CHAPTER FOURTEEN

1. "Independent Electoral Center."
2. "Democratic Party."
3. "Workers' Center of Motul."
4. The Morenista program was the political program espoused by Delio Moreno Cantón.
5. *La Gaceta de la Costa* was a weekly review published in Motul by Julián Alcalá Sabido between 1896 and 1897.
6. "Juárez Penitentiary."
7. Followers of Francisco I. Madero. See chapter 3, note 18.
8. Félix Palavicini, *Mi vida revolucionaria* (Mexico City: Ed. Botas, 1937).
9. Mexico's oldest existing newspaper, founded in Mexico City in 1916.
10. Sobriquet of Francisco I. Madero.
11. "Press Journalists of the States."
12. Carlos R. Menéndez, *Noventa años de historia de Yucatán: 1821–1910* (Mérida: Cia. Tipográfica Yucateca, 1937).
13. "Farmers and workers."
14. Robert Ross. *Francisco I. Madero: Apostle of Mexican Democracy* (New York: Columbia University Press, 1955).
15. "Poppies."
16. "Porfirista" refers to aspects of the thirty-one-year dictatorship of Porfirio Díaz.
17. The Spanish word for "chewing gum." *Chicle* was formerly obtained from the sap of the *chicozapote* tree, before the introduction of a synthetic version.
18. "Jungle."
19. "Arms Square."

CHAPTER FIFTEEN

1. Edward H. Thompson, *Archaeological Researches in Yucatan*, Memoirs of the Peabody Museum of American Archeology and Ethnology, vol. 3, no. 1 (Cambridge, Mass.: Harvard University, 1904).
2. Those who harvest the latex *(chicle)* of the *chicozapote*, or sapodilla, tree.
3. "A good collaborator."
4. "Labor union."

CHAPTER SIXTEEN

1. "Pamphlets."
2. "Esteemed comrade."
3. *La huelga de junio* [The June Strike] (Mérida, 1922). This is evidently a pamphlet published by Carrillo's Socialist Party.
4. In the Yucatán, a *mecate*—literally, "cord"—is a square plot of land measuring 20 × 20 meters.
5. A British legal reformer and Socialist elected to Parliament in 1922.
6. The Palmer Raids were a number of attacks on Socialists and Communists in the United States from 1918 to 1921 and were named after Alexander Mitchell Palmer, U.S. attorney general during Woodrow Wilson's administration. Essentially, Palmer believed that Communist activity was at the heart of America's economic problems.
7. See chapter 6, note 4.

CHAPTER SEVENTEEN

1. "Porfiriana" is an adjective referring to the styles and customs of the times of Dictator Porfirio Díaz.
2. The Labor Code of the State of Yucatán was promulgated on October 14, 1926, and had been decreed by an act of Congress on September 16 of the same year. Its purpose was to defend worker's interests, as well as those of capital, and sought to find a just means between these two factors of production.
3. "Labor Code."
4. *Official Daily.*
5. "Honorable Chamber."
6. "Social Security."
7. "Committee Room. Chamber of Deputies."
8. "Labor Party."
9. Obregonistas were supporters of Mexican general and later president of the Republic, Álvaro Obregón.
10. Here *señores* (sirs or lords) refers to the landed gentry who had ruled Yuca-

tán with an iron fist until the Mexican Revolution.

11. Carrillo Puerto is possibly referring to Don Clemente de Jesús Munguía (1810–1868), the first archbishop of Morelia and contemporary of Melchor Ocampo.

12. Carrillo Puerto is referring to Melchor Ocampo.

13. "Agrarian Party of Campeche."

14. The Toltecs were a highly influential Mesoamerican culture situated in Tollán, today's Tula, in the Mexican state of Hidalgo. They developed an advanced civilization between the tenth and twelfth centuries A.D. and were much revered by the latecomer Aztecs, who traced their lineage back to them.

15. All are names of Spanish conquistadors known for their brave—if cruel—conquest of different parts of Mesoamerica.

16. The acronym for the National Revolutionary Party, founded by Plutarco Elías Calles in 1929. In Spanish, it was called the Partido Nacional Revolucionario (PNR) and in 1946 became the PRI (Partido Revolucionario Institucional, or Party of the Institutionalized Revolution).

17. "Confederation of Unions."

18. The PRI, or the Party of the Institutionalized Revolution (not the Party of Revolutionary Institutions, as Reed calls it), governed Mexico for nearly sixty years until being defeated in 2000 by the PAN (Partido Acción Nacional, or National Action Party) and its presidential candidate, Vicente Fox. Needless to say, the concept of an institutionalized revolution is curious if not paradoxical.

19. "Embrace."

### CHAPTER EIGHTEEN

1. This picturesque sobriquet of Yucatán is still used to describe the region today, although the pheasant and deer have all but disappeared, due to human development.

2. Apparently, Reed is referring to an adaptation of the Nahuatl term *macehualli*, meaning "peasant" or "commoner." In pre-Hispanic Mexico, the *macehualli* normally lived outside the cities and were vassals and tributaries to their leaders.

### CHAPTER NINETEEN

1. As I pointed out in my introduction, "Pixan Halal" is the Mayan name given to Alma Reed by Felipe Carrillo Puerto. It is the translation of "Alma" (soul) and "Reed."

2. For many years Chapultepec Castle served as official residence for Mexico's presidents, until the construction of Los Pinos, the actual official presidential residence, located nearby.

### CHAPTER TWENTY

1. "The Maya Race."

2. Whitney was a suffragist and political radical who was prominent in the founding and early activities of the Communist Party in the United States.

3. "Dragoncito" is the Spanish diminutive of "Dragon," and Carrillo Puerto was known as the Red Dragon with Eyes of Jade. "Dragoncita" is the feminine equivalent, which he apparently adopted as yet another pet name for Reed.

4. Literally, "House of the Child."

### CHAPTER TWENTY-ONE

*Besides assigning my own title to this chapter, I should point out that it is also the spliced version of two fragmentary chapters, one included in the typescript I uncovered in Richard Posner's apartment and the other given to me by Rosa Lie Johansson. After comparing these documents, it became clear to me that Reed had yet to put the final touches on these final sections, and I have reconstructed them to the best of my ability, while respecting what I believe were her original intentions.*

1. "Porter."
2. "Embrace."
3. "Manager."

4. "The financier."
5. "Thousand summits."
6. "High plateau."
7. Literally, "hot land."
8. "Secretary of the Treasury."
9. Alfonso Taracena, *La verdadera revolución mexicana* (Mexico City: Ed. Jus, 1960), with prologue by José Vasconcelos.
10. Alonso Capetillo, *La rebelión sin cabeza: Génesis y desarrollo del movimiento delahuertista* (Mexico City: Imprenta Botas, 1925).
11. An inexpensive alcoholic drink usually distilled from sugarcane.
12. Beginning with this chapter, in which Reed narrates events she did not witness, certain inconsistencies appear with regard to the names of the individuals who accompanied Carrillo Puerto. Because of this, I have corroborated this information with that included in the death sentence composed by the War Council and have corrected names that Reed either spelled incorrectly or failed to include.
13. "Chato," or "flat-face," is a term of endearment in Mexico and other parts of Latin America for a snub-nosed person.
14. In Mexico an *ingenio* is a sugar plantation and refinery.

### CHAPTER TWENTY-TWO

1. "Guarantees"; in this case, guarantees related to the physical care of the prisoners.
2. John W. F. Dulles, *Yesterday in Mexico: A Chronicle of the Revolution, 1919–1936* (Austin: University of Texas Press, 1961).
3. Carlos R. Menéndez, *Historia del infame y vergonzoso comercio de indios, vendidos a los esclavistas de Cuba por los políticos yucatecos, desde 1848 hasta 1861: Justificación de la revolución indígena de 1847; Documentos irrefutables que lo comprueban* (Mérida: Talleres Gráficos de la Revista de Yucatán, 1923).
4. "Presiding Judge."
5. This is the first and only time that Vicente Coy's name appears in Reed's text. Therefore, whether he was one of Carrillo Puerto's confidants and why he was not condemned to die are unknown. The same situation occurs later on with Francisco Tejeda, who is mentioned among the men sentenced to death but who had never been mentioned before. It is also the case with Fernando Mendoza; although he was apprehended with Carrillo Puerto, as Reed mentioned in chapter 21, he was not judged by the War Council nor condemned. This occurs with several other people mentioned only once by Reed.
6. Note that although Reed refers to Hermenegildo Rodríguez as a colonel here, elsewhere in this chapter and in chapter 21, she describes him as a general.
7. Ethel Turner, widow of John Kenneth Turner and a close friend of Alma Reed's who was helping Reed proofread her book, made this suggestion regarding the conclusion of this chapter: "Alma: Add here or above what Doña Adela said about the mangled bodies, and so end the chapter."

### CHAPTER TWENTY-THREE

1. As on other occasions when Reed spelled a person's name more than one way, she used the spelling "Sumurano" in this paragraph for what is assumed to be "Zamorano."
2. Sinclair Snow, *The Pan-American Federation of Labor* (Durham, NC: Duke University Press, 1964).
3. Samuel Gompers of the Pan-American Federation of Labor. See chapter 10, note 4.
4. Literally, "barbed-wire neighborhoods." This term was evidently used to refer to a wartime arrangement whose exact definition has eluded this editor.
5. In another note written to Reed, Ethel Turner made this suggestion: "Alma: Tell about the procession every year to the graves."

# INDEX

*Page numbers in italics refer to photographs.*

www.ingramcontent.com/pod-product-compliance
Lightning Source LLC
LaVergne TN
LVHW090024310826
846742LV00010B/22
*9780292726154*